Lecture Notes in Computer Science 9926

Commenced Publication in 1973
Founding and Former Series Editors:
Gerhard Goos, Juris Hartmanis, and Jan van Leeuwen

More information about this series at http://www.springer.com/series/7409

Günter Wallner · Simone Kriglstein
Helmut Hlavacs · Rainer Malaka
Artur Lugmayr · Hyun-Seung Yang (Eds.)

Entertainment Computing – ICEC 2016

15th IFIP TC 14 International Conference
Vienna, Austria, September 28–30, 2016
Proceedings

 Springer

Editors
Günter Wallner
University of Applied Arts Vienna
Vienna
Austria

Simone Kriglstein
Vienna University of Technology
Vienna
Austria

Helmut Hlavacs
University of Vienna
Vienna
Austria

Rainer Malaka
University of Bremen
Bremen
Germany

Artur Lugmayr
Curtin University
Perth, WA
Australia

Hyun-Seung Yang
KAIST
Daejeon
South Korea

ISSN 0302-9743   ISSN 1611-3349   (electronic)
Lecture Notes in Computer Science
ISBN 978-3-319-46099-4   ISBN 978-3-319-46100-7   (eBook)
DOI 10.1007/978-3-319-46100-7

Library of Congress Control Number: 2016950415

LNCS Sublibrary: SL3 – Information Systems and Applications, incl. Internet/Web, and HCI

Printed on acid-free paper

This Springer imprint is published by Springer Nature
The registered company is Springer International Publishing AG Switzerland

Preface

This volume collects all contributions accepted for ICEC 2016, the International Conference on Entertainment Computing. ICEC 2016 was the 15th event in a series of successful conferences on entertainment computing, previously held in São Paulo, Brazil (2013); Sydney, Australia (2014); and Trondheim, Norway (2015).

This year's event was held in Vienna, Austria on September 28–30, 2016. ICEC 2016 was hosted by the University of Vienna, the oldest university in the German-speaking world, celebrating its 650th anniversary last year. It is Austria's largest research institution and home to more than 94,000 students.

The papers brought together in this edited volume span a variety of topics pertaining to different aspects of entertainment computing, including but not limited to games for health and learning, player behavioral analysis, and technological aspects. This once again shows that entertainment computing is a diverse and thriving research area bringing together experts from a wide range of disciplines. In this regard, ICEC 2016 served as a lively forum for multidisciplinary exchange to advance our understanding of this exciting field.

Overall, we received 46 submissions by authors from 22 countries across Europe, North and South America, Asia, and Australia. Each submission received at least three reviews by members of the international Program Committee. Eventually, 16 submissions were accepted as full papers, 13 as short papers, and two as posters. In addition, several demonstrations, three workshops, and a doctoral consortium were held during the conference.

The conference program was further complemented by two invited keynotes, held by Dag Svanæs from the Norwegian University of Science and Technology and Kris Staber from Arx Anima, an animation studio located in Vienna.

Finally, we would like to thank all members of the Program Committee and all external reviewers for their commitment and contribution to making ICEC 2016 a success. We also would like to thank our sponsors, the Austrian Computer Society and the International Federation for Information Processing (IFIP), for supporting this year's conference.

July 2016

Rainer Malaka
Artur Lugmayr
Hyun-Seung Yang
Helmut Hlavacs

Organization

General Chair

Helmut Hlavacs   University of Vienna, Austria

Program Chairs

Rainer Malaka   University of Bremen, Germany
Artur Lugmayr   Curtin University, Australia
Hyun-Seung Yang   Korea Advanced Institute of Science and Technology, South Korea
Helmut Hlavacs   University of Vienna, Austria

Local Chair

Simone Kriglstein   Technical University of Vienna, Austria

Publication Chair

Günter Wallner   University of Applied Arts Vienna, Austria

Publicity Chair

Letizia Jaccheri   Norwegian University of Science and Technology, Norway

Doctoral Consortium Chair

Esteban Clua   Fluminense Federal University, Brazil

Workshop Chair

Jannicke Baalsrud Hauge   University of Bremen, Germany

Program Committee

Sander Bakkes   University of Amsterdam, The Netherlands
Rafael Bidarra   Delft University of Technology, The Netherlands
Staffan Björk   University of Gothenburg, Sweden
Luis Carriço   University of Lisbon, Portugal

Marc Cavazza	University of Teesside, UK
Luca Chittaro	University of Udine, Italy
Sung-Bae Cho	Yonsei University, South Korea
Paolo Ciancarini	University of Bologna, Italy
Kendra Cooper	UT-Dallas, USA
Flavio S. Correa Da Silva	Universidade de São Paulo, Brazil
Monica Divitini	Norwegian University of Science and Technology, Norway
Jerome Dupire	CNAM - CEDRIC, France
Antonio J. Fernández Leiva	Universidad de Málaga, Spain
Chris Geiger	University of Applied Sciences Düsseldorf, Germany
Pedro González Calero	Complutense University of Madrid, Spain
Junghyun Han	Korea University, South Korea
Marc Herrlich	University of Bremen, Germany
Alexander Hofmann	University of Applied Science Technikum Wien, Austria
Haruhiro Katayose	Kwansei Gakuin University, Japan
Ines Di Loreto	Université de Technologie de Troyes, France
Joaquim Madeira	Universidade de Aveiro, Portugal
Maic Masuch	University of Duisburg-Essen, Germany
Irene Mavrommati	Hellenic Open University, Greece
Ryohei Nakatsu	National University of Singapore, Singapore
Anton Nijholt	University of Twente, The Netherlands
Valentina Nisi	University of Madeira, Portugal
Sobah Abbas Petersen	Norwegian University of Science and Technology, Norway
Johanna Pirker	Graz University of Technology, Austria
Matthias Rauterberg	Eindhoven University of Technology, The Netherlands
Teresa Romão	DI/FCT/UNL, Portugal
Walt Scacchi	University of California, Irvine, USA
Nikitas Sgouros	University of Piraeus, Greece
Elpida Tzafestas	University of Athens, Greece

Additional Reviewers

David B. Carvalho	Fabian Mertl
Katharina Emmerich	Mariela Nogueira-Collazo
Werner Gaisbauer	Konrad Peters
Christopher Helf	Alexandre Ribeiro Júnior Silva
Raul Lara	Luis Valente
Stefan Liszio	Hannes Wagner
Daniel Martinek	Rebecca Wölfle

Contents

Entertainment Technology

Short Papers

Posters

Games for Health, Learning, and Social Change

Using Gamification Mechanisms and Digital Games in Structured and Unstructured Learning Contexts

Ioana Andreea Stanescu[1(✉)], Antoniu Stefan[1],
and Jannicke Madeleine Baalsrud Hauge[2,3,4]

[1] Advanced Technology Systems, Str. Tineretului Nr 1.,
130029 Targoviste, Romania
{ioana.stanescu,antoniu.stefan}@ats.com.ro
[2] BIBA – Bremer Institut für Produktion und Logistik GmbH,
Hochschulring 20, 28359 Bremen, Germany
baa@biba.uni-bremen.de
[3] University of Bremen, Bibliothek Straße 1, 28359 Bremen, Germany
jmbh@uni-bremen.de
[4] Royal Institute of Technology, Alfreds Nobels Alle 10, Stockholm, Sweden
jannicke.baalsrud.hauge@kth.se

Abstract. The transition from the pre-defined and often inflexible tools and practices of institutionalized mass-education towards dynamic and flexible learning contexts remains a challenge. Enabling rich and engaging learning experiences that consider the different progression rates and routes of each student require new approaches in education. This paper analyzes opportunities for employing gamification and digital games to construct navigable dynamic learning channels and enable pathways towards turning users into adaptive learners able to reach learning goals both in structured and unstructured contexts.

Keywords: Lesson plan · Location-aware · Game customization · Tingo

1 Introduction

In recent years, games have found a new application, as the era of gamification has been launched. Gamification represents the application of game-thinking, game dynamics, and game mechanics in non-game contexts, with the purpose of engaging users, increasing participation, facilitating learning, and solving problems [1]. Gamification has emerged as a strategy across various disciplines such as education, environment, government, health, marketing, web, mobile applications, social networks, etc. Applying gamification in each of these contexts require a deep understanding of the relationship between the needs of the gamification project and the appropriate choice of game elements to apply [2]. Research on gamification has bloomed, and design practices, such as the 6G framework [3] brought the promise of successful gamification. At the core of gamification lies the following game element hierarchy [3, 4]:

- *Components*: the specific examples of the higher-level features, such as points, virtual goods, quests, etc.

G. Wallner et al. (Eds.): ICEC 2016, LNCS 9926, pp. 3–14, 2016.
DOI: 10.1007/978-3-319-46100-7_1

- *Mechanics*: the elements that drive player involvement and include elements like chance, turns or rewards.
- *Dynamics*: elements that provide motivation through features like narrative or social interaction.

Even if gamification brings the promise of engagement, there are also challenges to be considered when applying gamification mechanisms, especially in educational settings. Most elements used in gamification rely on competition and rewards. In games where competition lies as the core of the experience, we can identify two main categories: (a) head-to-head competition, where players compete directly against one another; (b) Asynchronous competition, where a player competes against other players by comparing the outcomes of their play [4]. These approaches cannot be applied as a universal solution. It is necessary to consider that each student has different needs and not all are motivated by competition [5]. Therefore, other mechanics need to be identified to lead motivation and engagement. Cooperative play experiences and chance-based play provide an alternative. In cooperative play, players can work simultaneously to achieve a common goal or take turns, in order to find success, while in chance-based games use randomness and chance to enhance the variety of decisions need to make. Such implementations reflect the basic human activity matrix that ranges from solo (hobby, audience, analysis) to competitive (job, sport, criticism) and collaborative activities (community, performance, teaching) [6]. Just like in non-digital or less technologized collaborative learning environments, where students work together on a collaborative assignment and at the same time they deepen their knowledge and their understanding [7], games have also the potential to increase participation in learning activities by enlarging availability of opportunities to collaborate; enhancing the accessibility of those opportunities, as well as the affordability [8].

Digital Educational Games build upon major learning theories [9]. In line with the behaviorism theory, games deliver stimuli to learners, gather their responses and provide feedback [10]. Following the constructivist approach, games involve learners in active processes, enabling them to construct new ideas or concepts based on their existing knowledge and experiences [11]. Social constructivism is applied in games by providing diverse cultural, language, and environmental contexts in which learning can take place. Connectivism is strongly represented in virtual environments [12], where the ability to make decisions [13], as well as nurturing and maintaining connections is explored to facilitate game achievements through continual learning.

While employing gamification to stimulate learning is the latest trend [14], the use of games in education has gained momentum in the last decade. However, designing games with a good game-play and immerse game players in a realistic setting while also encouraging re-playability is considered a true craft. Employing games in education require the consideration of the variables that influence learning and a learning theories need to be incorporated into the game design practices [15]. However, promising games are for the educational setting, a significant issue that needs to be addressed is the limited opportunities to tailor games for specific learning activities. Game customization remains a job for developers, even if efforts are being made to implement deeper levels of customization foe end-users [16–18].

Learning experiences span from effortless to difficult, where the gratification of accomplishment is delayed [19]. The challenge is not to motivate; it is to support them finding a path to success. Coupled with technology advancement, at strategy level, the priorities for Education and Training 2016–2020 focuses on more open and innovative learning and teaching; sustainable and efficient investments in educational systems; relevant and high quality skills and competencies; inclusive education, equality, and non-discrimination; as well as strong support for educators.

The European Qualification Framework [20] also recognizes the need to support validation of non-formal and informal learning towards core skills such as literacy, numeracy, science, foreign languages; and horizontal skills such as learning to learn, social and civic responsibility, creativity, to support learners in finding personal fulfilment, and later in life find employment and engage in society. All require new approaches in pedagogical practices and experimentation in smart, scalable, inclusive learning environments.

Key to addressing these challenges is the flexibility and elasticity of the learning space, of its contents and assessment methods that enable the learning space be reshaped based on learners' needs, performance, abilities, as well as on the learning objectives that have to be met. Digitally supported pedagogy today still relies on pre-defined (rigid) learning contents and assessment methods, and learning systems that are too assistive, leading to a distorted learning outcome. They do not adopt student-centred learning and do not present the required level of flexibility to accommodate both structured and unstructured learning.

In the context of this paper, structured learning contexts are constructs that are modeled by teachers in order to implement a certain learning plan. Unstructured learning contexts are constructed by students based on given assignments. Constructing consistent, yet dynamic learning spaces is an increasingly important issue in the context of the advancement and expansion of technologies for learning and skill development.

This paper reports work in progress on designing gamified lesson plans that are applied in structured and unstructured learning contexts. This approach creates new levels of flexibility in reaching learning objectives by employing emerging gamification mechanisms and digital educational games.

2 Constructing Structured and Unstructured Learning Contexts

The shift towards more flexible learning implies the adoption of new methodologies and practices. The emergence of gamification and gaming technologies offer opportunities to construct new approaches to learning, giving learners more freedom, strengthening collaboration skills, and stimulating their creative mind.

This section presents the transition from a traditional classroom-based approach to a gamified approach that employs technology to build specific language competencies. In the context of this paper, structured learning is learning that is continuously regulated by the teacher; while an unstructured learning context occurs when the teacher initiates the learning, but does not impose the steps to achieve the learning objectives and meet the assessment metrics.

2.1   Classroom-Based Lesson Plan

A significant part of the teaching activity relies on traditional methods, while the technology-oriented generations expect more engaging learning methods. Even if significant efforts are being made, the tradition from teacher-centers to student-centered education remains challenging. To address it, this paper follows the transition from conventional teaching methods to new approaches that integrate gamification and games as consistent stimuli for motivation and engagement.

Table 1 presents a lesson plan created for advanced English students in the 10th grade. The lesson plan details the curriculum objectives, the language skills that will be developed, the general and the specific objectives of the lesson plan, as well as the specific set of activities that will be carried out during the class.

2.2   Gamified Learning

Starting from the lesson plan presented above, to ease the transition to emerging teaching methods, a gamified approach has been constructed. Tables 2 and 3 present a set of activities that can be implemented to enhance student engagement and motivation to learn.

Table 1. Classroom-based English lesson plan

Lesson topic: Târgoviște City – past, present and future	
Subject: English	Grade: 10th
Level: Advanced	Time: 50 minutes (1 course)
Location: Classroom	ICT: PowerPoint presentation, video clips
Objectives set in the national language curriculum for the 10th grade, advanced level	**Language skills targeted by the lesson plan**
Objective 1. Comprehend oral and written messages in diverse contexts	Listening: receptive skill Reading: receptive skill
Objective 2: Speaking or writing on diverse topics	Speaking: productive skill Writing: productive skill
Objective 3: Oral or written collaboration	Speaking: productive skill Writing: productive skill
General objectives of the lesson: - To improve the student's vocabulary with words related to history, city architecture and civic responsibility - To develop communication and collaboration skills - To assess comprehension of oral and written messages - To enable students to use previous knowledge - To enhance civic engagement	
Specific objectives to be achieved by the end of the lesson: - Students will be able to use vocabulary related to history and city architecture	

(*Continued*)

Table 1. (*Continued*)

- Students will be able to recognize positive, negative, and neutral comments - Students will be able to describe historical events and historical figures - Students will be able to comprehend the oral and written messages given by the teacher concerning the history and architecture of Târgoviş te City - Students will be able to present ways in which they can participate in the life of the local community and can get involved in shaping the community's future.
Teaching techniques - Conversation - Questions and answers - Questionnaire - Discussion
Organization of the class **Activity 1 – Speaking** The teacher asks the students to comment on the role of the Târgovişte City as the former capital of Romania **Activity 2 – Reading** The students work individually. The students are asked to go scan a text that present the architectural styles of the buildings in the city and find out what is the topic of each new paragraph. After reading the text, the students do the exercise at the bottom of the text. **Activity 3 – Speaking, Listening** The students form pairs. They talk about different categories of buildings from Târgoviş te. They are asked to match names with building images. After discussing in pairs, the students present their feedback to the rest of the class. **Activity 4 – Listening, Speaking** Before listening to a text on civic responsibility, the students make predictions about what they are going to hear. The teacher reads the text on civic responsibility. Afterwards, the students discuss if/ how their perspective on civic responsibility has changed. **Activity 5 – Writing** The teacher asks the students to write a short composition on the buildings of Târgoviş te, historical figures and civic actions that can be taken to preserve the historical heritage of the city and support its future development.

An example of smartphone app that provides information about points of interest around the current location of a user is Field Trip. The application is a good indication of what can be achieved in terms of user experience for the students (https://play. google.com/store/apps/details?id=com.nianticproject.scout). However, it is not tailored for a formal learning environment and does not provide any kind of APIs or reporting that could be used by teachers to select the list of relevant topics that should be provided or to understand how students have engaged with the information and how long they have been following a particular topic.

Table 2. Structured indoor learning

Organization of the class **Activity: "Fill-in exercise" – Writing, Reading, Listening** Students will work in groups of four. Each group will choose a name for their team. Each team selects a letter. Each letter is associated with a different set of fill-in exercises. The set of exercises is divided into several levels of difficulty: **Level 1. Vocabulary practice. (10 points/ 1 badge)** The students will fill in the blanks with words they learnt in previous lessons. 1 point is given for each correct answer. 1 badge is given if the set of exercise is completed without errors. **Level 2. Vocabulary practice. (20 points/ 2 badges)** The students will match a given set of new words with the blank spaces. 2 points are given for each correct answer. 2 badges are given if the set of exercise is completed without errors. **Level 3. Vocabulary practice. (30 points/ / 3 badges)** The students will listen to an audio message/ watch a clip presenting the historical buildings in Târgovişte City and fill-in the blanks. 3 points are given for each correct answer, as the level of complexity increases. 3 badges are given if the set of exercise is completed without errors. *If the general and specific objectives of the lesson plan are extended to include grammar practice, the following levels can be added:* **Level 4. Grammar practice. (20 points/ 2 badges)** The students will fill-in the blanks with adjectives from a given list using the right degree of comparison. **Level 5. Grammar practice. (30 points/ 2 badges)** The students will fill-in the blanks with the right tense of the verb in brackets. *To make the activity more interesting, hints can be places in the classroom or within the school. The team that gathers the largest number of hints will get extra points. Time limits can be added to certain activities, in order to be able to comply with the estimated time of the lesson.* The team that collects the largest number of points or the largest number of badges wins the game. Special credit is given to the teams that have obtained best results per level.

2.3   Blending Technology into Unstructured Learning Contexts

One of the key challenges in providing students with unstructured learning is to set up an environment where users can have access to on-demand knowledge that is relevant to their current context and desired learning outcomes.

Existing technologies offer opportunities to create rich learning experiences at user level, building upon wide databases and supporting large-scale reuse. The tools proposed therein are:

Table 3. Unstructured outdoor learning

Activity: "Puzzle" – Writing, Reading, Listening, Speaking Students can play and collaborate to put together a map of Târgovişte City. Students will work in groups of six. Each group will choose a name for their team. Each team selects a different type of map: historical buildings, churches, modern buildings, favorite shops, memorial houses, parks, local markets, etc. All the documentation process is carried out outside the classroom. The role of the teacher is to set the goals of the game, without setting up rules or restrictions on how the research should be carried out or how the project should be elaborated. Each team has to document their project with information and pictures of the buildings they have identified. A team obtains or loses points based on the following criteria: - Number of buildings included in the project. (10 points per building) - Quality of information. (1-5 points per building) - The originality of the work. *E.g. if pictures are taken by the team members and not from the Internet.* (30 points) - Spelling mistakes. (-2 points per mistake) - Grammar errors. (-5 points per mistake) Evaluation is carried out by the competing teams and not by the teacher.

a. **DBpedia**, a project that provides semantically classified information that can be queried using a vast number of descriptors, including geo location. Because the resources contained in the datasets are classified semantically, it provides a straightforward way to retrieve these resources based on specific topic of interest and also to locate related content using knowledge graphs.

b. **Wikipedia,** the premier online open encyclopedia offers basic API functions that can search for articles that are in a specific radius from a particular geo location (https://www.mediawiki.org/wiki/Extension:GeoData#API). The limitation of this service is that it cannot be used to filter the results based on particular topics of interest. In some context this could be beneficial because students are exposed to the entire set of information that is available, but it can also be a factor that distracts their attention from the desired learning outcome.

c. **Wikimapia**, a service that aims to describe and categorize physical locations.

2.4   Game-Enhanced Learning with Tingo

Tingo is a Digital Educational Game developed by Advanced Technology Systems, Romania (http://desig.ats.com.ro/). The game was created to support foreign language learning, while coupling specific curricular competences and game activities.

A significant issue that occurs when teachers aim to employ digital games as support tools for learning is to adapt the game to the specific learning objectives within a lesson plan. To address this issue, the Tingo game has been designed to enable a basic level of customization, allowing teachers to create simple learning contexts. The applied scenario builds upon location-aware technology.

Starting from a simple map, several game objects can be added to create a fantasy map of the city (Fig. 1). Information dragged from the tools presented in the above section and GPS coordinates can be added for each of the buildings included in the map.

Fig. 1. Map of Târgoviște City in the Tingo game

When the player explores the virtual world, the background images changes color for the areas the players has visited (Fig. 2).

Fig. 2. Student activity within the game

When the player physically reaches a building, the game uses GPS coordinates from the device to determine the building and change its color on the map. If available, additional localization devices such as Bluetooth beacons or Wi-Fi base stations can also be used (Fig. 3).

Fig. 3. Student activity in physical locations

Table 4. Curriculum-based specific competences

Curriculum Objective 1. Comprehending oral and written messages in diverse contexts		
Reference	Specific competences	Support materials
1.1	Anticipate the information in a text based on its title or a visual stimulus	Provide texts of various lengths and diverse difficulty Provide audio/ video clips
1.2	Identify the message in a given text	Present dialogues Provide mass-media articles
1.3	Identify key information in original texts	Provide authentic texts extracted from books
1.4	Identify details from oral/ written messages	
1.5	Select information from several texts in order to fulfil a task	
1.6	Identify the logical structure from a given text	

In Tingo, individual players can set up their own bookcase. To collect books, players need to complete additional quests. Players can combine individual bookcases to form a public library.

Table 5. Unstructured outdoor learning

Reference	Game activities
1.1	The game displays several buildings and the player has to guess their category. The player is requested to match different activities with building categories.
1.2	The game displays a text message and the player has to act upon the information the game has provided.
1.3	The game displays a text message and the player has to identify words from a certain category: e.g. nouns, verbs; or categories of buildings.
1.4	The player listens to an audio message and is required to perform certain tasks, such as click on the building that has been described in the audio message.
1.5	The game displays text messages that provide information on historical buildings in Târgoviş te and the player is requested to classify them based on their architectural profile, the year they were built, etc.
1.6	The player is requested to identify the chronological order of the historical facts that are presented in several written or audio messages.

To increase motivation, the game enable players to set up an individual vocabulary. As they progress in the game and learn new words, their individual vocabulary becomes larger and larger. The game displays a scoreboard with the following categories of players: (a) players that have the largest collection of words; (b) players that have the largest number of unique words that do not appear in other players' vocabulary; and (c) players that have the largest number of similar words.

Starting from specific competences that are targeted (Table 4), the activities presented in Table 5 have been created using the wizard feature of the game.

These scenarios can be extended to support, for example, problem based learning. By coupling learning foreign languages with other disciplines such as math, the lesson plan on the architecture of the Târgovişte City can include specific tasks that address math topics.

3 Discussion and Next Steps

Students will invariably experience different progression rates and routes, which often lead to different learning outcomes than those expected. This can be a consequence of several factors including the pre-defined and often inflexible tools and practices of institutionalized mass-education, but above all else emerge two key considerations: on one hand, learning is a choice, an act of personal agency and even if the best blend of technologies is available, without sustained motivation, learners will not truly engage in deep learning processes; on the other hand, when technologies are not available or are not easy to integrate into learning spaces, the experience might prove too frustrating even for motivated learners.

To address these challenges, it is necessary not only to turn ICTs into navigable dynamic learning channels, but also to enable pathways towards turning users into adaptive learners able to reach learning goals without a high dependency on certain technologies. Technology is a guide for learners and a mean to reach learning goals. Therefore, technology dependency should be avoided. The aim is to foster self-regulated learning by assisting learners in how to comprehend and realize when they do not know something and to stimulate discovery such that learners seek out the necessary knowledge or information. The immediate benefit of such a learning environment is that it affords ambient leaning including adaptive and personalized teaching and assessment.

This approach contrasts to recent developments and solutions where the software is too assistive letting the learner know what is 'needed' in every step of the learning journey rather than letting the individual conduct reflective and summative learning. Removing agency from the equation of learning (and teaching) has implications from the pedagogical perspective. It limits the quality of the learning experiences by creating automatons and the consequential reliance of learners becoming highly dependent on software.

Instead, the approach proposed in this paper follows a completely different paradigm, where learners are given the freedom of choice based on a plug&learn approach (e.g. smartphone apps; digital games). It considers the fact that the outcomes of learning experiences that occur outside of formal, structured settings are not assessed and valuable information about the learner is lost. Moreover, the solution proposed herein builds upon the fact that many students own mobile devices. This offers a significant opportunity for bring-your-own-X (device, cloud, applications, etc.) enabling individuals to find one tool that performs every function they need, removing the hassle of working with problematic tools that do not address all their needs.

The paper presents lesson plan scenarios that employ gaming technology to construct engaging learning experiences. Future work involves the testing of the prototype and of the scenarios with students from different high schools, with the purpose of extending the learning scenarios for problem-based learning and enhancing the functionalities provided by the Tingo game.

Acknowledgement. The work presented herein is partially funded under the Horizon 2020 Framework Program of the European Union, BEACONING – Grant Agreement 68676 and by Unitatea Executiva pentru Finantarea Invatamantului Superior, a Cercetarii, Dezvoltarii si Inovarii (UEFISCDI) in Romania, Contract no. 19/2014 (DESiG).

References

1. Davis, D.Z., Gangadharbatla, H.: Emerging Research and Trends in Gamification. IGI Global, Hershey (2015)
2. Deterding, S., Sicart, M., Nacke, L., O'Hara, K., Dixon, D.: Gamification: using game design elements in non-gaming contexts. In: CHI 2011 Extended Abstracts on Human Factors in Computing Systems, pp. 2425–2428. ACM, New York (2011)
3. Hunter, D., Werbach, K.: The Gamification Toolkit: Dynamics, Mechanics, and Components for the Win. Wharton Digital Press, Philadelphia (2015)
4. Sharp, J., Macklin, C.: Introduction to Game Design LiveLessons (Video Training). Addison-Wesley Professional (2014). Rogers, S.: Level Up! The Guide to Great Video Game Design, John Wiley & Sons (2014)
5. Information Resources Management Association: Gamification. IGI Global (2015)
6. Koster, R.: Theory of Fun for Game Design. O'Reilly Media Inc., Sebastopol (2013)
7. Barkley, E.F., Patricia Cross, K., Howell, C.: Major Collaborative Learning Techniques: A Handbook for College Faculty. Jossey-Bass, San Francisco (2014)
8. Connolly, T., Okada, A., Scott, P.: Collaborative Learning 2.0. IGI Global, Hershey (2012)
9. Trentin, G.: Networked Collaborative Learning. Elsevier Science, New York (2010)
10. DeSmet, A., Van Cleemput, K., Bastiaensens, S., Poels, K., Vandebosch, H., Malliet, S., Verloigne, M., Vanwolleghem, G., Mertens, L., Cardon, G., De Bourdeaudhuij, I.: Bridging behavior science and gaming theory: using the intervention mapping protocol to design a serious game against cyberbullying. Comput. Hum. Behav. **56**, 337–351 (2016)
11. De Gloria, A., de Freitas, S., Obikwelu, C., Read, J.C.: The serious game constructivist framework for children's learning. In: 4th International Conference on Games and Virtual Worlds for Serious Applications (VS-GAMES 2012) (2012). Procedia Comput. Sci. **15**, 32–37
12. Isman, A., Techakosit, S., Wannapiroon, P.: Connectivism learning environment in augmented reality science laboratory to enhance scientific literacy. In: International Conference on New Horizons in Education, INTE 2014 (2014). Procedia Soc. Behav. Sci. **174**, 2108–2115 (2015)
13. Leadbetter, A., Pshenichny, C., Diviacco, P., Fox, P.: Collaborative Knowledge in Scientific Research Networks. IGI Global, Hershey (2014)

14. Urh, M., Vukovic, G., Jereb, E., Pintar, R.: The model for introduction of gamification into e-learning in higher education. Procedia Soc. Behav. Sci. **197**, 388–397 (2015)
15. Bishop, J.: Gamification for Human Factors Integration. IGI Global, Hershey (2014)
16. Kleinsmith, A., Gillies, M.: Customizing by doing for responsive video game characters. Int. J. Hum. Comput. Stud. **71**(7–8), 775–784 (2013)
17. Behr, K.M., Huskey, R., Weber, R.: Creative interactivity: customizing and creating game content. In: Green, G.P., Kaufman, J.C. (eds.) Video Games and Creativity, pp. 285–299. Academic Press, San Diego (2015). Chap. 14
18. Nagle, A., Wolf, P., Riener, R.: Towards a system of customized video game mechanics based on player personality: Relating the Big Five personality traits with difficulty adaptation in a first-person shooter game. Entertainment Comput. **13**, 10–24 (2016)
19. Burke, B.: Gamify: How Gamification Motivates People to Do Extraordinary Things. Bibliomotion, Brookline (2014)
20. http://ec.europa.eu/education/library/publications/monitor15_en.pdf

The Challenge to Nurture Challenge

Students' Perception of a Commercial Quiz App as a Learning Tool

Heinrich Söbke[(⊠)] and Laura Weitze

Bauhaus-Institute for Infrastructure Solutions (b.is),
Bauhaus-Universität Weimar, Weimar, Germany
{heinrich.soebke,laura.weitze}@uni-weimar.de

Abstract. Commercial quiz apps show characteristics, which could contribute to a promising game-based learning tool. Among these characteristics are huge popularity, easy accessibility and adaptivity to any content domain. We used the commercial quiz app QuizUp in an explorative study to clarify acceptance and requirements for the usage of these apps for educational purposes. We developed a topic-specific question corpus. Over a period of 12 days four topic affine students used QuizUp regularly and focused on learning. We observed them in three common gaming sessions. Furthermore, three interviews and a questionnaire were conducted. A main observation has been a self-reported decrease of motivation after a phase of curiosity. In general, we conclude that successful usage of such a quiz app requires a purposeful integration in an educational setting to ensure its continuous use. Additionally, we point to a set of further relevant research topics.

Keywords: Quiz apps · Educational content · Mobile learning · Explorative study

1 Introduction

Quizzes are established as an assessment tool. Not so common, but remarkable as well are their applications as learning tools [1, 2]. The quiz format can be used regardless of the technical area of the knowledge. In this context we argued for a common technical infrastructure to facilitate quizzes, especially in educational contexts [3]. Furthermore, recently raised proliferation of mobile internet has enabled the ubiquitous and enormous spread of quiz apps (e.g. *Quizkampen* [4] or *QuizUp* [5]). In a previous study [6] we found that quiz app players enter the game with an expectation to learn. Additionally, competition with friends has been identified as one main motivation for users of such apps [6]. Thus commercial quiz apps can be considered as potential educational tool.

In 2015 the commercial quiz app *QuizUp* has been opened for user-defined topics [7]. We used this feature in two engineering university courses. As a result, we found that players can be categorized in two groups: *learners* – who accomplish their quantum of educational content and then leave the app – and *gamers* – who get stuck in the game after having fulfilled their learning duties [8]. Further results have not drawn a

G. Wallner et al. (Eds.): ICEC 2016, LNCS 9926, pp. 15–23, 2016.
DOI: 10.1007/978-3-319-46100-7_2

clear picture. On one hand the integration of the app into the course has been appreciated by students as an enrichment, on the other hand the actual usage of the app – trackable via public ranking lists – has not been overwhelming. This ambivalence provided no answer to the question, to what extent quiz apps can contribute to intrinsic motivation in learning contexts. Furthermore, more detailed insights in usage experiences of such apps within educational settings would be helpful for the purposeful design of effective application scenarios. Therefore, the aim of the following explorative study is to contribute to a set of general conditions, necessities and requirements, which could frame the usage of game-like quiz apps as educational tools.

2 Study Design

The employed app *QuizUp* uses multiple choice questions with three distractors. Two players can compete in a match of seven questions all belonging to a certain topic. If currently there is no other player available, the system automatically assigns as opponent a bot. A question has to be answered within 10 s. The less time is needed for the correct answer, the more points are earned. A match takes on average three minutes.

As a prerequisite, we have developed a corpus of 57 questions about three areas of basic knowledge in the engineering topic of *Ecological Sanitation*. (The publicly available topic in QuizUp is called "NASS" – *New Alternative Sanitation Systems*). This corpus contains questions of different difficulty levels: there are questions about simple factual knowledge like abbreviations. On the other hand there are more complex questions which require the comparison of systems. Questions differ in text length, but they cannot exceed a system provided maximum length. During the study the corpus remained unchanged.

As participants 4 students (2 male, 2 female) of engineering courses of study were recruited by means of online pin boards. Prerequisites for participation were being a student, interested in quiz apps and technical topics, the possession of a smartphone and being available for a determined time frame. As a compensation a € 25 online-shopping voucher was promised. Those four persons, who responded most quickly, have been selected. Except for one person they had no prior experience with *QuizUp*. However, all of them were active players of *Quizkampen*. Although such a small sample size clearly limits the reliability of the results, we have chosen this approach to enable a familiar environment during the gaming sessions very quickly.

Within 12 days three meetings have been scheduled. One part of each of these meetings has been an attended gaming session of 30 min. Additionally, these meetings have been used to perform semi-structured interviews [9] with the participants. The interviews have been roughly guided by the main categories *Content*, *Motivation* and *Learning outcome*: These topics constitute main pillars of games in educational contexts. In the last session, participants had to answer a questionnaire. After Sessions 1 and 2 they have been provided with extra tasks for the next meeting in order to keep up the engagement with the app over time. In the following we refer to the period between Sessions 1 and 2 as *home period 1* and to the period between Sessions 2 and 3 as *home period 2*.

Session 1. Here we conducted a semi-structured group interview (and asked additionally for prior knowledge, expectations and experience) and a play session of 30 min. Participant played against each other, they connected to each other in QuizUp and established a chat group with the purpose of coordination. A 20-page brochure containing an overview of the topic NASS [10] was handed out to the participants. The task for home period 1 was to play at least one match a day. Outside of the gaming sessions, players were free to play against other participants or bots The intention of this task was to establish regular play and to point students to a bonus which is issued by QuizUp to reward daily play.

Session 2. This session took place seven days after the first session. Besides the play session, we interviewed them about their experiences since the last sessions. The task for home period 2 was to reach 25,000 points which is equivalent to 50 matches (if students play each day and are rewarded with the bonus). Intention of this instruction was on one side to investigate, how participants react to becoming the game a task instead of being fun. On the other side, we wanted to know if the habit of daily play has been kept up. This was the case, 3 of 4 participants still declared in Session 3 to have played on a daily base.

Session 3. In this session, held five days after Session 2, we conducted an interview about their experiences in the last five days. After the play session, a questionnaire has been answered.

There have been no variations of the experimental setting during the study. The only condition we changed was the specific task to accomplish during the home periods.

3   Results

Sessions, interviews and questionnaire revealed various, partially very detailed aspects. In the following we give an overview about selected aspects. Although categorization has been partly ambiguous, we assigned each aspect to one out of three main topics: *Content* (Knowledge has to be expressed by means of multiple choice questions (MCQs)), *Motivational aspects* (Quiz apps use game mechanics, therefore fostering of motivation, especially intrinsic motivation is a relevant aspect) and *Learning outcomes* (Learning is the purpose for employing quiz apps in this context). These were the main categories of the semi-structured interviews. Subcategories have been developed a posteriori according to the found results.

3.1   Content

After having defined three basic learning fields, the according questions corpus has been designed due to the recommendations of Haladyna and Rodriguez [11]. Nevertheless, there are further observations. In the following we describe them and suggest possible improvements.

Text length. Questions with short texts for question stem and answer options were preferred by participants, as they do not require much reading effort. This is especially critical as there is time pressure and limited space on the display. Long questions require more time for reading and are printed in smaller letters. Both increases the felt difficulty of answering. The allowed time to answer could be adjusted programmatically – e.g. linearly according to the length of the question stem and answer options.

Negation. Further, although negation in question should be avoided in general [11], one participant gave an example of such a question, which he considered as very informative: *Which is not an appropriate usage of treated stormwater? Body care – Washing machine – Toilet flushing – Cleaning.* He stated that the correct answer is not a far-fetched appropriate usage, so all options have to be considered carefully, which contributes to learning.

Level design. Not knowing the correct answer frustrates (One participant uttered often apparently almost in desperation "How should I know that?!"). So there is the need to order questions by complexity and release them stepwise. Questions, which refer to further, not included complex knowledge, can be seen as critical. Figure 1 depicts such a question: the question asks for a specific sanitation system, which fulfills a particular characteristic. Each answer option names such a system. If these systems are not described by other questions, the question pool is not self-contained. External knowledge is required. However, participants have not looked up additional knowledge on their own. Our conclusion is that not self-contained question pools require embedding in a formal educational setting.

Fig. 1. Sample question with references to external knowledge.

3.2   Motivational Aspects

Motivation is a key issue for a game based learning app, because motivation encourages engagement with the app and therefore causes indirectly a learning outcome. In general, the app together with its educational content is experienced as a game, as indicated by the results of the Game Experience Questionnaire (GEQ) [12]. We included the GEQ-in-game variant in the questionnaire. Among the results (see Fig. 2) are high values especially for *Positive affect* (3.63) and *Challenge* (3.13), whereas *Tension* (1.88) is rated low. Although the sample size is by far too small for reliable quantitative findings, received values seem to be game-typical, except for the quite high value of *Negative affect* (2.88).

One participant compared the regular play of the educational topic with the healthy habit of eating fruits: "Sometimes it tastes good, sometimes not". In the following, further observed aspects are described.

Competition. Matches against other persons have been indicated as more interesting as matches against bots. However, in many cases a specific bot, which imitates a perfect opponent (answering all questions within the lowest time possible) has been assigned. So there was no chance to win a match. A participant stated that such a bot assignment strategy made him quitting the gaming session. Another aspect of competition is caused by ranking lists: One participant reached more than 35.000 points in the first week. This is equivalent to 150 matches or 7.5 h of gaming. His dedicated intention was to conquer the top rank. Another player experienced a software failure,

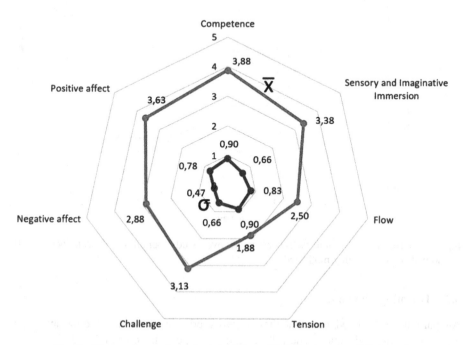

Fig. 2. Mean value and standard deviation of GEQ categories [12] (n = 4)

which prevented him from having a look at the ranking lists. As a consequence, he reported a decreased motivation.

Social Presence. In the play sessions students competed against each other and teased each other verbally. This was described by the participants as highly motivating.

Direct encouragement. In the first play session participants reported to be motivated by a textual app feedback after a match. However, this effect has not been mentioned in later sessions.

Focus and engagement. During a match the participants almost did not talk and seemed to be quite focused, especially in the first session. As an indicator for engagement, they uttered anger about false answers and cursed from time to time. Furthermore, working with the app requires attention: percentage of correct answers lowered, when there was a distraction, e.g. a switched-on TV during the home periods.

App-internal distraction. Besides our educational topic, QuizUp contains the original entertainment topics. In the first home period, three of four participants played entertainment topics at the same rate as technical topics. In the second home period, the number of matches about entertainment topics even increased.

Challenge. Especially in the third session the decreased motivation has been mentioned. Participants stated that the game has been receipted as boring, because 90 % of the questions could be answered from memory. Figure 3 mirrors the decrease of motivation over time.

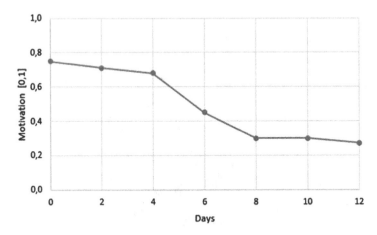

Fig. 3. Course of motivation (self-assessment) over study period on a scale between 0 (unmotivated and 1 (highly motivated)

3.3 Learning Outcome

All participants pointed out, that they have experienced learning in quiz apps and especially during this study. The following detail aspects have been found.

Level of knowledge. Participants stated that mostly factual knowledge can be taught with quiz apps. Simple questions, e.g. naming abbreviations, have been learned easily and could be answered in Session 3 without providing answer options. Questions about more complex topics could be answered after a while. However, especially in the case of complex topics, participants admitted, that they knew the correct answer, but did not gather the meaning of the question and missed an overview of the topic.

Learning curve. Already in the course of the first session effects of learning could be observed, participants could provide more and more correct answers. In the beginning of Session 1, mostly 1 to 2 questions of a match (seven questions) have been answered correctly. At the end of the first session, after approximately 10 matches, this rate increased to 4 to 5 questions per match.

Intervals of usage. One participant, which played in the home period 2 only on two days, observed fading memorization of knowledge after longer breaks. The answers could not be retrieved easily from memory, but she had to think again about the possible answers to the questions. There are two possible interpretations for this observation. First, it could be a sign of surface learning, which does not lead to long-term memorization. On the other hand, it could be a learning strategy for deeper learning, as repeated considerations for finding the correct answers could help to think thoroughly about the question.

Situated learning. During the play sessions, participants started discussions about missed questions and their correct answers. These face-to-face discussions contribute to learning [13].

External knowledge sources. Additional sources for topic-relevant knowledge have almost not been used. The established chat group did not show discussions about the technical topic. The brochure about the topic which has been handed out to participants has not been used. In the second and third session participants had not questions about the content – despite their statement, that they had not a thorough comprehension of the content of many questions. Although, students indicated that they had a better overview about the topic compared to the beginning of the study, it has to be investigated, if and in how far deeper learning processes can be triggered by a quiz app.

Time pressure. The limit of ten seconds to answer the questions and its relevance for the reward seems to hinder learning. Participants reported that the urge to answer fast, leads at least partly to superficial reading and to a kind of visual pattern recognition: The shape of question and answer options is recognized, but the question is not read thoroughly. However, this would be necessary for learning.

4 Discussion, Conclusions and Outlook

The most limiting restriction of this study is the low number of participants. Even for an exploratory approach four persons are quite a small sample. However, this small number of participants led to familiar atmosphere during the gaming sessions, which may have caused a more authentic behavior. Nevertheless, all findings have to be valued in consideration of this small sample size. The relative small size of the question corpus may have influenced findings as well. The grade of challenge may have not fallen that fast in the presence of a larger corpus. However, in this case the grade of frustration may have decreased the motivation of participants. Due to such a potential ambiguity, we consider the findings as hints, which require more detailed investigations.

In general, this study confirms learning effects of quiz apps. However, there are multiple aspects still to be discussed. On a more technical level, such aspects are partially related to the limitations and features of the studied app, *QuizUp*. So, learning algorithms – as implemented in flash card systems [14, 15] – are missing. More statistical data about answered and failed questions has been indicated as potentially being motivational. The role of time in the match process needs to be balanced carefully. Direct time pressure seems to be counterproductive. Further, the foreseen reading time should be adjusted specifically to current text length and question complexity.

In a broader range there is the process of content generation: an important aspect is the kind of knowledge which can be transformed into MCQs. Complex knowledge may have to be conveyed in other ways (e.g. lectures). Questions do not provide sufficient possibilities to teach all kinds of knowledge. An enrichment through graphics and pictures would improve current possibilities. Furthermore, we have found a relatively fast decreasing motivation among participants in this study. As a countermeasure we suggest the embedding of quiz apps into educational settings, which determine e.g. level design, regular play sessions and concrete app-related goals. In general, proven settings still have to be defined. Another important aspect, which has to be discussed is the role of entertainment topics: are they a distraction from or an enrichment for the learning process? Further, there is the basic aspect of type-dependency: the grade of motivation a quiz app can foster in a person depends on their individual preferences. Relevant in an educational context is to reach a sufficient motivation for any learner. Consequentially, a quiz app has to compete with genuine question-based learning tools like Skive [16], StudyBlue [17] or Quizlet [18]. In a further step we currently conduct a comparative study between a quiz app and a dedicated learning app regarding efficacy and acceptance. Commonly, app supported learning – no matter if game-based or not – can offer the advantages of adaptivity, ubiquitous accessibility and –at least basic – collaboration. Therefore, further research should help to mitigate current limitations.

Acknowledgements. We thank Lukas Hartung, who pursued the question design and the interviews with great commitment [19]. Parts of the activities described in this article have been supported by the German Federal Ministry of Education and Research (BMBF) under the grant agreement FKZ 033W011E. The authors gratefully acknowledge this support. Moreover, we thank the anonymous reviewers of this contribution for their valuable and helpful comments.

References

1. McDaniel, M.A., Agarwal, P.K., Huelser, B.J., McDermott, K.B., Roediger, H.L.: Test-enhanced learning in a middle school science classroom: the effects of quiz frequency and placement. J. Educ. Psychol. **103**, 399–414 (2011)
2. Wiklund-Hörnqvist, C., Jonsson, B., Nyberg, L.: Strengthening concept learning by repeated testing. Scand. J. Psychol. **55**, 10–16 (2013)
3. Söbke, H., Londong, J.: One size could fit it all: a common infrastructure for quiz apps. In: Busch, C. (ed.) Proceedings of the 8th European Conference on Games Based Learning, pp. 546–554. Academic Conferences and Publishing International Limited, Reading (2014)
4. FEO Media AB: QuizClash | Challenge your friends! http://www.quizclash-game.com/
5. Plain Vanilla: QuizUp - Connecting people through shared interests. https://www.quizup.com/
6. Söbke, H.: Space for seriousness? Player behavior and motivation in quiz apps. In: Chorianopoulos, K., et al. (eds.) ICEC 2015. LNCS, vol. 9353, pp. 482–489. Springer, Switzerland (2015)
7. Woods, B.: QuizUp launches tools for creating your own trivia categories and questions. http://thenextweb.com/apps/2015/09/24/quizup-launches-tools-for-creating-your-own-trivia-categories-and-questions/#gref
8. Weitze, L., Söbke, H.: Quizzing to become an engineer - a commercial quiz app in higher education. In: Pixel (ed.) Conference Proceeding. New Perspectives in Science Education, 5th edn., Florence, pp. 225–230. libreriauniversitaria it Edizioni (2016)
9. Schmidt, C.: The analysis of semi-structured interviews. In: Flick, U., von Kardorff, E., Steinke, I. (eds.) A Companion to Qualitative Research, pp. 253–258. SAGE Publications, London (2004)
10. DWA: Do we need New Alternative Sanitation Systems in Germany? Deutsche Vereinigung für Wasserwirtschaft, Abwasser und Abfall e.V. (DWA), Hennef, Germany (2010)
11. Haladyna, T.M., Rodriguez, M.C.: Developing and Validating Test Items. Routledge, New York (2013)
12. IJsselsteijn, W.A., De Kort, Y.A.W., Poels, K.: The game experience questionnaire: development of a self-report measure to assess the psychological impact of digital games (manuscript in preparation, 2013)
13. Lave, J., Wenger, E.: Situated Learning: Legitimate Peripheral Participation. Cambridge University Press, Cambridge (1991)
14. Leitner, S.: So lernt man lernen. Der Weg zum Erfolg. Herder, Freiburg (2011)
15. Fritz, C., Passey, D., Morris, P.: Independent Research Report: outcomes of using phase-6, Lancaster (2009)
16. qLearning Applications GmbH: Skive (2016). https://goskive.com/
17. StudyBlue Inc.: Studyblue - Conquer Your Course (2016). https://www.studyblue.com/
18. Quizlet LLC: Simple free learning tools for students and teachers | Quizlet (2016). http://quizlet.com/
19. Hartung, L.: "NASSUp" Entwicklung eines Fragenkatalogs zum Thema NASS für eine kommerzielle Quiz App. Bauhaus-Universität Weimar, Germany (2016)

Game System of Coordination Skills Training for Elderly People

Nobumitsu Shikine[1]([envelope]), Yuki Hayashi[2], Takeshi Akiba[3],
Mami Tanasaki[3], and Junichi Hoshino[2]

[1] Graduate School of Integrative and Global Majors,
University of Tsukuba, Tsukuba, Japan
shikine-shikine@entcomp.esys.tsukuba.ac.jp
[2] Faculty of Engineering, Information and Systems,
University of Tsukuba, Tsukuba, Japan
yuki-hayashi@entcomp.esys.tsukuba.ac.jp,
jhoshino@esys.tsukuba.ac.jp
[3] Product Department, System Instruments Co.,Ltd, Tokyo, Japan
{t.akiba,m.tanasaki}@sic-tky.com

Abstract. In this paper, we propose upper-limb-grasp motion as coordinated movement of five fingers and upper limbs. This coordination skill is important of daily living and we use unconscious. We divide upper-limb-grasp motion into 6 motion elements game system analysis and visualize with upper-limb-grasp motion measurement controller and game contents. We compared elderly and younger people and consider the result. As the result, we research exercise menu and game contents, technique of visualization.

Keywords: Elderly people · Coordinated movement · Upper-limb-grasp motion · Training · Game system

1 Introduction

In our daily lives, actions such as holding objects, opening doors, reaching for things from high places, cooking, driving a car, and other various activities are carried out by moving the upper-limbs and fingers based on visual information. However, it is known that our faculty to carry out these cooperative motions decreases with age [1]. Therefore, there is a need for older people to train the cooperative motions between the arms and fingers. This has become a particularly important issue as the populations of Japan, and other developed nations, begin to age [2].

In the scope of cooperative motion between the arms and fingers, it is has been found after measurements were carried out that focussed on the adjustment of strength in the fingers, there is a decrease in function with age [3], and training is carried out to focus on dexterity [4]. There are also limitations on arm movements, and a measurement of physical function using an actuator and training are performed [5]. The motion algorithm of hand-eye coordination is also being researched [6]. Furthermore, it has been made clear that training carried out through a game designed to improve cognitive function can also help improve the multitasking capabilities necessary for cooperative

© IFIP International Federation for Information Processing 2016
Published by Springer International Publishing AG 2016. All Rights Reserved
G. Wallner et al. (Eds.): ICEC 2016, LNCS 9926, pp. 24–37, 2016.
DOI: 10.1007/978-3-319-46100-7_3

motion even in the elderly [7]. However, while there is a need to break down and investigate each aspect of physical movement for the arms and fingers so that the cooperative motion between the two can be trained, as well as for an analysis of how they move cooperatively, this is no easy task. Therefore, it's very difficult to develop a system that trains for cooperation between them.

This paper defines the cooperative motion of the upper-limbs and fingers based on visual information as upper-limb grasp motion. And propose a game system to support training with a dumbbell-shaped controller, which is easy to grasp with both hands and game contents. We examined the movements that make up the cooperative motions between the upper-limbs and fingers, did an analysis and visualization for elderly people. And through it we support the implementation of healthy exercise and the self-awareness of motion characteristics for upper-limb grasp motion training.

By breaking down the elements that make up upper-limb grasp motions into 6 items; the pressure and balance of the fingers, the exercise capabilities of each finger, the smoothness of upper-limb movement, mobility range of the shoulders, cooperation between the upper-limbs and fingers, and the coordination of both hands, changes in the physical capabilities are analyzed.

In order to evaluate the effectiveness of this system, the upper-limb grasp motion of the elderly will be measured, and by comparing the analyzed results with a younger age range, the change in physical capabilities with age will be investigated, and the performance indicators and visualization method examined. Furthermore, the giving of visual feedback either to the user or care manager about their motion characteristics and how they stand physically compared to other users is useful in the promotion of healthy exercise, an increase in attentiveness to their daily activities, and the creation of a long-term training care plan.

2   Previous Studies

2.1   Decline in Physical Capabilities with Age

Through the results of the Jebsen-Taylor hand function test, which investigates the correlation between finger function and ageing, it is known that finger function begins to decline from the age of 60 [8]. In the research that focuses on function in the fingertips, such as pinch strength and accuracy, it was suggested that pinch strength declines with age and it becomes more difficult to keep hands still due to a loss of feeling in the fingertips [9], which leads to a drop in accuracy [10, 11].

Though it is a recognized fact that motor function declines with age, it's also reported that there are individual and crosswise differences [13], and that as there are also differences in the tendency towards this decline, it is important to take precautions to prevent it [12]. In addition to this, upon suggesting that motor function declines with age, it was also stated that there is also a scope for improvement [14].

2.2   Research Concerning Upper-Limb and Finger Coordination

In hand-eye coordination research, the movement of the eye and the upper-limbs when pointing to a dot was analyzed [6]. The result of this research was that it showed that the method of pointing is powered by feed-forward control.

Hand and upper-limb rehabilitation is effective in stroke rehabilitation and attempts are being made to restore physical faculties [15]. Many methods are proposed, including both-side training, one-sided training, and rhythm training.

2.3   Game Systems that Improve Physical and Cognitive Function

In the game Neuro Racer [7], cognitive function is shown to improve as the user has to push buttons at the correct time while racing, forcing them to do multiple actions at once. However, as this game only focuses on multitasking, the amount of motor function that the user is using is limited.

Games are also now being brought out onto the market that have been developed specifically to improve physical faculties and cognitive function. The standing up game "Rehabilium Kiritsukun", which is often used in stroke treatment, and is based on everyday movements, has also made its way onto the market [16]. As the user goes through the game making standing movements they can observe their form on the screen and carry out training of this function. In addition to this, there is a piece of equipment called the "digital mirror" that allows them to see their own physical functionality as they make certain movements. Through imitating the instructors movements while checking their form in a screen that forms a half-mirror and a set of balance scales on the floor, effective rehabilitation can be carried out.

2.4   Analysis of Movements and Cognitive Function in the Elderly

In research that studies the reaching movements of hemiplegia patients, a chronological data analysis is carried out, as well as an RMS and autocorrelation linear study, and a non-linear analysis that assumes dimensionality reduction through minimizing nearest-neighbor error [17]. A significant correlation with the clinical rating scale can be seen and as a rating scale it shows useful things. Furthermore, muscle potential is also used to analyze arm movement. In research that measured muscle potential by asking participants to perform simple movements, such as rotating a rod that they were grasping by 90°, there was a scattering in results [18].

As a performance indicator for the smoothness of movement, a minimum-jerk model is proposed to work as a rating scale for the sum total of the multiplication of jerks [19]. This model proved useful for evaluating stability in an experiment that looked at the stability of the walk of an elderly person to examine the smoothness of movement [20]. In regards to simple rotation of the arm, in research that looked in detail at the greatest angle the arm could reach, its speed, and its acceleration, it was found that there was little difference between elderly and young people when they were asked to rotate their arms at a slow speed of their choice, but the difference got much greater as they were asked to speed up.

Furthermore, when the dual-tasking ability of posture and attentiveness was investigated over 4 poses, it was found that the older someone was, the more difficult it was for them to hold their attentiveness as they held complicated poses.

Cognitive function is also analyzed, and analyses concerning fingertip movement and the relationship between motor capabilities and cognitive function were carried out by using fMRI and EEG.

Although research that aims to improve physical and cognitive function in the elderly like that above, which has been conducted from a variety of viewpoints, is being carried out, there is still no analysis or visualization that focuses on the cooperative motions between the fingers and upper-limbs or support for long-term training. This document proposes a system that covers these functions.

3 System Summary

3.1 Upper-Limb Grasp Motion

In this document, even within the scope of visiomotor coordination, upper-limb grasp motion refers to the coordinated movements between vision and the fingers and upper-limbs. We have sorted the physical elements of upper-limb grasp motion into 6 types, the details of which are explained below:

1. Balance of finger pressure
   This is the deviation of the maximum grip strength in each finger when gripping an object using all fingers on both hands. It's known that when elderly people put force on various parts of an object at the same time, that force is less then when they put that force on a more restricted area. A bilateral deficit is also reported. In this paper, because the pressure sensor of the controller has constant area, the physical quantity we measured by fingers is force [N].

2. Finger exercise capacity
   This is related to the ability to join together and move all of the fingers on both hands. It is the ability to move the intended finger at the intended timing, in the intended way. In everyday life people don't only grasp things, sometimes they often need to power 2 fingers to make a pinching motion, or a specific fingers to cook, or even specific fingers in order to operate machines. It's reported that the strength and accuracy of the fingers declines with age [9–11].

3. Upper-limb exercise smoothness
   This is when an upper-limb is moved at a fixed speed, and concerns the fragmentation that occurs if this movement is not smooth. It's reported that for elderly people, if it's very difficult for them to demonstrate a constant speed which reduces the smoothness of their exercise. Acceleration and jerks [19] are often used as performance indicators for smoothness.

4. Shoulder movement scope
   This is an element of movement that focuses on the shoulder and the scope in which it can be rotated up, down, left, or right. It's said that the range in which the shoulder can be moved upwards decreases with age. Movable region measurement is carried out in

physiotherapy, and the exercise direction that will be examined in this research is the bend of the shoulders (and shoulder girdle) as well as their inner and outer rotations.

5. Upper-limb and finger coordination

   This is an essential element of movement when moving the fingers and an upper-limb at the same time, and is related to the movement of gripping something as it is moved. It is the ability of how accurately and how far the hand can go as it grips an object and is moved by joints such as the elbow and shoulder. When a person ages, their movements become slow, and accuracy also decreases. This element of movement is usually examined using the pegboard test.

6. Hand-eye coordination

   This relates to the movement carried out by confirming the position of an object through sight and moving hand accurately and at the intended timing to grasp it, and also to grasp objects that are in motion. Adjustment of the position of the hands encompasses both feed-forward control and feed-back control. Feed-forward control is required for actions such as catching a ball that is flying towards you, while feed-back control is required when adjusting the angle of the hand to prevent a glass of water from spilling as it is carried.

3.2 Exercise Support System Summary

The images of the game system that measures, analyzes, and visualizes the upper-limb grasp motion of elderly people in use are shown in Fig. 1. The user sits in a chair, grasps the controller that will measure the upper-limb grasp motion, and proceeds through the game content that is displayed on the screen. The exercise process is explained by a character in the game who acts as an instructor. The game analyzes the characteristics of each user's upper-limb grasp motion, and gives feedback to either the user or their care manager.

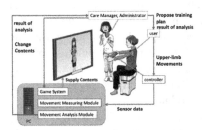

Fig. 1. System image

The upper-limb grasp motion is analyzed and visualized and supports the comprehension of the gap in capabilities in the upper-limb grasp motion of the elderly and the young. It measures the motion characteristics found in upper-limb grasp motion in all users, including the young, and by updating the performance indicators, can check the user's motion type, as well as make clear its relation to the state of their health.

3.3   A Controller that Measures Upper-Limb Grasp Motion

In order to be able to measure finger pressure, upper-limb movement, or upper-limb grasp motion, which is a combination of the two, it's necessary to be able to measure each finger's pressure and the movement of the arm. In this document, we have developed a controller like that in Fig. 2 together with System Instruments Ltd. The area where the controller is grasped has a rubber cover, and it's shaped to fit all 5 fingers. The pressure sensors buried into the area where the controller is gripped measures finger pressure [N], and upper-limb movement is calculated by 3-axis internal sensors that measure acceleration [m/s^2], angular velocity [rad/s], and geomagnetism. Using the body as a center point, the position of the user's up, down, left, and right arm rotations is calculated by information from the acceleration and angular velocity sensors. The data from each sensor is sent to computer via Bluetooth, where it is stored, calculated, and reflected on the screen (Fig. 3).

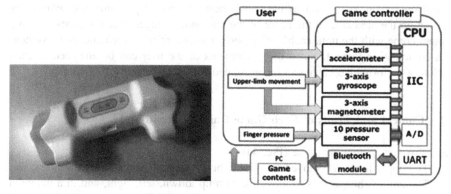

Fig. 2. Upper-limb-grasp motion measurement controller (System Instruments Co., Ltd.)

Fig. 3. Block diagram

The values from the sensors are converted by this formula (1) (2) (3) (4) in to the rotational angle (roll, pitch, yaw) [deg] of the arm using the shoulder as a center point. The roll and pitch directions use the acceleration value. For the yaw direction, the value of the angular velocity sensor is integrated to estimate the current position, and for this reason the game needs to be calibrated before the game content starts.

$$\theta_r \fallingdotseq c_r a_x \tag{1}$$

$$\theta_p \fallingdotseq c_p a_y \mid c_p > a_y \tag{2}$$

$$\theta_p \fallingdotseq c_p a_z \mid c_p \leq a_y \tag{3}$$

$$\theta_r \fallingdotseq c_y \int \left(g_x(t) \cos \theta_r - g_y(t) \sin \theta_p \cos \theta_r - g_z(t) \cos \theta_p \cos \theta_r \right) dt \qquad (4)$$

a_x, a_y, a_z: triaxial acceleration [m/s^2], g_x, g_y, g_z: triaxial angular velocity [rad/s], $\theta_r, \theta_p, \theta_y$: posture (roll, pitch, yaw) [deg], c_r, c_p, c_y: proportionality constant.

4   Configuration of the Game Unit

4.1   Game Unit Overview

A game unit is created to measure upper-limb grasp motion, and each game unit is used to acquire data concerning each element of movement related to upper-limb grasp motion. Each game unit features a character who acts as an instructor, re-enacting all of the movements that the user performs, and encourages the appropriate exercise via voice instruction. Furthermore, the user can see the state of their movements through the controller and interface displayed within the game (Fig. 4). The controller is displayed on screen in relation to its actual location. Finger pressure is displayed by lighting up the area around the name of the respondent finger in red. 6 types of game content come with the unit, each corresponding to one of the 6 elements of movement or a combination thereof. Since the movements of the user can be analyzed in each section, a performance value can be calculated for each element of movement.

4.2   Content and Traits of Each Game Unit (a)(b)(c)(d)(e)(f)

(a) Movement imitation game (Fig. 4a)
     The upper-limbs are moved to imitate the movements directed by the instructor. The aim of the game is to move the arm up, down, left, right, and in a diagonal direction using the shoulder as a center point (Fig. 5). The game last for 5 min and examines upper-limb exercise smoothness, shoulder movement scope, and flexibility.
(b) Simultaneous maximum finger pressure game (Fig. 4b)
     The controller is grasped using all 5 fingers on each hand, and the maximum finger pressure for each is calculated. The measurement is taken twice to imitate a real finger pressure examination. This examines the balance of finger pressure.
(c) Finger reaction game (Fig. 4c)
     The screen indicates one finger from both of the users hands, which they must then press down as fast as they can. The time between the direction being given and the finger being pressed is then measured. This game examines finger exercise capacity.
(d) Object moving game (Fig. 4d)
     This game compels the user to pick up an object in the game and move it to the specified location. The main element of movement that is examined here is upper-limb and finger coordination. The in-game catcher is moved by either rotating the arm in a pitch or yaw direction and closing in upon the object. When the catcher is close to the object, it can be grasped by applying pressure that totals

a value greater than that already fixed. The movement to transfer the object to the designated area is performed 3 times from left to right, and 3 times from right to left. The amount of time taken to complete the task and the number of times the object has been dropped are then calculated.

(e) Catch ball game (Fig. 4e)

The user catches the ball that is flying towards them 3 times within the game. The position of where the ball will land is fixed, and it always comes towards the user in the game. This game examines hand-eye coordination and feed-forward control capability is necessary for getting the grasp timing right. The amount of time between the users catch timing and an accurate timing is measured.

(f) Ball rolling game (Fig. 4f)

The controller is tilted backward and forwards and from left to right to cause the in-game ball to roll towards the target area. This game is repeated 3 times, and the ball starts at a different position each turn. This game examines hand-eye coordination as it requires the user to use the visual information in front of them to alter the direction of the ball and the ability of feed-forward control so the user knows when to tilt the controller. The game measures how long it takes the user to get the ball to the target area.

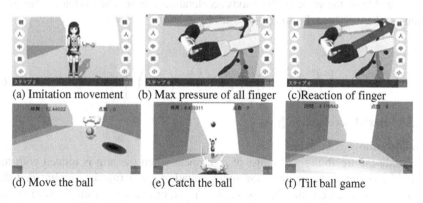

(a) Imitation movement   (b) Max pressure of all finger   (c)Reaction of finger

(d) Move the ball   (e) Catch the ball   (f) Tilt ball game

Fig. 4. Game contents base vision (Color figure online)

5 Analysis and Visualization of Upper-Limb Grasp Motion

5.1 Motion Analysis

An analysis is carried out on the data measured by the games and the performance values for the elements of movement calculated. To visualize the parameters for each element of movement, they are put into 5 levels of evaluation. The method for the analysis is shown below:

1. Balance of finger pressure

   Studies the scattering in maximum pressure from each finger when the user puts pressure on all fingers in the simultaneous maximum pressure finger examination game (b), and standard deviation is calculated from the average pressure of each finger (5). The value of the standard deviation is then evaluated into one of 5 levels.

$$\sigma = \sqrt{\frac{1}{10} \sum_{i=1}^{10} (F_i - \mu)^2} \tag{5}$$

   σ: Standard deviation, $F_1 \sim F_{10}$: each finger pressure (F_1 is right thumb, F_{10} is left pinkie) [N], μ: The mean value of each fingers' maximum pressure [N].

2. Finger exercise capacity

   In order to investigate whether the user can move each finger as instructed in the finger reaction game (c), the amount of time taken between the direction being given and the maximum finger pressure for the relevant finger being exerted is evaluated into one of 5 levels.

3. Upper-limb exercise smoothness

   In order to study the smoothness of the arm movements when the shoulder is centered during the movement imitation game (a), the minimum jerk model is calculated from the value of the 3-axis acceleration sensor. The evaluation function value is then evaluated into one of 5 levels.

$$C = \frac{1}{2} \int_0^{t_f} \left\{ \left(\dot{a}_x(t) \right)^2 + \left(\dot{a}_y(t) \right)^2 + \left(\dot{a}_z(t) \right)^2 \right\} dt \, [\text{m/s}^3] \tag{6}$$

   a_x, a_y, a_z: triaxial acceleration [m/s²].

4. Shoulder movement scope

   To study the flexibility and range of movement when the arm is rotated with the shoulder centered during the movement imitation game (a), the amount that the controller was moved either up, down, left, right, or at a slant from its place on the knees is evaluated. The evaluation is based on the reference angle of the outer rotation of the joint movement region measurement, and evaluated into one of 5 levels. A value is calculated from the average of each direction.

5. Upper-limb and finger coordination

   To study hand-eye coordination in the object moving game (d), the amount of time taken to move the ball and the number of times that it is dropped is evaluated. The time required is evaluated into one of 5 levels, and a level is dropped for each time the ball was dropped.

6. Hand-eye coordination

   In order to study feed-back control capabilities within the scope of hand-eye coordination during the ball rolling game (f), the time taken to roll the ball to the target area is evaluated into one of 5 levels.

5.2   Supporting Training by Visualization

So that each user can easily comprehend the characteristics of their elements of movement, their data is made into an easy-to-understand spider chart (Fig. 5). The average data for each generation and for young people can also be displayed, making it easier for the user to see where they stand when compared to others.

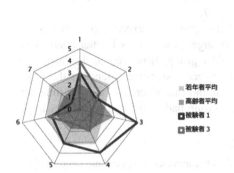

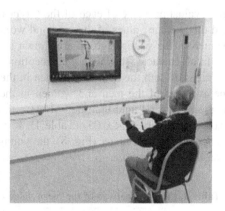

Fig. 5. Upper-limb-grasp motion cobweb chart

Fig. 6. Experimental situation

6   Evaluation Experiment

6.1   Experiment

To test the effectiveness of the measurement of upper-limb grasp motion, analysis, and visualization of results using the created system, a comparison was carried out between the elderly and the young.

6.2   Target Group

The research content was explained orally and through literature to the target group, and 12 healthy young and elderly people who gave their consent were selected. The elderly group was made up of 6 people (3 men and 3 women with an average age of 79.3 ± 5.7) who weren't prevented from exercising by their doctors, and the younger group was also made up of 6 people (3 men and 3 women with an average age of 24.3 ± 2.7) who were healthy university students.

6.3   Method

The content of the game was displayed on a large screen via PC, and the target group took part in the experiment by taking the controller and sitting in a chair 2 m away from the display (Fig. 6). The way to use the controller was explained. The games played were the 6 that were described in Chap. 4. The elements of movement of both the younger and older group were measured using the controller and game content, and an evaluation was calculated relating to each of the 6 types of motion characteristics.

6.4   Results

The evaluation value of each of the 6 types of motion characteristics were calculated, and the average values of the men and women from the older group, and the men and women of the younger group are shown in Fig. 7.

In all characteristics with the exception of the upper-limb exercise smoothness, the averages of both the men and women in the younger group yielded better results than the averages of the men and women in the older group. However, in the inspection analysis, it was found that the only trait that showed a significant gap was the finger exercise capacity ($p < 0.05$) (Table 1). It was found that when the reaction time was compared for each finger (Fig. 8), the younger group had better results in every finger than the older group.

Table 1. The comparison of the mean value of each parameter of upper-limb coordination

	Elderly	Young	P value
Balance of finger pressure [N]	212.693	186.952	0.3967
Finger exercise capacity [s]	1.808	1.210	0.0145
Upper-limb exercise smoothness [m/s^3]	14003893	17854048	0.38517
Shoulder movable scope [deg]	91.783	73.268	0.09963
Upper-limb-finger coordination [s]	25.815	6.1230	0.05929
Eye-hand coordination [s]	54.775	15.260	0.15183

Furthermore, when each trait was analyzed in detail, a significant difference ($p < 0.05$) between the older and younger group was found in the flexibility and movement scope of the shoulder in the up and down direction only (Fig. 9).

7   Investigations

We analyzed by quantifying 6 motion elements composing upper-limb movement. Although every subject's result was different from each other, elderly people group's result was more varied than younger group. So that we found, even they are same generation, elderly people's exercise capability and characteristic are not the same for each person. The only trait which showed a significant difference was the finger exercise capability component, it's thought that this is because there is a big scattering in the capabilities of those in the older group.

Furthermore, in relation to the finger exercise capability characteristic, which showed a significant difference, although it's thought that the older group's delay in reaction speed is also part of the cause, it's also thought that due to the larger disparity of results when compared to the younger group, the older group find it difficult to move

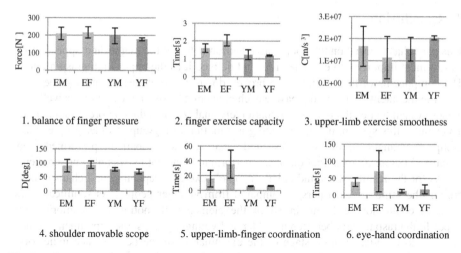

1. balance of finger pressure   2. finger exercise capacity   3. upper-limb exercise smoothness

4. shoulder movable scope   5. upper-limb-finger coordination   6. eye-hand coordination

Fig. 7. The comparison of upper-limb coordination EM (elderly male), EF (elderly female), YM (young male), YF (young female)

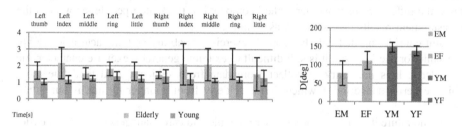

Fig. 8. Finger exercise capacity

Fig. 9. Shoulder movable scope (up-down)

their finger by their reflexes (Fig. 8). In fact, during the experiment itself, it was observed that the older group would move their fingers after vocalizing the direction, or move the wrong finger by mistake. It could be thought that the older group need to comprehend which finger to move and then move the finger after thinking about it. Therefore, there's a possibility that it's difficult for them to move their fingers intuitively in their private lives (e.g. using a remote control, chop stick, scissors).

Though in this paper we didn't impression evaluation, elderly who use our system said "Interesting" "I want to continue to use" "I want to buy". It seems that we can urge to do training by giving a game system entertainment.

8 Conclusion

This paper has focused on the cooperative motion between the fingers and upper-limbs, a movement important to everyday life, and defined it as the upper-limb grasp motion. The components of this motion were broken down into 6 elements, and a game controller and contents that could measure each element of movement created, as well as a games system that evaluated and comparatively analyzed this data before visualizing it. To evaluate this system, the upper-limb grasp motion of a group of older people and a group of younger people was measured, analyzed, a comparison performed, and visualized before an examination of the performance indicators was also undertaken.

As for the results, we found elderly people's exercise capability and characteristic are not the same for each person compared from younger people. As significant differences could not be found in all of the elements of motion that comprise the upper-limb grasp motion between the older and younger groups, the experiment did not progress to the visualization stage or the examination of the performance indicators. However, from the larger disparity found in the measured values in each element of movement in the older group when compared to the younger group, it was found that there is an individual gap between upper-limb grasp motion capabilities that bears no relation to age. Furthermore, it was also found that in the finger exercise capability tests, the difference in movement when compared to the young people, as well as the measurement results themselves, was significant.

But considering that elderly people's exercise capability and characteristic are not the same for each person, it is still difficult to examine generally exercise characteristic of elderly. It is necessary to collect more data from subjects. And to define more suitable performance index which divides elderly from younger by that is our future work.

In the future it will have found, elderly people and care managers can make it easier to see their characteristic or where they stand when compared to others by using this system. Furthermore, it can be expected that this system will be useful for the people who makes long-term care plan.

References

1. Seidler, R.D.: Motor control and aging: links to age-related brain structural, functional, and bichemical effects. Neurosci. Biobehav. Rev. **34**(5), 721–733 (2010)
2. 文部科学省: 生涯にわたる心身の健康の保持増進のための今後の健康に関する教育及びスポ ーツの振興の在り方について保健体育審議会 答申). http://www.mext.go.jp/b_menu/shingi/old_chukyo/old_hoken_index/toushin/1314691.htm
3. Shim, J.K.: Age-related changes in finger coordination in static prehension tasks. J. Appl. Physiol. **97**(1), 213–224 (2004). Published
4. Ranganathan, V.K.: Skilled finger movement exercise improves hand function. J. Gerontology Med. Sci. **56A**(8), M518–M522 (2011)
5. Lo, A.C.: Robot-assisted therapy for long-term upper-limb impairment after stroke. N. Engl. J. Med. **362**, 1772–1783 (2010)

6. Crawford, J.D.: Spatial transformations for eye-hand coordination. J. Neurophysiol. **92**(1), 10–19 (2004)
7. Anguera, J.A.: Video game training enhances cognitive control in older adults (NeuroRacer). Nature **501**, 97–101 (2013)
8. Hackel, M.E.: Changes in hand function in the aging adult as determined by the Jebsen Test of Hand Function. Phys. Ther. **72**, 373–377 (1992)
9. Ranganathan, V.K.: MSE: effects of aging on hand function. J. Am. Geriatr. Soc. **49**(11), 1478–1484 (2001)
10. Ketcham, C.J.: Age-related kinematic differences as influenced by task difficulty, target size, and movement amplitude. J. Gerontol. Psychol. Sci. **57B**(1), P54–P64 (2002)
11. Bernhardt, J.: Accuracy of observational kinematic assessment of upper-limb movements. Phys. Ther. **78**, 259–270 (1998)
12. Desrosiersa, J.: Age-related changes in upper extremity performance of elderly people: a longitudinal study. Exp. Gerontol. **34**(3), 393–405 (1999)
13. Poston, B.: Movement structure in young and elderly adults during goal-directed movements of the left and right arm. Brain Cogn. **69**, 30–38 (2009)
14. Voelcker-Rehage, C.: Motor-skill learning in older adults—a review of studies on age-related differences. Front. Hum. Neurosci. **5**, Article 26 (2011)
15. P.G. Levine: Stronger After Stroke. Demos Medical Pub., New York (2008)
16. メディカ出版: リハビリウム起立くん. http://www2.medica.co.jp/topcontents/kirithu/
17. 矢島大輔: 時系列データ解析による脳血管障害患者のリーチ動作の運動解析, 理学療法科学 **23**(6), 765–772 (2008)
18. Darling, W.G.: Control of simple arm movements in elderly humans. Neurobiol. Aging **10**, 149–157 (1989)
19. Cooke, J.D.: Kinematics of arm movements in elderly humans. Neurobiol. Aging **10**, 159–165 (1989)
20. Flash, T., Hogan, N.: The Coordination of arm movements: an experimentally confirmed mathematical model. J. Neurosci. **5**(7), 1688–1703 (1985)

A Grammar-Based Framework for Rehabilitation Exergames

Victor Fernandez-Cervantes$^{(\boxtimes)}$, Eleni Stroulia, and Benjamin Hunter

University of Alberta, Edmonton, AB, Canada
{vf,stroulia,bkhunter}@ualberta.ca

Abstract. Numerous serious exergames advocate the use of engaging avatars to motivate a consistent exercise regimen. However, the process of specifying the prescribed exercise, implementing it as avatar animation, and developing an accurate feedback-providing mechanism is complex and requires a high level of expertise in game engines, control languages, and hardware devices. Furthermore, in the context of rehabilitation exergames, the requirements for accurate assessment and timely and precise feedback can be quite stringent. At the same time, the Kinect^{TM} motion-capture sensor offers a natural interface to game consoles, and its affordability and wide availability represents a huge opportunity for at-home exergames. In this paper, we describe our work towards a system that envisions to simplify the process of developing rehabilitation exergames with Kinect^{TM}. The system relies on a language for specifying postures and movements between them, and includes an editor that enables rehabilitation therapists to specify the prescribed exercise, by editing a demonstration of the exercise. This exercise-specification grammar is used to drive the animation of an avatar and the provision of quality feedback, by comparing the player's postures (as captured by the Kinect^{TM}) against those of the coaching avatar and the grammar.

Keywords: Kinect-based gameplay · Interface · Serious games · Rehabilitation

1 Introduction

The concept of "serious games" refers to digital games whose purpose is more than entertainment [1]. The core intuition behind the serious-game paradigm is that, when learning tasks are embedded within a gameplay scenario, learners, motivated by the mechanics of gameplay such as "scoring points", "clearing levels", and "getting badges", spend more time learning, which facilitates the acquisition of new knowledge and skills.

A particularly interesting type of serious games are "exergames", i.e., games designed to encourage physical activity towards improving physical ability and

© IFIP International Federation for Information Processing 2016
Published by Springer International Publishing AG 2016. All Rights Reserved
G. Wallner et al. (Eds.): ICEC 2016, LNCS 9926, pp. 38–50, 2016.
DOI: 10.1007/978-3-319-46100-7_4

fitness, or towards systematizing athletes' training, or towards rehabilitation from injury or other health challenges. The development of exergames is a quite demanding software-engineering task: in addition to requiring the design of engaging avatars, animations and game mechanics, it also demands knowledge about specialized hardware sensors and controllers, game engines, algorithms for processing the sensor signals, producing feedback for the user and controlling the game state. Even more importantly, it relies on the specialized domain knowledge of exercise experts, such as trainers and physical therapists.

Exergames have received substantial attention recently, as controllers that use full-body motion, such as the very popular and relatively inexpensive Wii and Kinect^{TM}, have become increasingly available at-home. The latter, in particular, represents an extremely attractive platform for exergames [9] since it enables adequate skeleton tracking, and its SDK and user community offer substantial software-development support. Recognizing this opportunity, a variety of exergames have been developed that cover a broad design spectrum: on one hand, one can find complex systems with no evident gameplay [6]; on the other hand, some games [7,8] offer engaging gameplay but with restricted and limited movements, and, therefore, limited potential for physical conditioning.

It is our belief that the Kinect^{TM}-based gameplay for exergames suffers from a feasibility gap: today, there is no toolkit to support the integration of personalized animation, guidance feedback, and valid exercise assessment. As a result, even though the sensor is cost-effective, widely available, and sufficiently accurate, its potential is not yet fully met. Motivated by this position, the key objective of this work is to introduce Avatar Grammar Animation System (AGAS), our Kinect^{TM}-based toolkit for supporting the development of rehabilitation exergames in Unity. Our system offers an editing tool that enables casual computer users, with expertise in physical exercise but no software-engineering expertise, to specify an exercise script, including key postures and the movement between them. This editor, in effect, enables users to annotate a pre-recorded demonstration of the exercise with rules about the angles of the important joints in each step of the exercise. The resulting exercise script, represented in terms of the underlying AGAS grammar, an extension of the grammar reported in [8], is then used by the Unity game engine to (a) animate a coach avatar that demonstrates the exercise at run-time during gameplay, and (b) provide timely and accurate feedback to the player about his/her posture and movement.

The rest of this paper is organized as follows. Section 2 places our work in the context of related research, reviews Kinect^{TM} as the underlying hardware of our system, and motivates the use of fuzzy logic for assessing the user's movements. In Sect. 3, we describe the architecture of our system and our experience with it to date. Finally, in Sect. 4, we close with a summary of the key contributions of our system and our plans for future work.

2   Related Research and Background

Exergames: In 2006, the Wii console evolved the gameplay paradigm with an interactive control-system that established a rapport between the player and a digital avatar [2]. This rapport was shown to motivate exercise consistency and perseverance of seniors, who reported increasing levels of enjoyment during the 6-weeks training program with Wii Fit Plus games [3]. Another study reported similar results with overweight children who improved their exercise habits playing a virtual running game, featuring a slim and toned avatar design [4].

In late 2010, the affordable motion-capture Kinect^{TM} changed the gameplay once again to a natural body-motion interface. Even though the videogame console, Xbox, did not exploit this new capability –gameplay in games such as JUST DANCE[1] or ZUMBA fitness[2] is the same across all the main videogame consoles, and does not take advantage of the unique features of each console– the Kinect^{TM}'s potential for serious games has been amply demonstrated. In [5], the data from multiple tracking devices is combined to recognize dance patterns, using a Hidden Conditional Random Fields (HCRF) classifier. In [6], "seated Tai Chi" is presented as a Kinect-based physical rehabilitation exercise. The system was designed for patients with movement disorders and assessed their ability with a very simple measure: it evaluated whether some angles of interest in the patient skeleton were equal (within a threshold) to some pre-defined values. As a result the system can only give very simple feedback on eighteen postures. The same control system with more innovative game-flow design was presented in the sorcerer's apprentice [7], which was designed for patients with SIS (Subacromial Impingement Syndrome). The prescribed movements are specified as boundaries preconfigured by the therapist. The gameplay allows the patient to focus on playing, while achieving the goals in the rehabilitation exercises. In our own previous work [8], we focused on a more realistic mechanism for providing high-quality feedback in rehabilitation serious games. To that end, we developed a fuzzy grammar for evaluating the correctness of postures and movements. Our original grammar was, however, limited to analyzing mostly static postures and dynamic transitions through changes of a single angle between three joints. We also developed an intutitive user-interface feedback guide: a fill-up bar, attached to the corresponding joint, which fills up following the movement of the player and presents the correct angle with an arrow. In this paper, we describe an extension of our original grammar that can capture more complex exercises (such as TaiChi) and we develop an editor to enable exercise experts to define exercise scripts in this grammar.

Avatar Animation: The topic of avatar animation is quite vast and, in this section, we cannot but mention only an eclectic collection of works, on two broad topics. On the topic of movement animation, there is work on inverse kinematics for maintaining balance [10]; skeleton animation with walking cycles [11]; falling and landing with concern for self-preservation [12]; and realistic mass and balance properties of physical characters [13]. On the topic of the character appearance, there is work on animating non-human characters based on skeleton semantics [14]; representing avatars as arbitrary 3D mapping points [15] or with visually highly realistic bodies [16] and facial expressions [17]; and animating

---

[1] http://just-dance.ubi.com.

[2] http://zumbafitnessgame.com/.

3D puppets based on real-time motion capture [18]. In the context of serious exergames for rehabilitation, our interest in avatar animation stems from the need to communicate in an intuitive and unambiguous manner the movements to be mimicked by the player. In effect, our goal is to develop a system that will enable non-computer experts to animate a precise coach avatar demonstrating the prescribed exercise and providing timely and accurate feedback to the player.

A few platforms have been proposed to facilitate this task. The Flexible Action and Articulated Skeleton Toolkit (FAAST) [19] is a middleware that integrates full body control. Unfortunately, the gestures captured with the Kinect^{TM} are only substitutes for keyboard commands or a virtual mouse. XDKinect [20] is a similar toolkit, with an online framework service to recognize gestures. In [21], a multimedia environment for children rehabilitation is described. The system controls an avatar in Second Life to demonstrate the therapy exercises. The system is limited in terms of the exercises it can cover: the exercise postures focus on a single joint angle and so does the assessment. The motion-tracking evaluation system presented in [22] uses Unreal Engine 4 to compare the player's skeleton as recorded with the Kinect^{TM} sensor with the in-game avatar. This system requires a developer to program the avatar and offers very coarse-grained feedback regarding the correctness of the player's movements: simply red and green colors over the avatar's joints. This simple feedback makes it almost impossible to discern the specific corrections required in each posture. The Dual-Task Tai Chi game suffers from similar limitations, but with more interesting game play [23], using Kinect^{TM}-based full-body control with a cognitive task, i.e., 4×4 Sudoku. In this game, the user has to reach a specific posture in order to select a number with the right hand or foot, and then place this number on the Sudoku grid with the left hand or foot. The posture sequence during the game are similar to tai-chi.

The Kinect^{TM} Sensor: The Kinect^{TM} V2, on which AGAS is based, presents many improvements over its predecessor [24]. It is composed by infrared and color camera, with a resolution of 512×424, and 1920×1080 respectively. The sensing process is orchestrated by a fast clock signal whose strobes an array of three laser diodes, which simultaneously shine through diffusers, bathing the scene with short pulses of infrared light. The sensor also calculates the ambient-lighting, the final image invariant to lighting-changes. The accuracy of the Kinect^{TM} V2 in computing the joints' positions is lower than motion-capture systems, however it is "good enough" for some of the regimen exercises, or therapy. the discrepancy could go from $13\,mm$ to $64\,mm$ [25].

The Kinect^{TM} SDK version 2.0 estimates the position and orientation of 25 joints, organized in a hierarchy, centered at the spine base (SB), as shown in Fig. 1(a). This hierarchy causes difficulties with several postures, due to occlusion or, more generally, lack of information regarding the root of a particular joint and its hierarchical rotation, i.e., the amount of rotation in the 3D space that the joint inherits from its parent joint.

Fuzzy Logic: In order to assess the player's exercise style and provide feedback to motivate and improve it, an efficient mechanism for continuously comparing the player's actual posture against the "correct" one is required. In this work, similar to our previous work [8], we adopt a fuzzy-logic paradigm for that purpose, in order to avoid simplistic angle comparisons (as used in [6]). The fuzzy-logic paradigm considers that uncertainty is unavoidable when concepts are imprecisely expressed in natural language: in the context of the rehabilitation-exercise specification, the concepts of "correct" and "incorrect" posture are expressed with a real value between "1" and "0" indicating a degree of correctness.

3   Software Architecture

The AGAS system consists of three components: (a) a recording component through which an *expert demonstration* of the exercise is captured in a form that can be viewed and manipulated in Unity;[3] (b) an editor, implemented in Unity, through which a exercise expert reviews the demonstration to produce an *exercise script*, including *key postures*, their *important joints*, and the transitions between them; and (c) a game-playing engine, also implemented in Unity, during which the player's movement is compared against the coach avatar, i.e., the exercise script animation, and the rules around the important key-posture joints.

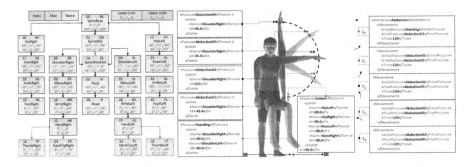

Fig. 1. (a) Kinect^{TM} skeleton tracking SDK 2.0 (Position, Orientation, Hierarchy, and Rotation); (b) Exercise-script animation

3.1   Exercise Demonstration and Recording

The motion-capture-and-recording component records 30 fps, each of which includes the complete information regarding all joints shown in Fig. 1(a). Each frame record includes (a) the frame timestamp in milliseconds, with the first

---

[3] The AGAS recorder is based on the examples of https://www.assetstore.unity3d.com/en/#!/content/18708 for how to use Kinect^{TM} V2 in Unity, including examples for how to start the camera, how to record data, and how to control the avatar based on the recording.

frame defining time 0; and (b) a sequence of joint records, each one consisting of the joint's identification number, and its orientation in three-dimensional space, centered at the 0_{th} joint, at the *SpineBase*.

3.2   The Exercise-Script Editor

In our AGAS system, an exercise specialist can review and edit the *exercise demonstration*, through the editor, shown in Fig. 3. The AGAS editor reads as input the demonstration frame sequence and provides a user interface through which an exercise expert, can review the the demonstration and identify the exercise *key postures*, selecting the appropriate frames where these postures are demonstrated.

Reviewing Avatar Postures: Through the AGAS editor, the exercise expert can replay, stop, move to next and previous frames of the demonstration record. When reviewing the avatar posture in a particular frame, the user can inspect the posture from multiple camera views and can review each avatar joint.

As shown in Fig. 1(a), the avatar is a rigid body with 25 interconnected joints. The orientation of each joint is relative to its parent joint in the skeleton hierarchy of Fig. 1(a). This implies that a change in the orientation of a joint affects the positions of all its descendant joints. For each joint j_i, in each frame of the recorded exercise demonstration, the following information is available:

$$j_i = \{Name, \theta_x^i, \theta_y^i, \theta_z^i\} \tag{1}$$

where *name* is the joint's label (and implicitly its position in the joint hierarchy) in the Kinect^{TM} skeleton, and the angles $\theta_x, \theta_y, \theta_z$ correspond to the orientation of the joint in the specified axes, in the frame under examination.

Specifying Key Postures and Transitions: The main purpose of the editor component is to produce an *exercise script*, based on the expert's demonstration of the exercise. The exercise script consists of a succession of *key postures*, starting with the *initial posture* demonstrated by the expert. The intuition behind the definition of the exercise script is that the player going through the exercise **has to** reach some key postures, which are defined in terms of their *important posture joints*, i.e., a subset of joints that have to be at precise orientation angles in this key posture. These major posture joints move from one key posture to the next, according to the demonstrated timing. The exercise expert, using the editor, (a) identifies the key postures; (b) specifies the major joints for each posture; (c) reviews and corrects the precise orientation angles of the major joints - in case the demonstration is not perfect; and, implicitly, (d) records the timing between these major postures.

The various elements involved in the specification of an exercise script are illustrated in Fig. 1(b). *Posture* elements specify the static skeleton configurations that the user must reach during the exercise. *Movement* elements specify the timing of the dynamic transition between two consecutive postures, expressed in the number of lapsed frames between the two postures. For every exercise script, there are two special postures: the *initial posture* is the first skeleton configuration of the recorded demonstration, and the *final posture* is the final skeleton configuration, correspondingly. The two may be the same, in fact they often are for exercises that start and finish at the same position, after going through a sequence of other intermediate postures. Each posture is characterized by a descriptive *name* element, and its unique *id* attribute. Each posture element is composed of a set of *joint* elements, a proper subset of the 25 Kinect^{TM}-skeleton elements, whose exact orientations are important for the posture to be considered correctly achieved. For each joint, its name is specified (as shown in Fig. 1(a)) as well as some (or all) of the *X-axis, Y-axis, Z-axis* orientation angles, relative to its parent joint.

```
<posture initial=true id=1>
    <name>posture name</name>
    <joint important=true>
        <name>joint name</name>
        <axis>angle</axis>
    </joint>
    <joint> ... </joint>
    ...
</posture>

<movement>
    <source><ref:posture ref=1></source>
    <target><ref:posture ref=100></target>
    <time>frames</time>
</movement>
```

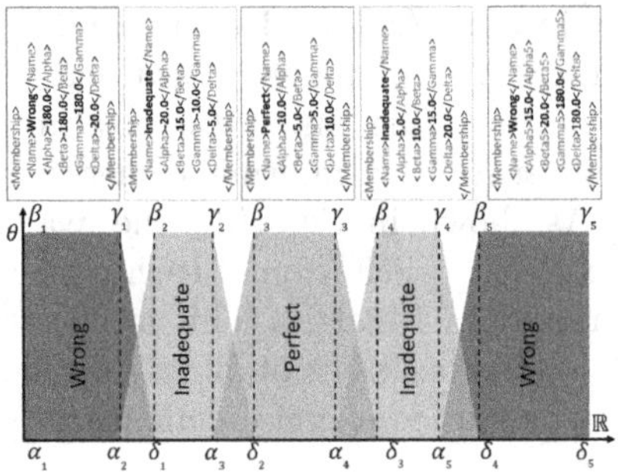

Fig. 2. The exercise script language (Color figure online)

The key postures are identified by the exercise expert as he/she reviews the exercise demonstration (see Sect. 3.1). As the expert moves through the frames of the demonstration record, he/she recognizes a key posture and, through the user interface in Fig. 3, selects the important joints, i.e., the defining joints for the posture. If a particular joint is not in a "perfect" position, the expert may also edit its orientation angles. Through this interaction, the key postures of the exercise are collected in the exercise script. The movement elements are inferred implicitly, based on the data between two consecutive key postures. The initial and final key postures are identified, by default, as the postures on the initial and final frames of the demonstration record. Finally, it is important to note that the specification of an *important joint* in a *key posture* gives rise to a corresponding fuzzy *assessment rule*, to be evaluated during game play at run time.

Coach-Avatar Animation: The coach avatar mimics the demonstrated exercise as a prearranged animated sequence, described in the exercise script.

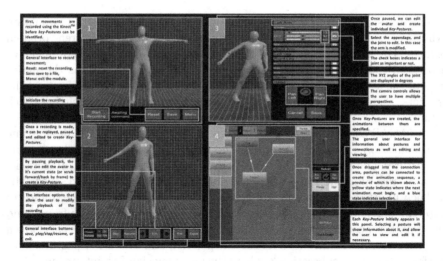

Fig. 3. The AGAS exercise-script editor

The coach avatar is composed of 33 joints. In addition to the twenty-five main joints of the Kinect^{TM} avatar, eight more joints are used for the animation of muscle movement, in key areas such as hips, legs, and shoulders, enabling a more realistic appearance of body movement.

The coach avatar initially appears with the standard T-Posture; in this posture, all Kinect^{TM}-skeleton joints are assumed to be in their corresponding 0,0,0 position. The animation process is controlled by the exercise script, as follows.

(a) At each step, the coach avatar moves from one key posture (source) to the next (target).

(b) The transition from the source to the target key posture is completed in the number of frames prescribed by the corresponding animation element in the exercise script.

(c) All major joints of the source key posture move synchronously until they reach their orientation in the target key posture. In principle, there are two directions of movement between any two angles; the direction of the movement is chosen so that the distance the joint travels is minimized. In order to produce a naturalistic animation, corresponding joints in subsequent key postures should not be more than 90° away (in any angle).

(d) Finally, the deltas of the joints' movements, between two frames, in all axes are equal. In effect, the animation component extrapolates a number of intermediate postures, at a rate of 30 fps, between every two consecutive key postures, to create the appearance of a smooth and fluid movement.

The animation process starts with the default T-posture which transitions to the first key posture of the exercise, and then iterates through all key postures until the last one.

An interesting feature of the AGAS component for exercise-script animation is that the same exercise script can potentially be applied to different original postures. For example, one could apply a script for upper-arm movement to an original sitting posture, for wheelchair-bound users. As long as the major joints of the key postures in the exercise script do not involve movements of the leg joints, the exercise could be demonstrated by a standing or a sitting coach avatar.

The AGAS editor user interface, shown in Fig. 3, enables all the design-time functionalities, i.e., exercise recording and replaying, identifying and reviewing key-postures, and specifying the transitions between them. In Fig. 3, subsection 1 shows the recording interface, where the movements are recorded and saved. The playback interface is shown in subsection 2, where the user has the ability to pause the playback, adjust its speed and direction, scrub frame-by frame, and export all key postures created. When playback is paused the user is also given the option to edit the avatar in its current position and save a key posture. This interface is shown in subsection 3, where the user may signify joints as important as well as select them to observe and modify the corresponding X, Y, and Z angles. Camera controls allow multiple views of the posture and a save option lets the user save the current pose as a key posture. Finally, subsection 4 shows the interface for reviewing and animating created key postures. Here the user can review and edit each posture, or finally preview and specify the transitions between two key-postures to create the animation script for gameplay.

3.3 Kinect-Based Gameplay

During gameplay, the coach avatar demonstrates the exercise in the context of the game background, the user performs the exercise and his/her avatar reflects his/her movements right next to the coach avatar, and the assessment component evaluates the correctness of the player's performance and provides appropriate feedback, through highlighting of the user's skeleton's joints (see Fig. 1(b)). We have explained the coach avatar demonstration in Sect. 3.2 and the replay of the Kinect^{TM}-captured user movement in Sect. 3.1. In this section, we describe the assessment component of our AGAS system.

The AGAS exercise-assessment component performs two types of evaluation of the user's performance, according to two measures: (a) the frame-by-frame similarity of the user's skeleton to the coach-avatar skeleton, and (b) its adherence of the user's skeleton to the rules around the orientation of the major joints of each key posture.

Conformance to Key Postures: In general, the complete assessment of a *key posture* relies on a collection of rules, each one corresponding to a major joint of the posture, J_2, and its angle relative to its parent and child joints, J_1, and J_3. The joints J_1 and J_3 form a interior angle with J_2, and the rule defines the correct angles θ among these joints in the corresponding axes: $\theta_x(left - right)$, $\theta_y(up - down)$, $\theta_z(front - back)$. The assessment rules are fuzzy: they specify smooth transition between correct and incorrect joint orientation, as opposed to defining a sharp boundary to separate these two states. For each important joint, a fuzzy rule, illustrated by the five overlapping trapezoid functions, shown in Fig. 2, defining a range of transitions from perfect to wrong. At run time, the game-playing component continuously evaluates the rules for all major joints for the next anticipated key posture, and identifies the frames at which each of the rules is met "perfectly" or "adequately" or "not at all" and provides feedback by annotating the joints with a color, ranging from green(perfect) to yellow(inadequate) and red(wrong), with a smooth color transition in between functions.

Frame-by-Frame Dynamic Angle Similarity: In parallel with the rule-based assessment of the key-posture joints, a second assessment measure is applied to the major arm and leg bones of the player. At each frame, the orientations of these bones in the player's avatar skeleton are compared against the orientations of the corresponding bones in the coach avatar skeleton.

During game play, the feedback component uses the frame-by frame assessment to highlight the arms and legs of the user's avatar. A configurable "difficulty" parameter modifies a threshold which defines what is perfect (green), neutral (yellow), or incorrect (red). For each compared bone, the average of the absolute differences of the three corresponding angles is compared against this threshold to determine the color shown to the user; the closer to 0 the absolute average difference is, the better the player has matched the coach.

3.4   Experience and Reflection

The AGAS tool enables the development of the basic elements of a serious exercise game, based on a demonstration of the game exercise. The display in Fig. 4 shows the product of this process, placed on a background. At this point, the game is playable, and it enables valid exercise by giving basic feedback on its correctness; yet, further work is needed to make it engaging and motivating. To complete the game, the aesthetic elements of the game have to be developed, including the background visuals, the music, and the body(ies) of the coach and player avatar. This remaining development is primarily the responsibility of designers; in effect, AGAS systematizes and simplifies the developers' tasks, so that an exercise expert can actually accomplish them based on their domain knowledge. To date, we have used AGAS to develop a set of simple upper-body exercises, similar to the ones found at http://eldergym.com/elbow-exercises. html. We have also developed a small TaiChi game, consisting of few simple TaiChi moves. The former game was relatively easy to develop, since the key postures are relatively clear to identify (in fact for most of the above exercises the eldergym web site identifies the key postures with still pictures), each posture consists of few important joints, and the orientation angles of these joints are simple to describe. In fact for most of these exercises the joints' orientations between key postures change only in one dimension. The TaiChi game is, however, much more challenging: the key postures are much more complex and multiple joints move between any two of them.

Fig. 4. Run-time posture assessment and feedback (Color figure online)

4   Conlcusions

In this paper we described AGAS, a tool for supporting the development of serious exergames, that can be used for rehabilitation purposes. These games must communicate in an intuitive and unambiguous manner the movements of the player's rehabilitation regimen, as prescribed by an exercise expert. In developing AGAS, our goal was to enable non-computer experts to animate a precise coach avatar demonstrating the prescribed exercise and providing timely and accurate feedback to the player. At the core of our tool is a simple grammar for postures and transition movements between them. Specifications of an exercise in this grammar can be constructed by an exercise expert using the AGAS editor to inspect and annotate a demonstration of the exercise. These specifications are then fed into the AGAS game-playing component, which is responsible for observing the player's movements, comparing them to the specification as well as to a coach-avatar simulation and providing feedback to the player so that he can improve his posture and movement.

In the future, we plan to improve the feedback component to provide more accurate feedback with respect to timing, and we will extend the editor to support the exercise experts with hints as to which the best key postures might be.

References

1. Susi, T., Johannesson, M., Backlund, P.: Serious games: an overview (2007)
2. Karoussos, K.: Mii & you. In: Proceedings of the 3rd International Conference on Digital Interactive Media in Entertainment and Arts, pp. 496–498. ACM (2008)
3. Nicholson, V.P., McKean, M., Lowe, J., Fawcett, C., Burkett, B.: Six weeks of unsupervised Nintendo Wii Fit gaming is effective at improving balance in independent older adults. J. Aging Phys. Act. **23**(1), 153–158 (2015)
4. Li, B.J., Lwin, M.O., Jung, Y.: Wii, myself, and size: the influence of Proteus effect and stereotype threat on overweight children's exercise motivation and behavior in exergames. Games for Health Res. Develop. Clinical Appl. **3**(1), 40–48 (2014)
5. Kitsikidis, A., Dimitropoulos, K., Douka, S., Grammalidis, N.: Dance analysis using multiple kinect sensors. In: 2014 International Conference on Computer Vision Theory and Applications (VISAPP), vol. 2, pp. 789–795. IEEE (2014)

6. Lin, T.Y., Hsieh, C.H., Lee, J.D.: A kinect-based system for physical rehabilitation: utilizing tai chi exercises to improve movement disorders in patients with balance ability. In: 2013 7th Asia Modelling Symposium (AMS), pp. 149–153. IEEE (2013)
7. Fikar, P., Schoenauer, C., Kaufmann, H.: The Sorcerer's Apprentice A serious game aiding rehabilitation in the context of Subacromial Impingement Syndrome. In: 2013 7th International Conference on Pervasive Computing Technologies for Healthcare (PervasiveHealth), pp. 327–330. IEEE (2013)
8. Fernandez-Cervantes, V., Stroulia, E., Oliva, L. E., Gonzalez, F., Castillo, C.: Serious games: rehabilitation fuzzy grammar for exercise and therapy compliance. In: 2015 IEEE Games Entertainment Media Conference (GEM), pp. 1–8. IEEE (2015)
9. Obdrzalek, S., Kurillo, G., Ofli, F., Bajcsy, R., Seto, E., Jimison, H., Pavel, M.: Accuracy and robustness of Kinect pose estimation in the context of coaching of elderly population. In: 2012 Annual International Conference of the IEEE Engineering in Medicine and Biology Society (EMBC), pp. 1188–1193. IEEE (2012)
10. Baerlocher, P., Boulic, R.: An inverse kinematics architecture enforcing an arbitrary number of strict priority levels. Vis. Comput. **20**(6), 402–417 (2004)
11. Multon, F., France, L., Cani-Gascuel, M.P., Debunne, G.: Computer animation of human walking: a survey. J. Vis. Comput. Anim. **10**(1), 39–54 (1999)
12. Dykes, S.B.: U.S. Patent No. 8,228,336. U.S. Patent and Trademark Office, Washington, DC (2012)
13. Kenwright, B.: Real-Time Physics-Based Fight Characters
14. Wang, X., Ma, Q., Wang, W.: Kinect driven 3D character animation using semantical skeleton. In: 2012 IEEE 2nd International Conference on Cloud Computing and Intelligent Systems (CCIS), vol. 1, pp. 159–163. IEEE (2012)
15. Rhodin, H., Tompkin, J., In Kim, K., Varanasi, K., Seidel, H.P., Theobalt, C.: Interactive motion mapping for realtime character control. Comput. Graph. Forum **33**(2), 273–282 (2014)
16. Teran, J., Sifakis, E., Blemker, S.S., Ng-Thow-Hing, V., Lau, C., Fedkiw, R.: Creating and simulating skeletal muscle from the visible human data set. IEEE Trans. Vis. Comput. Graph. **11**(3), 317–328 (2005)
17. Kalra, P., Magnenat-Thalmann, N., Moccozet, L., Sannier, G., Aubel, A., Thalmann, D.: Real-time animation of realistic virtual humans. IEEE Comput. Graph. Appl. **18**(5), 42–56 (1998)
18. Leite, L., Orvalho, V.: Anim-actor: understanding interaction with digital puppetry using low-cost motion capture. In: Proceedings of the 8th International Conference on Advances in Computer Entertainment Technology p. 65. ACM (2011)
19. Suma, E.A., Lange, B., Rizzo, A.S., Krum, D.M., Bolas, M.: Faast: the flexible action and articulated skeleton toolkit. In: 2011 IEEE Virtual Reality Conference (VR), pp. 247–248. IEEE (2011)
20. Nebeling, M., Teunissen, E., Husmann, M., Norrie, M.C.: XDKinect: development framework for cross-device interaction using kinect. In: Proceedings of the 2014 ACM SIGCHI Symposium on Engineering Interactive Computing Systems, pp. 65–74. ACM (2014)
21. Abdur Rahman, M., Qamar, A.M., Ahmed, M.A., Ataur Rahman, M., Basalamah, S.: Multimedia interactive therapy environment for children having physical disabilities. In: Proceedings of the 3rd ACM Conference on International Conference on Multimedia Retrieval, pp. 313–314. ACM (2013)
22. Alabbasi, H., Gradinaru, A., Moldoveanu, F., Moldoveanu, A.: Human motion tracking evaluation using Kinect V2 sensor. In: E-Health and Bioengineering Conference (EHB) 2015, pp. 1–4. IEEE (2015)

23. Kayama, H., Okamoto, K., Nishiguchi, S., Nagai, K., Yamada, M., Aoyama, T.: Concept software based on Kinect for assessing dual-task ability of elderly people. Games for Health Res. Develop. Clin. Appl. **1**(5), 348–352 (2012)

24. Butkiewicz, T.: Low-cost coastal mapping using Kinect v2 time-of-flight cameras. In: Oceans-St. John's 2014, pp. 1–9. IEEE (2014)

25. Xu, X., McGorry, R.W.: The validity of the first and second generation Microsoft Kinect for identifying joint center locations during static postures. Appl. Ergon. **49**, 47–54 (2015)

Two Experimental Virtual Paradigms for Stress Research: Developing Avatar-Based Approaches for Interpersonal and Evaluative Stressors

Oswald D. Kothgassner[1], Helmut Hlavacs[2], Leon Beutl[2], Lisa M. Glenk[3,4], Rupert Palme[5], and Anna Felnhofer[6(✉)]

[1] Department of Child and Adolescence Psychiatry, Medical University of Vienna, Vienna General Hospital, Vienna, Austria
[2] Research Group Entertainment Computing, University of Vienna, Vienna, Austria
[3] Comparative Medicine, Messerli Research Institute, University of Veterinary Medicine Vienna, Medical University of Vienna, University of Vienna, Vienna, Austria
[4] Karl Landsteiner Research Institute for Neurochemistry, Neuropharmacology, Neurorehabilitation and Pain Treatment, Landesklinikum Mauer, Amstetten, Austria
[5] Unit of Physiology, Pathophysiology and Experimental Endocrinology, University of Veterinary Medicine Vienna, Vienna, Austria
[6] Department of Pediatrics and Adolescent Medicine, Medical University of Vienna, Vienna, Austria
anna.felnhofer@meduniwien.ac.at

Abstract. In light of the rather limited ecological validity of paradigms traditionally used for social stress research, the current paper set out to introduce virtual analogues of the Cyberball-Game (Williams 2007) and the Trier Social Stress Test (Kirschbaum, Pirke, and Hellhammer 1993). Both were tested in samples of healthy adults using salivary cortisol, self-reported stress and presence as dependent measures. Results indicate a significant rise in cortisol levels and subjective stress; presence, however, was not correlated with stress reactivity. In sum, this study clearly supports the use of virtual environments in stress research as they offer both the internal control and ecological validity needed to generalize findings to real-world settings.

Keywords: Virtual reality · Social stress · Stress induction · Stress research · Cyberball-Paradigm · Trier Social Stress Test (TSST)

1 Introduction

Given its role in the development of various diseases, social stress has been a subject of extensive research in past decades (c.f., Ruiz et al. 2010). The exposure to a psychosocial stressor is known to result in an acute physiological stress response, involving the activation of the Sympatho-Adrenal-Medullary (SAM) axis and the

© IFIP International Federation for Information Processing 2016
Published by Springer International Publishing AG 2016. All Rights Reserved
G. Wallner et al. (Eds.): ICEC 2016, LNCS 9926, pp. 51–62, 2016.
DOI: 10.1007/978-3-319-46100-7_5

Hypothalamus-Pituitary-Adrenal (HPA) axis. The SAM-system causes an immediate increase in heart rate, whereas the HPA-axis activation entails a rise in blood and salivary cortisol levels (Kudielka and Kirschbaum 2005).

Generally, two kinds of social stressors may be distinguished: social-evaluative threats versus interpersonal (rejection) stressors (c.f., Dickerson and Kemeny 2004). The first usually occurs in a performance context such as public speeches or job-interviews. It involves being potentially exposed to negative evaluations and even failure. Studies show that cortisol reactivity is particularly large and recovery rates are low when confronted with social evaluative threats, especially if they are perceived as uncontrollable (Dickerson and Kemeny 2004). In everyday situations, however, these performance based social evaluations are not as common. More frequently, individuals may be exposed to (quite subtle) forms of social rejection. These may involve disapproval and criticism by peers or even being ignored by others. It has been shown, that social exclusion is particularly threatening for fundamental social needs like belonging and self-esteem (Williams 2007). Also, a repeated exposure may lead to cardiovascular diseases (Kemp et al. 2012) and depression (McEwen 2005).

1.1 Experimental Paradigms in Social Stress Research

In light of its pathogenic significance, it is not surprising that in recent years research on social stress has gained in numbers (c.f., Ruiz et al. 2010). Traditionally, paradigms such as arithmetic tasks or public speaking scenarios (Dickerson and Kemeny 2004) have been used to induce stress in laboratory settings.

One of the most widely applied experimental paradigms for social stress induction is the Cyberball-Game (Williams 2007). It represents a computer-based ball-tossing game, in which the participant is excluded from the game by two computer-animated players. As such, it is a perfect example of an interpersonal rejection stressor. Past studies have demonstrated the paradigm's effectiveness in evoking a number of stress related responses (e.g., Eisenberger, Lieberman and Williams 2003; Geniole, Carré and McCormick 2011; Moor, Crone and Van der Molen 2010; Wesselmann et al. 2012; Williams 2007; Zwolinski 2012). However, the task has also been criticized for its lack of mundane realism (Parsons 2015). The abstract stimulus bears only minimal resemblance to face-to-face social interactions and is, thus, regarded as limited in its ecological validity.

Another commonly used protocol for social stress induction is the Trier Social Stress Test (TSST; Kirschbaum, Pirke, and Hellhammer 1993). It requires a participant to prepare a five minute speech which s/he then delivers in front of two to three confederate actors; also, the participant performs a five minute arithmetic task. The TSST constitutes a typical social evaluative threat which is mostly perceived as uncontrollable because of the actors' neutral facial expressions and lack of predictability and which results in significant levels of stress (Kudielka et al. 2004a, b). Yet, the drawback of this method is that it requires the actors to hold their reactions constant in each trial. It is a prerequisite which is difficult to achieve across studies and may, thus, limit inter- and intra-individual comparisons (Ruiz et al. 2010).

1.2 Virtual Reality Based Solutions for Stress Research

A viable solution for these methodological problems is proposed by immersive virtual environments (IVEs). On the one hand, IVEs may provide a standardization of stimuli by introducing computer-controlled characters which reduce human error and circumstantial variations (Bohil, Alicea, and Biocca 2011). On the other hand, they allow for a real-time, dynamic interaction which approximates real-life social encounters (Parsons 2015). As such, IVEs constitute a loophole for the intricate problem of combining ecological validity and experimental rigor.

However, the precondition for IVEs to be considered ecologically valid is that they evoke reactions in users which are comparable to real-life situations. A phenomenon which has extensively been discussed to be responsible for the success of IVEs is the so called sense of presence. Presence may be defined as a sense of being there in the IVE. It is seen as a basis for a concordance between an emotion experienced in an IVE and one experienced in a comparable physical environment (Slater 2003). Yet, the debate regarding the nature of the relationship between presence and emotions is still ongoing (e.g. Diemer et al. 2015).

For both paradigms (Cyberball and TSST), attempts have been made to develop virtual counterparts. So far, three studies introduce a virtual Cyberball-Game and present preliminary results on its usefulness (i.e., Kassner et al. 2012; Kothgassner et al. 2014; Segovia and Bailenson 2012). However, Kassner et al. (2012) did not use physiological markers to assess stress reactivity, and Kothgassner et al. (2014) only assessed the SAM axis reactivity. Given that cortisol is particularly sensitive to social stressors (Dickerson and Kemeny 2004), the generalizability of both studies is limited and further empirical support is needed.

Similarly, virtual TSST versions have been introduced by different research groups (e.g. Delahaye et al. 2015; Fich et al. 2014; Kelly et al. 2007; Jönsson et al. 2010; Montero-López et al. 2015; Ruiz et al. 2010). However, the virtual TSSTs used in these studies differ with regards to content. While Fich et al. (2014) and Jönsson et al. (2010) used three virtual interviewers each, other authors used five (Kelly et al. 2007) or even 80 avatars (Delahaye et al. 2015) instead of the formerly proposed two to three interviewers. Also, these studies tend to alter the experimental setup by including an audience that is 'restless' rather than neutral (e.g. Ruiz et al. 2010). Hence, it is possible, that these alterations confounded the observed stress reactions.

1.3 Objective

In sum, social stress research is in need of ecologically valid stress induction scenarios. As traditional paradigms suffer from a number of disadvantages, IVE based counterparts are increasingly considered as valuable alternatives. This study set out to create virtual analogs for the two most commonly used and most well researched social stress paradigms, the Cyberball-Game and the TSST protocol. The objective was to provide support for their effectiveness using a multimodal assessment of stress responses (including subjective and objective markers). Also, by covering two complementary social stressors (social-evaluative threats vs. rejection stressors), more far-fetched conclusions about social stress reactivity in IVEs as well as generalizations to other paradigms were supported.

2 Methods

Two experimental psychological studies were conducted to explore the virtual paradigms' effectiveness in evoking social stress. Study 1 evaluated a virtual Cyberball-Game and Study 2 involved a virtual TSST. In accordance with the Declaration of Helsinki, subjects signed an informed consent and received course credits.

2.1 Study 1 (Cyberball)

Participants. Eight female (4 each group) German speaking undergraduates with an age ranging from 22 to 25 years participated in the current study.

Measures. To assess physiological stress reactions, salivary cortisol samples were taken via cotton swabs (Salivette®, Sarstedt, Wiener Neudorf, Austria). Participants were instructed to put the swabs into their cheek pouch and wait for 80 s to ensure sufficient saturation of the cotton with saliva. Prior to further processing, the samples were stored at -20 C. Sample analyses were centrifuged at room temperature (at 3000 g for 15 min) and then analyzed according to a sensitive cortisol enzyme immunoassay (see Palme and Möstl 1997). A total of 10 µl of a 1:10 clear saliva dilution were used and all samples were assayed in duplicates. To assess the virtual experience, a single item from the iGroup Presence Questionnaire (IPQ, Schubert, Friedmann, and Regenbrecht 2001) was used ("In the computer generated world I had a sense of 'being there'). Additionally, a single question ("Are you stressed?") served as an indicator for the subjective stress response. Another single item assessed the participants' perception of exclusion during the study ("Do you feel rejected and excluded?") on a visual analogue scale (VAS, 10 cm length).

Procedure. Upon their arrival at the VR-lab, participants were randomly assigned to one of two conditions (1) inclusion vs. (2) exclusion. They were asked to fill out a demographic screening and the VAS stress question before being donned the head-mounted-display (Sony HMZ-T1, Sony, Japan) with an external head-tracking unit (TrackIR 5, NaturalPoint, US). A wireless control unit (F710, Logitech, Switzerland) allowed tossing the ball. The left key had to be pressed to toss the ball to the left player and vice versa. Participants in the exclusion condition only received 4 ball tosses (duration: 45−60 s) before being excluded from the game with no further tosses until the end of the 5-minute interval. The remaining participants received a pre-programmed amount of ball tosses (30 %). Afterwards, participants were asked to fill out the remaining psychometric measures (IPQ and VAS stress question).

Cortisol samples were collected at 4 time points: (1) 20 min before the IVE exposure, (2) immediately before exposure, (3) 20 min and (4) 35 min post exposure. The overall procedure lasted approx. 80 min; all experiments were conducted in the afternoon (1:30–3:30 p.m.) to account for diurnal variation in cortisol release.

2.2   Study 2 (TSST)

Participants. Five German speaking students (3 females, 2 males) with an age ranging from 24 to 26 years were assessed via the VR-TSST.

Measures. Salivary cortisol samples also served as an indicator for social stress in this experiment. The extraction method as well as subsequent analyses did not differ from Study 1; the time points for sample collection are described below. Again, the IPQ item "sense of being there" (Schubert, Friedmann, and Regenbrecht 2001) and the VAS stress question assessed the subjective experience.

Procedure. Prior to exposure, participants filled out the pre-experimental questionnaires (demographics, VAS stress). Subsequently, they were informed about the job interview and a preparation time of 5 min was provided. Analogous to study 1, the same HMD and head tracking unit were used. At the start of the simulation, the two virtual interviewers (1 female, 1 male) entered the room, sat down and asked the participant why s/he was the best candidate for the job. Like in the original TSST, participants passed a job-interview in the first half of the task (5 min), for the remaining 5 min, they conducted an arithmetic task (subtract 13 from 1022). The avatars retained neutral expressions throughout the interview; their answers included instructions such as "This is incorrect. Please start over from 1022". After the procedure, participants answered the IPQ item and the single stress-question; 20 min post procedure, subjective stress was measured again. Cortisol samples were collected at 6 time points: (1) 20 min prior to stressor onset, (2) 10 min, (3) 20 min, (4) 25 min, (5) 40 min and (6) 60 min post exposure. The overall procedure lasted 80 min.

2.3   Technical Implementation

The applications use the open source render engine Ogre3D for real-time rendering of the scenes. The source code is written in C++ using the express version of Visual Studio. OpenAL, the well-known audio library was used for playing the sounds. All objects and animations in the scenes were created using Blender3D.

Options Cyberball

1. **Mood:** The park can be rendered in 5 different 'moods': (1) happy, (2) anger, (3) boredom, (4) sadness, (5) fear. The moods are masked by numbers to prevent the users from seeing the chosen option. Happy will render the park with a clear sky and pleasant surroundings. Anger is the same as happy, but there will be loud construction sound playing and construction vehicles will be visible. Sadness renders the park with a dark cloudy sky and rain. Boredom renders a concrete floor surrounded by concrete walls. Lastly, fear renders the park scenario at night. For this study, the default setting 'happy' with a sunny park was used.

Fig. 1. The virtual Cyberball-paradigm (left) and virtual TSST (right)

2. **People**: If this option is selected, other virtual characters (i.e., agents) will walk around the park, yet interacting with them is not possible for the user.
3. **Ballplayers**: This option is the core of the Cyberball-scenario (Fig. 1). It will render two additional virtual humans (1 male, 1 female) which will engage the user in a short football game. In the 'inclusion condition' the players keep playing with the user, in the 'exclusion condition', however, the avatars continue to play only with each other and further exclude the user from the game.

Options TSST

1. **Interviewer**: This setting allows specification of the interviewers' gender.
2. **Speaker**: This option specifies the interviewer who does the talking.
3. **Emotions**: Sets the interviewers' facial expressions to the emotion they are supposed to express. By default neutral is selected, other options are happy or hostile.
4. **Ally**: If this option is selected, another person (an ally) will participate in the interview. Again, the gender can be chosen. The ally is seated directly next to the user and s/he will answer the questions if the user fails to do so.
5. **Helper**: This option will make the ally more supportive, encouraging the user with some predefined phrases (i.e., "You are doing great").

3   Results

The results for the stress reactivity in both studies are presented in Fig. 2.

3.1   Study 1 (Cyberball)

The repeated measures ANOVA showed a significant increase of salivary cortisol concentration ($F(18,3) = 6.262$; $p < 0.004$), especially in the excluded group ($F(18,3) = 4.069$; $p = 0.023$). There is a distinct interaction effect, displaying that excluded participants showed significant increases in saliva cortisol (+51 % to baseline), whereas included participants had a lower increase after the Cyberball game (+22 % to baseline). Moreover, there is a significant increase in self-reported stress levels ($F(5,2) = 12.298$; $p < 0.001$), but only excluded participants rated the Cyberball game

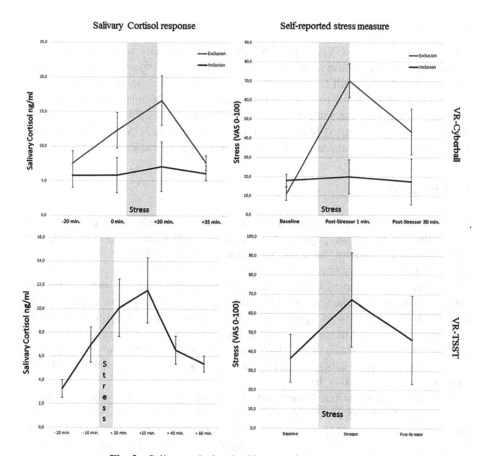

Fig. 2. Saliva cortisol and self-reported stress response.

as stressful ($F_{(5,2)} = 10.821$; $p = 0.002$) and stated, that they felt excluded ($F_{(8,1)} = 28.612$; $p = 0.002$). Table 1 shows a null finding regarding the relationship between the sense of being there and cortisol stress reactivity as well as the self-reported measure after social exclusion and inclusion.

Table 1. Correlations between sense of being there and stress measures*

		VR-TSST			VR-Cyberball		
		1	2	3	1	2	3
1	Self-report stress#	–	0.518	-0.263	–	0.283	0.131
2	Salivary cortisol#		–	-0.099		–	0.575
3	Sense of being there			–			–

* No significance within an Alpha of 5 %.
\# Measured during stressor; self-report stress is measured by the single-item question immediately after the stressor (VAS); salivary cortisol values point out mean salivary cortisol levels during speech and math task or the saliva sample immediately after the Cyberball stressor.

3.2 Study 2 (TSST)

A repeated measures ANOVA with a subsequent Greenhous-Geisser correction depicts a significant stress response in salivary cortisol ($F(7.345,1.836) = 5.247$; $p = 0.040$). Both the speech and math task seem to evoke a stress response in salivary cortisol concentration of 68 % for the speech task and 83 % for the math task respectively compared to the baseline sample measure. Furthermore, participants had significant stress ratings post exposure ($F(4,2) = 7.051$; $p = 0.017$; $\eta^2 = 0.23$). Again, Table 1 shows no correlation between presence and cortisol or the subjective stress response.

4 Discussion

In light of the rather limited ecological validity of paradigms traditionally used for social stress induction, the current paper set out to introduce virtual analogues of two popular, well researched paradigms, the Cyberball-Game (Williams 2007) and the Trier Social Stress Test (TSST, Kirschbaum, Pirke, and Hellhammer 1993). The present findings suggest that both the virtual Cyberball and the virtual TSST may be used as effective tools for social stress induction. All TSST-participants as well as those excluded from the Cyberball-Game showed significant increases in salivary cortisol during exposure to the stressor and reported to feel stressed. These observations are largely in line with prior research (e.g., Jönsson et al. 2010; Ruiz et al. 2010), and the current effect sizes are comparable to those achieved with the original tasks (Beekman, Stock, and Marcus 2016; Kudielka et al. 2004a, b).

The findings on the virtual Cyberball-task particularly constitute a valuable addition to the body of data on cortisol responses to social exclusion. To date, there is no consensus on whether the experience of social exclusion under laboratory settings results in an increase in cortisol (c.f. Dickerson, and Zoccola 2013). Prior studies using the original Cyberball-Game (i.e., Beekman, Stock, and Marcus 2016; Zöller et al. 2010) produced conflicting findings. A more ecologically valid virtual scenario, however, may lead to different results than the minimalistic original. Thus, the present study offers first evidence that virtual social threats – similar to real life-threats – may result in a considerable HPA axis activity. Certainly, a drawback of this study is the fact that possible gender differences in stress reactivity could not be considered as the sample consisted only of women. In order to substantiate the claim that cortisol increases are larger in women when confronted with social rejection, whereas men react more to achievement stressors (Stroud, Salovey, and Epel 2002), future VR research is challenged to balance participants' gender.

Another issue that was not considered in the current paper was the question of whether participants believed to interact with an avatar (i.e., a human-controlled character) or an agent (i.e., a computer algorithm). The Threshold Model of Social Influence (Blascovich et al. 2002) assumes that the degree of agency attributed to the virtual other influences the interaction. Other authors, however, have succeeded in demonstrating that it does not matter whether the Cyberball-players are controlled by a human or a computer (e.g., Kothgassner et al. 2014). In contrast to the virtual Cyberball and to the best of our knowledge, agency was not yet evaluated in studies on virtual TSST versions.

Hence, additional research is needed to further substantiate the claim that there is no difference in stress responses to avatars or agents for both virtual tasks.

A further concern is the validity of the findings. Generally, IVE stress induction paradigms have been found to produce medium to large effect sizes, approximating those of real-life-scenarios (c.f., Parsons 2015). Even though the present results are in line with those achieved with the original TSST (e.g., Kudielka et al. 2004a, b), a direct comparison of the virtual and real TSST would be the method of choice to establish validity. Also, comparing the virtual Cyberball to a face-to-face version would allow for a more thorough examination of its ecological validity. A first attempt (Kothgassner et al. 2014) has shown that virtual exclusion may result in similar stress responses (heart rate) as real exclusion, but results on cortisol reactivity are still missing.

Finally, presence was not correlated with the salivary cortisol response or subjective stress in the current study. This result corresponds with a virtual TSST study (Ruiz et al. 2010) which found no connection between the experience of presence and cortisol. Similarly, another study (Felnhofer, Kothgassner et al. 2014) found no correlation between presence, subjective anxiety and heart rate. Hence, rather than directly increasing the intensity of the emotional reaction, presence seems to serve as a precondition for an emotion or stress reaction to occur at all in IVEs. This study supports these findings and extends them to yet another indicator of stress –salivary cortisol. Future research should, however, complement questionnaire measures of presence with a multimodal approach (i.e., using behavioral markers) to shed more light on this issue. Also, the assessment of presence could be supplemented by another related yet distinct construct which could proof to be useful especially in avatar based IVEs: social presence (c.f., Biocca, Harms, and Gregg 2001).

4.1 Limitations and Conclusion

The present results once again strongly encourage the use of IVEs for diverse research purposes. Apart from traditional laboratory-based stress research, the introduced virtual counterparts may well be applied especially in fMRI studies. While being scanned, participants are usually confined to an enclosed space with little to no interaction. By creating Internet based shared IVEs, within which participants located kilometers apart may interact with each other, scientist may study neural responses simultaneously and under more ecologically valid circumstances (Bohil, Alicea, and Biocca 2011). For instance, the Cyberball-Game could consist of three participants actually playing with each other, and the TSST could make use of an extra function – an ally who sits right next to the interviewee and supports him/her.

Everyday social encounters involve a broad array of cues such as verbal and non-verbal reactions, joint attention, theory of mind as well as representation of self and others (Parsons 2015). Even though IVEs have come a long way to approximating real-life settings, they are still challenged to convincingly implement mechanisms of social interactions. In this study, basic avatar models were used with minimal facial and behavioral variability; spontaneous reactions were limited and the user was not able to freely engage the avatars. Yet, still, our participants responded with considerable stress to the virtual character. The Media Equation Concept (Nass and Moon 2000) may provide an explanation as to why image fidelity is not a key issue for a social response to computer generated images of others. This theory suggests that humans are evolutionarily prepared to react socially to even very minimal social cues (e.g. the impression of a face). This is alleviation for IVE programmers, as even low quality IVEs may trigger a substantial emotional and behavioral reaction in users as long as they are present. A study (Kothgassner, Felnhofer et al. 2016) assessing heart rate and cortisol responses to a public speech task in three groups (real audience, virtual audience, controls) further supports this assumption: it shows that stress responses in IVEs may solely be attributed to the confrontation with the social stimulus and not to the VR apparatus or other factors. Hence, the paradigms introduced here may also be used for therapeutic purposes, e.g. learning how to control one's stress level when confronted with social cues which are unpredictable and uncontrollable.

In sum, this study provided strong support for the implementation of virtual paradigms for social stress induction. The virtual analogues may on the one hand overcome the lack of ecological validity stemming from the minimalistic and abstract material; on the other hand, they may ensure an appropriate degree of control in order to enhance internal validity by providing interactions with no inter-subject variations.

Acknowledgements. We would like to thank Anna-Katherina Heinzle, Ellen Gerlach, Farina Flick and Johanna Rudyk for their support in the acquisition of parts of the data.

References

Beekman, J.B., Stock, M.L., Marcus, T.: Need to belong, not rejection sensitivity, moderates cortisol response, self-reported stress, and negative affect following social exclusion. J. Soc. Psychol. **156**(2), 131–138 (2016)

Biocca, F., Harms, C., Gregg, J.: The networked minds measure of social presence: pilot test of the factor structure and concurrent validity. In: 4th Annual International Workshop on Presence, Philadelphia, PA (2001)

Blascovich, J., Loomis, J., Beall, A.C., Swinth, K.R., Hoyt, C.L., Bailenson, J.N.: Immersive virtual environment technology as a methodological tool for social psychology. Psychol. Inq. **13**(2), 103–124 (2002)

Bohil, C.J., Alicea, B., Biocca, F.A.: Virtual reality in neuroscience research and therapy. Nat. Rev. Neurosci. **12**(12), 752–762 (2011)

Delahaye, M., Lemoine, P., Cartwright, S., Deuring, G., Beck, J., Pflueger, M., Graf, M., Hachtel, H.: Learning aptitude, spatial orientation and cognitive flexibility tested in a virtual labyrinth after virtual stress induction. BMC Psychol. **3**(1), 22 (2015)

Dickerson, S.S., Kemeny, M.E.: Acute stressors and cortisol responses: a theoretical integration and synthesis of laboratory research. Psychol. Bull. **130**(3), 355–389 (2004)

Dickerson, S.S., Zoccola, P.M.: Cortisol responses to social exclusion. In: DeWall, C.N. (ed.) Oxford Handbook of Social Exclusion, pp. 143–151. Oxford University Press, Oxford (2013)

Diemer, J., Alpers, G.W., Peperkorn, H.M., Shiban, Y., Mühlberger, A.: The impact of perception and presence on emotional reactions: a review of research in virtual reality. Front. Psychol., **6**(26) (2015)

Eisenberger, N.I., Lieberman, M.D., Williams, K.D.: Does rejection hurt? An FMRI study of social exclusion. Science **302**, 290–292 (2003)

Felnhofer, A., Kothgassner, O.D., Hetterle, T., Beutl, L., Hlavacs, H., Kryspin-Exner, I.: Afraid to be there? Evaluating the relation between presence, self-reported anxiety, and heart rate in a virtual public speaking task. Cyberpsychology, Behav. Soc. Netw. **17**(5), 310–316 (2014)

Fich, L.B., Jönsson, P., Kirkegaard, P.H., Wallergård, M., Garde, A.H., Hansen, Å.: Can architectural design alter the physiological reaction to psychosocial stress? A virtual TSST experiment. Physiol. Behav. **135**, 91–97 (2014)

Geniole, S.N., Carré, J.M., McCormick, C.M.: State, not trait, neuroendocrine function predicts costly reactive aggression in men after social exclusion and inclusion. Biol. Psychol. **87**(1), 137–145 (2011)

Jönsson, P., Wallergård, M., Österberg, K., Hansen, Å.M., Johansson, G., Karlson, B.: Cardiovascular and cortisol reactivity and habituation to a virtual reality version of the Trier Social Stress Test: a pilot study. Psychoneuroendocrinology **35**(9), 1397–1403 (2010)

Kassner, M.P., Wesselmann, E.D., Law, A.T., Williams, K.D.: Virtually ostracized: studying ostracism in immersive virtual environments. Cyberpsychology, Behav. Soc. Netw. **15**(8), 399–403 (2012)

Kelly, O., Matheson, K., Martinez, A., Merali, Z., Anisman, H.: Psychosocial stress evoked by a virtual audience: relation to neuroendocrine activity. CyberPsychology Behav. **10**(5), 655–662 (2007)

Kemp, A.H., Quintana, D.S., Felmingham, K.L., Matthews, S., Jelinek, H.F.: Depression, comorbid anxiety disorders, and heart rate variability in physically healthy, unmedicated patients: implications for cardiovascular risk. PLoS One **7**(2), e30777 (2012)

Kirschbaum, C., Pirke, K.M., Hellhammer, D.H.: The 'Trier Social Stress Test'–a tool for investigating psychobiological stress responses in a laboratory setting. Neuropsychobiology **28**(1–2), 76–81 (1993)

Kothgassner, O.D., Felnhofer, A., Hlavacs, H., Beutl, L., Palme, R., Kryspin-Exner, I., Glenk, L.M.: Salivary cortisol and cardiovascular reactivity to a public speaking task in a virtual and real-life environment. Comput. Hum. Behav. **62**, 124–135 (2016)

Kothgassner, O.D., Kafka, J., Rudyk, J. Beutl, L., Hlavacs, H., Felnhofer, A.: Does social exclusion hurt virtually like it hurts in real life? The role of agency and social presence in the perception and experience of social exclusion. In: Challenging Presence. Proceedings of the International Society for Presence Research, pp. 45–56 (2014)

Kudielka, B.M., Kirschbaum, C.: Sex differences in HPA axis responses to stress: a review. Biol. Psychol. **69**(1), 113–132 (2005)

Kudielka, B.M., Buske-Kirschbaum, A., Hellhammer, D.H., Kirschbaum, C.: HPA axis responses to laboratory psychosocial stress in healthy elderly adults, younger adults, and children: impact of age and gender. Psychoneuroendocrinology **29**(1), 83–98 (2004a)

Kudielka, B.M., Schommer, N.C., Hellhammer, D.H., Kirschbaum, C.: Acute HPA axis responses, heart rate, and mood changes to psychosocial stress (TSST) in humans at different times of day. Psychoneuroendocrinology **29**(8), 983–992 (2004b)

McEwen, B.S.: Glucocorticoids, depression, and mood disorders: structural remodeling in the brain. Metabolism **54**(5), 20–23 (2005)

Montero-López, E., Santos-Ruiz, A., García-Ríos, M.C., Rodríguez-Blázquez, R., Pérez-García, M., Peralta-Ramírez, M.I.: A virtual reality approach to the Trier Social Stress Test: contrasting two distinct protocols. Behav. Res. Methods, 1–10 (2015)

Moor, B.G., Crone, E.A., van der Molen, M.W.: The heartbrake of social rejection heart rate deceleration in response to unexpected peer rejection. Psychol. Sci. **21**(9), 1326–1333 (2010)

Nass, C., Moon, Y.: Machines and mindlessness: social responses to computers. J. Soc. Issues **56**(1), 81–103 (2000)

Palme, R., Möstl, E.: Measurement of cortisol metabolites in feces of sheep as a parameter of cortisol concentration in blood. Int. J. Mammal Biol. **62**(Suppl. 2), 192–197 (1997)

Parsons, T.D.: Virtual reality for enhanced ecological validity and experimental control in the clinical, affective and social neurosciences. Front. Hum. Neurosci. **9** (2015)

Ruiz, A.S., Peralta-Ramirez, M.I., Garcia-Rios, M.C., Muñoz, M.A., Navarrete-Navarrete, N., Blazquez-Ortiz, A.: Adaptation of the Trier Social Stress Test to virtual reality: psychophysiological and neuroendocrine modulation. J. CyberTherapy Rehabil. **3**(4), 405–415 (2010)

Schubert, T., Friedmann, F., Regenbrecht, H.: The experience of presence: Factor analytic insights. Presence **10**(3), 266–281 (2001)

Segovia, K.Y., Bailenson, J.N.: Virtual imposters: responses to avatars that do not look like their controllers. Soc. Influence **7**(4), 285–303 (2012)

Slater, M.: A note on presence terminology. Presence Connect **3**(3), 1–5 (2003)

Stroud, L.R., Salovey, P., Epel, E.S.: Sex differences in stress responses: social rejection versus achievement stress. Biol. Psychiatry **52**(4), 318–327 (2002)

Wesselmann, E.D., Wirth, J.H., Mroczek, D.K., Williams, K.D.: Dial a feeling: detecting moderation of affect decline during ostracism. Personality Individ. Differ. **53**(5), 580–586 (2012)

Williams, K.D.: Ostracism. Annu. Rev. Psychol. **58**, 425–452 (2007)

Zöller, C., Maroof, P., Weik, U., Deinzer, R.: No effect of social exclusion on salivary cortisol secretion in women in a randomized controlled study. Psychoneuroendocrinology **35**(9), 1294–1298 (2010)

Zwolinski, J.: Psychological and neuroendocrine reactivity to ostracism. Aggressive Behav. **38**, 108–125 (2012)

Success Factors for Applied Game Projects - An Exploratory Framework for Practitioners

Ralf Schmidt[1]([⊠]), Mirco Zick[1], Burkhard Schmidt[2],
and Maic Masuch[1]

[1] Entertainment Computing Group, University of Duisburg-Essen,
Duisburg, Germany
{ralf.schmidt,mirco.zick,maic.masuch}@uni-due.de
[2] Hochschule für Internationales Management- International University
Heidelberg, Heidelberg, Germany
b.schmidt@himh.de

Abstract. Applied games are an increasingly utilized approach to develop applications and concepts of organizational learning. However, which factors support the successful planning and execution of such projects within the organizational landscape remains unclear. This study initiates explorative research towards a success-factor model for applied games. The data is based on nine expert interviews within the DACH-region as well as a thorough literature review. The resulting factors are organized in a two-dimensional model, presenting the process of developing applied game projects and major organizational abstraction layers. The model aims to support the development of research and industry applied games productions in organizational context. Next steps are further validations as well as the development of a maturity model.

Keywords: Applied games · Gamification · Serious games · Game-based learning · Success factors · Best practices · Organizational learning

1 Introduction

Organizations continuously need to adapt to economic, technical and social changes that challenge established structures and its individuals alike [1]. Organizational development (OD) describes attempts of guided changes in organizations, which enable the personnel to cope with such environmental-based changes [2]. Typical goals are increases in performances, satisfaction or problem-solving [3]. Establishing organizational learning cultures is considered a constant contribution to OD and potential mechanism to achieve these goals [4].

Applied games [5] are still relatively new in organizational development and organizational learning. The original idea of using electronic and digital games for purposes other than entertainment roots in the 70 s. The early 2000 s then mark the beginning of the new generation of technically and educationally advanced, and heavily diversifying forms of applied games. Gameful applications [6] mark but the latest branch. A prominent European example was the serious game "Airline Company". The game transports the business model of Lufthansa AG to its employees.

© IFIP International Federation for Information Processing 2016
Published by Springer International Publishing AG 2016. All Rights Reserved
G. Wallner et al. (Eds.): ICEC 2016, LNCS 9926, pp. 63–74, 2016.
DOI: 10.1007/978-3-319-46100-7_6

"Module X" is a gamification learning platform incorporating applied gaming and web-based trainings at Bayer AG.

Multisensory stimulation, experiences of continual improvement and perceived proficiency are but a few of the many attributes applied games potentially inherit from their entertainment counterparts [7], which can be utilized in OD. Most research focuses on positive characteristics of games [7], best practices [8], frameworks guiding a successful design [9, 10] and questions of evaluation end effect [11]. Literature on how to successfully set up and conduct applied games projects is comparatively scarce. Therefore the aim of this study was to explore success factors described by experts in the field and to condense those into a model for practitioners.

2 Methodology

This study is based on an exploratory, qualitative approach. First experts with experience in conducting applied game projects needed to be identified. The search radius was narrowed to persons with a recent history (approximately 2010) of 10+ projects within an organizational context in the DACH-region (Germany, Austria, and Switzerland) to reflect probable cultural specialties. The search criteria resulted in a total of nine experts between 30 and 61 years with a history of 10 to 50 projects within search radius. Four held an academic title (4S). Backgrounds ranged from an explicit vitae in game design and development (2S), media and arts (1S) over economics and informatics (2S), to pedagogy (1S) and management (3S).

To solidify and ground previous findings an extensive literature research for success factors was conducted as a second step. It included relevant databases such as ACM DL, IEEE Xplore, ScienceDirect or SpringerLink. A first iteration concentrated on literature on applied games, such as gamification, game-based learning and serious games developed for organizational contexts. As the results were not extensive, a second iteration was conducted, to see what could be learned from other recent professions that share attributes with applied games. Those were: Relatively novel and innovative to organizations; a potential to contribute to organizational challenges mentioned above; a focus on the design of experiences; respecting the end user's needs. The selection resulted in the professions of user experience design [12] and design thinking [13].

Third a half-standardized interview questionnaire was developed based on the literature research and the underlying structure of a six-phase procedure model [14]. The questionnaire was assembled by all authors of the study.

Two types of interviews were conducted. The first series of seven interviews resulted in a wide range of statements that was processed according to the qualitative content analysis of Mayring [15]. The results were clustered distinctively to the phases of the process model as a horizontal structure. Next a type-structuring was conducted; clustering and counting similar expressions which resulted in a first iteration of the success-factors. A second series of four interviews, including two interviewees from the first series, aimed to revise and enhance the model. The interviewees were asked to comment on the success-factors found so far which resulted in some rearrangements, condensation and changes in wording of the factors.

Last the factors were classified along organizational abstraction layers, as defined below. The layers represent the second, vertical dimension concluding the two-dimensional success-factor model (Fig. 1).

Abbreviations. Throughout the further paper following abbreviations are used: "AG" = Applied Games; "SP" = Service Provider; User Experience = UX; Design Thinking = DT. A number followed by the letter "S" (e.g. 5S) highlights the collated number of subjects associated with a statement.

2.1 Two-Dimensional Framework

The horizontal dimension follows a six-phases procedure model [14]. It consists distinct and sequentially organized phases typical for applied game projects. For each phase input, throughput and output definitions are given. Iterations within each phase are strongly encouraged and common. Each end of a phase marks a possible exit of the procedure if results so far are not convincing or reasons demand ending the project. The idea of having closed phases while still iterating increases the plannability of an AG project. The model encourages a strict user-centered approach to AGs. It further aims at reducing known complexity regarding the solution and costs, with a close-to-100 % predictability at the end of the design phase. The vertical organization of the success factors follows three self-defined abstraction layers with an ascending level of influence by a SP.

First the organizational layer summarized factors, which are related to the culture, structure and external influences of an organization. The properties of these factors are rather consistent and hard to grasp, such as culture. Organizational factors exert an implicit influence on the AG project. Second the operational layer describes factors that frame the AG project, such as organizational goals, decrees, processes and workflows, teams and responsibilities. These factors follow mostly fixed rules and are usually well documented. Third the project layer refers directly to the AG-project and is about processes, human factors, methods, etc.

3 Literature Review

3.1 Applied Games

Michael & Chen [16] cite Quinn's most important preconditions for a project: A specific need for training, the perception and believe that a game approach could help and financial resources. Prensky, among other things argues for an openness and acceptance of the younger generation's play attitude towards serious contexts, such as work and learning [8]. Usually an organization needs to be convinced of a game-based solution and need to discuss an exit strategy for players who successfully finished a game [17]. Nicholson suggests to start a project with the desired outcome and a set of open questions to get there [18]. He and others also argue for a user-centered approach that addresses the target-user's needs and goals [10]. Other factors are facilitating a common ground among stakeholders about audiovisual quality and costs [16]. Academics again stress the necessity but also complexity of an early planning and implementations of evaluations [16, 19, 20] as the overall evidence of successful applied games remains rare [7, 21]. There is much more literature on the actual design of games for learning [7, 16], but that is outside scope of this paper.

3.2   User Experience

Likewise applied games, convincing customers is an important first step [22] in UX-projects [12]. Both is often new to organizations. A transparent and clear communication throughout the project avoids mistrust and gains the crucial management support [23]. Scholz and Wallach propose a five-step process for user-centered design [24]. It includes a thorough scoping, analysis of users and products, iterative design, evaluation and delivery of the product. Abele et al. focus on a systemic approach and a strict user-focus and propose communication of successful projects within the organization to advertise and establish the approach [25].

3.3   Design Thinking

Design Thinking is more a philosophy than an exact process [13, 26]. It describes a shift in one's attitude and thinking to approach a problem, likewise Schmidt et al. [14]. However, there are a number of rules, resources and methods such as ways for organizing information, working in small, mixed teams, well defined project scopes and a structured, time-bound and moderated process [13]. Flexibility, tangibility of ideas and prototypes and putting people first are other, very important constants of DT [13]. Others authors stress the importance of management commitment and clear communication to guide stakeholders through the probably unaccustomed way of thinking [26]. That includes the possibility of failure [27]. The idea of design thinking will feel less uncomfortable if an organization already established and innovative culture [28].

4   General Project Characteristics

All projects were declared innovation-projects and took place across industries (9S). Mid- to large-size organizations dominate the customers, presumably because of an earlier perception of the idea and larger personal and financial resources (9S). The experts did not disclose exact information on budgets but from the information given, ranges are between lower four-figure to mid six-figure amounts with a presumable typical range between 30.000–50.000 € and a project duration between three to six months. Interestingly, gamification budgets were rated 10-20 % cheaper in comparison to serious games projects (2S), probably because of smaller expected costs for audio-visual content. The most typical project-goal seems to be the increase of the overall performance and efficiency regarding learning goals. The designs therefore address motivation and behaviour of the learners to increase their engagement in the learning activity (8S). Most projects address younger people and are offered on top existing learning settings. Only rarely the organizations aim to replace a classic setting, such as seminars, completely. Six experts mentioned the additional political use of applied game projects, to support the company's public image (6S).

5   Success Factors

5.1   Overall Success Factors

Organizational layer – A culture of Innovation and Learning (9S). Similar to Prensky [8] for game-based learning and Hilbrecht and Kempkens for DT [28], all interviewees noted that a culture of innovation and learning in a customer's organization is advantageous (9S) on several levels. There seems to be a greater openness towards new ideas and ways to tackle problems and present learning scenarios frequently integrate new media. Most importantly those organizations follow an established innovation process that provides guidance to plan and conduct the project.

Operational layer – Managerial Support (9S). All interviewees and most literature stress the importance of managerial support of department and company heads to ensure the allocation of resources for the project (9S) [17, 26]. SPs must be aware that in a number of cases the contact person only explores the possibility of applied games and needs a business case before addressing superiors. Managerial support for AG projects cannot be taken for a fact within the organization and usually SPs are to earn and keep that support. Showstoppers, apart from missing managerial support, are a loss of interest in the topic or changes within organizational strategy and focus (3P).

Operational layer – Flexibility of Resources (4S). Fixed budgets are quite common with smaller organizations (2S) while bigger companies tend to allow flexibility (2S). There is a preference towards flexible budgets and other resources among the SPs while especially enterprises naturally prefer predictability. Two SPs (2S) try to negotiate each phase of the project separately and sequentially as suggested by Schmidt et al. [14]. Such practice may also foster the trust-building process but will sometimes be prohibited by organizational policy.

Operational layer – Transparency and Trust (5). Building and keeping up trust towards the idea of AGs and a SPs ability is indispensable across hierarchies. AGs are usually cooperative projects and therefore need a common sense among stakeholders, developed by the SPs. The overall project flow and next steps should be transparent at all times and invite customers to take part. Similar suggestions are found in [26, 29].

Operational layer – Moral and Ethics (2S). AGs are often criticized because of their manipulative nature [30]. Despite only explicitly mentioned by two interviewees, it was decided to include this factor as everyone working with persuasive designs should know about its advantages and downsides and therefore develop a clear position regarding project goals and morality.

5.2   Phase 1: Exploration

Both partners aim for a common understanding of the problem, project goals and success criteria. They discuss the motivation and chances for AGs as a possible solution to the problem and agree on milestones and financial parameters. A vision statement is a recommended outcome of this phase and foundation to a contract [14].

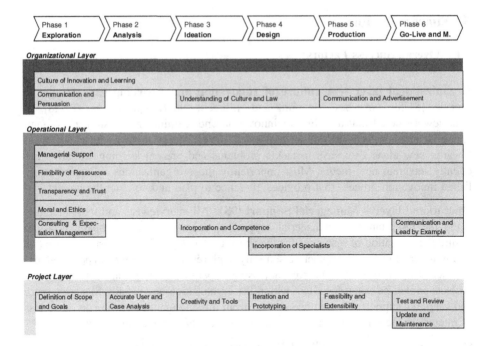

Fig. 1. Success-factor model

Organizational layer – Communication and Persuasion (5S). Quite often SPs must argue for AGs as a possible solution for learning and change in organizations. Inter-viewees stressed the sensibility of the word "game" and suggested to use other terms, such as motivational design or else (3S). Games and play are strongly connected with leisure time and work is attributed with seriousness and effectiveness in Germany (and elsewhere) (2S). Citing positive and competitor examples as well as stressing the idea of pleasure being a good precursor of job satisfaction and work performance, are common among SPs to argue for AGs (e.g. Schubert et al. [22]). However, some inevitable uncertainties about conventional problem solutions and cost pressure will naturally support the SPs argumentation (2S).

Operational layer – Consulting and Expectation Management (4S/6S). Consul-tancy is needed regarding chances, challenges and risks of a project and its coherence to company culture (4S) [28]. Moreover, most interviewees notice misleading thoughts about the complexity of game design and the expectable audiovisual quality of a product in the light of the budget ranges outlined above (6S). At last, two interviewees also discuss the necessity of an iterative process that accepts unconventional ideas and failing of ideas, likewise design thinking [13, 27] (2S).

Project layer – Definition of Scope and Goals (5S). Most interviewees discussed the relative vagueness of goals in the early stages of a project. The definition of distinct and measurable goals [16] within a specific project scope is accordingly part of the con-sulting and expectation management and will often differ from original ideas.

For example, the project lifetime has an important influence on the design of AGs (1S). Then again, goals need to be readjusted when new information is available (5S). Specifically referring to gamification, two SPs do not believe in cross-departmental projects (2S). Overall interviewees report a certain realism regarding goals and expectations towards behavior change and performance goals.

5.3   Phase 2: Analysis

A thorough context and target user-group analysis is conducted using qualitative and sometimes quantitative methods. The overall goal is to outline multiple perspectives from different stakeholders towards the problem and current solution and document the results with suitable artifacts such as user-journeys, use-case descriptions or technical specifications [14].

Project layer – Accurate User and Case-Analysis (9S). All SPs ensured to follow a user-centered approach. However, in most cases budgets and logistics do not allow for a thorough user-research process. Instead domain experts such as department managers provide contextual facts and information about users (9S). One interviewee explicitly highlighted the risk of inaccuracy of second-hand information for the success of the project (1S). Another mentioned the importance of choosing efficient methods, such as contextual inquiry and job shadowing, if given the chance (1S). First hand context and user information is a key factor in user-centered design and design thinking, too [13, 24, 25]. Standardized quantitative methods on the other hand appear not existent as these are thought to be less efficient.

5.4   Phase 3: Ideation (Idea + Creation)

The ideation uses the information of exploration and analysis to review and probably adjust the projects goals. A creative team incorporating multiple professions and domain experts aims to create a number of gameful solutions to the problem in workshop and creative sessions. Ideas are mixed, further elaborated and documented in a structured and comparable format, such as a canvas or exposé sheet, including visuals and first hand low-fi prototypes [14].

Organizational layer – Understanding of Culture and Law (4S). SPs need a thorough understanding of culture and law, both rural and organizational wise and a sensibility for the context and codes of conduct (4S). For example, in Germany strict data security rules mostly forbid ideas with a competitive nature. The following, non-extensive list of legal-fields is relevant to AGs in enterprises: (i) The Right to informational self-determination concerning the survey and use of personal data and questions of data ownership; (ii) Workplace-related rights usually enforced by employee-organizations and unions, such as rights of co-determination; (iii) IT-regulations and employee-agreements on ownership and use of outcomes conducted with a software; and (iv) Usage agreements and contractual rights between organization and SP.

Operational layer – Incorporation and Competence (4S). Besides finding a common ground like discussed above, SPs seek to raise competence levels regarding AGs on the customer side (4S). They do so to incorporate and partner up with the customer during the following project phases for purposes of easier mutual agreements on decisions and their consequences, likewise suggested by Wilke et al. [29]. Interviewees preferred to have at least one domain expert on their team who also may represent the target group. Workshops during which both parties ideate together are common. Some SPs are more cautious about incorporating customers, especially during the creativity processes, for effectiveness reasons (2S). DT likewise [13] argues for variety on the team and domain experts are requested in user experience projects [25].

Project layer – Creativity and Tools (5S). Interviewees suggested workshops as a primary format to iterate and ideate. These follow common rules for creativity sessions, such as no early critic, time-boxing and early visualization (5S). However, crazy ideas too early in the process could create doubts within conservative organizations. Warm ups exercises and discussing personal game experiences may help to start the activity and build a gameful attitude, which is important. (1S) [8, 13, 14].

5.5   Phase 4: Design

The design phase starts with a decision for one or more ideation results. The ideas are further elaborated and tested in a number of prototypes to test function, effectiveness, affective reactions of users and the overall experience they provide with respect to the projects goals. This phase includes feedback with target users and aims for a fully documented design concept, prototypes, content plan and technical specification that lays ground for a viable production planning [14].

Operational layer – Incorporation of Specialists (5S). When going further with one or more selected ideas, specialists should be added to the design team. On an administrative level the conformity of an idea to rules and regulations is required (employee organizations, stakeholders from IT, compliance and legal) (5S). Domain experts and pedagogical experts consult the team on a content level (4S).

Project layer – Iteration and Prototyping (4S). Likewise ideation the team should plan for a number of iterations during the design phase. Early low-fi and later hi-fi prototypes ensure the communication of functionality and emotionality of an idea (4S). It is important to regularly review the vision and goals of the project and respect common guidelines for usability and accessibility (1S). Other than suggested by literature, but coherent with the critic of phase two, target-users are only introduced late or not at all until the design is fixed (2S) [13, 17, 18, 25].

5.6   Phase 5: Production

The production is separated from the former creation phases. It is a predictive phase in terms of time and necessary resources where the product is actually implemented. Parallel to production the product's launch is being prepared [14].

Organizational layer – Communication and Advertisement (6S). Starting early to advertise the project across the target group and organization is a crucial factor for its later success [25] (4S), but regularly neglected from the experience of the SPs (2S). It is suggested to address management and set up a core communication team. Despite the importance of this aspect SPs usually are not incorporated (2S).

Project layer – Feasibility and Extensibility (3S). Overall the interviewees did not consider technical feasibility as a problem or risk (3S). A careful decision for a specific technology is of course important (2S). Requests for mobile or cross-platform development increase (1S). Three SPs stressed the need for a solid IT-architecture that allows for easy extension of features and contents after launch (3S).

5.7   Phase 6: Go-Live and Maintenance

The launch of the product concludes the project and should be accompanied by strong communication within the organization. An evaluation is conducted to control and review goals the contractors agreed on during project exploration and ideation. Probably maintenance and update conditions are negotiated [14].

Operational layer – Communication and Lead by Example (4S). Most AG projects are an additional offer above standard procedures, such as e-learning or seminars. When going live, department managers and core users are important multiplicators for project advertisement and role models (4S).

Project layer – Test and Review (5S). The majority of interviewees report tests of direct measurable data only, such as attendance or test results (5S). Other measures on soft factors, such as motivation or satisfaction are usually not applied. Academic methods, especially quantitative ones, can become costly. Organizations rather rely on informal indicators such as sensed satisfaction, which was criticized (3S).

Project layer – Update and Maintenance (4S). A periodically data collection and processing is common in the games world. The information suggests improvements and updates necessary to keep a product alive. The same would count for an AG that also wears of over time, like all technical products. Because of the nature of innovative projects unfortunately no budget is planned for maintaining the product (4S).

6   Discussion

The success-factor model reflects first hand practical experiences of conducting an AG project across a wide range of organizations and budgets. The findings show that project goals mostly seem concerned with organizational learning, probably followed by product marketing and issues of human resources [17]. However, AGs are far from established yet in the DACH-region and SPs mostly offer such services complementary to others, such as UX or e-learning. All projects were declared as innovation projects and show some typical characteristics accordingly [29].

Managerial support, communications and clear goal definitions are preconditions to a project in general. But SPs for applied games should take transparency and communications even more serious to gain trust and understanding towards the process and the only gradually revealing outcome of an AG project. It is suggested to educate customers towards the unfamiliar game-perspective and to incorporate them in creation and decision making. Times and budgets are relatively small and often do not allow for a thorough analysis on case and users. Without, it is difficult to design meaningful experiences and motivate on a deeper psychological level which fosters shallow designs as rightfully criticized [30]. Applied Games tend to process user data. Legal issues and company specific rules and culture therefore can have serious implications and might interfere with design ideas. Overall most of the qualitative factors presented could be backed up with literature, supporting the notion of a high-level comparability of UX, DT, and AG projects as presumed. However, the complexity of AG-projects suggests experience to be an additional important success-factor.

Since this is an exploratory study some limitations need to be addressed. First this kind of study is not able to and was not planned to infer causality. Second the number of expert interviewees (n = 9) is relatively small. This can partly be explained by the relative novelty of applied games and consequently a rare number of projects and partly by the narrow search radius of highly experienced experts. Therefore, we are confident to have identified a relevant sample for the DACH-region. Clearly, an international search would yield more representative results. Third no objective success criteria were mentioned as these differ widely across the projects. Standardized, practicable methods are not available apart from individual and indirect indicators, such as attendance. Fourth interviewees of the second series generally agreed on the two-dimensional framework but mentioned individual differences in the definition of the ideation and design phases.

AG projects remain a promising endeavor to organizational development, potentially improving the attractiveness and effectiveness of applications and processes of organizational learning, guided changes and enterprise software. Expectations regarding their quality and power to foster motivation and create meaningful experiences and outcome [7, 18] are high. When conducting such projects, much can already be learned from experts and other disciplines as referenced here. But budgets and circumstances need further adaption in some projects to actually transfer game-like experiences to the enterprise context. To contribute the further success of AGs, the results of this explorative research need further empirical and practical validation. A prioritization of the validated factors then eventually would allow for the design of a maturity model that helps enterprises and service providers to identify risks and areas of development of future projects. Cross-country studies would further help to differentiate general from rural and cultural depended aspects. Outside scope, this study suggests further research on design practices and standardized evaluation methods [11, 20] as well as on reasons and counterstrategies of weary effects.

Acknowledgements. We thank all interviewees for their time and valuable information and Thannos Rammos for the extensive background on legal aspects. We also thank the German Federal Ministry of Economic Affairs and Energy (BMWi) and DLR Project Management Agency for supporting this research.

References

1. Bundesministerium für Arbeit und Soziales: Grünbuch - Arbeit weiter denken (2015)
2. Nerdinger, F.W.: Organisationsentwicklung. In: Nerdinger, F.W., Blickle, G., Schaper, N. (eds.) Arbeits- und Organisationspsychologie, pp. 159–169. Springer, Berlin (2014)
3. Cummings, T.G., Worley, C.G.: Organization Development & Change. South-Western/Cengage Learning, Mason (2009)
4. Reichwald, R.: Innovative Arbeitsgestaltung im Unternehmen der Zukunft. In: Arbeiten und Lernen, pp. 39–54 (2001)
5. Schmidt, R., Emmerich, K., Schmidt, B.: Applied games – in search of a new definition. In: Chorianopoulos, K., Divitini, M., Hauge, J.B., Jaccheri, L., Malaka, R. (eds.) ICEC 2015. LNCS, vol. 9353, pp. 100–111. Springer, Heidelberg (2015)
6. Deterding, S., Dixon, D., Khaled, R., Nacke, L.: From game design elements to gamefulness. defining "gamification". In: MindTrek 2011, Proceedings of the 15th International Academic Conference on Envisioning Future Media Environments, ACM Press, New York (2011)
7. Whitton, N.: Digital Games and Learning. Routledge, New York (2014)
8. Prensky, M.: Digital Game Based Learning. Paragon House, St. Paul (2007)
9. Freitas, S.D., Liarokapis, F.: Serious games: a new paradigm for education? In: Ma, M., Oikonomou, A., Jain, L.C. (eds.) Serious Games and Edutainment Applications, pp. 9–23. Springer, London (2011)
10. Oprescu, F., Jones, C., Katsikitis, M.: I play at work - ten principles for transforming work processes through gamification. Front. Psychol. **5**, 14 (2014)
11. Ritterfeld, U.: Serious Games: Mechanisms and Effects. Routledge, New York (2009)
12. Hassenzahl, M.: Experience Design: Technology for all the Right Reasons. Morgan & Claypool, San Rafael (2010)
13. Brown, T., Katz, B.: Change by Design: How Design Thinking Transforms Organizations and Inspires Innovation. Harper Collins, New York (2009)
14. Schmidt, R., Brosius, C., Herrmanny, K.: Ein Vorgehensmodell für angewandte Spielformen. In: Strahringer, S., Ley, C. (eds.) Gamification. HMD Praxis der Wirtschaftsinformatik, pp. 826–839. Springer, Heidelberg (2015)
15. Mayring, P.: Qualitative Inhaltsanalyse : Grundlagen und Techniken. Beltz, Weinheim (2015)
16. Michael, D., Chen, S.: Serious Games: Games that Educate, Train, and Inform. Thompson Course Technology, Boston (2006)
17. Herger, M.: Enterprise Gamification. Createspace, Lexington (2014)
18. Nicholson, S.: A RECIPE for meaningful gamification. In: Reiners, T., Wood, L.C. (eds.) Gamification in Education and Business, pp. 1–20. Springer, Cham (2015)
19. Stokes, B., Walden, N., O'Shea, G., Nasso, F., Mariutto, G. Burak, A.: Impact with Games: A Fragmented Field. ETC Press under CC License. http://gameimpact.net/reports/fragmented-field/
20. Hamari, J., Koivisto, J., Sarsa, H.: Does gamification work? – a literature review of empirical studies on gamification. In: Proceedings of 47th Haiwai International Conference on System Sciences (2014)
21. Kapp, K.M.: The Gamification of Learning and Instruction: Game Based Methods and Strategies for Training and Education. Pfeiffer, San Francisco (2012)
22. Schubert, U., Groß, M., Pötzsch, S.: User experierence and user-centered design at DATEV eG. In: Maedche, A., Botzenhardt, A., Neer, L. (eds.) Software for People. Fundamentals, Trends and Best Practices, pp. 169–180. Springer, Berlin (2012)

23. Gulliksen, J., Boivie, I., Persson, J., Hektor, A., Herulf, L.: Making a difference. In: Raisamo, R. (ed.) NordiCHI 2004, Proceedings of the Third Nordic Conference on Human-Computer Interaction, pp. 207–215. ACM, New York (2004)

24. Wallach, D., Scholz, S.C.: User centered design: why and how to put users first in software development. In: Maedche, A., Botzenhardt, A., Neer, L. (eds.) Software for People. Fundamentals, Trends and Best Practices, pp. 11–38. Springer, Berlin (2012)

25. Abele, P., Hurtienne, J., Prümper, J.: Usability Management bei SAP-Projekten. Grundlagen Vorgehen Methoden. Friedr Vieweg & Sohn Verlag | GWV Fachverlage GmbH Wiesbaden, Wiesbaden (2007)

26. Uebernickel, F., Brenner, W.: Design thinking. In: Hoffmann, C.P., Lennerts, S., Schmitz, C., Stölzle, W. (eds.) Business Innovation: Das St. Galler Modell, pp. 243–265. Springer Fachmedien, Wiesbaden (2016)

27. Kolko, J.: Design thinking comes of age. Harvard Bus. Rev. **93**(9), 66–71 (2015)

28. Hilbrecht, H., Kempkens, O.: Design thinking im Unternehmen - Herausforderung mit Mehrwert. In: Keuper, F., Hamidian, K., Verwaayen, E., Kalinowski, T., Kraijo, C. (eds.) Digitalisierung und Innovation, pp. 347–364. Springer, Wiesbaden (2013)

29. Wilke, P., Stracke, S., Beile, J., Voß, E.: Innovation als Voraussetzung für Erfolg. In: Nerdinger, F.W., Wilke, P., Röhrig, R., Stracke, S. (eds.) Innovation und Beteiligung in der betrieblichen Praxis, pp. 277–288. Gabler, Wiesbaden (2010)

30. Ferrara, J.: Games for persuasion: argumentation, procedurality, and the lie of gamification. Games Cult. **8**, 289–304 (2013)

Use and Evaluation of Digital Entertainment

Integrating and Inspecting Combined Behavioral Profiling and Social Network Models in *Destiny*

André Rattinger[1], Günter Wallner[2], Anders Drachen[3(✉)], Johanna Pirker[1], and Rafet Sifa[4]

[1] Graz University of Technology, Graz, Austria
andre.rattinger@gmail.com, jpirker@iicm.edu
[2] University of Applied Arts Vienna, Vienna, Austria
guenter.wallner@uni-ak.ac.at
[3] Aalborg University & The Pagonis Network, Copenhagen, Denmark
drachen@hum.aau.dk
[4] Fraunhofer IAIS, Sankt Augustin, Germany
rafet.sifa@iais.fraunhofer.de

Abstract. In this paper two key venues of investigation in game analytics are combined: behavioral profiling and social network analysis. Both venues of research are well developed but combined they permit pattern evaluation across player performance and networks. Here, competitive networks covering almost 3.5 million players of the hybrid online shooter game *Destiny* are developed and combined with behavioral profiles based on match performance metrics and defined using archetypal analysis. The profiles are embedded in the networks along with other performance indicators for *Destiny* players. The social behavior of different archetypes is described. Network visualizations are presented which target the problem of making dense networked results actionable.

Keywords: Social network analysis · Destiny · Network visualization · Multi-player · Profiling · Game analytics

1 Introduction

With the introduction of telemetry tracking in digital games, game analytics has become a cornerstone of game development [18]. Visualization of behavioral analysis on high-dimensional datasets is challenging because of the typical complex behavioral phenomena in games [2,6,8,11,18,26]. This challenge is a well-described problem in game analytics, where major commercial titles can give rise to thousands of different features [11]. To counter this problem a variety of methods have been adopted and adapted from other domains. Of these, *behavioral profiling* plays an established role. The focus here has been on condensing varied, volatile and high-volume data into condensed profiles which encapsulate

© IFIP International Federation for Information Processing 2016
Published by Springer International Publishing AG 2016. All Rights Reserved
G. Wallner et al. (Eds.): ICEC 2016, LNCS 9926, pp. 77–89, 2016.
DOI: 10.1007/978-3-319-46100-7_7

player behavior and highlight key patterns of use for the specific purpose. The location of patterns in the behavior of players, and how to translate these to business action, using them to inform game AI or informing human behavior research, remains however a major line of inquiry [11]. The specific purpose of player profiling varies substantially, from top-down explorative analysis to hypothesis-testing [2,11]. Multiple examples have been described across a variety of games and using a variety of techniques, with unsupervised techniques such as clustering being the most common [2,11,17]. Cluster models allow segments to be developed which can describe the behavior of players according to specific behaviors and are driven by specific research questions, and they can be translated into behavioral descriptions of the different player segments. Behavioral profiling is notably useful in persistent online games, where the success of a title relies on its ability to keep a population of users engaged longitudinally and thus requires constant monitoring. This is also the situation in *Destiny*, a hybrid online shooter game which forms the case for the work presented here. *Destiny* is a persistent online game and the to date most expensive digital title to be developed worldwide, with a player base of roughly 30 million active players. As a hybrid title blending design aspects of multiple genres and featuring varied gameplay, e.g., multiple modes of play, *Destiny* forms an ideal basis for evaluating new frameworks and models for investigating player behavior.

Behavioral profiling work in games tends to focus on individual players, ignoring the connections between players, which are instead treated separately through social network analysis (SNA) [12]. From the perspective of SNA in games, the information about the players is generally limited, and the focus is instead on the links that connect players. This means that SNA typically views users as users, and ties minimal contextual information to the nodes of a network (demographics forming a common exception). In SNA, pattern recognition is as important as in behavioral profiling, and cluster analysis is used for defining groups and patterns in networks [5,12,13].

For behavioral profiling and SNA, a central challenge rests in the visualization of the results of analysis. In both instances, data and the patterns in them need to be presented to a user such that they are interpretable and actionable [11,12]. In this paper, a step is taken towards combining game-based behavioral profiling and game-based SNA. This, however, means that the visualization problem is amplified as the relative scope of analysis is increased. However, combining these two lines of investigation in games research has the advantage of providing a framework for exploring in-game behavior of players along with the connections between players. This permits a more detailed understanding of the individual player, in essence providing a lens that permits the observation of network behavior as well as general in-game behavior. This, in turn, informs the evaluation of design, engagement analysis, monetization decisions and similar factors in games.

Contribution. In this paper, game-based SNA, behavioral profiling, and data visualization is combined for the purpose of investigating the network behavior of competitive *Destiny* players as a function of the patterns in their performance, and ultimately develop novel visualizations that aim at making the results of combined SNA-profiling analysis interpretable by game designers and the *Destiny* players themselves. Towards this, competitive networks are constructed based on data from the Player-versus-Player (PvP) game modes, covering almost 3.5 million players. Using archetypal analysis, behavioral profiles are defined for each player, based on a range of performance indicators which includes information about behavior with the different weapon classes in *Destiny*. Given the shooter-type nature of the game, weapon performance is a key indicator of player skill. The profiles are embedded in the competitive networks and used to analyze the player network as a function of profiles. Furthermore, other metrics are integrated in separate analyses and visualized.

2 Related Work

The work presented here builds on previous work in three domains: (1) behavioral profiling in games; (2) social network analysis in games; (3) visualization of complex behavioral datasets and networks. For reasons of space this section will focus on key related work.

Behavioral Profiling in Games: Cluster analysis is a method for dimensionality reduction and pattern recognition and has been readily applied across disciplines. As an unsupervised method, it permits the exploration of data and can identify groups of players with similar behaviors or detect features that constitute such behaviors [2,23]. Behavioral profiling in game analytics has explored a variety of cluster models, including a few comparative studies [2,10]. There is no standard for which model to employ in which situation, but previous work has highlighted that various models are useful for different situations and problems [2,10]. For example, Thurau and Bauckhage [24] explored the evolution of guilds in *World of Warcraft* using matrix factorization which provided condensed views on how guilds change their composition over time. For example, Sifa et al. [22] identified clusters of players based on their relative playtime distribution across games on the Steam distribution platform using k-means clustering. Thawonmas and Iizuka [23] employed multidimensional scaling (CMDS) and KeyGraph to generate visualizations of player clusters. Drachen et al. [8] employed simplex volume maximization and k-means, developing behavioral profiles for two games. Normoyle and Jensen [17] used Bayesian Clustering. Moving into spatio-temporal clustering, Bauckhage et al. [3] developed waypoint graphs and adopted DEDI-COM for behavior-based partitioning of player trajectories. Archetypal analysis (AA) was adopted by Drachen et al. [10] and Sifa et al. [20], who noted the desirable properties of the model for investigating extremal behaviors and permitting soft clustering, i.e. the expression of behavioral profiles in terms of their belongingness to multiple cluster centers. In this paper, AA is adopted as the cluster model.

Social Network Analysis: SNA of relations between people has in recent years become a commonly employed tool, with large-scale online platforms such as

Facebook and *Twitter* providing a direct vehicle for investigation. Prior work has targeted not only analysis of social networks themselves, but also their potential for recommendation and prediction of user behavior. SNA has clear application in games, where the value of the different types of relations between players that exist in multi-player or massively multi-player online games to, e.g., player retention and user experience has been shown in a number of studies (e.g., [27]).

Due to the hybrid nature of *Destiny* there is no prior work that is directly comparable with the study presented here. Furthermore, the integration of detailed behavioral features into the network structure is also unexplored. Furthermore, most previous work has focused on analyzing social structures in persistent online communities, rather than competitive team-based games. However, Iosup et al. [16] examined networks in *DOTA* and *StarCraft* with a specific focus on modeling social structure and network robustness toward retention. Similarly, Jia et al. [13] introduced networks generated from team-based match data, including networks based on players being in the same match, on the same or different side in a match.

Visualization of Player Behavior: Visualization of player behavior in game analytics has covered a variety of goals but the majority of the work is focused on the spatio-temporal components of behavior. Wallner and Kriglstein [26] provide a recent review of the area, noting the wide range of techniques employed. Drachen and Schubert [9] reviewed spatio-temporal visualizations in use in game development. In general, the emphasis in the context of games is on pattern recognition and visualization of these patterns in a way that is actionable to the relevant stakeholder.

In network analysis, a wide range of visualizations have been proposed, but with an overall focus on link properties as compared to node properties. There are two common forms of display (cf. [12]): (1) The most common visualization is based on node-link diagrams where the nodes represent the social actors, and lines connections between them; (2) Matrices, where rows and columns represent social actors and various coal connections linking them. Recent years have seen the convergence of SNA and visualization, combined with interaction, but remains generally focused on network properties, including labeling, rather than node properties [7].

3   Background: *Destiny*

Destiny is a science-fiction themed game where players need to defend the Earth from various alien threats, taking on the role of *Guardians*. Humanity is reduced to one last city, and it is up to the players to make sure the city stays safe, while working for the overall goal of reviving a Deathstar-sized sphere being called the *Traveler*, who protected human civilization in the past but currently lays dormant. Players journey to different planets, complete missions, daily events, and perform a variety of different tasks to build up their characters and help eliminate the alien threat. *Destiny* is a hybrid digital game that blends features from a number of traditional game genres but which is first and foremost a shooter.

The main components of the gameplay is focused on tactical single-player or small-team combat, and the number of weapons, modifications and customizations in the game is staggering.

Weapons are divided into over a dozen different classes, each specialized for specific situations. For example, sniper rifles offer high power at long range, but are virtually useless at close range and require player skill to aim precisely. The utility of different weapon classes varies between game modes and in-game situations. Notably, the amount of damage that players in PvP can absorb can be dramatically different from the damage it takes to eliminate tough aliens in Player-versus-Environment (PvE) mode. In general, players are free to switch between any combination of weapon types, allowing for adjustment to in-game scenarios while at the same time reflecting individual behavior and preferences. Weapon-related performance metrics thus form one possible starting point for behavioral profiling of *Destiny* players, which targets the core shooter gameplay. Here, weapon class data is augmented with further performance metrics to provide a broad profile for developing profiles focusing on player performance in the game.

For reasons of limited space, the focus here is on those parts of *Destiny* that relate directly to PvP combat, but it should be pointed out that the game also has multiple PvE modes. PvP in *Destiny* is played in the *Crucible* – a central hub for the various PvP match types. These are commonly played in so-called *fireteams* comprised of 3 players on each side. Typically players can bring three different weapons to a PvP match. In the *Crucible*, players can earn medals (awards), points, and in-game currency by accomplishing tasks, winning matches, performing specific tasks, or feats of skill. *Destiny* features three different player classes, each with distinct abilities. Each class is divided into three subclasses. Players can level up their characters until level 40, unlocking new abilities and gradually becoming more powerful along with obtaining new weapons and other equipment through gameplay. In both PvE and PvP game modes, players are rewarded with new weapons and items through random drops or by completing specific tasks.

4   Behavioral Profiling with Extremes

Considering the large scale nature of today's behavioral datasets and the vast diversity of play-styles, finding profiles gives us the flexibility to manage, understand, and group the common behavioral patterns for the process of informed decision making. In this section we give a brief overview of Archetypal Analysis and it's use for player profiling. Archetypal analysis [1] is a constrained matrix factorization method that allows for soft clustering and is based on representing the data points as a convex combination of extreme datapoints that are called archetypes. Formally, given a data matrix $\mathbf{X} \in \mathbb{R}^{m \times n}$ we aim to find factors minimizing the matrix norms

$$\left\| \mathbf{X} - \mathbf{XBA} \right\|^2 = \left\| \mathbf{X} - \mathbf{ZA} \right\|^2,$$

where $\mathbf{Z} \in \mathbb{R}^{m \times k}$ represents the archetypes, $\mathbf{A} \in \mathbb{R}^{k \times n}$ and $\mathbf{B} \in \mathbb{R}^{n \times k}$ are column stochastic and represent the mixing coefficients respectively for archetypes and datapoints that represent the archetypes. Various techniques have been proposed to find appropriate factors for the above decomposition and its approximations. Examples of these include methods using pure alternating least square updates [1], active set updates [4], or distance geometry [25]. In the context of game analytics, archetypal analysis is used to profile players [8,15,20], build recommender systems [21], and generate human like bots [19]. In this study, as proposed in [8,20], we will concentrate on the use of archetypal analysis for finding player profiles in Destiny, in which we are interested in finding prototypical players that are encoded in $\mathbf{Z}$ to define particular player styles and belongingness coefficients represented in $\mathbf{A}$ showing how much each player belongs to the profiles defined in $\mathbf{Z}$.

5 Player Networks and Characteristics

In multi-player games players interact, play together or against each other, build different in-game groups and are thus forming complex relationships and in-game structures. We can map such relationships to networks to measure and analyze these interactions. To illustrate player interactions in *Destiny* we can build networks based on different forms of interactions. One way to illustrate in-game relationships is to build an undirected, weighted graph based on the information how often players play matches against or – as done in this paper – with the same players. In the network, players are represented as nodes, and their match relationships are modeled as weighted (based on the number of matches played together) links.

5.1 Network Measures

For the following analysis three different networks were created. Links for all networks are built between players that played matches together in the same team. The first network (main network, MN) describes the social structure of all 3,362,636 players based on match information of 930,720 matches. The second network (connected network, CN) illustrates a fully-connected friendship network based on three well-connected players. These players were used as starting point for a breadth-first-search and connected players were added to this network up to a network size of 1,000 nodes. 11 players were removed from the resulting network because of missing weapon information. The third network (random network, RN) was built based on 10,000 randomly picked players. Table 1 gives an overview of the network characteristics of the three player networks. The *largest connected component (LCC)* describes the largest self-contained subgraph in the network. A large LCC refers to a well-connected main graph. Looking at the number of nodes and links in the LCC the MN is well-connected, CN is fully connected (as designed), and RN is barely connected. The *degree (k)* of a player refers to the number of links to other players. The *average degree* refers to the

Table 1. Methodological comparison of the three networks, (a) the main network with over 3 million players, (b) a well-connected network, and (c) a random selection of 10,000 players (LCC = largest connected component)

	MN	CN	RN
Nodes	3,362,636	989	7,479
Nodes in LCC	3,347,226	989	407
Links	22,638,062	2,321	1,601
Links in LCC	22,614,017	2,321	432
Network size	3,362,596	989	1,991
Average degree	13	4	0.428
Diameter	15.0	4.0	23

MN = main network, CN = connected
network, RN = random network

Table 2. Overview of the different archetypes

Archetype	Description
Ranged Elites (AT1)	pretty good scores, auto-rifle focus, higher killing spree, unique precision kills, kill/death ratio, and win rate than AT3
Melee (AT2)	melee focused, medium performance, win rate similar to AT4
Mixed Weapon Elites (AT3)	high scores everywhere, more medals than AT1, better weapon scores except for auto-rifle, slightly lower win rate
Short Range (AT4)	medium performance, heavy use of shotgun, some melee
Newbies (AT5)	low performance everywhere

average number of links to other players. The *diameter* describes the longest of the shortest paths between two nodes and can be used to illustrate the linear size of a network.

5.2   Archetypes

Using archetypal analysis (AA) we identified five player archetypes (see Table 2) based on their most distinguished properties. 15 features from the *Destiny* dataset were selected (such as precision kills, scores, medals, kill/death ratio, and weapon preference) to be used with AA. Those features describe the in-game behavior and success of *Destiny* players in PvP matches. Figure 1 illustrates the five archetype profiles across the 15 selected behavioral features. Those features can be split into success-based features and weapon usage features. It further illustrates the varying weapon usage behavior between the archetypes.

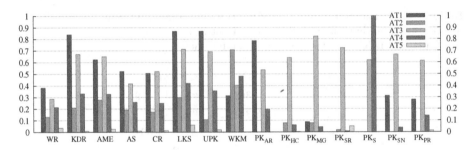

Fig. 1. Archetype profiles for *Destiny* across behavioral features. WR = win rate, KDR = kill/death ratio, AME = all medals earned, AS = average score, CR = combat rating, LKS = longest killing spree, UPK = unique precision kills, WKM = weapon kills melee, PK = precision kills with auto rifle (AR), hand cannon (HC), machine gun (MG), scout rifle (SR), shotgun (S), sniper rifle (SN), and pulse rifle (PR)

Table 3. Weapon use of the five different archetypes

Archetype	Short-range	Mid-range	Long-range
AT1	$M = 0.45$, $SD = 0.38$	$M = 0.45$, $SD = 0.32$	$M = 0.094$, $SD = 0.49$
AT2	$M = 0.41$, $SD = 0.28$	$M = 0.46$, $SD = 0.23$	$M = 0.13$, $SD = 0.38$
AT3	$M = 0.42$, $SD = 0.12$	$M = 0.45$, $SD = 0.10$	$M = 0.13$, $SD = 0.15$
AT4	$M = 0.45$, $SD = 0.17$	$M = 0.46$, $SD = 0.15$	$M = 0.095$, $SD = 0.20$
AT5	$M = 0.48$, $SD = 0.11$	$M = 0.42$, $SD = 0.10$	$M = 0.097$, $SD = 0.14$

Table 3 lists the differences in weapon usage between the archetypes for the different weapon ranges (short-, mid-, and long-range). The majority of weapon use for each archetype focuses on short and mid-range weapons, but there are a few exceptions. For instance, some players use long-range weapons almost exclusively.

In order to investigate if players belonging to a specific archetype have a tendency to play with the same group of players or if they rather play with random players we tried to map the archetypes to social network metrics. For that purpose, we calculated the weighted arithmetic mean $\bar{a}$ to determine how likely it is that a player plays with the same group of players, that is *sum of weights/k*. However, we could not find notable differences between the behavior of players from certain archetypes when matching up with team members, with $\bar{a}$ being 1.226 (AT1), 1.225 (AT2), 1.219 (AT3), 1.224 (AT4), and 1.233 (AT5).

6   Visualizations and Network Integration

Figure 2 shows a node-link visualization of the CN network which represents each node as a donut chart. This donut chart denotes the weapon usage (short-, mid-, and long-range) of a player. The size of a node is proportional to the number of matches played, that is, players playing more often are represented by

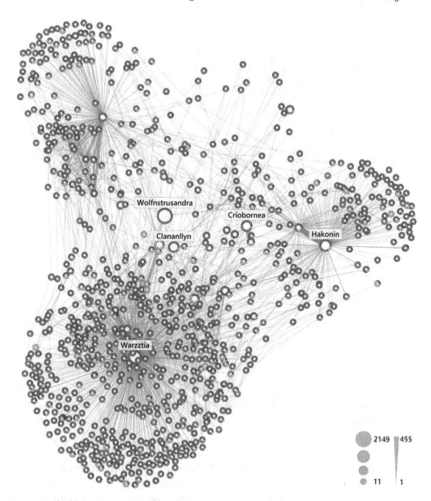

Fig. 2. Visualization of the fully-connected friendship network with 964 nodes. Donut charts at each node show the weapon usage for the individual players (■ short range, ■ mid range, ■ long range). Labels are shown for players who played more than 1000 matches. Player names were anonymized. (Color figure online)

larger nodes. Edges show which players played in the same team. The thickness of the edges corresponds to the number of matches played together, i.e. players who play together more often are connected by thicker edges. Edges are rendered semitransparent whereas the degree of transparency is weighted based on the number of matches in order to accentuate stronger relationships. As can be inferred from Fig. 2 players in this particular network prefer short-range (■ blue) and mid-range weapons (■ red) over long distance weapons (■ yellow).

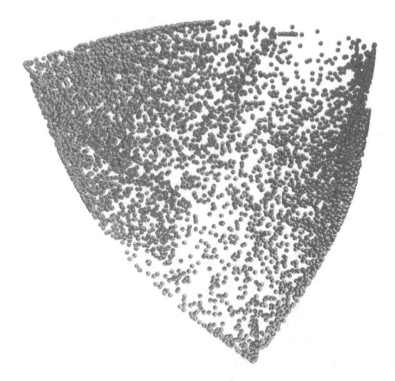

Fig. 3. Players' degree of membership to each of the five archetypes (▰▰ AT1 – Ranged Elites, ▱▱ AT2 – Melee, ▰▰ AT3 – Mixed Weapon Elites, ▰▰ AT4 – Short Range, ▰▰ AT5 – Newbies). (Color figure online)

Figure 3 depicts the result of the AA for the random network (based on a subset of 7479 players). The degree of membership to each of the five archetypes is depicted through pie-charts. The spatial arrangement of nodes has been derived using multidimensional scaling (e.g., [14]) such that players with similar archetype membership are placed in proximity of each other. To this end, the probabilities of belonging to each archetype were treated as a five-dimensional feature vector. The similarity of two players with feature vectors **A** and **B** was then measured using cosine similarity (see, e.g., [21]), that is, $s_{AB} = \mathbf{A} \cdot \mathbf{B} / \|\mathbf{A}\| \|\mathbf{B}\|$. From Fig. 3 it can be observed that players form three major groups: (i) players mainly belonging to the novice archetype (upper right corner), (ii) players mainly being considered melee focused but also sharing traits of the ranged elites and to a lesser degree of novices (lower right corner), and (iii) players primarily sharing characteristics of the mixed weapon elites and short range archetypes (upper left corner) with some of them exhibiting characteristics of either the novices, ranged elites, or melee archetype. The latter group also accounts for the largest of the three groups in the investigated network. Players sharing traits of four or even five archetypes are more uncommon as reflected by the sparse area in the center of the figure. While this indicates specialization to a certain extent it is also apparent that players can rarely be attributed to a single archetype.

7 Conclusion and Discussion

In this paper behavioral profiles have been constructed based on performance telemetry data from the PvP activities of 10,000 players, randomly selected from those who had played for at least two hours, of the persistent online FPS game *Destiny*, using Archetypal Analysis. A five-cluster solution was found, which showcases how performance-based profiling in the PvP component of *Destiny* can be closely related to the choices players make with respect to which weapons they use, as well as their relative skill, as expressed, e.g., via their kill/death ratios. Each of the players can be expressed in terms of their degree of membership to each archetype. The profiles have been embedded in a competitive player network covering the almost 3.5 million players that the 10,000 are connected to. The competitive network maps the tendency of people in *Destiny* to play with the same people or random groups across the various PvP modes of the game. In addition, a number of behavioral metrics has been examined in terms of their distribution in the network, notably weapon use distribution, which is a key indicator in *Destiny* as the main gameplay revolves around combat.

Future work will focus on evaluating player performance and network structure as a function of the number of players PvP matches. Initial dataset analysis indicated a relationship between performance metrics and the number of matches played. Furthermore, players tend to gravitate from using specific weapon classes during early matches to other weapon classes after having played many PvP matches. Both of these patterns will be verified and investigated in future work. Furthermore, the current work developed profiles for 10,000 players in a 3.5 million player network, and it is therefore an obvious next step to scale up the profiling to all the players in the network. This would substantially increase the sample size but also requires algorithms that scale well to such large datasets. Finally, the visualizations presented here will be further evaluated and expanded on, and a web-based interface developed which will target both game designers and players of competitive multi-player matches for performance evaluation.

Acknowledgments. The authors would like to extend their sincere gratitude to Bungie for making detailed behavioral telemetry from *Destiny* available.

References

1. Adele Cutler, L.B.: Archetypal analysis. Technometrics **36**(4), 338–347 (1994)
2. Bauckhage, C., Drachen, A., Sifa, R.: Clustering game behavior data. IEEE Trans. Comput. Intell. AI Games **7**(3), 266–278 (2015)
3. Bauckhage, C., Sifa, R., Drachen, A., Thurau, C., Hadiji, F.: Beyond heatmaps: spatio-temporal clustering using behavior-based partitioning of game levels. In: IEEE Conference on Computational Intelligence and Games, pp. 1–8 (2014)

4. Bauckhage, C., Thurau, C.: Making Archetypal analysis practical. In: Denzler, J., Notni, G., Süße, H. (eds.) DAGM 2009. LNCS, vol. 5748, pp. 272–281. Springer, Heidelberg (2009)

5. van de Bovenkamp, R., Shen, S., Iosup, A., Kuipers, F.: Understanding and recommending play relationships in online social gaming. In: Fifth International Conference on Communication Systems and Networks (COMSNETS), pp. 1–10 (2013)

6. Cleveland, W.S.: Visualizing Data. Hobart Press, Summit (1993)

7. Correa, C.D., Ma, K.L.: Visualizing social networks. In: Aggarwal, C.C. (ed.) Social Network Data Analytics, pp. 307–326. Springer, US (2011)

8. Drachen, A., Sifa, R., Bauckhage, C., Thurau, C.: Guns, swords and data: clustering of player behavior in computer games in the wild. In: IEEE Conference on Computational Intelligence and Games, pp. 163–170 (2012)

9. Drachen, A., Schubert, M.: Spatial game analytics. In: Seif El-Nasr, M., Drachen, A., Canossa, A. (eds.) Game Analytics: Maximizing the Value of Player Data, pp. 365–402. Springer, London (2013)

10. Drachen, A., Thurau, C., Sifa, R., Bauckhage, C.: A comparison of methods for player clustering via behavioral telemetry. In: Proceedings of the FDG, pp. 245–252 (2013)

11. Drachen, A., Thurau, C., Togelius, J., Yannakakis, G.N., Bauckhage, C.: Game data mining. In: Seif El-Nasr, M., Drachen, A., Canossa, A. (eds.) Game Analytics: Maximizing the Value of Player Data, pp. 205–253. Springer, London (2013)

12. Freeman, L.C.: Visualizing social networks. J. Soc. Struct. **1**, 1–15 (2000)

13. Jia, A.L., Shen, S., Bovenkamp, R.V.D., Iosup, A., Kuipers, F., Epema, D.H.J.: Socializing by gaming: Revealing social relationships in multiplayer online games. ACM Trans. Knowl. Discov. Data **10**(2), 11:1–11:29 (2015)

14. Kruskal, J.B., Wish, M.: Multidimensional Scaling. Sage Publications, Beverly Hills (1978)

15. Lim, C.U., Harrell, D.F.: Revealing social identity phenomena in videogames with archetypal analysis. In: Proceedings of AISB Symposium on AI and Games (2015)

16. Losup, A., van de Bovenkamp, R., Shen, S., Jia, A.L., Kuipers, F.: Implicit social networks in multiplayer online games. IEEE Internet Comp. **18**(3), 36–44 (2014)

17. Normoyle, A., Jensen, S.T.: Bayesian clustering of player styles for multiplayer games. In: Proceedings of the AAAI, pp. 163–169 (2015)

18. Seif El-Nasr, M., Drachen, A., Canossa, A. (eds.): Game Analytics - Maximizing the Value of Player Data. Springer, London (2013)

19. Sifa, R., Bauckhage, C.: Archetypical motion: Supervised game behavior learning with archetypal analysis. In: IEEE Conference on Computational Intelligence in Games, pp. 1–8 (2013)

20. Sifa, R., Drachen, A., Bauckhage, C., Thurau, C., Canossa, A.: Behavior evolution in tomb raider underworld. In: IEEE Conference on Computational Intelligence in Games, pp. 1–8 (2013)

21. Sifa, R., Bauckhage, C., Drachen, A.: Archetypal game recommender systems. In: Proceedings of the 16th LWA Workshops: KDML, IR and FGWM, pp. 45–56 (2014)

22. Sifa, R., Drachen, A., Bauckhage, C.: Large-scale cross-game player behavior analysis on steam. In: Proceedings of the AIIDE, pp. 198–204 (2015)

23. Thawonmas, R., Iizuka, K.: Visualization of online-game players based on their action behaviors. Int. J. Comput. Games Technol. **2008**, 5:1–5:9 (2008)

24. Thurau, C., Bauckhage, C.: Analyzing the evolution of social groups in World of Warcraft. In: IEEE Conference on Computational Intelligence and Games, pp. 170–177 (2010)

25. Thurau, C., Kersting, K., Bauckhage, C.: Yes we can: simplex volume maximization for descriptive web-scale matrix factorization. In: Proceedings of the 19th ACM International Conference on Information and Knowledge Management, CIKM 2010, pp. 1785–1788. ACM (2010)
26. Wallner, G., Kriglstein, S.: An introduction to gameplay data visualization. In: Lankoski, P., Björk, S. (eds.) Game Research Methods, pp. 231–250. ETC (2015)
27. Yee, N.: The demographics, motivations, and derived experiences of users of massively multi-user online graphical environments. Presence: Teleoper. Virtual Environ. **15**(3), 309–329 (2006)

How Playstyles Evolve: Progression Analysis and Profiling in *Just Cause 2*

Johanna Pirker[1], Simone Griesmayr[1], Anders Drachen[2(✉)], and Rafet Sifa[3]

[1] Graz University of Technology, Graz, Austria
jpirker@iicm.edu, simone.griesmayr@student.tugraz.at
[2] Aalborg University & The Pagonis Network, Aalborg, Denmark
andersdrachen@gmail.com
[3] Fraunhofer IAIS, Sankt Augustin, Germany
rafet.sifa@iais.fraunhofer.de

Abstract. Evaluating progression of players in a game can take a variety of forms, but ideally combines playstyle or performance analysis with one or more aspects of progression, e.g. through a level- or mission-based structure. Furthermore, visualization of the results of analysis are essential to ensure that action can be taken on them. In this paper behavioral profiling through Archetype Analysis is combined with progression analysis, expanding on previous work in the area, and extending it into the context of Open-World Games. The proposed methodological framework is applied to the case of the action-adventure title *Just Cause 2*, focusing on the main storyline. The results show how players navigate the content of the title, and how some playstyles remain constant throughout the game, whereas others emerge or disappear with player progress. Additionally, player performance as a function of progression is evaluated across a number of key metrics.

Keywords: Game analytics · Progression · Playstyle · Player behavior · Cluster analysis · Visualization

1   Introduction

Progression is a key element of game design, vital to balancing, and therefore an important focus of investigation in Game Analytics [16]. The concept of progression in game design can refer to a variety of components, however, adopting the definition of Lopez [15], generally refers to a pattern of advance towards a goal as well as the act of navigating towards the goal. This structure is important in ensuring the user experience and player engagement. Progression ties directly in with other elements of the game, including mechanics, rewards and risk, difficulty/complexity, etc.

From a behavioral analytics standpoint, evaluating progression can be performed in a variety of ways, but fundamentally combines performance analysis

© IFIP International Federation for Information Processing 2016
Published by Springer International Publishing AG 2016. All Rights Reserved
G. Wallner et al. (Eds.): ICEC 2016, LNCS 9926, pp. 90–101, 2016.
DOI: 10.1007/978-3-319-46100-7_8

and measures of progression, e.g. through a level- or mission-based structure [2,13,16–18]. The performance component can be developed in a variety of ways depending on the involved number of behavioral features and the specific questions asked of the analysis. A commonly adopted approach is profiling, which seeks to condense high-dimensional behavioral datasets into user profiles that contain the underlying patterns of variance in the data. Towards this, a number of studies have investigated approaches such as description, segmentation as well as machine learning, for the latter notably cluster analysis [2,7,9,17,18].

Being able to analyze and visualize progression is notably important in large development teams, where different stakeholders (designers, artists, programmers etc.) need to collaborate on constructing the indented progression ramp, and the need for checking if the design intent is implemented across all of the components of a game. Essentially the behavior of the player needs to be modeled on an ongoing basis as the player navigates through the content of the game, and results compared against design intent or combined with e.g. churn prediction models. This is the case for all digital games, irrespective of their genre, design or platform. A key element in progression analysis is acknowledging the dynamic nature of gameplay and the impact this has on progression, i.e. that as long as players are active, progression is taking place, either directly by moving through the content of the game, or indirectly, by considering and thinking about how to address particular challenges of puzzles. Progression inertia or even cessation is one of the major sources of player frustration, and therefore not a desirable situation [1]. Furthermore, visualization of the results of analysis are essential to ensure that action can be taken on them [13,16,19]. In the work presented here, behavioral profiling and progression analysis are combined towards evaluating player progression and visualizing analysis results.

1.1 Contribution

In this paper behavioral profiling through the clustering with Archetypal Analysis (AA) is combined with progression analysis, expanding on previous work in the area, and extending it into the area of Open-World (or Sandbox) Games. The proposed methodological framework is applied to the case of the major commercial action-adventure title *Just Cause 2*, using the main storyline of the game as a proxy measure of progression along multiple vectors. Results are visualized using Sankey flow diagrams, which permit visual inspection of the patterns in the behavioral data. The results show how players navigate the content of the title, and how some playstyles remain constant throughout the game, whereas others emerge or disappear as a function of player progress. Additionally, player performance as a function of progression and player profile are evaluated across a number of key metrics.

1.2 Just Cause 2

Just Cause 2 (JC2) is an action-adventure game set in an open-world environment, also commonly referred to as a *sandbox* game. Similar to other sandbox titles such as the *Elder Scrolls-* and *Grand Theft Auto*-series, it is characterized by free-roaming gameplay in a large 3D environment, in the current case covering over 1000 square-kilometers. The game was published by *Square Enix* in 2010 and sold over six million units, retaining an active player base today. The gameplay is reminiscent of other action-adventure third-person shooters, with the player controlling the game protagonist as he travels around the Panau environment whether to complete missions, explore, collect items, or just have fun with the mechanics of the game. There are computer-controlled enemies everywhere, and a substantial part of the gameplay is combat-focused, which also means that combat performance metrics are important for the current aim of developing behavioral profiles.

A complete description of the gameplay of JC2 is out of scope of this paper, but in brief, JC2 is set in the fictional tropical island nation of Panau. Panau is ruled by a ruthless dictator. The player, taking on the role of Rico Rodriguez, an agent for an outfit referred to as the Agency, is tasked removing the dictator from power. This is done via progressing along different vectors notably the seven Agency-related missions, as well as missions from a number of Rebel Factions which helps wrest control from the dictators forces and into the hand of the factions. At the end of each mission chain for each Rebel Faction is a Stronghold mission, which form some of the most difficult tasks in the game. Upon completion of a Stronghold mission, the control of an administrative district is gained by the local Rebel Faction.

Progression in JC2 follows a directed gameplay approach [15], where all mechanics in the game are available from the beginning of the game, but that the player is gradually encouraged to use and become familiar with the mechanics of the game progressively. Overall, progression in the game towards reaching the point where the dictator can be toppled, is determined by *chaos*, a measure of the overall efforts of the player towards destabilizing Panau, whether through completing faction missions, attacking military posts, searching for and blowing up status of the dictator, etc. Thus the overall chaos achieved by a player provides a proxy measure of progress across the various progression vectors in the game. Furthermore, Agency missions unlock with chaos progression. Throughout the game, the player is via missions encouraged to navigate around Panau, which can be done using a wide variety of vehicles operating in the water, on land and in the air. Barring a few missions players can travel via any means they can capture. The player also has a grappling hook and reusable para-sail/parachute which can be used for aerial movement as well as in combat.

2   Profiling and Progression: Related Work

Behavioral profiling in games has been explored by a number of researchers across academia and industry, providing a number of case studies showcasing how profiling can be performed using different techniques and in varied game contexts [4,7,9,10,14,16].

There are particular challenges associated with behavioral profiling in major commercial game titles, notably related to volume, variety, and volatility [5].

These problems have been approached using a variety of techniques from description and segmentation to machine learning. In the latter category, cluster algorithms [8] and other dimensional reduction techniques have been broadly applied across different game formats. Cluster analysis is an exploratory approach to building behavioral profiles, and aims at identifying groups for players with similar behaviors and identify the most important behavioral features in terms of the underlying patterns in the dataset [4,6,9,14].

The work presented here forms an extension of earlier work on behavioral game research, notably: Sifa et al. [17], who investigated player progression in the action-adventure, single-player *Tomb Raider: Underworld*, and Drachen et al. [2], who investigated player progression in the browser-based Massively Multi-player Online Game (MMOG) *Glitch*. Sifa et al. [17] utilized Simplex Volume Maximization (SIVM) to develop behavioral profiles of the seven levels of *Tomb Raider: Underworld*, finding some behavioral profiles to be present across the levels, others to be present in only some of the levels. They noted that the variations in the profiles present for a level appeared related to the specific challenges and gameplay of these levels. Drachen et al. [2] adopted a similar approach, but focused on time rather than in-game segments. The authors developed profiles on the auction house behavior of players using k-means clustering, and used Sankey diagrams to develop interactive visualization of the pattern of players moving into and out of profiles across monthly time bins. This visualization approach is adopted here. The work in the above mentioned publications in turn rests on other research in game analytics focused on behavioral profiling in games, e.g. [4,6,14].

3   Dataset and Features

The dataset was provided by Square Enix, the publisher of JC2. The data comprises complete play histories from over 5000 JC2 players who played the game in 2010. A vast amount of behavioral features were collected including the in-game geographical coordinates for all player actions registered, as well as timestamps for these events. The dataset contains a detailed set of metrics from the gameplay, e.g. the total kills, the total chaos gathered by the player, the kilometers driven or the number of stronghold takeovers the player completed, and more.

3.1   Feature Definition and Pre-processing

The gameplay of JC2 gives rise to a huge variety of potential behavioral measures, across spatio-temporal navigation, combat performance, progression through the main storyline and numerous side quests to general exploration. This means that progression analysis can target a number of dimensions in the game, however, for all the free-roaming gameplay, JC2 features a central storyline, experienced across seven Agency missions. Progressing along these missions in turn require the player to reach specific levels of Chaos, which in turn means completing Rebel Faction missions and causing mayhem and destruction in general, which means that the Agency missions work as a proxy for multiple vectors of progression in the game, and it was therefore chosen to make these the vector of progression in the work presented here.

In order to keep the profiling task manageable, a subset of features was selected based on the core mechanics of the game, following the principles of Drachen et al. [6], and the focus on the main storyline. This means for example including measures of distance traveled and locations discovered, which informs whether players focus on straight navigation between story points or are exploratory in their behavior, as well as combat performance metrics such as kill/death ratios (K/D ratio) and player death frequencies, and finally features related to more advanced mechanics such as base jumping, stunt driver points and the variety of vehicles used. The specific feature set chosen here does not impact on the analytical framework, which can be employed for any feature-set in any game context, but of course impacts on the kinds of conclusions that can be derived from analyzing them [2,17]. The features are described in Table 1.

Table 1. Overview of the behavioural features used for AA

Feature	Description
Total playtime	Total time played until the completion of the corresponding agency mission
Chaos/minute	Chaos gathered per minute (Chaos increases by completing missions, destroying buildings)
Kill/Death Ratio	(K/D ratio), the number of kills the player has scored divided by the number of deaths suffered
Kills/minute	Number of kills the player has scored per minute
Deaths/minute	Number of deaths the player has suffered per minute
Hijackings	Number of times the player hijacked a vehicle
Base jumps	Number of times the player used the game feature base jumps
Stunt driver points	Number of points the player gathered by performing stunts with vehicles
Stronghold takeovers	Number of completed stronghold takeovers
Kilometers driven	Distance covered by the player in kilometers
Locations discovered	Number of discovered locations
Locations completed	Number of completed locations

In further pre-processing, all players with scores outside the 1–99th percentile were excluded from the analysis, in order to remove extreme outliers. Outliers can in other contexts be the focus of study, but in the current case the most extreme outliers were caused by faulty tracking and similar errors, and therefore excluded. The behavioral features were normalized using regular variance normalization, following the principles of [4,9].

4   Analysis

We applied AA models to all seven agency mission bins. For each the optimal number of clusters (k) was determined. To identify the number of clusters for the AA, we analyzed the residual sum of squares for all k values less than or equal to 20 and chose the number of clusters by utilizing the elbow criterion. The residual sum of squares indicated that the data consists of three main archetypes.

4.1   Progression Profiling via Cluster Analysis

Profiling game player behavior is an important practice in game analytics to obtain insights about how players interact with the game [3,9]. Unlike the commonly used predefined-segmentation based profiling methods, clustering based profiling approaches reveal more interpretable and actionable insights about the game play behavior. Cast as low-rank matrix decomposition problems, many clustering methods can be grouped under the same formalism for better comparison. In this work we will concentrate on two factor decompositions as the methods we used here follow that scheme. That is, given a data matrix $\mathbf{X} \in \mathbb{R}^{m \times n}$, our aim is to find two lower rank matrices $\mathbf{P} \in \mathbb{R}^{m \times k}$ and $\mathbf{C} \in \mathbb{R}^{k \times n}$ such that $\mathbf{X} \approx \mathbf{PC}$. For the purpose of profiling, the factor matrix $\mathbf{P}$ contains the prototypical players that define the profiles and are selected by special procedure enforced by the algorithm whereas the matrix $\mathbf{C}$ contains the mixing or belongingness coefficients indicating how much a player belongs to the particular profiles defined by $\mathbf{P}$ [3,9]. It is important to note that under this framework we can categorize the algorithms with respect to their constraints. For Archetypal Analysis [11] $\mathbf{P}$ is constrained to contain extreme vectors that are defined as convex combinations of particular data-points whereas $\mathbf{C}$ is constrained to be column stochastic. Additionally, keeping the stochasticity constraint for $\mathbf{C}$, for a more relaxed archetypal decomposition such as Simplex Volume Maximization, $\mathbf{P}$ is selected to be a datapoint lying on the data-simplex [12]. For more information about constrained matrix decomposition and clustering we refer the reader to [3,9,17].

In this study we present a profiling analysis with two components: (1) Behavioral profiling of the JC2 players via the application of archetype analysis (by analyzing the resulting $\mathbf{P}$-matrices) and the (2) generation of a Sankey diagram-based visualization (by using the resulting $\mathbf{C}$-matrices) for the temporal behavior of the players across the defined profiles.

4.2   Player Profile Descriptions

The analysis with AA shows that the player profiles change over the different missions. Archetypal analysis provides an indication of the number of clusters between 4 and 6. Table 2 gives an overview of the distribution of the various main profiles among the different missions. One particular player group ("Low Performers") stands out in mission 2–3.

With AA we can identify eight main clusters, which appear and disappear in different missions and can have slightly different metrics depending on the mission-design. **Average Player:** This player cluster only appears in mission 6 and describes players with overall average values. **Drivers:** Players that drove the most kilometers and also performed the most base jumps and black market orders (cluster appears in mission 2). **Elite Players:** Players that played on the highest difficulty level with the highest kill/death ratio, for the rest of the features average values. They have an average exploration performance. In later missions (3 and 4) they also have higher values in hijacking cars and stunt driving points and less black market orders, base jumps (mission 5) and completed below average faction missions and stronghold takeovers (missions 6) and have a small number of kilometers driven (mission 7). **Explorers:** This player type is very constant and can be observed in slightly different forms over all missions. This cluster can be described as players with the slowest pace, a kill/death ratio above average, but the least amount of chaos collected per minute. They hijacked the most vehicles and discovered the most locations. In mission 2 they've already played in average three times longer than other player types and collect most stunt driver point. From mission 3 they have played at least twice as long as other player types and completed far most faction missions and stronghold takeovers and have discovered and completed nearly three times as many locations. **Low Performers:** Players with the worst kill/death ratio of all player types and most deaths per minute. Average values for the rest. One can also observe average or slightly above average performance regarding exploration and driving (mission 3 –7). **Low Performance Drivers:** This cluster only appears in mission 1. Players with a fast pace, a very low kill/death ratio and most deaths per minute, but collected a lot of chaos per minute. They drove with many different vehicles and on average drove more kilometers than other clusters. **Rushers:** This player group is also very constant and appears in all missions but mission 6. It described players that completed the game the fastest. They collected the most chaos per minute, achieved a high kill/death ratio and the most kills per minute. They care little about exploring the world and discovered and completed the least locations (mission 3–5). **Stunt Drivers:** This group is only observed in the first mission and describes players who collected the most stunt driver points, drove with more different vehicles than the other player types, and also drove the most kilometers. Skill scores pretty similar to player type "Low Performance Drivers".

4.3 Player Progression Along the Missions

Figure 1 gives an overview of various metrics, which can give the players feedback on their progress and/or their performance. *Progress* describes the a predefined in-game metric to describe the actual progress along the game. *K/D-ratio* describes the ratio between kills and deaths. In particular missions three and four seem to be "rich of action". In particular the last two missions seems to require the players to drive a lot according to the average metrics *Kilometers driven*.

Table 2. Overview of main AA types by missions (in %)

	Mission						
Type	1	2	3	4	5	6	7
Average Players	-	-	-	-	-	44.57	-
Drivers	-	2.27	-	-	-	-	-
Elite Players	19.00	-	3.69	6.15	12.43	21.71	14.74
Explorers	2.84	3.37	2.78	4.49	4.36	10.86	3.91
Low Performers	1.23	70.62	55.81	43.42	45.04	22.86	47.97
Low Performance Drivers	18.10		-	-	-	-	-
Rushers	56.23	23.74	37.72	45.94	38.17		33.38
Stunt Drivers	2.61	-	-	-	-		

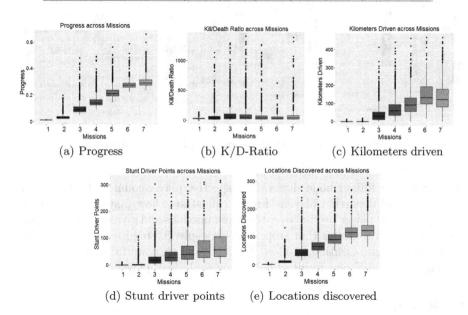

(a) Progress   (b) K/D-Ratio   (c) Kilometers driven

(d) Stunt driver points   (e) Locations discovered

Fig. 1. Player progression over the missions based on different in-game metrics

Stunt driver points can be collected by extreme driving activities. In particular in early missions more new locations (*Locations discovered*) are discovered.

4.4 Visualizing Player Behavior Along the Main Story Line

Sankey diagrams consist of nodes, in our case our clusters, and links, the flow of players between these clusters. The diagram was developed using an rCharts implementation of the d3.js sankey plugin for the R language[1]. Hovering the

---

[1] https://github.com/timelyportfolio.

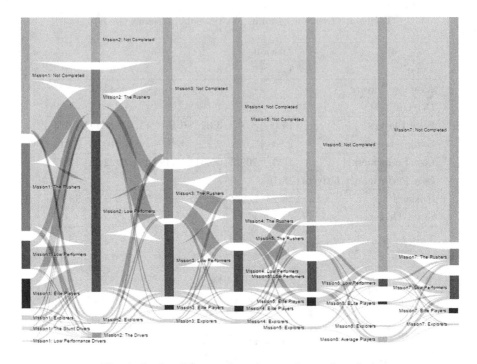

Fig. 2. Sankey Diagram based on archetypal analysis

mouse over any link or node shows the respective player count and information about new and departing players. Figure 2 illustrates how players change their playstyles (their player profile) over the seven missions and gives also a very good overview of player-groups that stop, how they split in subgroups, or merge. As an interactive visualization, Sankey diagrams are an powerful and easy-to-use tool supporting different forms of behaviour analysis of players.

5   Results

Based on the performed analysis and visualizations different results with focus on player behaviour along the game progress can be presented.

5.1   Player Behaviour over the Missions

The analysis clearly indicates variations in the player behaviours over the duration of the game, despite the consistent presence of the three main clusters throughout all agency mission bins. Players do not remain in a single cluster when they progress through the game, they move relatively freely across clusters from agency mission to agency mission. While the dominance in the exploration based features stays the same for the Cluster "Explorer", the other features, like the skill features change over the course of the main storyline from agency

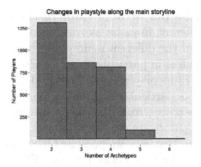

Fig. 3. How players change clusters along the main storyline: all players change the cluster at least once

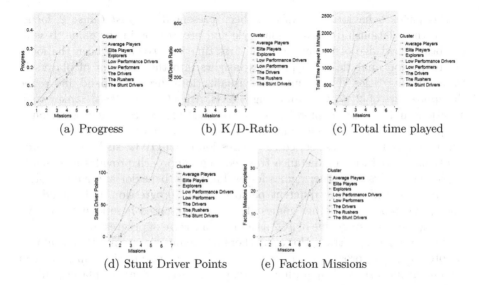

(a) Progress   (b) K/D-Ratio   (c) Total time played

(d) Stunt Driver Points   (e) Faction Missions

Fig. 4. Player progression over the missions based on AA clusters

mission to agency mission. Another quite consistent feature for all three clusters is the total time played, the "Explorer" cluster yields in the highest values of total play time across the whole main story line.

How many profiles enter players on average over the course of the game? The analysis indicates that all players change their in-game behaviour along the storyline. As illustrated in Fig. 3 all players change the cluster at least once. On average players enter 2.91 clusters over the course of the game.

How does in-game behaviour and performance change over the various missions? The analysis and the visualization clearly indicate that player behaviour changes over the different missions, which is also due to the nature of the mission design. The Sankey Diagram (Fig. 2) illustrates how players change the player types along the course of the seven missions.

How can we describe player behaviour of the different player pro-files? Fig. 4 refers to different in-game metrics and how these metrics change over the seven missions for the different main player profiles as described above. *Progress* is a metric, which is in particular high for Explorers. *Kill/Death-Ratio* is a distinct feature for Elite players. As illustrated in subfigure (c) the *total time played* (in minutes) is particular high for Explorers. Starting from mission 2 they start to strongly separate from the other clusters. This value is very low for Rushers. *Stunt driver points* are also very high for Explorers, but also for the group of Drivers. *Factions Missions* are popular for Explorers, but interestingly, only in Mission 6, also for the Low Performers and Elite Players.

6   Conclusion and Discussion

In this paper behavioral analysis has been presented for *Just Cause 2*, focusing on the relationship between playstyle and progression in the game. It is to the best knowledge of the authors the first time an OWG has been the focus of progression analytics, and provides insights into the behavior of players in these kinds of titles. The results and visualizations directly expand and refine the approaches of [2,17] via combining OWGs, Archetype Analysis, Sankey visualizations and in-depth exploration of key behavioral metrics. The progression of the player clusters exhibiting similar playstyles has been explored across a number of behavioral metrics related to progression in an OWG, such as discovered locations, K/D ratios or distance traveled. The approach provides a template for similar analyses in other games for evaluation of behavior and game design. Future work will explore different perspectives of progression and extend the work presented here to other games. The work presented here focuses initially on using the main story line of JC2 as a proxy measure of progression, expanding to integrate other metrics. However, there are many viewpoints that could be adopted on player progression in games. For example, progression can also mean gradual acquisition and upgrading of weapons, developments of player skill, or exploration of the environment. Similarly, in other games, progression is a viewpoint that can be applied in a range of situations. Irrespective of the game and the specific aspect of progression studied, it is a key aspect of game design and vital to balancing. The work presented here combines profiling and progression towards enabling the detailed evaluation of player progression.

Acknowledgments. The authors would like to express their sincere gratitude to Square Enix for making the Just Cause 2 dataset available for analysis.

References

1. Canossa, A., Drachen, A., Srensen, J.R.M.: Arrgghh!!! blending quantitative and qualitative methods to detect player frustration. In: Procedings of the FDG (2011)
2. Drachen, A., Baskin, S., Riley, J., Klabjan, D.: Going out of business: auction house behavior in the massively multi-player online game glitch. J. Entertainment Comput. **5**, 20–31 (2014)

3. Drachen, A., Sifa, R., Thurau, C., Bauckhage, C.: A comparison of methods for player clustering via behavioral telemetry. In: Proceedings of the FDG (2013)
4. Drachen, A., Sifa, R., Bauckhage, C., Thurau, C.: Guns, swords and data: clustering of player behavior in computer games in the wild. In: Proceedings of the IEEE CIG (2012)
5. Drachen, A., Thurau, C., Togelius, J., Yannakakis, G., Bauckhage, C.: Game data mining. In: El-Nasr, M.S., Drachen, A., Canossa, A. (eds.) Game Analytics: Maximizing the Value of Player Data, pp. 205–253. Springer, London (2013)
6. Drachen, A., Canossa, A., Yannakakis, G.: Player modeling using self-organization in Tomb Raider underworld. In: Proceedings of the IEEE CIG (2009)
7. Normoyle, A., Jensen, S.T.: Bayesian clustering of player styles for multiplayer games. In: Proceedings of the AAAI AIIDE (2015)
8. Aggarwal, C., Reddy, C.: Data Clustering: Algorithms and Applications. Chapman & Hall/CRC, Boca Raton (2013)
9. Bauckhage, C., Drachen, A., Sifa, R.: Clustering game behavior data. Trans. Comput. Intell. AI Games **7**(3), 266–278 (2015)
10. Bauckhage, C., Sifa, R.: k-Maxoids clustering. In: Proceedings of the KDML-LWA (2015)
11. Cutler, C., Breiman, L.: Archetypal analysis. Technometrics **36**(4), 338–347 (1994)
12. Thurau, C., Kersting, K., Bauckhage, C.: Yes we can: simplex volume maximization for descriptive web-scale matrix factorization. In: Proceedings of the ACM CIKM (2010)
13. Wallner, G., Kriglstein, S.: An Introduction to Gameplay Data Visualization. Game Research Methods, pp. 231–250. ETC Press, Pittsburgh (2015)
14. Shim, K., Srivastava, J.: Behavioral profiles of character types in EverQuest II. In: Proceedings of the IEEE CIG (2010)
15. Lopez, M.: Gameplay Design Fundamentals: Gameplay Progression, Gamasutra, 26 November 2006. http://www.gamasutra.com
16. Seif El-Nasr, M., Drachen, A., Canossa, A.: Game Analytics - Maximizing the Value of Player Data. Springer, London (2013)
17. Sifa, R., Drachen, A., Bauckhage, C.: Behavior evolution in Tomb Raider underworld. In: Proceedings of the IEEE CIG (2013)
18. Sifa, R., Hadiji, F., Runge, J., Drachen, A., Kersting, K., Bauckhage, C.: Predicting purchase decisions in mobile free-to-play games. In: Proceedings of the AAAI AIIDE (2015)
19. Cleveland, W.S.: Visualizing Data. Hobard Press, Tasmania (1993)

EyeCo: Effects of Shared Gaze on Social Presence in an Online Cooperative Game

Bernhard Maurer[1]([⊠]), Michael Lankes[2], Barbara Stiglbauer[3], and Manfred Tscheligi[1]

[1] Center for Human-Computer Interaction,
University of Salzburg, Salzburg, Austria
{bernhard.maurer,manfred.tscheligi}@sbg.ac.at
[2] Department of Digital Media,
University of Applied Sciences Upper Austria, Hagenberg, Austria
michael.lankes@fh-hagenberg.at
[3] Department of Education and Psychology,
Johannes Kepler University Linz, Linz, Austria
barbara.stiglbauer@jku.at

Abstract. This paper investigates the effects of a shared gaze approach on social presence in an online cooperative game. We explored how a shared gaze visualization changes how players work together and form collaborative strategies based on different combinations of gaze interaction and verbal communication. Our study findings highlight the positive influence of a shared gaze visualization on team cohesion and involvement towards increased perceived social presence among cooperating team members. With our findings we want to inform game designers with insights on the inclusion of gaze-based interaction in remote gaming settings and whether this can strengthen the social bond between players. Our approach aims at fostering social couplings in remote collaborative gaming and investigates their potential to increase the connectedness between players.

Keywords: Cooperative games · Gaze-based interaction · Social presence · Shared gaze

1 Introduction

Playing games is an activity that is embedded in social and situated practices [18]. Game experiences are often driven by a certain social context where the presence of other players is an integral part of enjoyment. This results in social interactions between players (e.g., coordination of actions or encouraging another player) that are deeply rooted in natural human communication. In human-human collaboration gaze and eye contact are crucial factors building the foundation for social interaction [10, p. 86] and information flow [9, p. 67]. However, in remote settings, like online coop games, typical interpersonal means of face-to-face communication (e.g., gaze, mimic, etc.) that are prevalent in co-located gaming, are not or only limitedly present. These non-verbal signals have an impact on social presence and manifest themselves in various ways like

© IFIP International Federation for Information Processing 2016
Published by Springer International Publishing AG 2016. All Rights Reserved
G. Wallner et al. (Eds.): ICEC 2016, LNCS 9926, pp. 102–114, 2016.
DOI: 10.1007/978-3-319-46100-7_9

facial expression, gesture, head movement, body posture, etc., which are factors that can also influence how players perceive each other in cooperative gameplay. This is especially relevant in games that require players to act cooperatively in order to be successful. In cooperative gameplay social interactions are often targeted at creating a shared understanding of the current scene and to coordinate each other's actions. We argue that gaze interaction can play an important part in how such cooperative actions are coordinated and thus, also influences social presence.

The approach discussed in this paper uses a game in combination with a shared gaze visualization as a shared embodied resource in order to foster social presence and connectedness between players. By giving the gaze of a cooperating player a "body" and a representation within the game we aim at exploring this gaze-based interaction modality as a means for collaboration. We argue that by providing a means of non-verbal communication (i.e., a shared gaze visualization) within a game, even if not actively part of the gameplay itself, a new layer of non-verbal communication for the players is created, that can result in new forms of human-human collaboration in online games.

In this paper, we investigate the impact of a shared gaze on social presence in a remote cooperative game setting. Further, we want to find out how a shared gaze visualization changes how people collaborate (e.g., different strategies) and how it is used in combination with other communication modalities like verbal input. We aim at using gaze as a "moderator" and facilitator of cooperation, and use shared-gaze as a way to create a coupling between players in order to foster a shared sense making process towards increased social presence. With our findings we want to inform game designers with insights on how and why the inclusion of gaze-based interaction in remote game settings fosters the social bond between players.

1.1 Social Presence in Online Games

Several authors share the opinion that presence is composed of the three dimensions: social presence, spatial presence, and self presence [e.g., 20]. As this work specifically focuses on the social aspect of presence a more elaborated definition of the term shall be given. The concept of social presence was introduced by Short et al. and defined as "the degree of salience of the other person in the interaction and the consequent salience of the interpersonal relationships" [17, p. 65]. The researchers claimed that communication medium has an impact on the intimacy and immediacy. After Bulu [1] theories based on the work of Short et al. explain that the level of social presence increases as the communication capabilities of the medium increases, ranging from text-based, to face-to-face media or to computer mediated communication. Following Hudson and Cairns [6] social presence can be compared with the concept of "Shared Involvement", coined by Calleja [3]. Shared Involvement can be understood as a sense of being with subjects in a common environment, whether that involvement is composed of explicit communication, acting as a team, or by being aware that one's actions are taking place in a shared environment. Regarding the role of social presence in the context of games Hudson and Cairns [6] emphasize the importance of social presence by noting that social relationships between players as mediated by games (as well as social presence as its foundation) have a significant influence on the gaming experience. This does not only apply to massively multiplayer games but also to console & PC games (multiplayer, co-located play, etc.). Cairns et al. [2, p. 1069] state that "playing socially is a prevalent and important aspect of digital gaming." Furthermore, several studies identified a correlation between a positive game experience and a high degree of social presence and social interaction (e.g., [5, 14]).

1.2 Nonverbal Interaction and Gaze-Based Interaction in Games

Nonverbal communication manifests itself in a variety of forms such as facial expression, gestures, paralinguistic, body language and posture, proxemics, haptics, and gaze [4]. Several studies revealed that there is a relation between social presence and nonverbal communication [8]. Mansour et al. [13] argue that there is a positive relationship between the perception of social interaction (reciprocal processes in which humans negotiate and regulate the quality of their relationships) and the feeling of social presence in online multiplayer games. The authors note that the coordination of a conversation within games (e.g., clarifying mutual goals, discussing strategies, tactics, etc.) is a dynamic and complex process including exchanges of nonverbal communication. Their proposed framework shows that both verbal and nonverbal communication acts are two main components of social interaction among players. After Mansour et al. [13] the application of verbal and nonverbal behavior helps players to familiarize with their partners, fosters the management of the interaction flow and has a positive influence on the feeling of trust among players. Manninen and Kujanpää [12] suggest that an efficient combination of different communication channels enhances interaction among players. By combining various forms of interaction players would not have to rely on verbal communication alone, but have more flexible means in representing themselves and their ideas. Further, Shahid et al. [16] investigated the effects of mutual gaze on the game experience and perceived social presence during video-mediated and co-present gameplay. Their results indicate that the absence of mutual gaze dramatically affects the quality of interpersonal interaction in video-mediated gameplay settings. Including mutual gaze interaction in such a setting, on the other hand, leads to increased social interaction and mutual understanding among remote collaborators. They argue for the inclusion of mutual gaze interaction as an integral part of playful cooperative settings.

2 Contribution

Based on related research, we argue that there is much potential for gaze-based interaction in cooperative online gameplay. Research on gaze interaction is rather limited in the context of cooperative online gaming. Besides using gaze as a substitute and as enrichment for interaction we want to investigate whether the non-diegetic use of a shared gaze visualization can support social interaction in remote collaborative gameplay. In contrast to other research, we see gaze communication as an integral part of the gaming experience and explore its potential to be used as a means of explicit and implicit interaction. Further, we explore how a shared gaze visualization changes cooperative in-game communication and how teams appropriate the use and meaning of it.

We aim at using gaze as an input method to foster social presence and enhance team collaboration. We argue that by providing this additional communication channel in an online co-op can potentially increase connectedness between cooperating players. In that regard, the game acts as a mediatory artifact generating a social bonding between the cooperating team of players. In a remote setting, typical human face-to-face qualities and non-verbal communication (e.g., eye contact) is very limited. Incorporating eye-based interaction during cooperative online play (in our case visualizing another person's gaze point on a player's screen) can potentially enrich such remote co-op settings. With our approach and gaze-based interaction concept we aim at providing non-verbal information without distracting players but to support them in their gaming activities and explore shared gaze as a subconscious and implicit means of communication but also as an explicit tool for cooperation.

3   Experiment Description

In order to explore gaze-based collaboration in an online co-op game, we conducted an experiment that investigates the effects of shared gaze visualizations on social presence among the participants. The main idea behind the experiment was to visualize the cooperating person's gaze on the player's screen and vice versa (see Fig. 1). We chose the game *Ibb & Obb* [19] as a test bed for our experiment and gaze-based interaction concept. Ibb & Obb is a 2D platformer that lets two players cooperate online to succeed the different puzzle based levels. In this game, players have to coordinate each others actions quite carefully to be able to finish the puzzles the game presents.

Fig. 1. Left side: Picture of study participant playing the game while eye tracking is used to communicate with the other player. Right side: In-game visualization of gaze point indicated via a black circle rendered above the actual game

The experiment consisted of four conditions with varying communication modalities for the cooperating players which were completely randomized to the participants (i.e., randomized block factorial design): (1) no additional communication channels (condition name: none), (2) verbal communication (condition name: voice), (3) gaze (condition name: gaze), and (4) verbal communication + gaze (condition name: voice and gaze). In conditions with shared gaze (i.e., condition 1 and 3), the gaze of the other player (i.e., where the other player is currently looking at) was visualized in real-time on the other player's screen as a black circle (see Fig. 1, right picture). In conditions 2 and 3 participants could additionally communicate via online voice chat. After every playing condition, participants filled out a questionnaire regarding social presence (see section on Measures). The participant pairings played the levels of the game in ascending order to assure that players are always confronted with an increasing level of difficulty. The playing condition of every level was randomized for every participant pairing.

With this study experiment we wanted to investigate the following hypothesis: With the integration of gaze interaction (i.e., the visualization of the other person's gaze) in online co-op games, subjects will experience an increased level of social presence in comparison to a gaming scenario that is solely based on verbal and in-game interactions. We argue that with shared gaze, players receive an additional communication channel that is either used consciously or unconsciously, but which in any case, provides a means of non-verbal communication that is deeply rooted in natural human face-to-face communication. This potentially effects social presence during online co-op play and gives players a new tool to be used for e.g., in-game spatial referencing.

3.1 Participants and Procedure

The study was conducted at two separate research facilities. The sample consisted of 20 participants), age 21 to 37 years (6 female, mean age = 26.20, SD = 4.51). All participants were either students of the University of Applied Sciences Upper Austria (65 %) or research staff working at the University of Salzburg (35 %). Furthermore, subjects represented a variety of disciplines of education having a background in psychology, software engineering, or in digital arts. About half of the participants (11 persons) share an affinity to play video games as they indicated to play games at several times a week or daily, whereas only one participant stated to never play games.

Each evaluation session consisted of two subjects that played the game collaboratively in two separate rooms. The evaluation was divided into four parts based on the previously described conditions (none, voice, gaze, gaze and voice). By choosing a within-subject design, all participant teams had to play each of the mentioned scenarios (play time limit for each condition: 5 min). The order in which the teams were assigned to the conditions was randomized to limit the effects of the condition and game difficulty. As a first step, the experimenter provided a short introduction to give an overview of the overall procedure. After the eye tracking devices were calibrated the evaluation part started with a sandbox level ("limbo" level with level selection) showing the basic means of interaction. Participants were instructed about the setting and the game goals. As the control scheme and the genre itself (i.e., platform game) were easy to comprehend, subjects had no difficulties to get into the game. When subjects confirmed that the control scheme of the game was clear to them the experiment began. All subjects started with the first game level of Ibb & Obb in conjunction with one of the four conditions, followed by level 2, 3 and 4. After each level the condition was changed. For example, team 1 started the experiment with level 1 and the gaze condition, while team 2 played level 1 with the voice condition. This should enable players to get into the game (no steep learning curve), as well as make sure that at the beginning of the experiment subjects were not confronted with too difficult game situations.

After every condition, participants were instructed to fill out the CCPIG question-naire (see section on *Measures* for a detailed description). After finishing all conditions, participants had the possibility to give comments on the played conditions with a focus on social presence and their experience with the gaze visualization, via a team interview carried out by the experimenter. One experimenter was present during the whole study and took notes on observations and participants' interactions in every condition (i.e., how they used the gaze visualization and potential collaboration strategies emerging from the gaze visualization). The procedure took between 50 to 60 min.

3.2 Technical Setup

The technical setup for our experiment consisted of two Tobii EyeX eye trackers (http://www.tobii.com/xperience/) and two separate applications, one for data com-munication and another one for gaze visualization on each player's computer. The gaze position of a player (i.e., X and Y in screen coordinates) was captured by the eye tracker and visualized in real-time on the corresponding players screen "above" the actual game. The communication between the eye tracking application on one player's side and the gaze visualization on the other player's computer was realized via Spacebrew (docs.spacebrew.cc), which is an open-source websocket-based prototyping framework. In order to provide a smooth movement of the gaze visualization, we filtered the gaze point values before sending them to the visualization application. Figure 2 illustrates the overall technical setup.

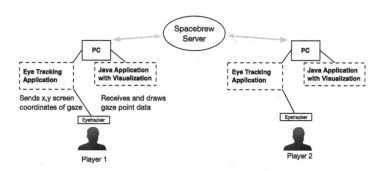

Fig. 2. Schematic of the technical study setup; Two separate applications sending and receiving gaze data for visualization within the game on each participant's side

3.3 Measures

To measure the social presence dimensions the Competitive and Cooperative Presence in Gaming Questionnaire (CCPIG v1.2), which is a validated scale developed by Hudson and Cairns [7], was employed. We decided to use this questionnaire, because it specifically aims at exploring social presence in the complex social environments that are team-based online games. It focuses explicitly on games and is not designed to be a general measure for social presence across multiple media. The CCPIG is composed of two parts: part 1 measures competitive social presence, which is the level of social presence experienced by players towards their opponents. The second part measures cooperative social presence, the level of social presence experienced by a participant towards their teammates. The authors of the questionnaire note that it is possible to use the two parts independently to investigate different kinds of games (competitive, cooperative). Since the game of our evaluation features cooperative and not competitive gameplay, we applied only the second part of the CCPIG. This part is made up of two modules. The first module measures the perceived level of team cohesion (25 items – example: "It was as much about the team as about my own game"), while module 2 measures team involvement (11 items – example: "The actions of my teammates affected my thoughts and actions"). All items were rated on a five-point Likert scale (ranging from 1 = "strongly disagree" to 5 = "strongly agree"). The internal consistencies were acceptable to good with Cronbach's alpha reliability estimates ranging from $\alpha = .67$ to $\alpha = .92$ (cf. Table 1).

Table 1. Means, standard deviations, zero-order correlations, and Cronbach's alpha reliabilities (in the diagonal) of the studied variables

Variable	M	SD	1	2	3	4	5	6	7	8	9	10	11	12
1. Gender	–	–												
2. Age	26.20	4.51	.19											
3. Occupation	–	–	.21	.80*										
4. Playing games	2.80	0.95	−.21	−.04	−.41†									
5. Cohesion (1)	3.99	0.57	.11	.28	.16*	−.19	(.92)							
6. Involvement (1)	4.12	0.46	.16	.39†	.53*	−.41†	.70*	(.86)						
7. Cohesion (2)	4.54	0.27	.06	.54*	.63*	−.12	.24	.24	(.74)					
8. Involvement (2)	4.39	0.30	−.03	.55*	.53*	.04	.15	.16	.68*	(.67)				
9. Cohesion (3)	4.09	0.44	.30	.20	.39†	−.22	.63*	.60*	.31	.41†	(.87)			
10. Involvement (3)	4.23	0.38	−.06	.22	.34	−.09	.72*	.64*	.26	.44†	.75*	(.85)		
11. Cohesion (4)	4.56	.031	.02	.16	.20	.11	−.06	−.03	.51*	.71*	.39†	.30	(.82)	
12. Involvement (4)	4.48	0.33	−.26	.03	.04	.06	−.12	.10	.25	.70*	.20	.43†	.74*	(.79)

Note. N = 20. † p < .10, * p < .05.

Gender: 0 = male, 1 = female.

Occupation: 0 = student, 1 = employed. Playing games: 1 = never, 2 = occasionally, 3 = several times a week, 4 = daily.

1 = condition without gaze and voice, 2 = voice, 3 = gaze, 4 = gaze and voice.

Apart from the CCPIG the evaluation also included an open interview at the end of the test session in order to gain a deeper understanding of the game experience and how participants perceived the gaze interaction. Participants were asked if the gaze visualization was a helpful tool to interact with their teammate as well as how they used it for communication. Additionally, the participants were asked if they felt their teammate as being more present in conditions with a gaze visualization and if they had any suggestions for improvements in regard to game design and the usage of the gaze visualization.

3.4 Data Analysis

All dependent variables were normally distributed, meeting the requirements for parametric analyses. Hence, data were analyzed by means of a repeated measure analysis of variance (rANOVA) with the experimental condition (4 conditions) as the within-subjects factor and the 2 indicators of social presence (team cohesion and team involvement) as the dependent variables. To account for violations in sphericity, the Greenhouse-Geisser correction of degrees of freedom was employed. Post hoc analyses on mean differences between each pair of the four conditions were conducted using Sidak's method. The conventional level of $p < .05$ was used when evaluating the results with regard to statistical significance.

4 Results

Table 1 reports the descriptive statistics and bivariate Pearson correlation coefficients between the variables. As expected, participants experienced higher levels in social presence in conditions with additional communication channels. Social presence was highest in conditions where voice communication was possible (i.e., conditions 2 and 4). Gender was not significantly related to social presence, but age was associated with higher levels in social presence, particularly in the voice condition. Moreover, the more frequently participants were playing games, the less team involvement they were experiencing in the condition without gaze and voice communication.

The results of the rANOVA revealed a significant main effect of experimental condition, $F(1.61, 35.70) = 12.42$, $p < .001$, and a significant interaction effect between experimental condition and the social presence indicators, $F(1.88, 35.70) = 6.03$, $p = .006$. Both effect sizes were large with part. $\eta^2 = .40$ for the main effect and $\eta^2 = .24$ for the interaction. Thus, social presence differed significantly between experimental conditions (main effect), and the effects of the experimental condition were different for team cohesion and team involvement (interaction effect). Figure 3 illustrates the results.

Although condition 3 (gaze) had higher ratings than condition 1 (none) post hoc tests regarding the main effect of experimental conditions demonstrated that condition 3 (gaze) did not result in significantly higher social presence experiences as compared with condition 1 (none), $M_{difference} = 0.11$, $SE_{difference} = 0.07$, $p = .613$. Moreover, condition 4 (voice + gaze) was significantly superior to condition 3 (gaze),

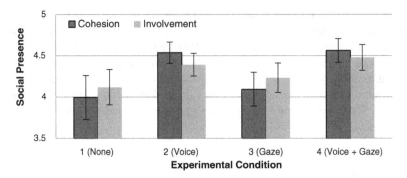

Fig. 3. Means of Social Presence in the four experimental conditions (error bars represent 95 % confidence intervals)

$M_{difference} = 0.36$, $SE_{difference} = 0.09$, $p = .003$, but not to condition 2 (voice), $M_{difference} = 0.06$, $SE_{difference} = 0.05$, $p = .894$. In sum, these results suggest that adding gaze as a communication channel tends to have positive effects on social presence experiences of players, however not significantly, which is contrary to expectations.

As far as the interaction effect is concerned, post hoc analyses revealed that the effect of the experimental condition was stronger for team cohesion as the dependent variable, $\eta^2 = .44$, than for team involvement, $\eta^2 = .25$. The differential effects of the experimental condition on team cohesion and team involvement became particularly evident when conditions 2 (voice) and 4 (voice + gaze) were compared with condition 1 (none): Team cohesion could be significantly improved by adding voice, $M_{difference} = 0.54$, $SE_{difference} = 0.13$, $p = .003$, or voice and gaze as communication channels, $M_{difference} = 0.57$, $SE_{difference} = 0.15$, $p = .007$. On the other hand, team involvement was significantly higher when voice and gaze were added simultaneously, $M_{difference} = 0.36$, $SE_{difference} = 0.12$, $p = .045$; adding voice only tended to be superior to condition 1 as well, but this difference failed to reach significance, $M_{difference} = 0.27$, $SE_{difference} = 0.10$, $p = .090$.

4.1   Qualitative Data Results

The qualitative data consisted of the answers from the team interviews as well as observations and notes taken during the study. The notes were assigned to one of four pre-defined categories (i.e., one for every condition) to gather the study observations in a structured way. During the study the observing experimenter wrote down how participants coordinated their actions (e.g., potential strategies) in every condition and what instructions they gave to each other (e.g., either through gaze or verbal communication). The observation data as well as the team interview after the playing sessions was analysed according to the basics of qualitative content analysis [15] in order to identify "common themes" and similarities among the participant teams in every condition.

The observations as well as the interviews showed that in conditions where voice communication was enabled (i.e., condition voice + gaze and condition voice), voice was the dominant information channel for the teams. Voice was used to negotiate actions, coordinate planning, turn taking, potential hazards, avatar capabilities etc. Further, teams also reported that they felt less verbal misunderstandings in the condition that combined gaze and voice input. This suggests a positive effect of the gaze visualization towards gaining a shared understanding among the team members. For instance, when the teams encountered new, yet unexplored level areas, players stopped their avatars, discussed and planned together, before executing the negotiated actions in a cooperative manner ("I think you have to jump right up there and then I can reach over here"). This step-by-step planning was supported by the gaze visualization as it was used to draw paths showing the team member how to proceed and link verbal input with spatial referencing. The more communication channels the teams had (within the different conditions), the more "planning ahead" occurred. In contrast to that, the condition with no additional communication channels (i.e., condition none) appeared to be most prone to trial and error behavior of the teams.

During the interviews, 9 out of 10 teams reported, that compared to the condition with no additional communication channels (i.e., *condition none*), conditions with a shared gaze visualization made them perceive the other player as being "more present". They reported that they tried to use the gaze visualization as a tool for communication, e.g., for pointing reasons to show the team member where to move. However, some participants felt that using the gaze as a tool was too difficult, as the meaning of, e.g., potential movements and gestures drawn via the visualization, could not be negotiated in advance with the teammate, thus, tended to be unclear to them. Further, the players' gaze was naturally more focused on their own avatar, except when they tried to use the gaze visualization as a tool for pointing and turn taking, in order to draw the other player's attention to something. The concept of perceiving the gaze visualization as a mere tool and not as a representation of the other player may also explain why the effect of social presence was not as pronounced as anticipated. Some players noted that it would be a good idea to visually link the other player's game character with the gaze information. A detailed discussion on the design possibilities in this regard can be found in Lankes et al. [11]. An issue participants had with the gaze visualization was its "always-on" behavior. They felt a strong loss of meaning in the partner's gaze visualization as it was constantly visible, thus, making it hard to distinguish between deliberate communication and unwanted inputs. In that regard, players highlighted that for future iterations of the prototypes they would like to see both, their own and their partner's gaze visualized, a visual link between the avatar and the gaze information, as well as having a way to activate/deactivate the visualization when necessary.

5   Discussion & Lessons Learned

Our study has shown, that gaze-based interaction bears much potential as an additional layer of collaboration in games with shared gaze showing positive influence on perceived social presence. We explored how the non-diegetic use of a shared gaze visualization can support social interactions in a remote setting. It proofed to be a viable means for communication, however, it needs improvements to act as a useful tool for explicit interaction and communication.

Gaze input needs affordances and activation strategies: In our prototype the partner's gaze was visualized in an abstract manner (i.e., via a black circle) without giving the gaze point a semantic meaning within the game world. We did this in order to explore how people react to this new interaction modality and how its use and meaning will be negotiated by the teams themselves letting the players freely appropriate the gaze input towards facilitating common ground. However, a crucial aspect towards making gaze a useful "tool" is to provide a certain affordance and meaning in order to let the players know how and when to use it appropriately. This could be done by, e.g., integrating the gaze point directly into the game world (e.g., letting avatars react to the gaze point) to assure that there is no disconnect between in-game interactions and player interactions. Additionally, one of the lessons learned from the study was that players didn't like the "always-on" aspect of the prototypes current implementation of the gaze visualization. Thus, we argue, that in order to be adopted as a tool by players, we also need to design for meaningful and understandable ways of activation of such a gaze-based interaction (e.g., the player can trigger the visualization actively).

Gaze as an additional layer of communication supporting team processes: Players used their gaze as a tool for communicating in situations that required e.g., exact pointing, or as a substitute to verbal interaction to establish a shared understanding between players and lessen the occurrence of misunderstandings due to potential ambiguous verbal communication. The more communication channels the teams had, the more negotiation between players was happening. This notion of gaze as an additional communication layer could in turn help players to connect and communicate with each other, e.g., in game settings where verbal input might be undesired but team coordination is still necessary (e.g., cooperative mobile online gaming in a public transport scenario).

Gaze as a subconscious non-verbal communication channel: Besides explicit gaze interactions like pointing, we believe that players can also form a kind of subconscious communication through an omnipresent gaze visualization of the other player. Over time players could potentially learn to understand the gaze movements and resulting gestures and intentions of another player, which could lead to a more integrated visual "team language" and connectedness. If and how such implicit gaze-based communication is established between two remote cooperating players will be part of future work, though. In that regard, we plan to do a study in a similar setup with more participants over a longer period of time in order to investigate if such a shared gaze visualization can be used and "learned" over time as a subconscious means communication.

Limitations: The questionnaire we used included many items regarding the players' feelings of acting together as a team. We are aware that the game we used in our study was already strongly based on working together as a team, which could have led to the increases in team coherence and presence in the questionnaire data being not significant among the different conditions. Although we found only little quantitative improvement in social presence between gaze and non-gaze conditions, post-play interviews nonetheless indicate that subjects reacted positively to the inclusion of shared gaze, particularly in conjunction with voice communication.

6 Conclusion

This paper reports on a study that investigated a shared gaze approach and its effects on social presence and collaborative interactions in online cooperative play. We explored different combinations of voice and gaze input as a communication channel for players during a team-based game. Our study findings show that shared gaze can have a positive influence on team cohesion and involvement, leading to players perceiving their team member as being more present when their partner's gaze is visualized. Participants tried to use the gaze visualization as a tool for communication, e.g., for spatial referencing, and described it as being a useful substitute to verbal communication. Based on our findings we argue, that shared gaze can foster social couplings in remote collaborative gaming settings which in turn can contribute to increased connectedness between collaborating players. The integration of such non-verbal interpersonal communication qualities such as gaze, is yet an underrepresented and underused design resource, but nevertheless, a promising direction for future game designs.

Acknowledgements. The financial support by the Austrian Federal Ministry of Science, Research and Economy, the Austrian Ministry for Transport, Innovation and Technology and the federal governments Vorarlberg, Salzburg, Steiermark is gratefully acknowledged (Comet - LiTech).

References

1. Bulu, S.T.: Place presence, social presence, co-presence and satisfaction in virtual worlds. Comput. Educ. **58**(1), 154–161 (2012)
2. Cairns, P., Cox, A.L., Day, M., Martin, H., Perryman, T.: Who but not where: the effect of social play on immersion in digital games. Int. J. Hum Comput Stud. **71**(11), 1069–1077 (2013)
3. Calleja, G.: In-Game: From Immersion to Incorporation. The MIT Press, Cambridge (2011)
4. Dunning, G.B.: Research in nonverbal communication. Theor. Pract. **10**(4), 250–258 (1971)
5. Gajadhar, B., de Kort, Y., IJsselsteijn, W.: Influence of social setting on player experience of digital games. CHI 2008 Extended Abstracts on Human Factors in Computing Systems (CHI EA 2008), pp. 3099–3104. ACM Press, New York (2008)
6. Hudson, M., Cairns, P.: Interrogating social presence in games with experiential vignettes. Entertainment Comput. **5**(2), 101–114 (2014)
7. Hudson, M., Cairns, P.: Measuring social presence in team-based digital games. In: Interacting with Presence: HCI and the Sense of Presence in Computer-mediated Environments, p. 83 (2014)
8. Kaye, L.K.: Exploring flow experiences in cooperative digital gaming contexts. Comput. Hum. Behav. **55**, 286–291 (2015)

9. Kendon, A.: Some functions of gaze-direction in social interaction. Acta Psychol. **26**, 22–63 (1967)
10. Kleinke, C.L.: Gaze and eye contact: a research review. Psych. Bull. **100**(1), 78 (1986)
11. Lankes, M., Mirlacher, T., Wagner, S., Hochleitner, W.: Whom are you looking for?: the effects of different player representation relations on the presence in gaze-based games. Proceedings of CHI PLAY 2014, pp. 171–179. ACM, New York (2014)
12. Manninen, T., Kujanpää, T.: Non-verbal communication forms in multi-player game session. In: Faulkner, X., Finlay, J., Détienne, F. (eds.) People and Computers XVI-Memorable Yet Invisible, pp. 383–401. Springer, London (2002)
13. Mansour, S.S., El-Said, M.: Building a bi-directional bridge between social presence and interaction in online games. In: IEEE 17th International Conference on Computer Games (CGAMES), pp. 202–207. IEEE, July 2012
14. Maurer, B., Aslan, I., Wuchse, M., Neureiter, K., Tscheligi, M.: Gaze-based onlooker integration: exploring the in-between of active player and passive spectator in co-located gaming. In: Proceedings of the CHI PLAY 2015, pp. 163–173. ACM, New York (2015)
15. Mayring, P.: Qualitative content analysis. In: Flick, U., von Kardoff, E., Steinke, I. (eds.) A Companion to Qualitative Research, pp. 266–269. Sage, London (2004)
16. Shahid, S., Krahmer, E., Swerts, M.: Video-mediated and co-present gameplay: effects of mutual gaze on game experience, expressiveness and perceived social presence. Interact. Comput. **24**(4), 292–305 (2012)
17. Short, J., Williams, E., Christie, B.: The Social Psychology of Telecommunications. Wiley, London (1976)
18. Sjöblom, B.: Gaming as a situated collaborative practice. Hum. IT **9**(3), 128–165 (2008)
19. Sparpweed Games. Ibb & Obb. [PC], Sparpweed Games, played January, 2016 (2014)
20. Tamborini, R., Bowman, N.: Presence in video games. In: Bracken, C., Skalski, P. (eds.) Immersed in Media: Telepresence in Everyday Life, pp. 87–109. Routledge, New York (2010)

Evaluating Experiences in Different Virtual Reality Setups

Volker Settgast[1(✉)], Johanna Pirker[2], Stefan Lontschar[3], Stefan Maggale[3], and Christian Gütl[2]

[1] Fraunhofer Austria, Graz, Austria
volker.settgast@fraunhofer.at
[2] IICM, Graz University of Technology, Graz, Austria
{jpirker,cguetl}@iicm.edu
[3] Graz University of Technology, Graz, Austria
{stefan.lontschar,stefan.maggale}@student.tugraz.at

Abstract. This paper describes the evaluation of three different scenarios in the fully immersive room-based virtual environment DAVE (Definitely Affordable Virtual Environment) and a head-mounted display, the Oculus Rift. The evaluation focuses on comparing the two immersive environments and three different scenarios (observation, emotion in a roller coaster, and interaction) in regards to typical virtual-reality characteristics, such as immersion, engagement, but also on cybersickness and the overall experience. First results indicate the DAVE environment better supports scenarios, which require the user to directly interact with the environment. The roller coaster scenario creates stronger immersion and a higher nausea-level, while the interactive task is more engaging in terms of fun.

Keywords: Virtual reality · Immersion · Cybersickness · Oculus Rift · CAVE

1 Introduction

Over the last years, the potential of immersive virtual environments (VE) has been described for various application scenarios. In particular the current trend of affordable head-mounted displays (HMD) allows a wide range of users to access different virtual reality (VR) applications. Such immersive experiences are not only interesting for entertainment, gaming, and simulations, but also for training and education scenarios [1,2].

However, in particular in learning and training applications different scenarios often require different interactions and activities in the virtual reality. For example, specific training tasks would require rich and realistic user interactions (e.g. learning how to use a specific machine). Other tasks require more freedom in the environment such as the possibility to freely examine the objects

G. Wallner et al. (Eds.): ICEC 2016, LNCS 9926, pp. 115–125, 2016.
DOI: 10.1007/978-3-319-46100-7_10

and the environments. For other experiences often only the observation and the experience of the virtual scenario is sufficient.

Different virtual reality devices and setups support different degrees of freedom, of immersion, and interactions with the environment. In a room-based fully immersive virtual environment (such as a CAVE) users are still able to see their own body and set in relation to the virtual world. It is possible to use additional tools in a natural way (e.g. a map or a smart phone) and interact directly with other users. Head-mounted displays support more flexible forms of experiences and activities, for example show a different body for the user or trick the sense of orientation. However, they often give users not the possibility to directly interact with the environment, since the representation of the own body is missing or poorly represented. Different forms of interaction are challenging, since consumer HMDs only give a limited range of sensors for tracking the body [3].

To design rich learning and training scenarios in a virtual environment it is not only necessary to focus on the different interactivities, but also to design the experience with consideration of different virtual reality characteristics and problems to create a sound user experience. This in particular includes immersion and cybersickness.

In this work we present a first comparison of different activities (observations, strong emotions, interactions) in two virtual reality systems (CAVE, Oculus Rift DK2) with focus on typical virtual-reality characteristics, such as immersion and engagement, but also on the potential issue of cybersickness.

2   Background and Related Work

Significant research and development efforts of different VR experiences have discussed and shown the potential of immersive VR already very early [5,6].

2.1   Comparing Experiences in Virtual Reality Environments

Tan et al. [4] compare and evaluate gaming experiences in the *Oculus Rift*. They used a Oculus Rift DK1 and a traditional computer with monitor setup to play a first-person shooter game (Half-Life 2). The test persons had to play the game on each system and then they answered two main question. Ten test persons were participating. The first main question was about the experience using the Rift compared to a standard PC setup. The second question was about what to take care about when designing games for the Rift based on the findings about the peoples experience. The study shows that most participants experienced cybersickness 8 on a scale from 1 to 10 and that cybersickness only occurs on the Oculus Rift. They say that: "cybersickness was a strong factor in modulating peoples gaming experiences using the Rift."

Kim et al. [7] compared three different VR Systems with two tasks for each system (A 3×2 study). The Systems used were a standard PC without any VR elements, a HMD with limited peripheral vision and a fully immerse CAVE environment (DiVE). The two tasks where a low stressful and a high stressful task where the participants had to find cards with a certain word-color combination. The difference was, that in the low stress task the color and name of the words was congruent and in the high stress task they were not. Additionally in the high stress version of the tasks, the participants were influenced by averse simulations (loud noises, flashes and occasional tactile vibrations). The study focused on cybersickness, presence, and emotional changes. Additionally the time to find the cards was tracked and a galvanic skin sensor was used to measure sympathetic autonomic arousal. The result showed, that there were higher emotional arousal values in the DiVE and HMD compared to the desktop system but there were also differences between the VR devices. In the DiVE the emotional changes were mainly positive whereas with the HMD the effects were negative. Overall the participants showed the highest SCR changes with the DiVE, with the HMD the changes were moderate. In the end the findings showed, that a CAVE like environment is best used to evoke happy emotions whereas a HMD device is advantageous to evoke negative emotion. The desktop system resulted in the smallest changes overall and moderate task performance. This knowledge can be used e.g. in psychological studies because it gives insight in which technologies are viable to use for which treatments. A HMD device can therefore maybe be used to treat anxiety disorders.

2.2 Cybersickness

As VR-devices become more and more popular, there is still a big obstacle to overcome to make it an enjoyable experience for everyone, namely cybersickness. Cybersickness symptoms in virtual reality environments are similar so motion sickness (e.g. nausea, disorientation, discomfort, vomiting). The sensitivity and grade of cybersickness differs from person to person and thus is hard to keep track of. Most studies rely on self-reported tests after using VR devices and so it highly depends on every participant, how the results of the study develop.

Davis et al. compare the two HMDs Oculus Rift DK1 and Oculus Rift DK2 [8]. In a follow-up paper Davis, Nesbitt, and Nalivaiko [9] introduce new techniques to explicitly measure cybersickness. The idea is to create certain tasks and actions that induce cybersickness and with help of these it would be possible to measure psychological conditions and objectively quantify cybersickness symptoms. The paper also refers to older studies and sets different approaches to measure this condition into contrast to find well suited ways of finding an objective measurement. The study was held with 30 participants and with the use of two different virtual roller coasters. With these two different coasters it was possible to find relations between e.g. the level of detail, the level of user interaction and the nausea condition of each participant.

In conclusion the study found, that the coaster with more complex realism (Helix) causes a higher level of nausea offset compared to the other and is therefore suggested for further studies regarding objective measurement of cybersickness. Such studies are necessary to bring VR further to the possibility of everyday usage because only with cost effective and objective measurements, which still have to be found, this will be achievable [9].

Polcar and Horejsi [10] compared three devices with a group of 45 students. The devices were a regular PC workstation, a Stereoscopic projection wall (CAVE, PowerWall, StereoWall) and an HMD (Oculus Rift DK2). After the test participants had to fill out a questionnaire about cybersickness, their symptoms, and the level of knowledge acquisition. The goal was to find a comparison of these devices. In the third part of the paper, they describe the effects of virtual learning and cybersickness. In conclusion there found no big difference of knowledge acceptance by doing a training exercise in reality or in a virtual world. While different controllers did not have much effect on the results, a larger display enhances the knowledge acceptance rate. In this study males achieved a better performance at this task than females. This effect decreased when the virtual environment was viewed on a bigger screen.

3   The Setting

For this study we used 2 ((a) Oculus Rift DK2, (b) DAVE) × 3 (tasks based on (1) observation, (2) emotion, (3) interaction) experiment setup with focus on comparing immersion, cybersickness, and the overall experiences.

3.1   Virtual Environments

Oculus Rift. The Oculus Rift is a Head Mounted Display developed by Oculus VR since 2012. The first commercial version was released in March 2016. For this paper the second pre-released developer kit (DK2) of mid 2014 was used[1]. In this version the display has a full HD resolution which is divided vertically showing the stereoscopic image for both eyes. Compared to prior HMDs the Oculus Rift was able to increase the field of view to 110° by using lenses and adjust the rendered images accordingly. An optical tracking system is used in combination with an orientation sensor for the localization of the users head. A sitting and a standing setup is possible but the range of movement is limited to less than two meters because of the cable-based video transmission.

DAVE. The Definitely Affordable Virtual Environment (DAVE) is an immersive projection room with three side walls and one floor projection [12]. The projection screens are 3.3 m wide and 2.7 m high. (see Fig. 1). Stereo projectors with HD resolution are updated at 60 Hz. Stereoscopic shutter glasses are used, similar to the ones also known from 3D TV sets or 3D cinemas. In addition, an optical head tracking system allows a correct parallax and creates an undistorted view for the main user. Within the 3.3 by 3.3 m the user can walk around an object to see it from all sides. A big advantage compared to most HMDs is the very wide field of view. Such a CAVE provides a visually convincing immersive experience and while allowing the user to see her own body.

---

[1] https://www.oculus.com/dk2/.

Fig. 1. The DAVE: A four-sided CAVE-like immersive environment

3.2   The Implemented Scenarios

For the study three different scenarios (see Fig. 2) were implemented with the goal to create three different experiences (observation, strong emotion, and interaction).

Fig. 2. The three scenarios from left to right: complex model for observation, roller coaster and catch-the-ball game

Task 1 (Observation). The first task was mostly focused on letting people become familiar with the systems. It was just a stationary scene where the participants had to find a certain object on a big model (see Fig. 3-a). Participants had to move around to find the object. The difference between the task with the Rift and in the DAVE was the object on the model they had to find.

Task 2 (Emotion). This was the dynamical task where the study participants had to take a ride in a virtual roller coaster once with the DK2 (see Fig. 3-b) and once inside the DAVE. The users only had to sit on a chair and experience the virtual ride. Afterwards they had to describe their feelings while riding. Some of the test persons experienced quite a lot of cybersickness during this task but for none it was enough to interrupt the ride. The task was exactly the same with the Rift and in the DAVE.

Task 3 (Interaction). The last task was a dynamical scene where the study participants had to interact with the virtual environment. The goal of this task was to catch or deflect as many balls as possible in a certain time. The balls came flying towards the user from a virtual canon. This task created mostly positive reactions from all participants because it was much fun to play. There was no difference between the task with the DK2 (see Fig. 3-c) and in the DAVE. In both setups a Microsoft Kinect was used for detecting the users hands.

4   Preliminary Study

To evaluate the different scenarios we devised a study setup which should shed light on the participants' experience in the two virtual environment setups with focus on different aspects, such immersion, nausea level, and engagement. The tasks, as described above, were designed to cover activities focusing on (1) observations, (2) emotions, and (3) interactions in virtual environments.

In a first study we compared the two different virtual reality environments with 8 persons. One environment was an HMD and the other one was the DAVE. The participants had to do three tasks in each of these two virtual environment. Before they started with task 1, they had to fill out a pre-questionnaire. After each task they rated the immersion, nausea level, overall experience, and fun. After completing all 3 tasks in the DAVE, they filled out a post-questionnaire At the end they had to fill out the task questionnaire of part two and a specific cybersickness questionnaire.

4.1   Participants

To evaluate the scenarios 8 participants (5 female) between 21 and 48 (M = 28.38, SD = 8.29) were recruited. After a first introduction, participants completed an pre-survey with demographic information (e.g. age, gender, profession), experience with games and virtual realities. 6 participants are students. On a Likert-scale between 1 (not at all) and 5 (definitely) the participants rated their experiences in computer usage with a arithmetic mean of 3.13 (SD = 1.36) and their experience wit video games with a mean of 2.0 (SD = 1.6). All of them mentioned that they are not experienced with Virtual Reality. Only 2 play often or relatively often computer games. 3 like playing video games. 4 have heard of a CAVE/DAVE environment, 1 of them has already used one. 4 have heard of the Oculus Rift, 3 have already used one.

(a) Task 1 - Observation

(b) Task 2 - Emotion

(c) Task 3 - Interaction

Fig. 3. The three different tasks as rendered in the Oculus Rift DK2.

4.2 Setup

The virtual reality Oculus Rift Developer Kit 2 (DK2) and the DAVE environment as described in Sect. 3 were used for the evaluation. For the task design the scenarios (Task 1: Observation, Task 2: Emotion, Task 3: Interaction) as described in the previous section were used. Figure 4 illustrates the three tasks in the DAVE.

Fig. 4. The tasks in the DAVE; from left to right: Task 1 - Observation: The participants were asked to find a specific part of the machinery by observing the scene; task 2 - Emotion: The participants had to ride a roller coaster; task 3 - Interaction: In a mini game the participants had to catch balls shot in a random angle at them.

4.3 Method

Immersion, Experience, and Engagement. To evaluate aspects such as immersion and fun we used two different measures. (1) After each task we asked the participant to rate immersion, fun, and if they have liked the experience on a Likert scale between 1 (not at all) and 10 (very) to receive immediate feedback. (2) After they have completed all three tasks for one device we asked them to complete slightly modified version of the Game Engagement Questionnaire (GEQ) [11]. GEQ is designed to measure engagement in games. It provides a set of 19 questions (we used 18 for our study) to measure absorption, flow, presence, and immersion. Since we measure the "game engagement" after the interaction with each setup we are able to compare these values for the two different virtual reality setups.

Cybersickness. As also described in [9] we used a subjective individual rating of the participant's perception of their nausea level to evaluate cybersickness. The participants were asked after each task to rate their nausea level between "0 - no discomfort" to "10 - feeling like vomiting".

5   Findings

5.1   Experiences

Immersion. Participants rated their immersion level on a scale from 1–10 after each tasks slightly higher in the DAVE. They rated in particular the rollercoaster experience as immersive (see Fig. 5(a)). Looking at the GEQ (see Fig. 6) the overall immersion-level in the DAVE is also rated higher compared to DK2.

Cybersickness. After each task the participants were asked to describe their nausea-level on a scale between 0 - no discomfort" to "10 - feeling like vomiting". Figure 5-b gives an overview of the participants' nausea level in the two different virtual environment. The value was for both devices very high after the Rollercoaster task (Task 2). The nausea level difference between DAVE and DK2 indicates that this feeling is only slightly higher in the DAVE.

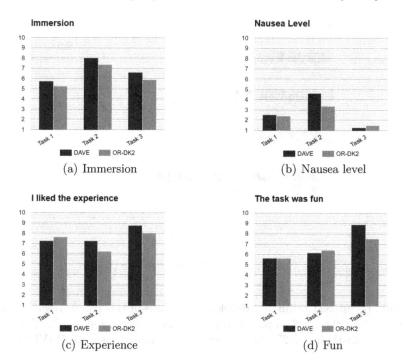

Fig. 5. Subjective rating of immersion, nausea level, experience, and fun after each tasks - 1 (not at all) 10 (very)

Fun and Overall Experience. As illustrated in Fig. 5(c) the participants mentioned to like all experiences, but task 3 was rated highest. They also mentioned to have most fun in the interactive experience (see Fig. 5(d)). Figure 6 illustrates the four main (absorption, presence, flow, and immersion) concepts as a result the 18 different GEQ-questions. All engagement metrics were described as slightly higher in the DAVE compared to DK2. In particular Immersion as factor of engagement was rated extremely high in the DAVE environment.

5.2 The Tasks

7 out of 8 participants would prefer the DAVE over DK2 for the observation tasks. Reasons for that were described as "more realistic interactions" or "better graphics". Participants rated the difficulty of finding the object in the DK2 (M = 2.5, SD = 1.41) slightly higher compared to the DAVE (M = 2.0, SD = 1.07).

7/8 rated their experience in the virtual roller coaster as a fun experience. Three had a fear emotion at some point of the ride. Four would want to use this simulation again. Two would prefer DK2 for this simulation ("movement more realistic in DK2"), six the DAVE ("feels more real").

On a scale between 1 (not at all) and 5 (very) participants described the fun while playing the minigame with an arithmetic mean of 3.88 (SD = 1.25).

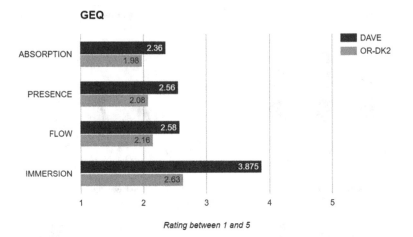

Fig. 6. Game Engagement Questionnaire (GEQ).

6/8 would be interest in further developed versions of this game. 7 would prefer the DAVE over the DK2 to play this game ("not so heavy glasses", "display of hands not realistic in DK2", "hand movements more realistic in DAVE").

6   Conclusion and Discussion

The presented study is designed as the beginning of many tests with this setup and gives a first overview. Early results indicate, that a DAVE environment gives participants more freedom in regard to body perception, small-scale movement, and more realistic images. However, all tasks were mainly designed for small movements in a limited space. While the roller coaster scenario (designed to create strong emotions) gives participants a strong feeling of immersion and creates a higher nausea level, the interactive playful task is rated as a more fun task.

Further studies should also include scenarios, which require participants e.g. to travel distances. Also due to the small study setup and the natural differences between the two virtual reality environments (HMD vs. room-based virtual environment) many key limitations are given. Given the current rapid development of HMDs, it will be important to extend the current study with the latest HMD-technologies and other platforms. Future studies investigating more specific emotions and different forms of interactions with a larger participant base will extend the present findings.

References

1. Stone, R.J.: Applications of virtual environments: an overview. In: Handbook of Virtual Environments: Design, Implementation, and Applications. Human Factors and Ergonomics, pp. 827–856, 1232 pp. Lawrence Erlbaum Associates Publishers, Mahwah (2002)

2. Kim, K., Rosenthal, M.Z., Zielinski, D.J., Brady, R.: Effects of virtual environment platforms on emotional responses. Comput. Methods Programs Biomed. **113**(3), 882–893 (2014)

3. McGill, M., Boland, D., Murray-Smith, R., Brewster, S.: A dose of reality: overcoming usability challenges in VR head-mounted displays. In: Proceedings of the 33rd Annual ACM Conference on Human Factors in Computing Systems, CHI 2015, pp. 2143–2152. ACM, New York (2015)

4. Tan, C.T., Leong, T.W., Shen, S., Dubravs, C., Si, C.: Exploring gameplay experiences on the Oculus Rift. In: Proceedings of the 2015 Annual Symposium on Computer-Human Interaction in Play, pp. 253–263. ACM (2015)

5. Sutherland, I.E.: The ultimate display. Multimedia: From Wagner to virtual reality (1965)

6. Bishop, G., Bricken, W., Brooks, F., Brown, M., Burbeck, C., Durlach, N., Ellis, S., Fuchs, H., Green, M., Lackner, J., McNeill, M., Moshell, M., Pausch, R., Robinett, W., Srinivasam, M., Sutherland, I., Urban, D., Wenzel, E.: Research directions in virtual environments. Comput. Graph. **26**(3), 153 (1992)

7. Kim, K., Rosenthal, M.Z., Zielinski, D., Brady, R.: Comparison of desktop, head mounted display, and six wall fully immersive systems using a stressful task. In: 2012 IEEE Virtual Reality Short Papers and Posters (VRW), pp. 143–144. IEEE (2012)

8. Davis, S., Nesbitt, K., Nalivaiko, E.: A systematic review of cybersickness. In: Proceedings of the 2014 ACM Conference on Interactive Entertainment, pp. 1–9 (2014)

9. Davis, S., Nesbitt, K., Nalivaiko, E.: Comparing the onset of cybersickness using the oculus rift and two virtual roller coasters. In: Proceedings of the 11th Australasian Conference on Interactive Entertainment (IE 2015), vol. 27, p. 30 (2015)

10. Polcar, J., Horejsi, P.: Knowledge acquisition and cyber sickness: a comparison of VR devices in virtual tours. MM Sci. J. **2015**(02), 613–616 (2015)

11. Brockmyer, J.H., Fox, C.M., Curtiss, K.A., McBroom, E., Burkhart, K.M., Pidruzny, J.N.: The development of the Game Engagement Questionnaire: a measure of engagement in video game-playing. J. Exp. Soc. Psychol. **45**(4), 624–634 (2009)

12. Lancelle, M., Settgast, V., Fellner, D.W.: Definitely affordable virtual environment. In: Virtual Reality Conference (2008)

Proposing a New Conceptual Model Predicting Consumer Videogame Engagement Triggered Through Playful-Consumption Experiences

Amir Zaib Abbasi[1], Ding Hooi Ting[1], and Helmut Hlavacs[2(✉)]

[1] Department of Management and Humanities, Universiti Teknologi PETRONAS,
Tronoh, Malaysia
amir_zaib_abbasi@yahoo.co.uk
[2] Research Group Entertainment Computing, University of Vienna, Vienna, Austria
helmut.hlavacs@univie.ac.at

Abstract. The aim of the study is to propose a conceptual model which predicts consumer videogame engagement triggered by the playful-consumption experience of videogame-play. The proposed conceptual model is based on a review of past literature on experience and engagement in videogame studies. Moreover, this study employs the hedonic theory of consumption experience and the concept of consumer engagement in order to conceptualize and operationalize the construct of playful-consumption experience and consumer videogame engagement and accordingly, develops the conceptual model. Based on the conceptual model, this study has drawn related hypothesis. This study is unique in its investigation as it examines the idea of experience from the perspective of hedonic theory of consumption experience and whereas, engagement is studied from the previous work on consumer engagement. Besides, this conceptual model is new in the field of videogame literature that examines consumer videogame engagement and playful consumption experience concurrently and this model also predicts consumer videogame engagement that is provoked by the playful-consumption experience of videogame play.

Keywords: Experience · Hedonic consumption experience · Playful consumption experience · Imaginal experience · Emotional experience · Sensory experience · Engagement · Consumer engagement · Consumer videogame engagement · Cognitive · Affective and behavioral engagement

1 Introduction

The prevalence of playing videogames such as computer, mobile, portable and console videogames, has been raised significantly in the past decade [1]. Due to the popularity of videogame playing, the total consumers' spending on games industry has increased to $22.41 billion [2]. This prominent growth in the videogame industry has encouraged

© IFIP International Federation for Information Processing 2016
Published by Springer International Publishing AG 2016. All Rights Reserved
G. Wallner et al. (Eds.): ICEC 2016, LNCS 9926, pp. 126–134, 2016.
DOI: 10.1007/978-3-319-46100-7_11

academicians to research on videogame related issues. One of the key issues in videogame literature that has much debated is exploring and measuring the consumer's experiences, which arise from the interaction of a player, playing a videogame [3].

In similar vein, numerous academicians have investigated the concept of experience in videogame studies; some of the studies have qualitatively explored the term experience [4, 5] while, some studies have quantitatively measured the notion of experience [6, 7]. The term experience has been studied through several theoretical constructs *"absorption and flow, presence, immersion and engagement, gameflow, immersion and flow, presence, immersion, flow and absorption"* by these studies [4, 5, 7–11] to measure the subjective-experience of videogame-play. Moreover, the study has related the notion of experience with immersion, which has been further explored in the application of new technologies. For instance, immersive virtual environments in digital humanities that further create a new human experiences by consuming the new media technology like interactive immersive environments with videogames [12].

In literature, there are other studies [13, 14] that have investigated the subjective experience of videogame-play but they termed as *"game-engagement"*. Authors of these studies [13, 14] have used the following dimensions *"presence, flow, immersion, absorption and involvement"* to measure the subjective game-play experience.

Doing a critical analysis of the past studies, the present study has found that the main issue in the previous studies is, they have studied two different concepts *(experience and engagement)* with similar theoretical constructs for instance; authors of the study [7] have measured the subjective experience of videogame-play through these theoretical lenses *(presence, flow, immersion and psychological absorption)* and named as immersion. Whereas, authors of these studies [13, 14] have measured the term *"engagement"* in videogames as game-engagement and used the following theoretical dimensions *flow, presence, absorption, involvement and immersion* in order to quantify the subjective game-play experience. The same viewpoint has also been raised in the recent study [15] in which authors of the study have stated that prior studies have applied the concept of experience/immersion and engagement interchangeably to examine the subjective game-play experience as well as player's engagement in videogame playing. Another issue in the previous studies [7, 13, 14, 16] is, they have restricted the construct of experience and engagement to the use of only psychological dimensions *presence, flow, immersion and psychological absorption*. Besides, these studies have ignored the importance of studying behavioral elements in both of the constructs.

The main purpose of the study is twofold; first, this study considers *engagement and experience* as a separate concept whereby, experience recognizes as consumer's consumption experience that occurs from the consumption of the product which influences a consumer to further engage in the product [17, 18]. These studies have also cleared the understanding between experience and engagement that consumption experience comes before the engagement in the product. This viewpoint is consistent with the following study [19] who has discussed in his study that consuming experience of ambient media leads consumers to further engage in the ambient media.

Moreover, this study follows the viewpoint of [20] who added that engagement arises from the experiences that come from the interactions of the main stimuli *(product or service)* and therefore, this study attempts to propose a new conceptual model that predicts consumer videogame engagement triggered by the playful-consumption experience of videogame play. Another objective of the study is to expand the conceptual model through conceptualizing and operationalizing the construct of playful-consumption experience and consumer video-game engagement.

2 Literature Review

Experience in videogame studies is a multifaceted construct, which has been explored and studied by several studies [4–7]. Among these studies, research done by [4] was first study in the videogame literature, who explored the experiences of videogame-players and defined such experiences as game immersion. In Addition, authors have further categorized the definitional construct of game immersion into three sub levels of experiences such as *"engagement, engrossment, and total immersion"*. Another study by [5] who investigated the concept of immersion to understand the basic essentials of videogame-play experience. The study resulted in three factors *"sensory-immersion, challenge-based immersion and imaginative-immersion"* affecting the construct of immersion.

Literature review reports that these studies [6, 7, 10, 21, 22] have examined the experiences of videogame-play for instance; the following studies [10, 21, 22] have considered the idea of experience as a multidimensional construct that comprises these dimensions *"imaginative and sensory-immersion, competence, challenge, annoyance/ tension, flow, positive and negative affect"*. Based on these dimensions, authors have developed and labeled a scale as game experience questionnaire (GEQ) for measuring the experiences of videogame play. But, the questionnaire lacks empirical validation [23]. In contrast to game experience questionnaire, these studies [4–7] have employed the theory of immersion to develop the instruments such as *"immersion questionnaire [7] and game immersion questionnaire [6]"* for describing the experiences of videogame-play. Moreover, immersion questionnaire has been developed through the efforts of [7] in which authors have applied such theoretical constructs *"flow, presence, cognitive absorption and immersion"* to develop a scale for measuring the experience of immersion in videogame-playing. While, another study [6] has employed the definition of immersion [4] to develop a scale for *"game immersion experience"* which is intended to measure the experiences of videogame-play. According to the study [4], immersion is defined as *"three sub-levels of experiences"* such as *"engagement, engrossment and total immersion"*.

Recently, the research done by [15] has debated that few studies have employed the notion of experience/immersion and engagement in a similar manner to examine the experiences of videogame-play. This can be supported by these studies [13, 14] who have applied the term engagement to quantify the subjective experience of videogame-play. Another interesting point that has been raised is, authors of these studies [13, 14] have applied similar dimensions *"flow, presence, absorption and immersion"* to measure the construct game engagement, which have already been employed in the following study [7] to measure the experiences of videogame-play.

A critical evaluation of past researches that have utilized the notion of experience/immersion and engagement in videogame studies, the current study has found the following issues for instance; first, the concept of experience/immersion and engagement have been used interchangeably to measure the subjective experience of videogame play [7, 13, 14]. Second, authors have applied similar theoretical dimensions *"flow, presence, absorption and immersion"* to measure the experiences as well as player's engagement in videogame-play. Besides, authors have applied only psychological dimensions in the construct of game engagement and experience/immersion.

To address the above stated issues, the next section aims to propose a unique conceptual model that studies the concept of experience and engagement as two separate theoretical constructs. In this conceptual model, the present study employs the concept of experience from the context of hedonic theory given by [24] and whereas, engagement from the work of following studies [25–27].

3   The Development of Conceptual Model and Study Propositions

The notion of experience was initially presented by [24] in the field of consumption and marketing. Now onwards, the studying of experience has turned into a significant component to realize consumer's behavior [28]. Formerly, the researchers of marketing and consumer field, have applied the idea of consumption in only purchasing decisions. But, this viewpoint of the consumption, has been extended by the study [24] who has introduced the experiential features of the consumption. Moreover, a study [29] has contributed that a researcher can investigate the idea of consumption in terms of buying, usage and disposal. In similar vein, the following studies [30–32] have also added that consumption experience occurs in numerous ways for instance; when consumers are looking for a product, when consumers purchase the product or acquire any service and lastly, when consumers make use of the product or service. Among these consumption experiences, the present study is mainly interested in investigating the consumption experience that comes from the use of the product. Applying the concept of consumption experience in context of videogame-play, the consumption experience is assumed to achieve through the playful-consumption of a videogame product because a study has added that *"playing a videogame is truly as experiencing a videogame"* [33]. Moreover, researchers [34, 35] have considered the act of playing a videogame or consuming videogames as *"playful-consumption experience"*. This is due to the reason that playful-consumption experience affiliates to intrinsically motivated consumer behavior that is usually done for its own benefit. Such consumption experience of videogame-play, further facilitates the videogame-consumers to experience a variety of hedonic elements relating to videogame-play such as imagination, emotional responses and multisensory attributes [35, 36]. Furthermore, these hedonic elements *"imagination, emotional responses and multisensory attributes"* come under the umbrella of hedonic consumption. Authors of these studies [24, 37], have defined hedonic consumption as *"those facets of consumer behavior that relate to consumers' emotive-responses, imaginary and multi-sensory aspects in using products"*. Besides, according to [24], videogame is one of the hedonic product because, the consumption of a videogame product as *"playful-consumption"* involves *consumers' emotive-responses, imaginary and multi-sensory aspects.*

In the following studies, researchers have further operationalized and categorized the hedonic consumption experience into three main experiences, explicitly, imaginal, emotional and sensory experiences [24, 38]. Imaginal experience states about mental events of visualizing things that are not considered as real and such visualizing is internal, personal and unspoken [39]. Hedonic consumption is connected with imaginal experience as a product has the potential to help consumers imagine actions that they want [24]. While, emotional experience denotes to emotive states that consumers experience with respect to particular activities. The following research [24] has added a product has the ability to arouse consumers' emotional state and therefore, emotional experience is linked with hedonic consumption. The last experience that is tied to hedonic consumption is sensory experience. Whereas, the study [24] has defined sensory experience as *"the receipt of experience in multiple sensory modalities comprising sense of touch, sight, and sound"*.

In earlier debate, the study has defined and operationalized the term experience as *"playful-consumption"* from the perspective of hedonic consumption theory given by [24]. However, the term engagement is less defined in the above studies and therefore, the next debate will shed light on the concept of engagement in videogame.

The current article studies the concept of engagement in videogame literature as *"consumer videogame engagement"*. This study takes a theoretical support from the following studies [18, 25, 26] in order to define and conceptualize the concept of consumer videogame engagement. According to the authors, *"engagement is a multi-dimensional construct which is subject to a context-specific expression of relevant cognitive, emotional and behavioral dimensions"*. Moreover, the study by [18] has further promoted that the process of engagement exhibits due to having two-way communications among the engagement-subject like *"consumer/customer"* and a specific engagement-object like a product, service or a brand, which finally helps in generating consumer engagement levels in terms of consumers' cognitive, affective and behavioral engagement. As a result of these definitions given by [18, 25, 26], this study defines consumer videogame engagement as *"A psychological state that triggers due to two-way interactions between the consumer and videogame product, which generates different level of consumer engagement states (cognitive, affective and behavioral)"*. According to the definition of consumer videogame engagement, the construct of consumer videogame engagement is further conceptualized as three main states of engagement comprising cognitive, affective and behavioral engagement.

In spite of the fact, consumers gain playful-consumption experience through the consumption of a videogame product as *"playing a videogame"*. Such playful-consumption experience refers to the notion of hedonic consumption experience, which relates to consumers' imaginal, emotional and sensory experience in the videogame-play. A study [40] has further added that this kind of experiences *(playful-consumption experiences)* are so interactive and co-creative that consumers get engaged cognitively, affectively and behaviorally in playing more videogames. On this basis, the present study proposes a unique conceptual model as shown in Fig. 1 that predicts consumer videogame engagement in terms of consumers' or video-gamers' cognitive, affective and

behavioral engagement triggered by consumers' or video-gamers' playful-consumption
experience in terms of their imaginal, emotional and sensory experience.

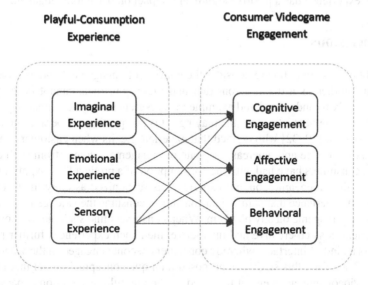

Fig. 1. Predicting consumer videogame engagement triggered by playful-consumption
experience

3.1   Conceptual Model

The following proposed conceptual model explains that when consumers play a videogame, they actually get an experience of playing which is termed as playful-consumption
experience. Playful-consumption experience is further categorized as imaginal experience, emotional experience and sensory experience. This is consumers' playful-
consumption experience that further motivates consumers to engage into videogame
playing. This engagement is coined as consumer videogame engagement in the proposed
conceptual model. The consumer videogame engagement is further classified into
cognitive engagement, affective engagement and behavioral engagement.

3.2   Study Hypothesis

According to the proposed conceptual as shown in the Fig. 1, this study develops the
following hypothesis.

Imaginal experience has a positive significant impact on cognitive engagement.
Imaginal experience has a positive significant impact on affective engagement.
Imaginal experience has a positive significant impact on behavioral engagement.
Emotional experience has a positive significant impact on cognitive engagement.
Emotional experience has a positive significant impact on affective engagement.
Emotional experience has a positive significant impact on behavioral engagement.

Sensory experience has a positive significant impact on cognitive engagement.
Sensory experience has a positive significant impact on affective engagement.
Sensory experience has a positive significant impact on behavioral engagement.

4 Conclusions

This study took an initiative to consider the concept of engagement and experience in videogame studies as a distinct construct and these constructs cannot be employed interchangeably to understand and examine the experiences of videogame-play as well as players' engagement in videogame playing. This perspective can be well understood from the work of [30–32] who defined that experience exits when customers consume the product or service and whereas, the state of engagement comes from such experiences that consumers have had with the consumption of a product [20]. Applying these concepts in the videogame context, experience is recognized as consumers' playful-consumption experience that gains when consumers consume the videogame product as *"playing"* a videogame on any platform. When consumers find such playful-consumption experiences as co-creative and interactive, then such experiences further provide consumers a kind of interface, whereby consumers become engaged in the videogame-play [40]. Therefore, this study has proposed a unique conceptual model that predicts consumer videogame engagement triggered by the playful-consumption experience of videogame-play.

5 Contribution and Future Research

This study contributes to videogame literature in several ways for instance; this study is first to employ the hedonic theory of consumption experience in the field of videogame studies, to examine the playful-consumption experience, namely, imaginal, emotional and sensory experience in videogame-play. Secondly, this study differentiates between the concept of experience and engagement in videogame studies because, previous researches [7, 13, 14] have applied the concept of experience and engagement interchangeably to examine the player's experiences and engagement in videogame play. This study further contributes to the past studies that experience comes first then such experiences further influence consumers to get engaged in the videogame-play. Moreover, this study employs the definition of consumer engagement that has been mentioned in the following studies [18, 25, 26] to conceptualize consumer videogame engagement in videogame literature. The new perspective of engagement as *"consumer videogame engagement"*, brings new insights in the previous studies [13, 14] that have studied the notion of engagement in their studies. Thirdly, all previous work in the field of videogame literature, especially on measuring experiences [6, 7, 10, 21] as well as engagement [13, 14], are scarce to simultaneously examine the notion of experience and engagement within a model, which the current study addresses in the proposed model that predicts consumer videogame engagement triggered by playful-consumption experience of videogame play. This study is conceptual in nature and therefore, future study is warrant to validate the proposed model and the study propositions. Moreover, future work is in progress to develop a scale on playful-consumption experience and consumer video-game engagement.

References

1. Takatalo, J., et al.: User experience in digital games differences between laboratory and home. Simul. Gaming **42**(5), 656–673 (2011)
2. Entertainment Software Association: Essential facts about the Computer and Video Game Industry, p. 20. Entertainment software association (2015)
3. Seo, Y., Buchanan-Oliver, M., Fam, K.S.: Advancing research on computer game consumption: a future research agenda. J. Consum. Behav. **14**(6), 353–356 (2015)
4. Brown, E., Cairns, P.: A grounded investigation of game immersion. In: CHI 2004 Extended Abstracts on Human Factors in Computing Systems, pp. 1297–1300. ACM (2004)
5. Ermi, L., Mäyrä, F.: Fundamental components of the gameplay experience: analysing immersion. Worlds Play: Int. Perspect. Digit. Games Res. **37**, 2 (2005)
6. Cheng, M.T., She, H.C., Annetta, L.A.: Game immersion experience: its hierarchical structure and impact on game-based science learning. J. Comput. Assist. Learn. **31**(3), 232–253 (2015)
7. Jennett, C., et al.: Measuring and defining the experience of immersion in games. Int. J. Hum.-Comput. Stud. **66**(9), 641–661 (2008)
8. Costello, B., Edmonds, E.: A tool for characterizing the experience of play. In: Proceedings of the Sixth Australasian Conference on Interactive Entertainment, p. 2. ACM (2009)
9. Funk, J.B., Pasold, T., Baumgardner, J.: How children experience playing video games. In: Proceedings of the Second International Conference on Entertainment Computing, pp. 1–14. Carnegie Mellon University (2003)
10. IJsselsteijn, W., et al.: Characterising and measuring user experiences in digital games. In: International Conference on Advances in Computer Entertainment Technology, vol. 2, p. 27 (2007)
11. Sweetser, P., Wyeth, P.: GameFlow: a model for evaluating player enjoyment in games. Comput. Entertainment (CIE) **3**(3), 3 (2005)
12. Lugmayr, A., Teras, M.: Immersive interactive technologies in digital humanities: a review and basic concepts. In: Proceedings of the 3rd International Workshop on Immersive Media Experiences, pp. 31–36. ACM (2015)
13. Brockmyer, J.H., et al.: The development of the game engagement questionnaire: a measure of engagement in video game-playing. J. Exp. Soc. Psychol. **45**(4), 624–634 (2009)
14. Procci, K.C.: The Subjective Gameplay Experience: An Examination of the Revised Game Engagement Model (Ph.D Dissertation). University of Central Florida Orlando, Florida (2015)
15. Hookham, G., Nesbitt, K., Kay-Lambkin, F.: Comparing usability and engagement between a serious game and a traditional online program. In: Proceedings of the Australasian Computer Science Week Multiconference, p. 54. ACM (2016)
16. Nordin, A.I., Denisova, A., Cairns, P.: Too many questionnaires: measuring player experience whilst playing digital games. In: Seventh York Doctoral Symposium on Computer Science & Electronics, vol. 69 (2014)
17. Bowden, J.L.-H.: The process of customer engagement: a conceptual framework. J. Mark. Theory Pract. **17**(1), 63–74 (2009)
18. Hollebeek, L.D.: Demystifying customer brand engagement: exploring the loyalty nexus. J. Mark. Manag. **27**(7–8), 785–807 (2011)

19. Lugmayr, A., et al.: Categorization of ambient media projects on their business models, innovativeness, and characteristics—evaluation of Nokia Ubimedia MindTrek Award Projects of 2010. Multimedia Tools Appl. **66**(1), 33–57 (2013)
20. Malthouse, E.C., Calder, B.J.: Comment: engagement and experiences: comment on Brodie, Hollenbeek, Juric, and Ilic (2011). J. Serv. Res. **14**(3), 277–279 (2011)
21. IJsselsteijn, W., et al.: Measuring the experience of digital game enjoyment. In: Proceedings of Measuring Behavior, Maastricht, Netherlands, p. 88 (2008)
22. Poels, K., de Kort, Y., Ijsselsteijn, W.: FUGA-the fun of gaming: measuring the human experience of media enjoyment. Deliverable D3. 3: Game Experience Questionnaire. FUGA project (2008)
23. Norman, K.L.: Geq (game engagement/experience questionnaire): a review of two papers. Interact. Comput. **25**(4), 278–283 (2013)
24. Hirschman, E.C., Holbrook, M.B.: Hedonic consumption: emerging concepts, methods and propositions. J. Mark. **46**(3), 92–101 (1982)
25. Brodie, R.J., et al.: Customer engagement: conceptual domain, fundamental propositions, and implications for research. J. Serv. Res. **14**(3), 252–271 (2011)
26. Brodie, R.J., et al.: Consumer engagement in a virtual brand community: an exploratory analysis. J. Bus. Res. **66**(1), 105–114 (2013)
27. Hollebeek, L.: Exploring customer brand engagement: definition and themes. J. Strateg. Mark. **19**(7), 555–573 (2011)
28. Addis, M., Holbrook, M.B.: On the conceptual link between mass customisation and experiential consumption: an explosion of subjectivity. J. Consum. Behav. **1**(1), 50–66 (2001)
29. Holbrook, M.B.: Consumer Research: Introspective Essays on the Study of Consumption. Sage Publications, Thousand Oaks (1995)
30. Holbrook, M.B.: The millennial consumer in the texts of our times: Experience and entertainment. J. Macromark. **20**(2), 178–192 (2000)
31. Brakus, J., Schmitt, B., Zhang, S.: Experiental attributes and consumer judgments. In: Schmitt, B.H., Rogers, D. (eds.) Handbook on Brand and Experience Management, pp. 174–187. Edward Elgar, Boston (2008)
32. Arnould, E., Price, L., Zinkhan, G.: Consumers—International Edition. McGraw Hill, Boston (2002)
33. Salem, K., Zimmerman, E.: Rules of Play. Mit Press, Cambridge (2004)
34. Buchanan-Oliver, M., Seo, Y.: Play as co-created narrative in computer game consumption: the hero's journey in Warcraft III. J. Consum. Behav. **11**(6), 423–431 (2012)
35. Holbrook, M.B., et al.: Play as a consumption experience: the roles of emotions, performance, and personality in the enjoyment of games. J. Consum. Res. **11**(2), 728–739 (1984)
36. Abbasi, A.Z., Ting, D.H., Jamek, A.B.S.A.: An integrated conceptual model for predicting behavioral learning triggered by video-game engagement: a mediating role of observational learning. In: Game Physics and Mechanics International Conference (GAMEPEC 2015), pp. 11–15. IEEE (2015)
37. Alba, J.W., Williams, E.F.: Pleasure principles: a review of research on hedonic consumption. J. Consum. Psychol. **23**(1), 2–18 (2013)
38. Wang, C.-L., et al.: The influence of hedonic values on consumer behaviors: an empirical investigation in China. J. Glob. Mark. **14**(1–2), 169–186 (2000)
39. MacInnis, D.J., Price, L.L.: The role of imagery in information processing: Review and extensions. J. Consum. Res. **13**(4), 473–491 (1987)
40. Caru, A., Cova, B.: A critical approach to experiential consumption: fighting against the disappearance of the contemplative time. Crit. Mark. **23**, 1–16 (2003)

Entertainment Technology

Avatar Density Based Client Assignment

Lutz Behnke[1](✉), Sven Allers[1](✉), Qi Wang[2], Christos Grecos,
and Kai von Luck[1]

[1] Department of Computer Science, University of Applied Sciences Hamburg,
Hamburg, Germany
{lutz.behnke,sven.allers}@haw-hamburg.de
[2] School of Computing, University of the West of Scotland, Paysley, Great Britain

Abstract. Scaling the number of supported users for Massive Multi-User Games (MMOGs) allows more users to experience its content together. Supporting this capability needs consider the chain of all components that constitute the system between the client software of any two users.

A large body of research has been created over the last decades on the problem of dividing the resultant workload of a MMOG to specific nodes in a cluster of server. Connecting clients to the most appropriate server of this cluster is as important. Clients will place widely varying, dynamically changing requirements on processing, storage and network bandwidth resource on the MMOG.

We propose a novel mechanism of assigning clients to servers in a MMOG as part of an load balancing effort. It allows the optimization of resource utilization while being able to handle overload situations in the face of high avatar density and adapt to change over time.

Keywords: DVE · MMOG

1 Introduction

Managing the amount of processing, memory and network resources to provide the platform for any MMMOG follows the proven divide-and-conquer approach. Trying to scale up the number of players that can play the game concurrently a long list of bottlenecks have to be considered and overcome. The following work is part of a larger effort to create a complete MMORPG system that (a) will allow the creation of a single virtual environment with support for far more than 100k concurrent users; (b) will provide a non-stop service with no planed down-time, (c) will handle component failure (hard- and software) with minimal service degradation; (d) will allow unparalleled level of flexibility of the contained environment.

Prior publications have targeted the partitioning of the actual server workload, the resultant storage requirements and the aggregate network bandwidth that is required for the communication between the components (see [1]).

© IFIP International Federation for Information Processing 2016
Published by Springer International Publishing AG 2016. All Rights Reserved
G. Wallner et al. (Eds.): ICEC 2016, LNCS 9926, pp. 137–148, 2016.
DOI: 10.1007/978-3-319-46100-7_12

The platform presented, QuP, will support a high number of concurrent players, as it allows large (>20) clusters of servers to maintain a single, continuous game environment.

QuP will also support a high local Avatar Density (the number of avatars in a given space), as it allows the same spatial area to be maintained on more than one server. This may lead to the next bottleneck: sending environment updates to the client computer, as this connection is usually the weakest link. To provide a minimal reduction user experience while greatly reducing the amount of change messages needed, we introduced Dynamic Budget Based State Aggregation [2]. While the concept is a generalized one, will it mostly benefit from situations that are present in may MMOs, where crowds of people or blocks of military units are moving in a similar fashion. Their action can easily be described as a group, with massive reduction of required messages.

QuP and DyBuBSA both benefit from an optimal assignment of clients to servers in order to group information about avatars that are in spatial proximity to a small subset of the whole cluster, idealy to a single server. This is due to the pre-fetching and pre-processing nature of both techniques. Client Assignment (CA) is a NP-complete problem [4], if encompassing a grouping problem it is even NP-hard [7].

Many existing solutions to CA in MMOGs are very application dependent. In many large-scale games, they range from the primitive, as in MMOBA-type (Massive Multiplayer Online Battle Arena) games like World-of-Tanks or Star-Craft, where very small groups of players (usually 4–40) are grouped into a large number of world instances. These instances only exist for a short time (usually less than 60 min) while a single battle lasts. MOBA CA usually follows a few computationally simple rules to group players of similar strength in order to optimize the entertainment value of the game.

In MMO-RPGs, the assignment is often done via a static shard selection (e.g. World of Warcraft). This selection may be changed by the user, if the vendor allows it. The selection usually is subject to capacity planing by the service provider. These shards, or replicated instances of the virtual world can than be distributed statically to pre-planed server instances.

When attempting to construct a MMOG that models a continuous or at least connected space, in which all users interact in a single, integrated, continuous environment, the CA is more difficult to pre-plan and requires constant monitoring and update while the game is running. To increase the number of concurrently supported players within the world, MMORPGs often used zoning to partition the game population together within the game world. Unfortunately this often fails to support scenarios, where the whole population gathers explicitly to partake in a single event (e.g. massive battles in EVE online [3]).

We present a MMOG platform that is able to separate the spatial location of the avatar within the game environment from the Game Server (GS) to which it is assigned (e.g. QuP [1]).

Within it, large synergistic effects may be gained by grouping avatars in spatial proximity on the same server while avoiding overload situations before they develop. To minimize the required network traffic further, we introduce a method to reduce the average number of replicas of games objects on the GSs. We aim to achieve this goal by attempting to group avatars of similar Areas of Interest (AoI) on the smallest subset of servers as possible. To handle overload of a single server, QuP does allow for the same spatial area of the game to be represented by more than one server, albeit with a certain amount of additional network overhead.

Striking a balance between tight grouping and avoiding overload is the task of the Client Assignment Manager (CAM).

2   Related Work

A number of approaches to partitioning the client population prior to assigning them to servers have been discussed by commercial vendors as well as scientific publications. Most commercial vendors opt for primarily static or pre-computed assignment.

A wide range of work has been done on the subject of load distribution and load balancing. Most publications propose the partitioning of the game world and thus the avatar population. These partitions are then assigned to servers within the system. [13] proposes to assign one region to one server, with the region being partitioned further into cells, which can be ceded to other servers in high load situations. The load information of each server are regularly submitted to a central load collector server. As [8] observes, the cells are only moved to neighboring servers and global state is not considered, thus underutilized servers may be ignored since they are not adjacent to the server in overload. To order to address these shortcomings, [8] proposes a hybrid approach in which the load is shed not only to neighbors, but appropriate servers are also chosen from a global set.

The work in [10] approaches load balancing via linear optimization, looking not only at server processing load, but the required communication overhead among the servers as well. The aim is to distribute the load evenly among servers while minimizing communication at the same time. They construct a graph based on the Area of Interest (AoI) of each avatar, connecting the graph when the AoIs overlap. [11] improve this by using an ant colony optimization algorithm, but also showed that there is a minimal size of avatar population and server cluster that limites the cost efficiency of more complex load balancing approaches.

[4] does not attempt to distribute load evenly, but rather to ensure that pre-defined levels of Quality of Service (QoS) are met by each server. These QoS include CPU utilization, network bandwidth consumption. They propose an appropriate partitioning and merging scheme.

Static partitioning is the state of the art of many commercial online games, but does not match the dynamics of an MMO-RPG. [5] investigate a number of algorithms and their fitness for approaching optimal distribution of clients to server. They show linear programming to be able to provide an optimal solution, but also that the required cost of computation is prohibitive for practical use.

[15] show that all the other algorithms are costly as well. In [6] they propose a method that uses a simulated heat flow model, based solely on local information.

All above approaches assume that all client connections and thus avatars produce a similar load and thus partition the avatar population by partitioning the environment space. A different approach is taken by [12]. Here a server is focused on the avatars that are assigned to it. The scheme first sorts the avatars by the number of AoIs they are present in. It then repeatedly moves the most interesting avatar, until a number of iterations is reached.

[9] states that regions do not reduce the inter-server communication to a sufficient degree. Instead they favor a simple load balancing scheme. They propose the use of a NAT-Server between server and client and the use of standard load balancing methods like round-robin. The proxy approach is also proposed by [14] to isolate the region-to-server assignment from the client-to-server assignment.

3 Requirements

As this work is based on QuP platform for large scale MMOGs, the AoI of each avatar is represented by its view box, an Axis Aligned Bounding Box (AABB). The CAM should group the assignments to the game servers according to the spatial grouping of their avatars within the virtual environment. This is expected to allow a reduction of retrieved state and subsequent state update messages to a given server as multiple avatars will access the same pre-fetched object and environment data through a local lookup rather than costly remote query.

The CAM must also ensure that the CPU load on a given server is within acceptable parameters. As the load created by a single client connection can vary widely, this will require feedback from the GS. Available main memory and network bandwidth must be considered as well.

Based on the requirements, we derive the following cost function to govern the client assignment. The client will be assigned to the server that will return the minimal value from the cost function below:

$$cost(a, s) = w_0 * -g(a, s) + w_1 * Load(s) - w_2 * MemFree(s) \qquad (1)$$

For an avatar a and the serve s the function $g(a, s)$ will calculate the Grouping Factor (GF). The GF represents similarity of the AoI of the new avatar to the AoI of the avatars that are already present on a given server. It is assumed that most of the objects in the AoI of the other avatars have already been loaded and that further updates on those objects will be relevant to both the existing and the new avatars. The actual computation of the GF will be discussed in Sect. 4.

Memory requirement is not given as the percentage used, but the amount of remaining memory instead, so that servers having large amounts of memory remaining are favored, regardless of their total amount of memory. w_0, w_1, w_2 are weights to control the priority of the potentially contradictory requirements of maximizing the grouping factor and not surpassing limits on CPU load and memory utilization. Network utilization is not considered as separate parameter here, as it directly relates of the grouping factor. More fine grained modeling on this may be an area for further study.

As the avatars move over time, the client assignment must be able to track validity of the calculation results over time. This may lead to the need for a reassignment of clients to new GS over time. Also any CAM solution should be able to scale with the MMOG to support a user population far in excess of 100k concurrent users, including the resultant churn, expected clustering of user log-in and number resultant number of GS.

4 Proposed Solution

We propose calculating the grouping factor, using a heat map. To construct the heat map, the virtual environment is partitioned into a set of blocks of equal size. This is similar to partitioning of the actual game environment into micro cells [5], but we use these blocks only for the grouping calculation. Due to the architecture of QuP, this is done in three dimensions. The diagrams below are restricted to two dimensions for the benefit of illustration only.

As the AoI of an avatar governs which objects in the game have to be pre-fetched to a server, we use the view boxes and their overlap to determine the grouping factor when considering a server for assignment.

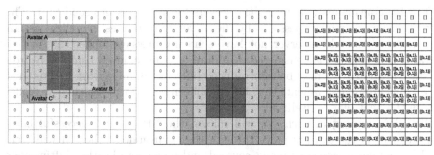

(a) Viewbox overlap and resultant heatmap for server A

(b) Heatmap for server B

(c) Combined heatmap for servers A and B

Fig. 1. View box overlap

Each block holds a set of servers that serve at least one avatar whose view box overlaps with the block. A tally of the number of intersecting view boxes is kept, as shown in Fig. 1c

In QuP and the LB all object coordinates are within a norm cube ($0 <= x, y, z < 1$). This cube is partitioned into n blocks per axis. For each block (identified by it coordinate between 0 and n-1) and each server, $T(x, y, z, s)$, a tally of avatar view boxes that overlap this block is maintained. This allows the calculation of the grouping factor for each server in a block.

As each client is requesting a server assignment, the view box of the avatar is queried from the world state (maintained by the QuP servers). As the server is chosen, its tally is updated in each of the blocks that the clients view box intersects with. As a server is considered to cover the view box of an avatar even if the view box only intersects the spatial area covered by the server, this method forms an overestimating heuristic. It allows the computation of the GF used in Eq. 1.

4.1 CAM Components

The CAM is partitioned into two different components: the Load Balancer (LB) and the Server Monitor (SM). In our experiment we only used a single LB instance (for further scalability see Sect. 7). One SM is assigned to each GS. See Fig. 2 for communication links and integration into the full system. The actual CAM components are shown in darker color.

As the central component, the LB holds the actual heat map and meta information on the known servers and the previously assigned clients. The Authentication Server queries the LB to receive a server assignment. The LB in turn maintain a lease on the client-server assignment to update the tallies for the heat map. This lease will be confirmed if an acknowledgement messages is received by the LB. This message will sent by the server once the client has connected to it.

The LB continuously monitors the servers for any messages send to it. This may either be heart beat messages by the server or responses to a client assignment requests. Should a server not have sent any message longer than a configurable threshold, it is considered dead and will be removed completely from the state of the LB. It may be reintroduced only by administrator command. If there are pending assignments that have not been confirmed yet, they are rolled back in the heat map as well.

The SM running in each GS will inform the LB of any successful client connections. As the avatars move through the environment, the SM will track which heat map regions are being covered and uncovered by the shifting view boxes of each avatar. The list of changes is reduced by applying inverse operations (e.g. the number of new avatars in a region is subtracted from the number of avatars that have left the region). The resulting difference list is sent to the LB in regular intervals.

4.2 Base Grouping Factor

The assignment algorithm has to weigh between placing an avatar on a server that already covers a spatial region or placing it on a new server to avoid overloading the former server. There are two special cases to consider when selecting servers for the client: (a) empty servers (i.e. without any clients) and (b) server whose covered area does not intersect with the avatar view box. Empty servers will not only occur after starting the system, but can also result from avatars congregating on small spatial areas of the game, leaving others completely empty and thus the corresponding servers idle, as reassignment incrementally groups the avatars on fewer and fewer servers to optimize the grouping factor.

Both cases are similar, in that they result in a grouping factor of 0, as no view boxes overlap. The client assignment would only be controlled by the CPU and memory resource utilization values.

We propose to use a grouping factor for empty servers, that represents the state in an idealized game, containing only equidistant avatars that are evenly distributed among the servers. For this we calculate a Distance value (for a world in 3 dimensions) from an ideal field count to an average field count of the actual servers in the running game:

$$IdealFieldCount = g_0 \frac{P^3}{ServerCount} + g_1 \frac{UsedFields}{ServerCount}$$

The heat map is split into precision P, given as the number of regions per dimension g_0, g_1 are weights so that $(0 < g \leq 1, g_0 + g_1 = 1)$. The weights represent the balance between two objectives: the even partitioning of the whole virtual environment among the servers and the even distribution of the regions already used among the servers. The optimal values are application specific.

From the ideal field count, a distance value can be computed.

$$Distance = \frac{\sqrt[3]{IdealFieldCount} - \sqrt[3]{AvgFieldCount}}{2} * \frac{1}{P}$$

As a large distance would be bad for grouping avatars, the grouping factor for empty servers is $g(a, s) = -Distance$

All server that are neither empty nor have a server view box that overlaps with the avatar view box are considered in turn for assignment by setting the cost to the Manhattan Distance from the fields that contain the avatars view box. The position of a given non empty server is calculated for each field it is assigned in.

4.3   Reassignment

After each avatar is assigned to a server, it is likely to move through the virtual environment. Thus the grouping factor of the servers will deteriorate over time. To counter this, our approach supports a protocol for client reassignment. Executing this protocol produces a small overhead. Reassignment may result on a negativ impact on the user experience, even if only for a limited time. Thus a certain amount of hysteresis is required to regulate the frequency of reassignments of a given client connection.

In order to track the quality of each assignment, as well as to monitor a user session, the LB maintains a (lightweight Erlang) monitor process for each connected client. In regular intervals, each process is activated in order to recalculate the server assigned to the client. Should the calculation result in a different server, the client is reassigned.

As the new avatar will shift the aggregate view box of the newly assigned server, the probability of assigning the same server on the recalculation increases. If needed, an additional weight against reassignment could easily be applied to the calculation.

The server will notify the LB when the client has disconnected. This will remove the monitoring process for the client session.

If the distance is greater than a pre-set threshold, a client reassignment process will be triggered. If the assignment results in a different server, the re-connection protocol is executed (see Fig. 3b).

The LB will also re-check the assignment of each avatar after a pre-set interval. This will slowly, but continuously, improve the assignment in the face of avatar movement. While this will regularly query the position of the avatar from the QuP subsystem, it will not suffer the very large bandwidth requirement of tracking each position change of each avatar.

A further method of initiating an assignment reevaluation will be triggered by the server directly. If it detects insufficient CPU, memory or bandwidth resources, it will send an emergency signal to the LB to trigger immediate assignment re-evaluation.

The reassignment protocol will notifiy the new server to start pre-fetching all object data required by the avatar. Then the client is informed by the old server of the need to switch. The message will include the contact details of the new server as well as a token string that allows the client to authenticate to the new server.

5 Experiments

We have implemented a prototype of each of the component's shown in Fig. 2. For the tests, the AS and the game clients were replaced by a test server in order to isolate the LB for measurements. Also, the LB was configured to contact a special QuP mock server in order to separate the time required for computing the server assignment from the time for the QuP look up. The mock was pre loaded with the position of the avatars, provided no redundancy and was co-located with the LB on the same maschine.

The test were done on three PC type virtual machines. The VM manager was configured to allow full CPU utilization during the test. The systems where running Erlang version OTP 18 on Ubuntu Linux.

Tests reflect the three types of avatar distribution introduced by [10]. We consider them sufficient representations of avatar behaviour in an MMOG. The distributions were adapted to three dimensions as supported by QuP. All avatars are place in a norm cube. Skewed distribution was set to 60 % of avatars in a cube occupying the lower 0.3 of each dimension; clustered set to 75 % of the avtars being in 10 evenly distributed groups; the remaining avatars were uniformly distributed in the whole environment.

Two test series with 10,000 and 100,000 avatars were set up. The heatmap was partitioned with a precision of $P = 10$ blocks per dimension. The smaller scale

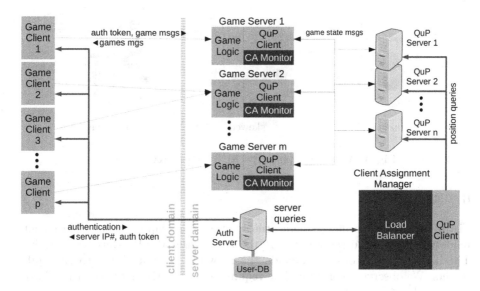

Fig. 2. proposed timadorus architecture

test was conducted with only three servers in order to allow manual verification of the assignment. The larger one to test the time requirements based on the number of clients previously assigned. The larger scale test used seven servers to inspect the increase of computation time for an increased number of avatars.

Increasing P results will an cubic increase the memory requirements of the LB. We assume that $P = 10$ will partition the space sufficiently to effectively distribute clients to a number of game servers in the order of 10 to 100. Any installation that outgrows this, would should have enough resources to support much higher values of P.

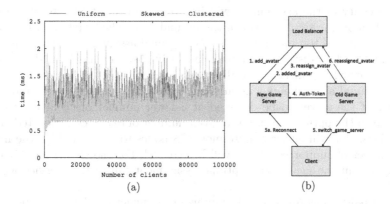

Fig. 3. (a) Reply times for all distributions, $P = 10$, (b) Reassignment process

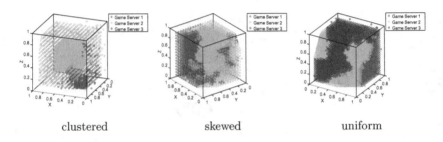

clustered   skewed   uniform

Fig. 4. Avatar grouping (P = 10, 3 servers, 1000 avatars)

6   Results

Figure 3a, shows the 99.9th percentile for the time elapsed from a placement request being sent to reply given by the LB. It uses P = 10, thus 1000 blocks. The measurement does not include the network communication to the QuP servers. We observe a constant time requirement once the data structures have been filled.

Figure 4 shows the distribution of the avatars to three servers in the smaller scale test environment for each of the three distributions.

7   Conclusion and Future Considerations

We have shown that, in combination with QuP [1] and DyBuBSA [2], our approach to client assignment provides the needed capabilities to drastically scale up the number of supported concurrent users in an MMOG with a single continous game environment, or distributed virtual environment in general.

For a given set of servers, the load balancer will return an assignment in constant time, regardless of the number of avatars currently active. The only prerequisite is a sufficient amount of memory to maintain the heatmap, but this is constant and can be controlled by the number of blocks per dimension.

The quality of the assignment will improve the utilization rate of the prefetched data on the target server in the normal case. The worst case, if data in the LB has drifted too much, an less than optimal assignment is given, further increasing the drift distance. If a sufficient drift distance has been detected, a reassignment will be initiated for all avatars concerned.

Sub-optimal assignments will only cause the CPU, memory and bandwidth resources of the server to be depleted at a lower number of client connection compared to the optimal case. For a given number of expected supported client connections, this will either require more GS nodes to be started, or the maximum number of supported clients will be redcued. For the clients already connected, even in the face of sub-optimal assignment full quality service will be proved.

The reassignment process will minimize the impact on the user experience, but may create small interruptions as the network connection is switched from one server to another.

When scaling up the system, the number assignment requests and reassignment protocol messages will increase with the number of connected game servers and the number of clients connecting to the system concurrently. This will result in an increased network bandwidth requirement placed on the LB. Access to the data structure that holds the heatmap and its ancillary data may pose a bottleneck, since it is held on a single compute node and not replicated. It receives updates sent by the monitor processes of each server, as well as all the client assignment requests. More importantly, creates a single point of failure for the whole system with regards to connecting new users and the continuous improvement of the resource utilization for the already connected clients.

We intend to undertake further work on eliminating this source of system failure and to support even larger user bases. One possible method is to use a Distributed Hash Table (DHT) to maintain the heat map in a small set of servers, as the changes to the map are generally small and localized. The authentication server would contact the LBs in a round robin fashion. Thus the ASs can itself be duplicated and contacted by the clients in a round robin fashion themselves. The re-calculation processes and possible re-assignment processes can be separated onto further server nodes as well.

References

1. Behnke, L., Grecos, C., Luck, K.V.: QuP: graceful degradation in state propagation for DVEs. In: Proceedings of International Workshop on Massively Multiuser Virtual Environments. ACM Press, Singapore (2014). http://dl.acm.org/citation.cfm?id=2577389
2. Behnke, L., Wang, Q., Grecos, C., von Luck, K.: Budget based dynamic state update aggregation. In: Proceedings of the 7th ACM International Workshop on Massively Multiuser Virtual Environments - MMVE 2015, pp. 25–26, Portland, Oregon (2015). http://dl.acm.org/citation.cfm?doid=2723695.2723696
3. CCP Manifest: A Weekend of Epic Destruction in EVE Online (2013). http://community.eveonline.com/news/dev-blogs/a-weekend-of-epic-destruction-in-eve-online, http://www.webcitation.org/6dK9gvgpD
4. Chen, J., Wu, B., Delap, M., Knutsson, B., Lu, H., Amza, C.: Locality aware dynamic load management for massively multiplayer games. In: Proceedings of the Tenth ACM SIGPLAN Symposium on Principles and Practice of Parallel Programming - PPoPP 2005, p. 289, New York, USA (2005). http://dx.doi.org/10.1145/1065944.1065982, http://portal.acm.org/citation.cfm?doid=1065944.1065982
5. De Vleeschauwer, B., Van Den Bossche, B., Verdickt, T., De Turck, F., Dhoedt, B., Demeester, P.: Dynamic microcell assignment for massively multiplayer online gaming. In: Proceedings of 4th ACM SIGCOMM Workshop on Network and System Support for Games - NetGames 2005, p. 1, New York, USA (2005). http://portal.acm.org/citation.cfm?doid=1103599.1103611
6. Deng, Y., Lau, R.W.H.: Dynamic load balancing in distributed virtual environments using heat diffusion. ACM Trans. Multimedia Comput. Commun. Appl. 10(2), 1–19 (2014). http://dl.acm.org/citation.cfm?doid=2579228.2499906
7. Falkenauer, E.: A new representation and operators for genetic algorithms applied to grouping problems. Evol. Comput. 2(2), 123–144 (1994). http://www.mitpressjournals.org/doi/abs/10.1162/evco.1994.2.2.123

8. Lau, R.W.: Hybrid load balancing for online games. In: Proceedings of the International Conference on Multimedia - MM 2010, p. 1231, New York, USA (2010). http://dl.acm.org/citation.cfm?doid=1873951.1874194

9. Lu, F., Parkin, S., Morgan, G.: Load balancing for massively multiplayer online games. In: Proceedings of 5th ACM SIGCOMM Workshop on Network and System Support for Games - NetGames 2006, p. 1, New York, USA (2006). http://doi.acm.org/10.1145/1230040.1230064, http://portal.acm.org/citation.cfm?doid=1230040.1230064

10. Lui, J., Chan, M.: An efficient partitioning algorithm for distributed virtual environment systems. IEEE Trans. Parallel Distrib. Syst. **13**(3), 193–211 (2002)

11. Morillo, P., Fernandez, M., Orduna, J.: An ACS-based partitioning method for distributed virtual environment systems. In: Proceedings International Parallel and Distributed Processing Symposium, p. 8, No. C, IEEE Comput. Soc. (2003). http://ieeexplore.ieee.org/lpdocs/epic03/wrapper.htm?arnumber=1213283

12. Morillo, P., Orduña, J.M., Fernández, M., Duato, J.: An adaptive load balancing technique for distributed virtual environment systems. In: Proceedings of the IASTED International Conference on Parallel and Distributed Computing and Systems (PCDS 2003), vol. 15, pp. 256–261 (2003). http://www.scopus.com/inward/record.url?eid=2-s2.0-1542537865&partnerID=tZOtx3y1

13. Ng, B., Si, A., Lau, R.W., Li, F.W.: A multi-server architecture for distributed virtual walkthrough. In: Proceedings of the ACM Symposium on Virtual Reality Software and Technology - VRST 2002, p. 163. New York, USA (2002). http://portal.acm.org/citation.cfm?doid=585740.585768

14. Quax, P., Cornelissen, B., Dierckx, J., Vansichem, G., Lamotte, W.: ALVIC-NG: state management and immersive communication for massively multiplayer online games and communities. Multimedia Tools Appl. **45**(1–3), 109–131 (2009). http://www.springerlink.com/index/10.1007/s11042-009-0299-3

15. Deng, Y., Lau, R.W.H.: On delay adjustment for dynamic load balancing in distributed virtual environments. IEEE Trans. Vis. Comput. Graph. **18**(4), 529–537 (2012). http://ieeexplore.ieee.org/lpdocs/epic03/wrapper.htm?arnumber=6165133

A Hybrid Game Contents Streaming Method: Improving Graphic Quality Delivered on Cloud Gaming

Kar-Long Chan[1]([✉]), Kohei Ichikawa[1], Yasuhiro Watashiba[1],
Uthayopas Putchong[1,2], and Hajimu Iida[1]

[1] Nara Institute of Science and Technology, Ikoma, Japan
{kar_long.chan.jr2,ichikawa,watashiba}@is.naist.jp, pu@ku.ac.th,
iida@itc.naist.jp
[2] Kasetsart University, Bangkok, Thailand
http://sdlab.naist.jp/

Abstract. The emerging Cloud Gaming Service provides highly accessible video gaming experience. However, in term of the gaming quality, Cloud Gaming is not competitive to rival with traditional gaming because of network constraints. Especially, 3D game contents streamed as encoded video sequence is suitable in a network environment, but the resulted lower graphic quality may not meet client's demand. Therefore, we propose a Hybrid-Streaming System that aims at improving graphic quality delivered on Cloud Gaming. By utilizing available rendering power from both Cloud Server and client's PC, the system distributes rendering operations to both sides to achieve the desired improvement. Quantitative results show the improvement of graphic quality from the proposed method, as well as reducing server's workload and attaining acceptable network bandwidth consumption.

Keywords: Cloud Gaming · Hybrid-Streaming · Graphic quality

1 Introduction

The emerging Cloud Gaming Service envisions an intriguing future of providing million clients with novel and highly accessible gaming experiences. By leveraging reliable, elastic and high-performance computing resources, Cloud Gaming shifts the intensive workloads of game processing from client's device to powerful Cloud Server. In its simplest form, which is shown in Fig. 1, the actual interactive gaming application is stored at the Cloud Server and gets executed once requested. The rendered game scenes are then streamed back to the client's device as encoded video sequence over a network. At the client's side, the control events input from devices such as mouse, keyboard, joystick are recorded and sent back to the Cloud Server for the manipulation of game logics.

© IFIP International Federation for Information Processing 2016
Published by Springer International Publishing AG 2016. All Rights Reserved
G. Wallner et al. (Eds.): ICEC 2016, LNCS 9926, pp. 149–160, 2016.
DOI: 10.1007/978-3-319-46100-7_13

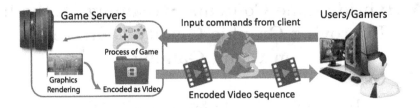

Fig. 1. Brief Structure of Cloud Gaming

The on demand feature of Cloud Gaming benefits both clients and game developers by easing the possible incompatibility issues between gaming software and hardware environment. Therefore, it has been not only an active topic both in industries [6] and research fields [7] in recent, but also a new area which possesses tremendous market value [5].

However, a challenging objective of developing a sustainable Cloud Gaming service is to maintain and improve client's Quality of Experience (QoE), as network constraints play critical roles in affecting the system performance [3,4]. In general, interaction delay and graphic quality are two significant criteria that determine client's QoE. In Cloud Gaming, rigid real-time responsiveness is demanded in order to achieve good enough QoE [2,7], so currently most related researches focus on alleviating interaction delay [1,9]. On the other hand, findings from a conducted subject test show that clients are sensitive to changes in graphic quality and smoothness during gameplay, which implies that graphic quality notably affects QoE of Cloud Gaming as well [8]. Furthermore, alongside the advancement of in-game visual effects and high resolution display, client's demands for gaming with more realistic graphics on their devices are uprising. However, in term of graphic quality, there is an obvious gap between traditional local rendering and Cloud Gaming's streaming encoded video, which the graphic quality is degraded from the original.

With this consideration, this study aims to enhance graphic quality delivered on existing Cloud Gaming system. Especially we address the use case of PC, which is not necessary to be a significant powerhouse, but rendering-capable to a certain extent. Based on the two existing streaming methods which will be introduced in later section, our approach is to allocate available rendering power at client's side to achieve the improvement of graphic quality. Furthermore, the distribution of rendering tasks also mitigates server's workload as well.

2   Existing Techniques

In general, two major streaming methods are used in Cloud Gaming: the Image-based Streaming and the Instruction-based Streaming. These two methods differ from each other in how the game contents are delivered from server to client.

2.1   Image-Based Streaming

In the Cloud Gaming environment adopting the Image-based Streaming, the game logics, which drive the progression of gameplay, are manipulated according to the client's inputs received by the server CPU. Afterwards, graphics are rendered through a dedicated Graphic Processing Unit. The rendered game contents are then encoded into video and streamed back to the client's device. Up on receiving the encoded video, the client's device decodes the contents and finally shows the corresponding frame on the display.

One advantage of Image-based Streaming is that the encoded video, in term of bandwidth consumption, is suitable to be streamed in a general network environment. Normally game contents are streamed as 720p video, while the quality can be raised to 1080p in a faster network environment. Another advantage is that since decoding can be processed by using low-cost decoder chips which are massively embedded in client's device, this approach is ideal for running on resource-constrained devices. Therefore, given the wide availability of this method, most commercial Cloud Gaming service providers apply Image-based Streaming to deliver game contents.

On the other hand, GamingAnyWhere is the first and the only available open source Cloud Gaming platform [7], which is based on the structure of Image-based Streaming. It is designed to be highly extensible and customizable that allows user to extend the capabilities of the platform with ease. In this research, Cloud Gaming, in general, refers to the system utilizing Image-based Streaming.

2.2   Instruction-Based Streaming

As for the Instruction-based Streaming, after game logics are processed at the server, every API call to perform the corresponding rendering task is intercepted. The intercepted API functions, or referred as graphics command, are compressed and sent to the client's device. Together with the graphics command, related 3D data such as geometry mesh and texture are streamed to the client's device as well. Soon after the arrival of the data, game rendering according to the received graphic commands is processed on-site at the client's device.

The biggest advantage of Instruction-based Streaming over Image-based Streaming is the preserved original graphic quality, as the actual rendering is operated at client's device. Furthermore, without the heavy burden of 3D graphics processing, Cloud Server is more effective at simultaneously handling more clients' requests. However, it requires client's device to be not only compatible with the delivered 3D graphics command, but also powerful enough to process high quality rendering, thus indicating less availability than the Image-based Streaming.

3   Hybrid-Streaming System

The goal of this research is to enhance graphic quality based on the structure of Image-based Streaming. As such, our proposed solution is to integrate the mechanism of Instruction-based Streaming to achieve the desired improvement.

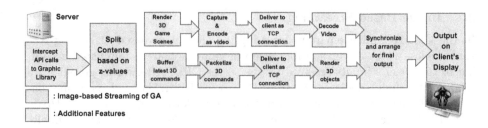

Fig. 2. Data Flow of Proposed Hybrid-Streaming (Color figure online)

This Hybrid-Streaming System, which stands for adopting both the streaming methods, distributes partial game contents to be streamed as graphic commands and rendered locally at client's PC. Simultaneously, it maintains partial rendering tasks at Cloud Server and the corresponding contents are streamed as a video sequence. The improvement of graphic quality is mainly contributed by the portion of game contents rendered at client's PC. Furthermore, by offloading some rendering tasks to client's device, server's workload is mitigated as well.

3.1   System Structure Overview

Figure 2 presents the overall structure of the Hybrid-Streaming System. The blue boxes indicate the original data flow of Image-based Streaming which our Hybrid-Streaming System is based on, while the orange boxes refer to the additional features for achieving the whole system.

Within the system, how the final representation of game contents is correspondingly composed from the products of two different streams is an important objective. It largely depends on the way of splitting game contents at the server. By comparing the depth value, all the objects are separated into two groups, the upper layer which contains shallower objects (closer to the client's view), and the lower layer which contains deeper objects (further away from the client's view). Considering that the contents delivered through Image-based Streaming result in video frame without any depth factor, the game contents represented in this form should be treated as the background. For this purpose, objects belonging to the lower layer are streamed as a video sequence, which undergoes the original process of Image-based Streaming. On the other hands, objects belonging to the upper layer are streamed as graphics command. Therefore, as soon as the rendering operation is completed at the client's PC, the products can be overlaid on top of the background filled by the contents from Image-based Streaming. The graphical representation of the final product is indicated by Fig. 3.

In the following subsections, the data flow of Image-based Streaming is explained by exploring GamingAnyWhere (GA), which is the open source Cloud Gaming platform that our work is based on. Furthermore, the additional features for achieving the Hybrid-Streaming System will be introduced as well.

3.2   Structure of GamingAnyWhere's Image-Based Streaming

In GA, the data flow refers to streaming audio and video frames from the server to the client. Here we focus on the graphics data manipulation throughout the data flow, which is indicated as the blue boxes in Fig. 2. After the game source is processed and rendered at the server, a designated video capturer implemented in GA is triggered to capture the contents in a polling manner. The captured data is then buffered and encoded by a customizable encoder module. Afterwards, the encoded video frame is delivered to the client through the network. At GA's client module, only the packets representing the most currently encoded video frame is buffered at the decoder. Once the video is decoded, the buffer is cleared for the next frame. On the other hand, audio streams and control inputs from client's device are the other two main streams that affect the overall gaming experience, but they are not the focus of this research. Compared with graphics data, these two streams consume significantly less network bandwidth in the GA structure.

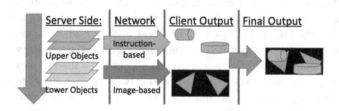

Fig. 3. Graphical representation of constructing the final output from two streaming

3.3   Additional Features

For achieving the Hybrid-Streaming System as shown in Fig. 2, features including splitting the game contents, Instruction-based Streaming, synchronizing the data from two streams and arranging the final output are mandatory.

Splitting the Contents. In order to distinguish if an object belongs to the upper layer or the lower layer during the game processing, it is necessary to dynamically intercept API calls to graphic library and looks for the most updated z-value of each object's center point. A threshold of z-value is defined for classifying which layer the object belongs to, and it can be defined by the developer to handle different in-game scenarios.

Contents' Processing Prior to Streaming. After the lower layer object is rendered at the server, it undergoes the normal process of Image-based Streaming of GamingAnyWhere, as mentioned in last subsection.

As for the Instruction-based Streaming, the intercepted OpenGL instructions that correspond to render the upper-layer objects are overridden for not sending to the server's GPU, but instead packetized for streaming to the client's PC. Considering that usually the same sequence of graphic commands are routinely called for performing a particular task, we encode the sequence as a fixed code which indicates the corresponding task. As such, rather than delivering every native OpenGL instructions individually to client, streaming a light-weight code with other necessary parameters can maintain smaller overhead.

Furthermore, regarding the other graphic data such as objects vertices and textures that potentially incur heavy network load, a copy of such data is streamed in advance and saved at the client's PC prior to actual gaming. Therefore, during the actual gameplay, only the graphics command set, which include the code and parameters, is streamed to the client's device and hence, reducing the overhead as well. The streaming through the network is based on a normal TCP connection, which is separated from the one of Image-based Streaming.

Data Synchronization. Synchronizing the data of two streaming is another critical design objective. In our Hybrid-Streaming System, the latest graphics command which is for rendering the upper layer objects is buffered and updated in every game processing cycle. Whenever GA's source capturing is triggered, the most currently buffered graphics command together with the related parameters is packetized and streamed to the client. After the graphics command is sent to the client, the buffer is cleared and continues for the next iteration of API interception. Since the contents of the two streams undergo separated TCP connection, a precise global time stamp is appended to the respective headers during the packetization. The global timestamp is for the client module to recognize the same-frame contents from the two streams.

Final Arrangement at Client's Device. After the video is decoded from Image-based Streaming, an additional step is to assign a suitable depth value to the video frame for maintaining the corresponding contents to be always at the back of the locally rendered objects.

For the on-site rendering, a parallel running thread is responsible for receiving inputs from Instruction-based Streaming and decoding the contents afterwards. Based on the decoded code which represents a particular rendering task, the corresponding sequence of graphic commands is called and assigned with the received parameters. As such, local rendering at the client's PC can be performed.

Finally, the embedded global timestamp is checked for the confirmation of the same-frame contents before updating the next game frames. Once the confirmation is made, the game frame, which is composed of the locally rendered objects' overlaying on top of the video frame, is updated on the client's display.

4   Implementation

Based on the Image-based Streaming structure of GA, we implemented a prototype to simulate the output of our system, which allows us to achieve the current main goal of evaluating the graphics quality. At this stage, graphic commands together with related parameters are streamed directly from the source of demo application. At the client side, the corresponding 3D objects are then rendered based on the received instructions together with necessary texture data which is saved at client's device in advance.

4.1 Instruction-Based Streaming

The current Instruction-based Streaming sends 3D graphics command directly from our created demo application which is OpenGL-based. At the client module, a separated thread for requesting graphic commands was developed. This thread, which operates in parallel with the original GA's thread for decoding video sequence, periodically sends requests to server for the latest graphic commands. Furthermore, a lock is used to synchronize the contents from the two streams.

As for the construction of 3D graphics command, a sequence of OpenGL instructions which are responsible for a particular function is represented as an ID. Functions here refer to changing the object's location, rotation, scale, environment lighting effects or camera positions. For the corresponding rendering operation to be performed properly at the client side, the data that should be packetized includes Object ID which indicates the object to be rendered, the Function ID which refers to the function to be performed, and the set of related parameters. In addition, multiple functions can be aggregated into a single packet by simply putting the function set, which includes the parameters, one after another. The current packet layout is designed only for the minimum required data in this preliminary implementation, as it can be adjusted for adopting more patterns in favor of more complex gaming application.

4.2 Arrangement at the Client Module

After decoding the received video frame, the contents of lower layer are mapped as a texture on an OpenGL-based rectangular-shaped polygon, which represents the background objects of our final output. By setting a suitable depth value for this polygon object, the background contents are always further away than any locally rendered 3D objects.

As for the contents of upper layer, the client module decodes the corresponding packetized graphic command sets. Afterwards, OpenGL functions are called accordingly to render the objects into a buffer, which also contains the polygon object representing the background contents.

Finally, once the buffered products are requested for updating the next frame on the display, the locally rendered 3D objects accordingly overlay on top of the background contents.

5 Measurement

As for our current primary goal, we compared the graphic quality of the prototype Hybrid-Streaming System to original Image-based Streaming system of

Fig. 4. Demo Application

GamingAnyWhere. Besides, we also preliminarily evaluated graphic card usage and network load on both systems. Considering that using existing game software as test case is sophisticated for the prototype stage of the system, we instead created a simple interactive demo application for evaluation.

5.1   Demo Application for Current Evaluation

Figure 4 shows the OpenGL-based demo application, in which three jet-fighters are presented. The main background, which includes the scene of mountain landscape, is the base element that is always classified as a lower layer object, which represents the background contents at the client side. Therefore, it is always delivered to the client by Image-based Streaming.

In addition, the location of all the jet-fighter objects can be explicitly defined in the demo, so we can also conveniently classify if the object belongs to the lower layer or the upper layer. For example, in Fig. 4, the two closer jet-fighters can be classified as upper layer objects, while the further one together with the landscape background is streamed as encoded video. Moreover, it is convenient to add more 3D objects in the scene, which enables us to perform testing under more complicated scenarios.

5.2   System Environment

As for the environment setup, the server machine is equipped with an Intel Core i7 4770 K 3.5 GHz CPU, a Nvidia GeForce GTX780 graphic card and 16GB system memory, running on a 64-bit CentOS Linux system. On the other hand, client machines include a Laptop A (2.6 GHz Intel Core i7 CPU, Nvidia GeForce GT750M with 16 GB system memory) and four Laptop B (2.1 GHz Intel Core i7, Intel HD Graphics 4000 with 8 GB system memory). Each machine is installed with a pre-compiled GA modules. The Image-based Streaming of GA is set to stream the demo application at the resolution of 1280×720. The testing was conducted within a campus network environment.

5.3   Procedure of Measuring Graphic Quality

Referring to previous researches related to Cloud Gaming, Peak Signal-to-Noise Ratio (PSNR) and Structural Similarity (SSIM) are measured to evaluate the graphic quality. PSNR refers to the ratio between the signal and the noise introduced by compression, with a typical range between 30 and 50 dB. On the other hand, SSIM is an index for determining the similarity between two images, which the value is ranged from -1 to 1. Both metrics are same in the way that the higher the value is, the better the graphics quality it indicates.

In order to take the measurement of PSNR and SSIM, a short video is captured for the output at the client's PC respectively when the contents are delivered as either Image-based Streaming or Hybrid-Streaming. As for the reference source, we capture a short video of the demo natively running on our Linux server as well. After acquiring a video source for each mode, we extracted every frame from each video source. Referencing to the frame of the original quality, a chosen frame each from Image-based Streaming and Hybrid-Streaming System is used for calculating PSNR and SSIM respectively. We took the measurement of PSNR and SSIM under three scenarios.

5.4 Measuring GPU Usage and Network Traffic Load

The Hybrid Streaming System is also expected to reduce server workload as well, since partial rendering tasks are offloaded to the client's PC. Therefore, we measure the respective GPU usages of the server and all the clients' devices by utilizing specified tools including nvidia-smi[1] and Intel-gpu-tools[2]

In addition, developing a Cloud Gaming system that is viable in common broadband network environment is another critical design objective. Since the implemented Instruction-based Streaming in our proposal can introduce additional overhead, it is necessary to measure the traffic load for evaluating the availability of the system in a broadband network. For this reason, IpTraf[3], which is a network monitoring software, is used to investigate the network bandwidth consumption during the streaming of game contents.

Both measurements were taken under the scenario of presenting 30 jet-fighters in the scene. At the Cloud Server, five instances of the demo application were executed and streamed to five clients' devices respectively. Furthermore, each client's device were distributed equal number of jet-fighters to be rendered locally, where the measured cases include 0 jet-fighter (Image-based Streaming), 6 jet-fighters, 12 jet-fighters, 18 jet-fighters, 24 jet-fighters and 30 jet-fighters.

6   Results

6.1   Results of PSNR and SSIM

Figure 5(a) shows the PSNR and SSIM of the test case with one jet-fighter displaying in the demo application. The proposed Hybrid-Streaming System, referred as HS in the table, in which the jet-fighter object is locally rendered at the client's PC, achieves 46.20 dB compared to 43.96 dB from GA's Image-based Streaming. As for the SSIM, the Hybrid-Streaming System also achieves better results than Image-based Streaming, but the difference is not very significant. It can be due to the reason that SSIM is sensitive in different aspect from PSNR.

---

[1] nvidia-smi: https://developer.nvidia.com/nvidia-system-management-interface/.

[2] Intel-gpu-tools: https://01.org/linuxgraphics.

[3] IpTraf: http://iptraf.seul.org/.

(a) With 1 jet-fighter   (b) With 2 jet-fighters   (c) With 3 jet-fighters

Fig. 5. Evaluation Results of Graphic Quality.

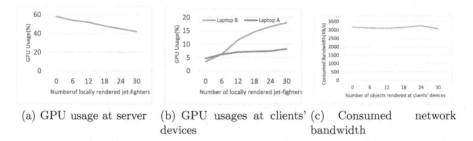

(a) GPU usage at server   (b) GPU usages at clients'   (c)   Consumed   network
                            devices   bandwidth

Fig. 6. Evaluation Results of GPU usage and Consumed Bandwidth.

As for the other two testing scenarios, the proposed Hybrid-Streaming System achieves overall better results than Image-based Streaming in terms of both PSNR and SSIM. Furthermore, while comparing only the scenarios of Hybrid-Streaming System, better graphic quality is indicated while streaming more jet-fighter objects as 3D graphics command. This is reasonable because local rendering at the client's PC preserves the original quality of the 3D object.

6.2 GPU Workload at Server and Client

As shown in Fig. 6(a), the measured GPU usages at the server and clients' PCs demonstrate expected behaviors. When more objects are distributed to clients' PC, GPU usage at the server, which is mainly leveraged by object's renderings and video encoding, decreases gradually. Simultaneously, as more objects are assigned to be rendered locally, GPU usage of each client's device, which mainly includes video decoding and objects' renderings, increases. Furthermore, Fig. 6(b) shows the respective GPU usages of Laptop A and Laptop B (Average value of 4 laptops). Since Laptop A is equipped with a more powerful GPU, the utilization is lower than the less capable built-in GPU of Laptop B.

6.3 Network Bandwidth Consumption

As for the results of measured network bandwidth, data presented in Fig. 6(c) do not indicate an increasing trend. As such, the overhead incurred by the additional

Instruction-based Streaming mechanism is relatively trivial. It is considered that the bandwidth is mostly consumed by delivering the contents as encoded video. We expect that more sophisticated graphics command in formal gaming application will likely lead to larger overhead. Even so, as Hybrid-Streaming System saves related graphical data such as textures and geometry meshes at clients' devices prior to actual gaming, low-bit overhead should be maintained by streaming only the light-weight graphics command set.

7   Discussion

7.1   Determination of the Z-Value Threshold

The depth threshold for determining if an object belongs to the upper layer or the lower layer is currently specified by game developers. However, in the case when an object may cross the depth boundary, the same object is required to be rendered both at the Cloud Server and the client's PC in order to align correctly. Hence, it may lead to redundant rendering. As a solution, we consider to use a different set of zNear and zFar at the server side to clip out the corresponding contents, thus reducing the redundancy. Furthermore, we plan to develop an approach to automatically decide the threshold according to the monitoring of GPU usages at client's PC and server. As such, the system should preserve as much the graphic fidelity without overloading the client's PC.

7.2   Compatibility with Other Genres of Games

The developed demo proves to be a perfect situation for evaluating the Hybrid-Streaming system. However, further in-depth testings with different genres of gaming applications are necessary. Especially we need to address if the difference in term of the graphic quality is significant. We consider that our system should benefit game genres such as 2D scrolling, fighting and FPS since these games usually have distinguishing background and foreground objects.

7.3   Significance of the Improvement

The current quantitative evaluation based on the demo shows the improvement of graphic quality, but the difference is not significant. Therefore, it is not yet valid to be conclusive about our work. We expect that with more complicated visual effects, our system should demonstrate more obvious advantages. Furthermore, qualitative evaluation is also planned to be conducted so the actual improvement can be evaluated more comprehensively from player's perspective.

8   Conclusion and Future Works

In this paper, we have presented a Hybrid-Streaming System for the purpose of enhancing graphic quality delivered on Cloud Gaming. Based on the more prevalent structure of Image-based Streaming, we integrated the mechanism of Instruction-based Streaming to construct the proposed system. As such, by distributing rendering tasks and utilizing graphics processing resource from both client's device and server, enhanced graphic quality of Cloud Gaming can be delivered. Quantitative results show that the implemented prototype of Hybrid-Streaming System achieves better graphics quality than GamingAnyWhere's Image-based Streaming, while maintaining insignificant overhead during network streaming. Furthermore, the Hybrid-Streaming System also alleviates server's graphics processing workload by offloading rendering tasks to client's device.

Currently, the Hybrid-Streaming System is still at the prototype stage, as more thorough investigations are needed to evaluate the system as a prospective Cloud Gaming platform. As future works, we plan to qualitatively evaluate the QoE of the system, as well as applying actual gaming softwares to conduct further testing. Moreover, we will continue to improve the applicability of the Hybrid-Streaming System by developing a more comprehensive framework.

References

1. Cai, W., Zhou, C., Leung, V., Chen, M.: A cognitive platform for mobile cloud gaming. In: 2013 IEEE 5th International Conference on Cloud Computing Technology and Science (CloudCom), vol. 1, pp. 72–79. IEEE (2013)
2. Chen, K.-T., Chang, Y.-C., Tseng, P.-H., Huang, C.-Y., Lei, C.-L.: Measuring the latency of cloud gaming systems. In: Proceedings of the 19th ACM International Conference on Multimedia, pp. 1269–1272. ACM (2011)
3. Chen, K.-T., Huang, C.-Y., Hsu, C.-H.: Cloud gaming onward: research opportunities and outlook. In: 2014 IEEE International Conference on Multimedia and Expo Workshops (ICMEW), pp. 1–4. IEEE (2014)
4. Clincy, V., Wilgor, B.: Subjective evaluation of latency and packet loss in a cloud-based game. In: 2013 Tenth International Conference on Information Technology: New Generations (ITNG), pp. 473–476. IEEE (2013)
5. Cloud Gaming Report 2012. Distribution and monetization strategies to increase revenues from cloud gaming (2012). http://www.cgconfusa.com/report/documents/Content-5minCloudGamingReportHighlights.pdf
6. Geron, T.: Sony to acquire cloud gaming startup gaikai for $380 million (2012). http://www.forbes.com/sites/tomiogeron/2012/07/02/sony-to-acquire-cloud-gaming-startup-gaikai-for-380-million/
7. Huang, C.-Y., Hsu, C.-H., Chang, Y.-C., Chen, K.-T.: Gaminganywhere: an open cloud gaming system. In: Proceedings of the 4th ACM Multimedia Systems Conference, pp. 36–47. ACM (2013)
8. Jarschel, M., Schlosser, D., Scheuring, S., Hoßfeld, T.: An evaluation of QoE in cloud gaming based on subjective tests. In: 2011 Fifth International Conference on Innovative Mobile and Internet Services in Ubiquitous Computing (IMIS), pp. 330–335. IEEE (2011)
9. Xu, L., Guo, X., Lu, Y., Li, S., Au, O.C., Fang, L.: A low latency cloud gaming system using edge preserved image homography. In: 2014 IEEE International Conference on Multimedia and Expo (ICME), pp. 1–6. IEEE (2014)

Anyboard: A Platform for Hybrid Board Games

Simone Mora$^{(\boxtimes)}$, Tomas Fagerbekk, Matthias Monnier, Emil Schroeder, and Monica Divitini

Department of Information Technology and Computer Science,
Norwegian University of Science and Technology, Trondheim, Norway
`simone.mora@ntnu.no`, `monica.divitini@idi.ntnu.no`

Abstract. Making hybrid board games that mix the interactivity of video games with the social impact of board games is challenging. While the design process needs to take into account elements from the digital and analog domains, building prototypes requires dealing with diverse technologies in the field of Tangible Interfaces and Interactive Tabletop and Surfaces. Anyboard provides theoretical tools to map traditional board game interaction to the hybrid medium and lightweight technology tools to facilitate game prototyping. Our platform provides augmented game pieces that work with traditional cardboards, allowing designers to easily build collaborative interactive games without requiring engineering skills.

Keywords: Hybrid game · Pervasive game · Design · Prototyping · Platform · Tangible interface

1 Introduction

Despite the popularity of computer games, board games still represent a significant part of the market [3]. The reason lies in board games providing a more human-oriented experience compared to computer games [15]. Playing board games is indeed a social ritual where families and friends get together; having low entry-barriers for cost and skills, board games represent a cross-generational form of entertainment.

Over the last twenty years, research has pointed at combining the interactivity of computer games with the benefits of board games [13,15] creating interactive and augmented board games; hereafter referred as *hybrid board games*. For a review see Haller et al. [8]. Hybrid games have been extensively implemented using interactive surfaces such as tabletop computers, recently complemented by novel technologies in the field of *Multi-Display Environments* (MDE) [20] and *Around-the-Device Interaction* (ADI) [5]. In hybrid games, large interactive surfaces recreate the social affordances typical of board games, whilst the use of active or passive playing pieces preserve physical affordances similar to traditional game pieces. However these technologies pose several constraints in terms of design space, mobility and cost; and high entry-barriers for developers.

Published by Springer International Publishing AG 2016. All Rights Reserved
G. Wallner et al. (Eds.): ICEC 2016, LNCS 9926, pp. 161–172, 2016.
DOI: 10.1007/978-3-319-46100-7_14

The objective of our research is to lower the barrier for developers to create hybrid games. In [18] we proposed the Interactive-Token approach (ITo) to hybrid games. The approach, grounded in Tangible User Interfaces frameworks [9,21], is based on the concept of *tokens, constraints* and *interaction events*. It proposes the design of hybrid games based on interactive game pieces only, without using interactive surfaces. In the approach, the board is preserved as a low-tech component. Because of not relying on interactive surfaces or external sensing infrastructures, ITo provides an extended design space and mobile alternative to interactive tabletops and surfaces.

In this paper we present *Anyboard*, a platform for creating hybrid board games based on the ITo approach. The platform supports design and prototyping of games. Anyboard design concepts help modelling hybrid game user interaction with technology-augmented game pieces, facilitating the transition between design and implementation. Anyboard software and hardware tools support prototype development with (i) a set of interactive physical game pieces that can be reused across different games, and (ii) a software library to support the coding of games. Our platform aims at reducing the gap between design and prototyping making it easier for designers to use technologies such as sensors and actuators that usually require engineering skills. It should be noted that Anyboard focuses on supporting interaction design rather than more "traditional" game development components such as game engines.

The paper is structured as follows. We first provide a definition of the ITo approach, followed by existing tools for supporting development of hybrid board games. Second we describe the architecture of Anyboard, listing the tools and APIs provided to developers. We evaluate the power of Anyboard illustrating how it could be used to implement common board game mechanics. We conclude highlighting future work.

2   Hybrid Board Games: The ITo Approach

With the dawn of the ubiquitous computing age, board games gained new interest. Advances in interactive surfaces enabled for the development of hybrid versions of board games with or without augmented playing pieces. For example in [2] players use interactive physical iconic or symbolic artifact as their avatars to perform actions in the game. In [11], players can interact on a virtual game board with smart-pens and combine physical and virtual objects to solve puzzle games.

In recent years the large adoption of smartphones and tablets fostered the creation of hybrid games for mobile platforms. To address the limited screen size that impedes co-located play, technologies in the field of Multi-Display Environments (MDE) [20] and Around the Device Interaction (ADI) [5] were adopted. In hybrid games such as *Capture the flag* [20], gesturing and juxtaposition of private smartphone screens onto a shared screen reveal hidden layers and provide player-custom perspectives into the game. ADI technologies have demonstrated the development of augmented game pieces capable to control the behavior of a smartphone game by manipulation over or around the screen. *Airsteroids* [6], a spaceship game, demonstrates how the game space can extend across several tablets brought in by players and the use of augmented cards to control spaceships' heading.

These examples show how hybrid games usually rely on a mix of private and shared interactive surfaces as a primary mean to convey interactivity, with augmented game pieces as helpers. This approach poses several limitation in terms of mobility and cost and it requires engineering skills to orchestrate the diverse technologies; limiting the adoption of hybrid games outside research labs.

In the ITo approach, game pieces (tokens) with embedded sensors and actuators are the primary means to add interactivity to board games, while the cardboard is preserved as passive. In this way the same tokens can be used to play multiple levels or games just printing a new cardboard with consumer-grade devices. Technology is used to enhance *control* and *representation* roles of game pieces. Tokens can *control* the state of a game by capturing players' interaction events. For example an accelerometer embedded in a dice can sense the result of a dice throw, and notify a computer game engine in a way that is transparent to the player. At the same time, tokens can *represent* the state of a game by producing *digital feedbacks*; e.g. via graphics, haptics or sound via embedded displays and actuators.

Distributing interactivity across multiple components opens for a wider space of possibility in designing game experiences. Tokens are active playing pieces and they can influence the state of a game not only when they sit on an interactive surface, but also when they are manipulated over and around it. Finally, because of relying on embedded technology not requiring external hardware, ITo offers a more mobile and cost effective alternative to tabletop and ADI technologies. For more information about the ITo approach see [19].

2.1   Challenges to the Development of Hybrid Games

The development of hybrid games based on the ITo approach poses several challenges, mixing issues typical of both board and computer games [12]. These challenges are often common to many pervasive [13] games. From a design point of view there is a lack of theoretical tools to model players' interaction as well as abstractions to describe common elements of games. In particular, the complexity of dealing with different low-level hardware and software technologies, for example to detect manipulation of augmented game pieces, makes game development hard to non-expert, creating a gap between design and prototyping tasks [16]. Further, besides game pieces and mechanics can be generic, the implementation is often so specific that cannot be re-used to develop similar games [12].

Software frameworks and game engines for development of video-games can partially help development, however special tools are often needed to exploit at full the design space. Tangible User Interfaces prototyping toolkits, such as *Arduino* [17] and *Phidgets* [7] can be used to implement interactive pieces, although they don't specifically address game development. Conversely, toolkits to support hybrid game development often focus on tabletop or tablet computing platforms; for example supporting object recognition and tracking as for game pieces [4], dealing with multiple screens [14], designing terrain composition and dealing with input management [12], or facilitates the development of games that feature playing pieces on and around a tablet screen [1].

Only a few toolkits [10,16] explicitly support the development of interactive game pieces required by the ITo approach, and only as complement to tabletop interactive surfaces. An integrated set of design and prototyping tool to support the development of ITo hybrid games could not be found.

3   The Anyboard Platform

Building on analysis of development tools available and our experience in building hybrid games [18] we created the Anyboard platform (Fig. 1). AnyBoard implements the ITo approach providing:

- *Design entities* to model interaction styles and provide a common terminology to describe games both in design and implementation phases
- *Interactive game pieces and cardboard templates* to support the construction of the game hardware (Fig. 2)
- *AnyboardJS library* to facilitate coding of games by abstracting the complexity of dealing with hardware and low-level programming

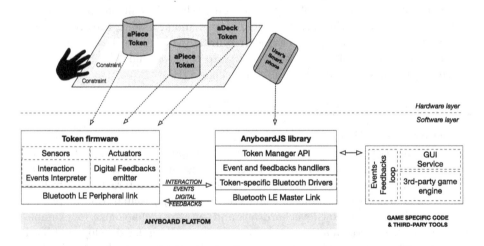

Fig. 1. Anyboard platform overview

3.1   Design Entities

Design entities derived from the ITo approach [18], listed below, constitute the foundation of a language to model interaction styles with Anyboard games. They have been mapped to traditional board games elements in Table 1, to help bridging the gap between game design and development.

Table 1. Mapping between Anyboard and board game concepts

Anyboard design entities	Traditional board game elements
Tokens	Game pieces
Constraints	Board tiles or sockets
Interaction Events	Player's actions

Tokens are technology-augmented artifacts which resemble traditional game pieces; ranging from elements of chance (e.g. an augmented dice in *Backgammon* or RFID-enabled cards in *Monopoly*) to game pieces, e.g. pawns augmented with an LCD displaying the player's rank in the game.

Constraints are either visual or physical confining regions in the board space. The association or dissociation of a token within a constraint can be mapped to digital operations to activate game dynamics. Examples of constraints are checks for *Chess* pieces and territories in *Risk*.

Interaction events are player-triggered manipulations of tokens, that modify the (digital and physical) state of a game. We define three types of events:

- *token event (TE)* - the manipulation of a single token on, over around the board; e.g. the action of rolling a dice or drawing a card
- *token-constraint event (TCE)* - the operation of building transient token-constraint associations by adding or removing tokens to a constrained region of the board; e.g. moving army pieces beyond a territory line as an attack action
- *token-token event (TTE)* - the operation of building transient token-token adjacency relationships, achieved by moving tokens on the board; e.g. moving a token next to another token to exchange a resource between two players.

An Anyboard game can be therefore defined as a sequence of player-initiated interaction events that modify spatial configurations of tokens with respect to board constraints and other tokens. As a consequence tokens' *intangible* (digital feedbacks) representations are updated.

Sequences of interaction events describe players' actions during the game and are mapped to specific game dynamics implemented in a game engine.

The game engine connects and exchange data with tokens using the AnyboardJS library (Sect. 3.3) running on the user's smartphone, for example activating specific game mechanics according with interaction events sensed by tokens or triggering digital feedbacks.

Design entities have driven the development of hardware and software tools to assist the making of Anyboard games.

3.2 Interactive Game Tokens and Cardboard Template

Anyboard currently prototypes two different types of interactive tokens: *aPiece*, an augmented game piece, and *aDeck*, an augmented card deck (Fig. 2).

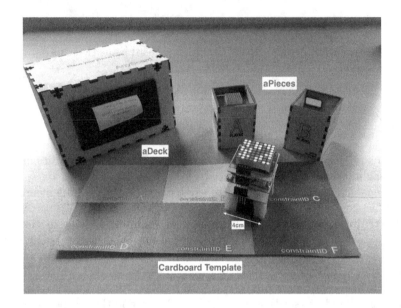

Fig. 2. Interactive game pieces and cardboard template prototype

Being two of the most common elements of board game they can be used to implement a wide range of games.

aPieces are a technology-augmented version of game pieces commonly found in most games. They are capable of capturing the set of interaction events and produce digital feedbacks. Tables 2 and 3 cluster interaction events and digital feedback supported by typology and provide a player-perspective description of their role. Possible mapping with dynamics commonly found in board games are also exemplified. For example the action of shaking an aPiece can be mapped to the draw of a random number or event.

aPiece has been designed and implemented using custom components. This choice allowed the use of miniaturised components, leading to aPieces with volume and affordances similar to traditional game pieces. aPiece embeds an ARM processor, which runs a custom-designed firmware, and a BTLE (Bluetooth Low Energy) radio transmitter. It implements algorithms to handle sensors data and drive feedback actuators as well as establishing wireless links with the game engine. The core unit is complemented by circuitry for battery charge and firmware upgrade.

TEs (Token Events) are recognised by a 3-axis accelerometer implementing algorithms for extracting features to identify physical manipulation events (e.g. SHAKE, TAP).

TCEs recognition is implemented by assigning and imprinting unique colors to different sectors of a game board (representing visual constraints to token's locations). A color-sensor located on the bottom of aPiece samples the color

Table 2. Interaction events implemented by aPiece

Type	Interaction event	Description	Sample mapping with game mechanics
TE	SHAKE	aPiece is shaken	Throw a random number
	TILT	aPiece is tilted upside down	Undo a previous action
	TAP	aPiece is tapped on the top side	Increase a resource by one unit
	DOUBLE-TAP	aPiece is double-tapped on the top side	Decrease a resource by one unit
TCE	ENTERS_[cID]	aPiece is moved inside a cID sector of the board	Signal player's placement and movements among
	LEAVES_[cID]	aPiece is moved away from cID sector	different board sectors
TTE	APCHES_[aID2]	aPiece is moved close to another one	Trade a resource between two players
	LEAVES_[aID2]	aPiece is moved away to another one	Break a relationship between two players

temperature of the surface the device is lying on, returning an unique color-code which is used as a fingerprint for board constraints, enabling to detect when aPiece is moved between two sectors. TCE detection also makes use of accelerometer data to ensure that color sampling is performed only when the device is steady on a sector, deactivating the sensing routine when aPiece being moved.

TTEs are recognised by computing the distance between two pawns using RSSI (Received Signal Strength) data from the radio transmitter.

Token digital feedbacks are implemented using three different devices: an RGB LED, a 8×8 LED Matrix and a vibration motor.

The aPiece firmware (Fig. 1) can be extended using Arduino code. In this way new functions can be added allowing implementing new interaction events and extending the range of feedbacks. Further, the firmware can be used as a template to develop new tokens. The appearance of aPiece can also be customized with handcrafted or 3D-printed models blending the digital feedback with a static iconic or symbolic shape.

aDeck is an interactive version of the card deck commonly found in board games. Instead of holding stacks of cards, aDeck prints out its own cards using a small thermal printer. aDeck provides visual feedbacks as listed in Table 4. Besides having textual and graphical information on card, aDeck can also be configured to print cards with 2D-barcodes that can be recognised by smartphone cameras or dedicated devices, and used in certain games to trigger game mechanics. This is not yet specifically addressed by our platform but can be easily implemented with third-party tools.

Table 3. Digital feedbacks implemented by aPiece

Type	Feedback (FEEDBACKID)	Description	Sample mapping with game mechanics
Visual	LED_[color]	aPiece lights up in the color defined by [color]	Show the status of a resource
	MATRIX_[text]	aPiece top side display shows the string [text]	Shows player's action point allowance
	MATRIX_[icon]	aPiece top side display shows the icon [icon]	Show the result of a dice roll
Haptic	SHRT_HAPTIC	aPiece produces a short haptic feedback	Signal a player to move to the next turn
	LNG_HATIC	aPiece produces a long haptic feedback	Signal a player an action not allowed

Table 4. Digital feedbacks implemented by aDeck

Type	Feedback	Description	Sample mapping with game mechanics
Visual	CARD[text]	A new card with textual information is printed	Inform the player about an event
	CARD[icon]	A new card with an graphical icon is printed	Represent a resource that the player owns
	CARD[barcode]	A new card with a barcode is printed	Trigger an action when barcode is scanned

aDeck is implemented using a thermal printer capable to print on conventional thermal paper up to 4.8 cm length, and an Arduino-compatible board.

Cardboard Templates provide support to creating custom cardboards that interact with iPieces. As mentioned above, Anyboard use color temperature sensing to implement constraint regions.

We therefore selected nine colors that provided satisfactory sensor recognition rate across different materials and printing techniques and associate them with unique IDs to be used in game development. A color palette to draw cardboard with custom constraint regions is provided as a template file that can be modified with vector graphic editors (example in Fig. 2).

3.3 AnyboardJS

AnyboardJS is a javascript library providing developer-friendly functions to code games (Fig. 3). It acts as an interface between the interactive tokens provided by the Anyboard platform and game-specific code developed as standalone or with third-party game engines. AnyboardJS provides two main functions. It establishes wireless links with aPieces and aDeck enabling data exchange using specific drivers for each type of token. It provides a *TokenManager* interface to enable developers to easily write javascript code to handle interaction events from tokens and generate digital feedbacks, to implement game-specific routines. The library is designed to be extensible, support to new interactive tokens can be added by writing driver modules. Although tokens are the primary user interface with a game, it is possible to code a secondary GUI to display extended information and controls on the smartphone screen; e.g. to be used to edit game settings, to display game rules and leader-boards. This functionality can be implemented with external libraries (e.g. jQuery mobile[1]).

A subset of the *TokenManager* interface functions is provided in Fig. 3.

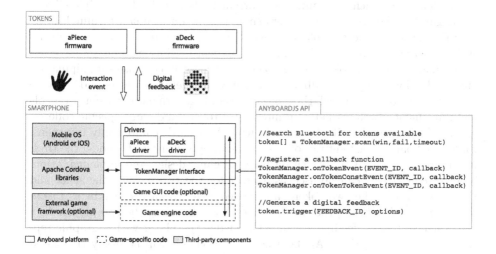

Fig. 3. AnyboardJS library internals and API

AnyboardJS is built on top of the *Apache Cordova* framework[2], and it can deployed on a number of mobile platforms. Further the library has been designed to be used with standard javascript code, to implement simple games, but it can also be integrated with third-party game development frameworks such as *UnityMobile*[3] or *Phaser*[4] for building complex games.

4 Discussion: Making an Anyboard Game

Making an hybrid game using Anyboard is a two-steps process. First it requires to model game pieces, rules and mechanics using the provided design entities

---

[1] jQuery mobile - https://jquerymobile.com/.

[2] Adobe Cordova - https://cordova.apache.org/.

[3] UnityMobile - https://unity3d.com/.

[4] Phaser - http://phaser.io/.

(Sect. 3.1). Second it involves prototyping the game using the provided interactive game pieces and the AnyboardJS library. Our platform saves developers from taking care of low-level implementation details, yet leaving freedom for customization.

As a working example, we consider the popular board game mechanic of resource trading, for example transferring the ownership of a property in a game like Monopoly. This mechanic could be implemented in hybrid board games by having two tokens, avatars of players, moved close to each other to symbolize the resource transaction between the two. Digital feedbacks can acknowledge the player with approval or failure (in case of no funds available) with visual or haptic feedbacks.

Implementing such mechanic with current tools would take multiple efforts. First, game designers and developers should agree on common terminology to describe the mechanic and playing pieces involved, because there's usually no such "resource trading" API in game development toolkits. Second, game developers should build the tokens and implement recognition of tokens manipulation and production of digital feedbacks, dealing with diverse hardware and software low-level technologies. Third, the developer should design data transfer protocols and implement interfaces between interactive tokens and game-specific code.

Developing the described mechanic with Anyboard requires only two steps. First, Anyboard design entities offer a choice of opportunities to model the trading mechanic, simplifying transition between game design and implementation. Two *aPieces* tokens can be used as avatars for the two players, the seller and the buyer. When the two tokens are moved close to each other in a *Token-Token Interaction Event*, the resource is exchanged among the two player. As a consequence, tokens' feedbacks can acknowledge the player with a graphic representation. Second, using AnyboardJS, the mechanic can be easily translated into code which handles interaction events and triggers feedbacks (Listing 1.1); acting as an interface with digital model of the game implemented in a game engine.

Listing 1.1. Example of game mechanic implemented with AnyboardJS

```
var trade = function(initToken, respToken, options){
    if (initToken.fundsAvailable())
    {
        transfer_property();
        initToken.trigger(MATRIX,"ICON_OK");
        respToken.trigger(MATRIX, "ICON_OK");
    }
}
TokenManager.onTokenTokenEvent("MOVE_NEXT_TO", trade);
```

This simple example can be further extended to leverage other Anyboard functions. For example, the trading action to be only allowed when both tokens are in a specific constrain sector, detected by a *Token-Constraint event*. Otherwise *aDeck* could be used to issue an "ownership certificate" reporting the name of the new owner and current property value.

Anyboard makes it easy for developers to explore design choices just editing a few lines of code. For example, the digital feedback in the example above, provided in a form of iconic visualization can be instead provided with haptic feedbacks or with color codes, using aPiece's LED. Information provided to the player can mix tangible and intangible representations. For example, static information like players identities or roles can be provided by customizing aPieces with 3D-printing and handcrafting work, instead action points or other dynamic information can be provided using digital feedbacks.

Anyboard has been designed to be extensible, experts can create interactive tokens of their own, with different sensors or feedback capabilities, tinkering with the Arduino-compatible firmware developed for aPieces and by writing *driver modules* for AnyboardJS.

5   Conclusion and Future Work

The Anyboard platform contributes to hybrid board game research with design and prototyping tools to create games based on the ITo approach. Design entities facilitate modelling game mechanics, while interactive tokens supported by a Javascript library shield developers from dealing with hardware complexities and low-level software development. We expect Anyboard to lower the thresholds of technical competences needed for game development.

Anyboard source code and hardware schematics are open source[5]. Future work will have multiple efforts. On one side we aim at better understanding the expressive power of Anyboard design entities by systematically modelling popular game mechanics, adding to the mapping already provided in Tables 2, 3 and 4. On the other side we plan to run game design workshop to evaluate developer friendliness and performances of the tools. Finally there are also plans to build new type of interactive tokens to further explore the space of opportunities provided by the ITo approach.

Acknowledgements. We thank Dr. Ines Di Loreto for her contribution to the ITo approach formalisation and her feedbacks on Anyboard.

References

1. Avrahami, D., Wobbrock, J.O., Izadi, S.: Portico: tangible interaction on and around a tablet. In: Proceedings of UIST, pp. 347–356. ACM (2011)
2. Bakker, S., Vorstenbosch, D., Van Den Hoven, E., Hollemans, G., Bergman, T.: Weathergods: tangible interaction in a digital tabletop game. In: Proceedings of TEI, pp. 151–152. ACM (2007)
3. Costikyan, G.: Don't be a vidiot: what computer game designers can learn from non-electronic games. In: Game Developers Conference, vol. 26 (1998)
4. Dietz, P., Leigh, D.: DiamondTouch: a multi-user touch technology. In: Proceedings of UIST, pp. 219–226. ACM (2001)

---

[5] Anyboard GitHub repository is available at http://anyboardgames.co.

5. Garcia-Sanjuan, F., Catala, A., Fitzpatrick, G., Jaen, J.: Around-device interactions: a usability study of frame markers in acquisition tasks. In: Abascal, J., Barbosa, S., Fetter, M., Gross, T., Palanque, P., Winckler, M. (eds.) INTERACT 2015. LNCS, vol. 9297, pp. 195–202. Springer, Heidelberg (2015)
6. Garcia-Sanjuan, F., Jaen, J., Catala, A., Fitzpatrick, G.: Airsteroids: re-designing the arcade game using markairs. In: Proceedings of ITS, pp. 413–416. ACM (2015)
7. Greenberg, S.: Collaborative physical user interfaces. In: Communication and Collaboration Support Systems (2004)
8. Haller, M., Forlines, C., Koeffel, C., Leitner, J., Shen, C.: Tabletop games: platforms, experimental games and design recommendations. In: Art and Technology of Entertainment Computing and Communication, pp. 271–297 (2010)
9. Ishii, H.: Tangible bits: beyond pixels. In: Proceedings of TEI. ACM (2008)
10. Krzywinski, A., Mi, H., Chen, W., Sugimoto, M.: RoboTable: a tabletop framework for tangible interaction with robots in a mixed reality. In: Proceedings of ACE. ACM (2009)
11. Leitner, J., Haller, M., Yun, K., Woo, W., Sugimoto, M., Inami, M., Cheok, A.D., Been-Lirn, H.D.: Physical interfaces for tabletop games. ACM Comput. Entertain. (CIE) 7(4), 1–21 (2009)
12. Lilis, Y., Savidis, A.: An integrated development framework for tabletop computer games. ACM Comput. Entertain. (CIE) 12(3), 1–34 (2015)
13. Magerkurth, C., Cheok, A.D., Mandryk, R.L., Nilsen, T.: Pervasive games: bringing computer entertainment back to the real world. ACM Comput. Entertain. (CIE) 3(3), 4 (2005)
14. Magerkurth, C., Stenzel, R., Prante, T.: STARS - a ubiquitous computing platform for computer augmented tabletop games. In: Proceedings of UBICOMP (2003)
15. Mandryk, R.L., Maranan, D.S.: False prophets: exploring hybrid board/video games. In: Proceedings of CHI Extended Abstracts, pp. 640–641. ACM (2002)
16. Marco, J., Baldassarri, S., Cerezo, E.: ToyVision: a toolkit to support the creation of innovative board-games with tangible interaction. In: Proceedings of TEI. ACM (2013)
17. Mellis, D., Banzi, M., Cuartielles, D., Igoe, T.: Arduino: an open electronic prototyping platform. In: Proceedings of CHI Extended Abstracts. ACM (2007)
18. Mora, S., Di Loreto, I., Divitini, M.: The interactive-token approach to board games. In: De Ruyter, B., Kameas, A., Chatzimisios, P., Mavrommati, I. (eds.) AmI 2015. LNCS, vol. 9425, pp. 138–154. Springer, Heidelberg (2015). doi:10.1007/978-3-319-26005-1_10
19. Mora, S., Di Loreto, I., Divitini, M.: From interactive surfaces to interactive game pieces in hybrid board games. J. Ambient Intell. Smart Environ. (2016, to appear)
20. Mueller, S., Dippon, A., Klinker, G.: Capture The flag: engaging in a multi-device augmented reality game. In: Proceedings of ITS, pp. 277–282. ACM (2015)
21. Ullmer, B., Ishii, H., Jacob, R.J.K.: Token+constraint systems for tangible interaction with digital information. ACM Trans. Comput. Hum. Interact. (TOCHI) 12(1), 81–118 (2005)

Accelerating the Physical Experience of Immersive and Penetrating Music Using Vibration-Motor Array in a Wearable Belt Set

Tomoko Yonezawa[✉], Shota Yanagi, Naoto Yoshida, and Yuki Ishikawa

Kansai University, Takatsuki-shi, Osaka 5691095, Japan
{yone,k463362,k030913}@kansai-u.ac.jp

Abstract. In this research, we aim to create a heightened and physical musical experience by combining electronic sound and time-lagged multiple vibrations that surround the user's neck, chest, and back. The purpose of the research is to elevate an immersive and extended experiences of music as though the sound source had a physical presence. We developed a wearable interface of a vibration-motor array with separately controlled multiple vibration motors to simulate both strong bass sounds and movement of the physical presence of the sound source. The control of intensity and the time differences among the motors produce not only the illusion of spatial presence but also the physical penetration of the ongoing sound. The results of the evaluations showed the effects of (1) the combination of vibration and sound in the musical experience and (2) time differences of the starting timings between the front and back vibrations when creating the illusion of physical penetration as though the sound had a physical presence.

Keywords: Sound and vibration · Vibration-motor array · Realistic sensation's expressions · Physical penetration and localization

1 Introduction

Since the 1980s when portable music players became popular, we have been to enjoy pre-recorded music with sophisticated and lightweight players in an easy and familiar way. These players have small speakers or need external headphones that are not advantageous for creating a high-powered deep bass sound, although musical experiences in live performances or movie theaters provide a strong presence of sound as a physical phenomenon with sensible vibrations. Such experiences are realized by a powerful output of volume using large-scale devices, such as large speakers or woofers, that are not suitable for personal use.

Humans perceive various stimuli as being multimodally combined. Subchannel stimuli can change the perception of the main stimulus, as can be seen in McGurk effect [5]. Consequently, we considered that the sound and music experience of live performance or theater with real mega volume is not perceived by

© IFIP International Federation for Information Processing 2016
Published by Springer International Publishing AG 2016. All Rights Reserved
G. Wallner et al. (Eds.): ICEC 2016, LNCS 9926, pp. 173–186, 2016.
DOI: 10.1007/978-3-319-46100-7_15

the sense of hearing alone. We especially focused on the sense of touch on sound vibration; as Merchel [6] discussed in relation to the influence of the listener's experience of whole-body vibrations, the natural feeling of sound and music is expected to provide vibrations to a greater or lesser extent.

To achieve the experience of realistic sound and music of massive volume but without expensive audio equipment, we have developed a wearable interface with a vibration-motor array that produces vibrotactile expressions in synchronization with the sound of music. Multiple vibrators provide a localized illusion of both sound and vibration. Furthermore, we focused on an illusion of the physical penetration of a sound source through the user's body based on fictive physical presence by the differences in starting times among the vibration motors. Not just massive volume at live concerts, localized vibration would aid in creating a realistic experience of immersive opera and parades with actors' movements. The physical penetration is also expected to emphasize the presence of virtual objects passing through the user's body in 3D theaters. As described above, the surrounding vibrations reproduce these physical experiences.

Thus, the localized vibration and illusion of physical penetration would also provide a novel music experience. Moreover, the sound localization would become easier not only based on normal differences of level and time (ILD: interaural level difference and ITD: interaural time difference) among multiple vibrations but also based on the illusion of the physical penetration from the ongoing sound.

As an application of this configuration, the use of the vibration-motor array as a monitor combined with sound feedback would help a player in a live performance, especially for directional and expressive assignments while the wearable device does not restrict the user's actions. As another application, the proposed method is also expected to give an impact on people with hearing difficulties. The vibration can individually express the rhythm of music even without any sound.

2   Related Works

First, we refer to studies that have suggested the importance of vibration to the experience of music. Merchel and Altinsoy [5] discussed the effect of whole-body vibrations on the listener's experience of listening to concert recordings with a box-type chair with a large vibrating system in it. Their results showed that music with vibration, –though only from the buttocks,– was judged better than simple sound alone. Chang et al. [1] suggested that audio-based vibrotactile feedback on a mobile phone is preferred to simple audio and is recognized as better sound. Thus, it is presumed that vibration improves the musical experience, especially with a small device and low volume. Yoshida et al. [11] provided vibration stimuli in the user's palm using an electromagnetic coil device driven by low-frequency components of the sound. Their evaluation showed that the different types of vibrations elevated the listener's sensitivity.

There are researches on educational systems in which vibration is used as a tool for learning music. Miura and Sugimoto [7] aimed to give each person a vibration of a particular rhythm of the assigned part to learn on an instrument in ensemble. They showed that a vibration device could become an effective tool for rhythm learning. Similar to their application, our proposed system is also expected to be adopted not only for rhythm learning but also for understanding sound localization to develop musical experiences, though our main purpose is not education itself.

Second, there are discussions on various fixed/wearable systems of haptic expressions for realistic sensation of sound and musical experience. Lindeman et al. designed VR immersive devices with multiple haptic feedbacks covering the user's upper body [8,9]. You et al. [12] developed a sound-specific vibration-array interface according to a sound stream using 16 oscillators. They found the shoulder was the most effective place to fix the attachment among the wrist, forearm, upper arm, shoulder or neck to increase immersiveness. There is also a palm-sized mobile haptic device with dual-band stimuli to produce low- and high-frequency bands for musical experiences [2]. The dual-band stimuli showed predominance in making a good impression; however, the user's action is limited while holding the device in the hand. In contrast, our wearable system does not restrict the action of the user. According to their dual-channel feedbacks, we applied different frequency bands to express various types of music. Sakuragi et al. [10] reduced vibration motors to a minimum setup with actuators only at the clavicle to efficiently provide wide vibrations with as far-reaching stimuli as possible. For more extended experiences, we focused on the vibration-motor array on not only the clavicle but also other places on the user's body.

The above three music devices [2,10,12] cover a narrow surface of the body from only one direction except Lindeman's VR garment [8], which was not for a musical experience. Even the 4x4 table vibration array has difficulty in generating distinct localizations because it covers only a narrow surface. The palm-sized device and the simple placement on the clavicle also cannot provide vibrations on a wide or surrounding surface. For an immersive experience and localization of the sound from various directions, we considered that a wider surface and arrayed multiple vibrations should be prepared. Accordingly, we adopted multiple vibration motors placed in various directions from the center of the body. Also, the three above studies used small vibrators that made it difficult to create strong and slow vibrations like real loudspeakers. In contrast, we adopted two types of vibration motors: low-frequency and strong vibrators for the low frequency band and a small brushless motor for the midrange frequency band.

Chair-type systems provide vibration stimuli with sound for a similar purpose. Karam et al. [3] suggested a chair-type haptic system fusing eight channels. The system expresses various vibrations of multiple musical instruments in music using haptic devices fixed on various parts of the body. There is also a chair-type vibration machine, Bodysonic [4], to extend the sense of hearing music. The chair-type device is considered to cover the user's body; however, the strong sound experience in a live performance provides the music experience with sound from the front to the back.

Differently to Karam et al., we focus on haptic vibrations from the front, back, left, and right to elevate sound localization and realistic sensation as though the user were surrounded with musical sound. The novel point of our proposed system is the differences in starting times of the vibrations among multiple vibration motors to create the illusion of physical penetration as though the sound had a physical presence.

3   Physical Experience System of Sound and Music

3.1   Summary of System Structure

In order to expand the sound and experience of using portable head-phones/earphones, we implemented a synchronized vibration-motor array system as follows. The system consists of (1) a sound analysis unit and (2) a control unit of a vibration-motor array (see Fig. 1). First, the sound-analysis unit analyzes the signal of ongoing music. Second, the control unit of the vibration-motor array (1) distributes the level of each vibration motor and (2) calculates the time delay for each motor based on the analyzed data and parameter settings. Finally, the original hardware device of the vibration-motor array produces vibrations in synchronization with the sounds of the music.

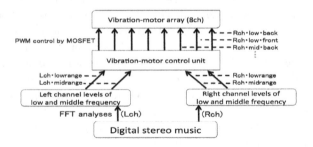

Fig. 1. System structure

3.2   Hardware Structure and Vibration-motor-array Device

The hardware of the system consists of a laptop PC, a set of headphones, an original wearable set of the vibration-motor array, an AVR microcomputer (Arduino UNO), and an Nch-independent MOSFET.

The proposed vibration-motor array device is configured as a wearable belt set for the chest with four vibration motors and a choker with four vibration motors (Figs. 2 and 3). Two dual-axis vibration motors of 6000 RPM (revolutions per minute), which are assigned to the low-frequency power of the sound, are also placed on the upper rubber band of the chest belt in the vicinity of the third and fourth ribs. Two of the same 6000 RPM motors are placed on the upper rubber

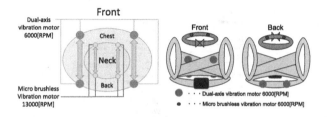

Fig. 2. Vibration motor array device

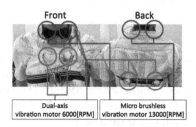

Fig. 3. Fixed wearable suit with vibration motor array device

band of the belt on the left and right sides of the back 15 cm from the center of the spine. On the choker, two micro-brushless vibration motors of 13000 RPM, which are assigned to the middle-frequency power of sound, are placed on the left and right of the front of neck near the clavicles. Two of the same motors are also placed on the left and right at the back of the neck. The left and right pairs of micro-brushless vibration motors are placed at 8 cm intervals.

The AVR microcomputer performs pulse width modulation (PWM) controls for each of eight channels through the Nch-independent MOSFET in synchronization with the volume levels of each frequency band based on the data sent by the sound-analysis unit. The left motors are operated by reflecting the level of sound source from the left channel. The right motors reflect the right channel. Accordingly, the difference in the intensity of vibration between the left and right channels is automatically reproduced, including several-millisecond differences, such as the interaural time difference between the left and right ears. Therefore, localized sound can be felt emphatically by the differences in the intensity of vibrations between the left and right sides.

3.3   Sound-Analysis Unit

The sampling rate of sound processing is 44100 Hz. The analysis window size is 1024 samples. The FFT analysis of the sound at every 43 Hz derived the levels for following frequency bands: the low-frequency band is from 43 to 86 Hz, and the midrange frequency band is from 258 to 301 Hz. The FFT analysis is processed for each channel (left and right). The four values of the levels, the left/right and low/midrange frequency bands, are converted into 0 to 255 levels to control

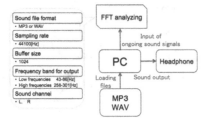

Fig. 4. Sound-analysis unit

each vibration motor. The music sound is output by headphones connected to the PC at the same time as the vibration stimuli (see Fig. 4). The system is basically using a sound file, but it can also operate real-time processes of external input with the audio interface system. Accordingly, the system is expected to be applied to improvements of realistic sensation in both interactive sounds during game play and real-time audio in watching TV.

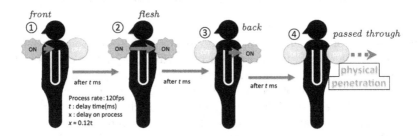

Fig. 5. Vibration-motor controls with delay for physical penetration

3.4   Vibration-Motor Control Unit

There are two methods of vibration-motor controls. The first is the direct conversion of the frequency power to each motor without special delay except the interaural time difference. The second is the unique method of time-lag among the motors that was adopted.

Vibration-motor control without additional delay: First, the sound-analysis unit sends the power levels of each frequency band of both the left and the right channels and converts them into levels from 0 to 255. Second, the vibration-motor control unit operates the PWM controls for each vibration motor. Thus, the eight motors are controlled to correspond to the sound-analysis result.

Vibration-motor controls with designed delay for generating illusion of physical penetration by sound: The vibration-motor control unit produces an illusion of physical penetration of sound by time lags in starting the vibrations among the motors. The processing frame rate is set to 120 fps. The delay time is set from 0 to 1000 ms every 100 ms. That is, the second vibration motor starts its operation after 0–1000 ms when the first vibration motor begins its vibrations (Fig. 5). When there is physical penetration by a real object through the human body, it is assumed that the first shock will be perceived on the front surface and the second shock will be perceived on the back surface after the passage through the flesh. Although sound and music do not have any physical presence, the assumed stimuli with the differences in starting times of vibrations are expected to create a physical penetration of sound.

To make the user perceive vibrations by an eccentric rotor, it takes $x - t$ ms (x is the time of the length of the sound, and t is the starting time among the vibration motors), which is a longer period than short-time pulse signals. Accordingly, there is an overlap between the timing of the front and back vibrations. Moreover, the overlapped timing is expected to create the feeling of passage through the body, as we aimed physical penetration.

4   Experiment

4.1   Evaluation of the Effect of Creating Realistic Sensations with Physical Vibrations in Synchronization with the Ongoing Music

Purpose of experiment: We tried to verify the effectiveness of vibration stimuli for creating realistic sensations of the ongoing sound of the music.

Hypothesis: The vibration stimuli covering the user's upper body will elevate the realistic sense of the sound's presence and power.

Participants: Twenty-five university students aged from 19 to 22 years old.

Conditions: We prepared 16 conditions according to two factors: (A) four different volumes of sound (s.none, low, middle, high) and (B) four different strengths of vibration (v.none, weak, medium, strong). The volume of sound for each condition was set as follows. The "s.none" means without any sound. The "low" is the lowest sound that the audio interface can output. The "middle" is 15 dB higher than low. The "high" is 5 dB higher than middle. The strengths of vibration for each condition were as follows. The "v.none" means without any vibration. The "medium" is the linear-mapped strength of the vibration synchronized with the volume levels of the sound converted from 0 to 255 levels. The "weak" is 0.5 times the power of medium. The "strong" is 1.5 times the power of medium. A branching table of the conditions is shown in Table 1. The 16 conditions with two factors were randomly arranged for counterbalance.

Procedures and Instructions: The participants were instructed to listen to the music for 40 s (rock music played for 20 s and then changed into ballad music for 20 s) through the headphones and our proposed vibration-motor array device for each condition. The time difference between the motors was not generated in this experiment. The combined conditions of sound volume and vibration using each level in each factor were performed in the repeated measurement.

Table 1. Conditions in the experiment of synchronized vibrations with music

	Sound(A)	Vibration(B)		Sound(A)	Vibration(B)
pt.01	none	none	pt.09	middle	none
pt.02	none	weak	pt.10	middle	weak
pt.03	none	middle	pt.11	middle	middle
pt.04	none	strong	pt.12	middle	strong
pt.05	low	none	pt.13	high	none
pt.06	low	weak	pt.14	high	weak
pt.07	low	middle	pt.15	high	middle
pt.08	low	strong	pt.16	high	strong

When the 40 s of music finished, the participants were instructed to evaluate the statements that followed. The other 15 conditions were repeatedly conducted with both listening and evaluation.

Evaluation Items: The participants made an evaluation using a five-point rating scale of the relevance (5: very relevant, 4: somewhat relevant, 3: even, 2: somewhat irrelevant, 1: irrelevant) of the following statements.

Q1 You felt you were in a live performance.
Q2 You felt the sound source was close to you.
Q3 You felt the sound surround you.
Q4 You felt the whole space vibrating from the sound.
Q5 You felt the sound had spread.
Q6 You felt the sound had moved.
Q7 You felt the volume was high.
Q8 It was easy to feel changes in the strength of the sound
Q9 You didn't feel anything unnatural about the vibration.
Q10 The vibration was consistent with the sound.
Q11 It was easy to listen to.
Q12 The sound was hollow.
Q13 You felt a change at exciting points in the music.
Q14 You felt power in the music.
Q15 You felt high.
Q16 Your body moved unconsciously.
Q17 You felt a sense of overdose on music.
Q18 You received a warm impression.
Q19 You felt comfortable with the sound.
Q20 You felt comfortable with the vibration.
Q21 You felt comfortable with the harmony of sound and vibration.

Results: The results of the mean opinion scores (MOS) are shown in Fig. 6. The results of the analyses of variance (ANOVA) with repeated measurement among the conditions ($p < .05$) are shown in Table 2.

The subjective evaluations showed significance for both factors except questions 11, 12, and 16. No significant result by vibration factor was found without sound. There were no significant differences in the conditions without vibration in the result of the evaluation questions 9, 10, 12, 16, and 21. Almost all of the evaluation items, except those above, showed significant differences between the with-sound and without-sound conditions at every vibration level. Besides the

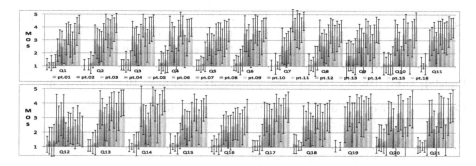

Fig. 6. MOS results in the experiment of synchronized physical vibrations with music

conditions with or without sound/vibration, there were significant differences among different sound intensities. In addition, there were interactions and simple effects between conditions with and without vibration at each volume. There were also significant differences in high-medium and high-weak strengths of the vibration. However, there was no significant difference in the vibration strength between medium and weak when the volume was in the middle for Q11 and Q19.

4.2 Evaluation of the Time Difference Among Vibration Motors for the Illusion of Physical Penetration of Sound

Purpose of experiment: We tried to verify (1) whether the new experience of physical penetration of sound could be created by the emphatic time lags of the starting times between multiple vibration motors, such as forward to backward, and (2) whether the proposed time improves the realistic sensation and the sense of sound image localization.

Table 2. Two-factor ANOVAs in the experiment of synchronized vibrations

	loudness(A)			strength of vibration(B)			Interaction		Multiple comparison based on simple main effects							
	F(24)	p	multi.comp.	F(24)	p	multi.comp.	F(24)	p	A(b1)	A(b2)	A(b3)	A(b4)	B(a1)	B(a2)	B(a3)	B(a4)
Q1	132.0	<0.01*	all	26.0	<0.01*	exp4-3	5.50	<0.01*	4-[1,2],3-[1,2]	exp4-3	exp4-3	exp3-2	—	[2,3,4]-1	[2,3,4]-1	all
Q2	147.0	<0.01*	all	17.4	<0.01*	[2,3,4]-1	5.24	<0.01*	exp2-1	[2,3,4]-1	exp3-4	all	—	[2,3,4]-1	[2,3,4]-1,3-2	4-[1,2]
Q3	143.0	<0.01*	all	55.6	<0.01*	[2,3,4]-1	5.97	<0.01*	4-[1,2],3-[1,2],1,4-3	exp4-3	[2,3,4]-1	exp3-4	—	[2,3,4]-1	[2,3,4]-1,3-2	[2,3,4]-1
Q4	77.8	<0.01*	exp4-3	14.5	<0.01*	[2,3,4]-1	8.93	<0.01*	4-[1,2]	[2,3,4]-1	[2,3,4]-1,3-2	exp4-3	—	[2,3,4]-1,2-4	[2,3,4]-1,3-2	[2,3,4]-1,4-2
Q5	83.4	<0.01*	exp4-3	10.5	<0.01*	[2,3,4]-1	2.54	<0.01*	[2,3,4]-1,4-2	exp4-3	[2,3,4]-1	exp4-3	—	[2,3,4]-1	[2,3,4]-1	[2,3,4]-1
Q6	101.0	<0.01*	exp4-3	31.0	<0.01*	[2,3,4]-1	6.71	<0.01*	4-[1,2],3-1	[2,3,4]-1	exp3-4	exp4-3	—	[2,3,4]-1	[2,3,4]-1	exp4-3
Q7	162.0	<0.01*	all	11.5	0.017*	4-[2,3]	8.38	<0.01*	exp2-1	exp3-2	all	all	—	[2,3,4]-1	exp2-1	4-[1,2,3]
Q8	96.1	<0.01*	exp4-3	13.5	<0.01*	[2,3,4]-1	4.29	<0.01*	4-[1,2],3-[1,2]	[2,3,4]-1	[2,3,4]-1	[2,3,4]-1	—	exp3-4	[2,3,4]-1,3-2	4-1
Q9	29.4	<0.01*	exp4-3	7.98	<0.01*	[2,3,4]-1	3.83	<0.01*	—	3-[1,2],4-1	[2,3,4]-1	exp3-2	—	3-1	[2,3]-1	[2,3,4]-1
Q10	67.1	<0.01*	exp4-3	25.8	<0.01*	[2,3,4]-1	8.84	<0.01*	—	[2,3,4]-1	[2,3,4]-1	all	—	exp2-3	[2,3,4]-1,3-4	[2,3,4]-1,4-2
Q11	127.7	<0.01*	exp4-3	2.398	0.075 +		1.96	0.046 *	[2,3,4]-1	exp4-3	[2,3,4]-1	all	—	3-4	—	[4,3]-1
Q12	18.9	<0.01*	exp4-3	1.610	0.195	-	1.66	0.100+	—	—	—	—	—	—	—	—
Q13	98.2	<0.01*	exp4-3	20.4	<0.01*	[2,3,4]-1	5.48	<0.01*	exp4-3	[2,3,4]-1	[2,3,4]-1	exp4-3	—	exp2-3	[2,3,4]-1	[2,3,4]-1
Q14	107.0	<0.01*	exp4-3	34.0	<0.01*	[2,3,4]-1,2-3	13.35	<0.01*	4-[1,2],3-[1,2]	[2,3,4]-1,2-3	exp3-4	exp4-3	—	exp3-4	all	exp4-3
Q15	94.5	<0.01*	exp4-3	10.7	<0.01*	[2,3,4]-1	7.41	<0.01*	4-[1,2],3-[1,2]	[2,3,4]-1	exp3-4	all	—	exp3-4	4-1,3-[1,2]	[2,3,4]-1,4-2
Q16	49.1	<0.01*	exp4-3	7.61	<0.01*	[2,3,4]-1	1.84	0.063 +	—	[2,3,4]-1	[2,3,4]-1	all	—	—	—	—
Q17	110.0	<0.01*	exp4-3	14.4	<0.01*	[2,3,4]-1	3.20	<0.01*	exp4-3	[2,3,4]-1	exp4-3	exp4-3	—	[2,3,4]-1	[2,3,4]-1,3-2	[3,4]-1
Q18	70.4	<0.01*	[2,3,4]-1	2.851	0.043*	3-1	3.28	<0.01*	[2,3,4]-1	[2,3,4]-1	[2,3,4]-1	exp4-3	—	—	[2,3,4]-1	[3,4]-1
Q19	106.0	<0.01*	exp3-[4,2]	3.78	0.014 *	3-1	2.36	0.0146*	[2,3,4]-1	[2,3,4]-1	[2,3,4]-1	exp3-2	—	3-[1,4]	—	[4,3]-1
Q20	51.4	<0.01*	exp4-3	21.6	<0.01*	[2,3,4]-1	5.64	<0.01*	—	[2,3,4]-1	[2,3,4]-1	all	—	exp3-2	[2,3,4]-1	[2,3,4]-1
Q21	93.9	<0.01*	exp4-3	21.236	<0.01*	[2,3,4]-1	9.78	<0.01*	—	[2,3,4]-1	[2,3,4]-1	all	—	3-[1,4],2-[1,4]	[2,3,4]-1	[2,3,4]-1,4-2

¶ expX-X means all combinations except X-X

Hypotheses: The emphatic time lags of starting times between forward and backward vibration motors (1) generate the feeling of physical penetration of the sounds, (2) improve the realistic sensation and (3) make clear the sense of sound image localization.

Participants: Twenty-five university students aged from 19 to 22 years old.

Conditions: We prepared 11 conditions of within-subject design according to a factor of time lag between forward and backward vibration motors: from 0 to 1000 ms every 100 ms. The conditions are shown in Table 3. The 11 conditions were randomly arranged for counterbalance.

Procedures and Instructions: The participants were instructed to listen to the sound of a bass drum for 30 s with headphones and the vibration-motor array device. The forward vibration motor was synchronized with the real-time sound, and the backward vibration motor was operated after the specified time lags for each condition. Accordingly, the backward vibration motors produced stimuli with one of the 11 different time lags. After each 30-second experience, the participants evaluated the impression for the statements of evaluation items that follow.

Evaluation Items: The participants made an evaluation using a five-point rating scale of the relevance (5: very relevant, 4: somewhat relevant, 3: even, 2: somewhat irrelevant, 1: irrelevant) of the following statements.

Q1 The backward vibration was later than the forward vibration.
Q2 The forward vibration was later than the sound.
Q3 The backward vibration was later than the sound.
Q4 You felt as though the sound passed through your body from forward to backward.
Q5 You felt the sound was just like the original sound of a bass drum.
Q6 You felt the bass drum was played in front of you.
Q7 The sound generated from the bass drum hit the front of your body.
Q8 The sound generated from the bass drum passed through your body.
Q9 You felt that the bass drum was close to you.
Q10 You felt a punch of the sound.
Q11 The vibration was natural in connection with the sound.
Q12 You felt the sound cover you.
Q13 The vibration was natural.
Q14 The sound passed through the flesh of your body.
Q15 The sound passed through the bones of your body.
Q16 You felt comfortable with the sound.
Q17 You felt comfortable with the vibration.
Q18 You felt comfortable with the harmony of the sound and the vibration.
Q19 You felt comfortable with the feeling of the sound passing through your body.

Results: The results of the MOSs and ANOVA with repeated measurements among the conditions ($p < .05$) are shown in Fig. 7 and Table 4. The evaluations

Table 3. Conditions in the experiment of physical penetration

Time difference	pt.01	pt.02	pt.03	pt.04	pt.05	pt.06	pt.07	pt.08	pt.09	pt.10	pt.11
(ms)	0	100	200	300	400	500	600	700	800	900	1000

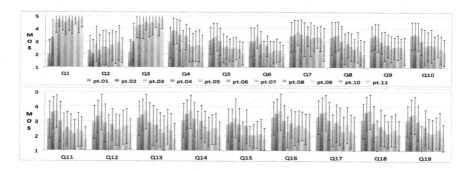

Fig. 7. MOS results in the experiment of physical penetration

except Q2 and Q7 showed significance. In particular, there were significant results in the 100–200 ms and 400–1000 ms lags. The most important results are Q13 and Q14, which showed the highest values in 200 ms lags as evaluations for hypothesis 1).

5   Discussion

5.1   The Effects of Vibration on the Realistic Sensation of Sound

From the results of two factorial analyses of variance, the sound with vibration provided a stronger feeling of immersion and realistic sensation than simple sound by itself. Therefore it is suggested that our proposed method of providing vibration from various directions can elevate the illusion of the physical presence of the sound. Moreover, we conjecture that the realistic sensation of the sound is improved and that the loudness of the sound is strongly perceived, especially when the volume of the sound is low.

The harmony between the vibration and the sound may stimulate comfortable feelings; however, if the vibration was too strong, this reduced the level of comfort. Moreover, there was no negative influence on the perception of the sound quality from the vibration. These results confirmed the hypothesis in Sect. 4.1. For further application for people with hearing difficulties, we should evaluate the musical perception using vibration without sound.

5.2   Illusion of the Physical Penetration of Sound

At first, from the results for Q2, there were no perceptional time lags from the musical sound stimuli and the vibration, while the vibration motors required

Table 4. One-factor ANOVAs in the experiment of physical penetration

	Time difference		
	F(19)	p	Multiple comparison (from pt.1 to pt.11)
Q1	26.049	<0.01*	[3,4,5,6,7,8,9,10,11]-[1,2],2-1
Q2	1.566	0.1174	–
Q3	19.402	<0.01*	[3,4,5,6,7,8,9,10,11]-[1,2],2-1
Q4	6.845	<0.01*	6-11,4-[5,11],3-[5,7,8,9,10,11] ,2-[5,7,8,9,10,11],
Q5	5.959	<0.01*	4-11, 3-[5,6,7,8,9,10,11] ,2-[7,8,10,11],1-11
Q6	7.448	<0.01*	4-11,3-[5,7,8,9,10,11],2-[5,7,8,11],1-[5,7,11]
Q7	1.464	0.1538	–
Q8	6.021	<0.01*	3-[5,8,10,11],2-[8,10,11],1-[10,11],4-11
Q9	5.115	<0.01*	3-[7,11],2-[7,8,9,10,11],1-[7,11]
Q10	5.760	<0.01*	3-[10,11],2-[5,8,10,11],1-[5,8,10,11]
Q11	9.516	<0.01*	4-11,3-[5,6,7,8,9,10,11], 2-[5,6,7,8,9,10,11],1-[8,11]
Q12	6.809	<0.01*	3-[4,5,6,7,8,9,10,11]2-[5,7,8,11],
Q13	7.590	<0.01*	3-[5,6,7,8,9,10,11],2-[7,8,10,11],1-[8,11],4-11
Q14	8.050	<0.01*	6-1,4-[8,11], 3-[5,7,8,9,10,11],2-[5,7,8,9,10,11],1-11
Q15	8.643	<0.01*	6-11,4-[5,7,8,11],3-[5,7,8,9,10,11],2-[5,7,8,9,10,11],1-11
Q16	7.343	<0.01*	3-[5,6,7,8,10,11],2-[5,7,8,9,10,11],1-[5,11]
Q17	7.600	<0.01*	4-11,3-[5,7,8,9,10,11],2-[5,7,8,10,11],1-[5,8,10,11],
Q18	10.037	<0.01*	3-[4,5,6,7,8,9,10,11],2-[5,6,7,8,9,10,11],1-[5,8,11]
Q19	10.270	<0.01*	4-[5,8,11],3-[5,6,7,8,9,10,11],2-[5,6,7,8,9,10,11],1-[5,7,8,11]

a few milliseconds for perceivable stimuli from the start of the rotation of the motor.

Next, from the results of the factorial analyses of variance, the time lag around 100–200 ms from front to back could provide a feeling as though (1) the sound passed through the user's body without any unnatural or incongruent feeling and (2) a bass drum were being played in front of the user.

Moreover, the participants could perceive the difference in the front and back vibrations even with only 100 ms of time lag. The significant difference in the feeling of physical penetration was confirmed in the statements regarding the penetration of both flesh and bone. Based on the results that the MOS for Q14 was higher than that of Q15, it is possible that the penetration of flesh is stronger than that of bone. This indicates that humans can feel an illusion of the physical penetration of sound.

From these results, the hypotheses in Sect. 4.2 were confirmed. We consider that the illusion of physical penetration of sound elicits both a realistic sensation and localization of the sound with an impression of physical presence. The advantage of multiple sound sources with each different direction of the physical penetration should be discussed in future work.

6   Conclusions

In this paper, we proposed a wearable system with a vibration-motor array in synchronization with sound to create an emphasized experience of music that included both a strong bass sound and the illusion of the physical presence of the sound source. The multiple vibration motors expressed not only strength and localization but also fictive penetration through the user's body. The vibration motors were placed surrounding the user's neck, chest, and back.

We evaluated the effects of (1) the combination of vibration with sound in the musical experience and (2) the differences in starting time between the front and back vibrations on creating the illusion of physical penetration. From the results, it is confirmed that (1) the surrounding vibration in synchronization with the sound of music produced both a realistic sensation and a punch of the musical experience and that (2) the appropriate time lags between the front and back vibration motors created an illusion of physical penetration of the sound; at the same time, sound localization and realistic sensation were also elevated.

In future work, we should consider the possibility of the proposed device for musical experience of people with hearing difficulties. It is also suggested that the proposed vibration-motor array could be combined with the visual presentation of sound through head-mounted displays.

Acknowledgments. This research was supported in part by JSPS KAKENHI 25700021 and JSPS KAKENHI 15H01698. The authors would like to thank the participants in the experiment.

References

1. Chang, A., O'Sullivan, C.: Audio-haptic feedback in mobile phones. In: CHI 2005 Extended Abstracts on Human Factors in Computing Systems, CHI EA 2005, pp. 1264–1267. ACM, New York (2005)
2. Hwang, I., Lee, H., Choi, S.: Real-time dual-band haptic music player for mobile devices. IEEE Trans. Haptics **6**(3), 340–351 (2013)
3. Karam, M., Branje, C., Nespoli, G., Thompson, N., Russo, F.A., Fels, D.I.: The emoti-chair: an interactive tactile music exhibit, pp. 3069–3074 (2010)
4. Komatsu, A.: Body-felt sound unit and vibration transmitting method therefor. US Patent 5,442,710, 15 August 1995
5. McGurk, H., MacDonald, J.: Hearing lips and seeing voices (1976)
6. Merchel, S., Altinsoy, M.E.: Auditory-tactile music perception. In: Proceedings of Meetings on Acoustics, vol. 19, p. 015030. Acoustical Society of America (2013)
7. Miura, S., Sugimoto, M.: Supporting children's rhythm learning using vibration devices. In: CHI 2006 Extended Abstracts on Human Factors in Computing Systems, CHI EA 2006, pp. 1127–1132. ACM, New York (2006)
8. Lindeman, R.W., Page, R., Yanagida, Y., Sibert, J.L.: Towards full-body haptic feedback: the design and deployment of a spatialized vibrotactile feedback system. In: Proceedings of VRST 2004, pp. 146–149 (2004)
9. Lindeman, R.W., Sibert, J.L., Mendez-Mendez, E., Patil, S., Phifer, D.: Effectiveness of directional vibrotactile cuing on a building-clearing task. In: Proceedings of ACM CHI 2005, pp. 271–280 (2005)
10. Sakuragi, R., Ikeno, S., Okazaki, R., Kajimoto, H.: CollarBeat: whole body vibrotactile presentation via the collarbone to enrich music listening experience. In: Imura, M., Figueroa, P., Mohler, B. (eds.) International Conference on Artificial Reality and Telexistence and Eurographics Symposium on Virtual Environments, ICAT-EGVE 2015. The Eurographics Association (2015)

11. Yoshida, R., Ideguchi, T., Ooshima, K.: An examination of a music appreciation method incorporating tactile sensations from artificial vibrations. In: Fourth International Conference on Innovative Computing, Information and Control (ICICIC), pp. 417–420, December 2009
12. You, Y., Lee, H., Sung, M.Y., Jun, K., Kang, J.-S.: Sound-specific vibration interface: its performance of tactile effects and applications. In: The 9th International Conference for Young Computer Scientists, pp. 1266–1271, November 2008

The Concept of Pervasive Virtuality and Its Application in Digital Entertainment Systems

Luis Valente[1(✉)], Bruno Feijó[2], Alexandre Ribeiro[3], and Esteban Clua[1]

[1] MediaLab/Institute of Computing/UFF, Niterói, Brazil
{lvalente,esteban}@ic.uff.br
[2] VisionLab/Department of Informatics/PUC-Rio, Rio de Janeiro, Brazil
bfeijo@inf.puc-rio.br
[3] Instituto Federal do Triângulo Mineiro, Uberaba, Brazil
alexandre@iftm.edu.br

Abstract. Virtual reality has received a lot of attention lately due to a new wave of affordable HMD devices arriving in the consumer market. These new display devices – along with the availability of fast wireless networking, comprehensive wearable technologies, and robust context-aware devices – are enabling the emergence of a new type of mixed-reality system for games and digital entertainment. In this paper we name this new situation as "pervasive virtuality", which we define as being a virtual environment that is extended by incorporating physical environments, physical objects as "proxy" elements, and context information. This new mixed reality paradigm is not well understood by both industry and academia. Therefore, we propose an extension to the well-known Milgram and Colquhoun's taxonomy to cope with this new mixed-reality situation. Furthermore, we identify fundamental aspects and features that help designers and developers of this new type of application. We present these features as a two-level map of conceptual characteristics (i.e. quality requirements). This paper also presents a brief case study using these characteristics.

Keywords: Pervasive virtuality · Pervasiveness · Context-awareness · Mixed-reality continuum

1 Introduction

Nowadays we are witnessing a growing interest in VR technologies, as several manufacturers have announced the development and shipping of high-quality head-mounted display (HMD) devices at affordable prices – examples include the Facebook Oculus Rift, Samsung VR, HTC Vive, and Sony PlayStation VR. The availability of these devices – along with fast wireless networking, comprehensive wearable technologies, and robust context-aware devices (e.g. sensor devices and the internet of things) – brings exciting potential to develop new digital entertainment applications.

Due to these advances, some initiatives have recently emerged by exploring the following pattern in mixed-reality environments: the players wear mobile HMD devices (seeing only virtual content) and are able to move freely in a physical environment, being

© IFIP International Federation for Information Processing 2016
Published by Springer International Publishing AG 2016. All Rights Reserved
G. Wallner et al. (Eds.): ICEC 2016, LNCS 9926, pp. 187–198, 2016.
DOI: 10.1007/978-3-319-46100-7_16

able to touch physical walls and interact with physical objects, while immersed in the simulation. On the industry side, The VOID [1] and Artanim Interactive's VR system [2] are notable examples. On the academia side, we developed a similar experience by creating an indoor navigation system for "live-action virtual reality games" [3, 4]. These three examples share similarities that we believe will become a current trend in digital entertainment.

To help in conceptualizing this new kind of entertainment application more precisely, this paper presents the concept of "pervasive virtuality (PV)". Essentially, PV means "a virtual environment that is extended by the incorporation of physical environments and objects as proxy elements". At first glance, PV seems to be another name for a well-known mixed-reality situation. However, this is not the case. Observing The VOID and Artanim's systems [1, 2] reveals a new mixed-reality situation (imprecisely named as "real virtuality" by Artanim [2]), which is not well understood by both industry and academia. Therefore, firstly we argue that "pervasive virtuality" is a more adequate term for this type of mixed reality. Secondly, we claim that the well-known Milgram and Colquhoun's mixed reality [5] should be extended to accommodate this new type of situation. Thirdly, we believe that pervasive virtuality (which is the situation found in [1, 2]) needs a more precise and useful definition. Our contribution stems from shedding some light in this new type of mixed reality, by creating a common vocabulary and identifying important aspects and features for designers and developers. Research on conceptual characteristics that help the design of mixed-reality applications can be found in other related areas, such as pervasive games [6–9]. Some conceptual characteristics presented in this paper have been inspired by the work in [9], whose authors discuss non-functional requirements (qualities) for pervasive mobile games and provide checklists to assess and introduce these qualities in game projects.

The present paper is organized as follows. Firstly, Sect. 2 defines and characterizes "pervasive virtuality". Next, Sect. 3 proposes a two-level map of characteristics (i.e. quality requirements), which can describe pervasive virtuality in a more precise way and help the design of new applications. Section 4 presents a brief case study using these characteristics. Finally, Sect. 5 presents conclusions and future works.

2   Pervasive Virtuality

Pervasive virtuality comprises a mixed-reality environment that is constructed and enriched using real-world information sources. This new type of mixed reality can be achieved by using non-see-through HMD devices, wireless networking, and context-aware devices (e.g. sensors and wearable technology). In PV, the user moves through a virtual environment by actually walking in a physical environment (exposed to sounds, heat, humidity, and other environmental conditions). In this mixed environment, the user can touch, grasp, carry, move, and collide with physical objects. However he/she can only see virtual representations of these objects. Even when a user is physically shaking hands with another user, he/she has no idea about the real characteristics of this other user (such as gender, appearance, and physical characteristics).

This new type of mixed-reality application has emerged recently, with several similar initiatives appearing almost simultaneously in the industry ("The VOID" [1] and "real virtuality" [2]) and academia ("live-action virtual reality game" [4]). An earlier similar academic initiative was "virtual holodeck" [10]. The experience in this new type of mixed-reality is extremely intense and immersive. However, being a new area, the literature lacks proper definitions, design principles, and methods to guide designers and researchers. This paper contributes to shed more light on these issues. We start by defining PV considering the traditional reality-virtuality continuum [5].

2.1 A New Reality-Virtuality Continuum Axis

Milgram and Colquhoun [5] proposed a mixed-reality taxonomy with visual displays in mind. Yet, most mixed-reality applications found in the literature simply juxtaposes real and virtual objects through the projection of visual artefacts. For instance, a common example of augmented virtuality is the video of a real human face projected on a 3D mesh of an avatar's head in a virtual world. Essentially, in these applications, "augmented virtuality" consists of a virtual world augmented with the mapping of an image or video from the real world in virtual objects, and "augmented reality" is the same process the other way round. Therefore, we need to extend Milgram and Colquhoun's taxonomy to accommodate other forms of mixed reality.

We need a taxonomy that can cope with situations where real physical objects are transformed into virtual objects, and vice-versa (i.e. virtual objects become real objects). We propose to identify the first situation as "pervasive virtuality" and the later situation as "ubiquitous virtuality". These situations represent a better fusion of reality and virtuality, which goes beyond a simple mapped visual projection. In these new environments, transformed objects should work like a proxy. Figure 1 illustrates a proposal to extend the Milgram and Colquhoun's taxonomy with our new concepts.

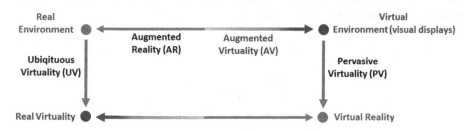

Fig. 1. Extending Milgram and Colquhoun's taxonomy of real and virtual environments

Augmented virtuality is different from pervasive virtuality, as in the first one real world objects are projected in virtual content and the HMDs that the user wears (if any) necessarily are see-through devices. Examples of augmented virtuality can be found in [11, 12].

Pervasive virtuality is different from the mixed-reality found in "pervasive games" [9], although they may share similarities (e.g. context-awareness). Essentially, pervasive games are based on the idea of a real-world augmented with virtual content (left of

Fig. 1) through context-awareness, made possible through sensor devices placed in the physical environment and carried by players (in mobile and wearable devices) while they move in the real-world.

Our concept of ubiquitous virtuality (UV) is aligned with well-known definitions of this term in the literature [13], which means that this type of mixed-reality integrates virtual objects seamlessly in the real environment and preserves as many human senses as possible. However, transforming virtual objects into real ones is a much more complicated affair and we have almost no examples to produce. Computational holography is a potential technology in this regard, but this is a research area still in its infancy. Smart materials that can change their shape in particular magnetic fields or change their texture in response to a voltage change could also be used, but they are in an experimental stage. In the realm of science fiction, UV would be the Star Trek Holodeck. Figure 1 illustrates that PV enhances visual virtual environments towards what we consider the true "virtual reality" – an environment with a strong sensation of immersion and presence due to the existence of several human senses. On the other hand, UV tends to evolve towards what we call "real virtuality" – a virtual world so convincing that we cannot easily distinguish it from the real world. As a last observation about Fig. 1, we can expect that a continuum of mixed reality situations connect its two ends (Real Virtuality and Virtual Reality).

PV transforms physical objects into virtual equivalents (also named "proxy objects" in [10]) by representing their geometry in the virtual environment and tracking them with wireless networking systems. Furthermore, pervasive virtuality maps the real environment into the virtual environment through the compression and gain factors that apply to a user during his/her immersion in virtual environments. For example, the user's real movements always occur over smaller (and curved) paths when compared to his/her virtual paths (Fig. 2). For example, these compression factors allow a user to walk through a long and intricate virtual map by walking in circles over a small physical area. Steinicke et al. [10] present several variables on which these factors apply, such as: user's head rotation, path curvature, scaling of translational movements, and scaling of objects (and/or the entire environment).

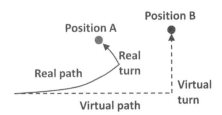

Fig. 2. Mapping real movements into virtual ones (inspired in [10])

2.2 Defining and Characterizing PV

In the context of the previous section, we define pervasive virtuality (PV) as follows. PV is a mixed reality where real, physical, objects are transformed into virtual objects by using real-world information sources through direct physical contact and context-aware devices (e.g. sensors and wearable technology). In PV users wear non-see-through HMDs all the time, which means that they do not see any real-world contents. PV usually requires intensive use of compression and gain factors on external world variables to adjust the transformation between reality and virtuality.

PV can be better understood by exploring its characteristics (as Sect. 3 describes), which are essentially "quality requirements" (or "non-functional requirements"). In this Sect. (2.2) we summarize the concepts underlying those requirements. While doing so we make references to subsections of Sect. 3 to correlate descriptions with specific characteristics/requirements, to help in understanding the new concepts better.

All content that a user experiences in PV is virtual – the simulation uses digital content and generates virtual content based on real world information sources. These information sources are: (1) the physical environment architecture; (2) physical objects that reside in the environment; and (3) context information (see Sects. 3.1 and 3.6).

PV takes place in a "simulation stage" (or "game stage", in the case of games), which consists of a physical environment (e.g. a room, school floor, or museum) equipped with infrastructure to support the activities (e.g. wireless networking, sensors, and physical objects). The simulation (or game) uses these elements to create the mixed reality.

In PV, a user wears a non-see-through HMD device and walks in the physical environment (Sect. 3.3), being able to touch physical walls and other elements. The user sees a 3D virtual world through the HMD and does not see the real world. The simulation constructs a virtual world based on the physical environment architecture (i.e. the first information source, as a 1:1 matching), keeping these two worlds superimposed (Sects. 3.1, 3.7). The simulation detects physical objects (e.g. furniture, portable objects, and users' bodies – the second information source) and maps them into virtual representations, which are then displayed to the user (Sect. 3.1). Users touch, grasp, carry, and move these physical objects, but they only see their virtual representation (Sects. 3.1, 3.5).

The third information source is context information [14] (Sect. 3.6), which the simulation may use to generate virtual content and to change the rules or simulation behaviour (i.e. unpredictable game experiences and emergent gameplay). Examples of context information include: (1) player information (e.g. physiological state, personal preferences, personality traits); (2) physical environment conditions (e.g. temperature, humidity, lighting conditions, weather); (3) information derived from the ways a player interacts with physical objects and input devices; and (4) information derived from relationships and interactions among players in the game (the social context).

A PV application may respond back to the user through various channels and various types of media (Sect. 3.4). Some of these channels may be worn or carried by users (Sect. 3.1), and some of them correspond to physical objects that are spread in the physical space (e.g. smart objects and environment devices, Sects. 3.4, 3.6). Finally, users may interact in PV through multiple modalities (e.g. voice, body movements, and gestures), ordinary physical objects, and context-aware devices, supporting tangible, body-based, and context-aware interaction paradigms (Sect. 3.5).

3   Pervasive Virtuality Characteristics

Figure 3 illustrates a map with two levels of characteristics, which can be understood as quality requirements to use for PV system design. Each one of the seven first-level characteristics is subdivided into further sub-aspects, which represent more specific issues. In future works, we intend to explore the interdependences among these characteristics, similarly as in [9]. This section presents a brief description of these characteristics (i.e. quality requirements).

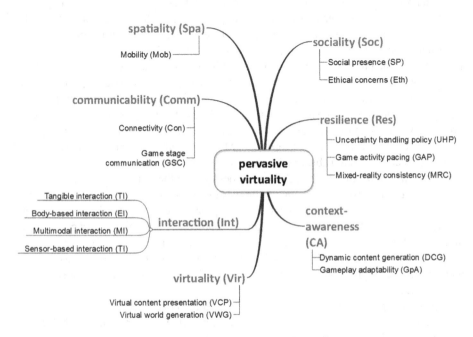

Fig. 3.   Important pervasive virtuality characteristics

3.1   Virtuality

Virtuality (Vir) regards handling the virtual aspects in PVs, including *Virtual world generation (VWG)* and *Virtual content presentation (VCP)*. *Virtual world generation* regards procedures to generate the 3D virtual world based on physical world structure, which may be a real-time process or may be a pre-configuration step (i.e. mapping the environment before the simulation runs), for example. *Virtual content presentation* concerns issues about how the simulation presents the virtual world and virtual content to users. For example, PV may present content through HMDs, wearable devices (capable of providing haptic feedback), the underlying physical structure, and physical objects (e.g., touching physical walls, tables, and holding small objects). In case of HMDs, there are issues that the simulation must address properly, such as adverse effects on users (e.g. nausea, motion sickness). Hearing may be stimulated by isolating or non-isolating headphones and smart objects (Sect. 3.4). VCP also relates to presence in virtual environments [15].

3.2 Sociality

Sociality (Soc) refers to social aspects and social implications of the simulation. *Social presence (SP)* concerns *"how people experience their interactions with others and refers to conditions that should be met in order to experience a sense of co-presence (i.e. mutual awareness)"* [16]. Social presence may happen among real people and/or among users and virtual characters. For example, a simulation may foster social relations by providing team play activities that require collaboration. A stronger possibility in this example may be activities that require collaboration due to complimentary user roles.

Finally, *Ethical concerns (Eth)* regards topics related to the well-being of users and ethical issues. For example, Madary and Metzinger [17] discuss issues about virtual environments influencing user's psychological states while using the system, lasting psychological effects after the simulation is over (e.g. long-term immersion effects, lasting effects of the illusion of embodiment, undesired behaviour change).

3.3 Spatiality

Spatiality (Spa) regards aspects related to the physical space usage. In particular, *Mobility* concerns issues related to the free movement of players in the physical environment. Some examples are providing adequate network support that covers the entire simulation stage, requirements of user movement due to physical space size and interaction with physical objects, and how to simulate a large virtual environment in a confined space (e.g. redirected walking techniques [18] as in Fig. 2).

3.4 Communicability

Communicability (Comm) concerns aspects about the infrastructure that the simulation uses to communicate with users and other simulation components. *Connectivity (Con)* refers to the networking infrastructure that is required to support activities in the simulation (and associated issues). For example, PVs may require wireless local networking with specific requirements (e.g. low latency).

Game stage communication (GSC) refers to the communication channels that the game uses to exchange information with players in the game stage. For example, environment devices [9] are objects placed in the physical environment and may output information (e.g. audio), generate effects in the physical world (e.g. smells, wind, heat, cold, spray water, open doors, and move elevators).

3.5 Interaction

Interaction (Int) refers to interaction paradigms in PV. So far we identify these important paradigms that contribute to create the "live-action play" aspect of PV: *Tangible* interaction *(TI)*, *Body-based interaction (BI)*, *Multimodal interaction (MI)*, and *Sensor-based interaction (SI)*. These interaction paradigms may be facilitated through wearable devices (e.g. smart bands, motion sensors) and dedicated infrastructure (e.g. motion-capture cameras).

Multimodal interaction (MI) corresponds to interaction through multiple modalities such as voice input, audio, and gestures. *Tangible interaction (TI)* represents the "tangible object metaphor" as first defined by Ishii and Ullmer [19]. In TI, a user interacts with the simulation by manipulating context-aware mobile devices (e.g. portable device equipped with sensors) and ordinary physical objects (e.g., wood sticks, rocks). In PV, the simulation tracks all these devices and displays a correspondent virtual representation to the user through a HMD. For example, a real wood stick could become a virtual sword in the simulation. *Body-based interactions (BI)* represent interactions through body movements such as jumping, spinning, walking, running, and gestures. *Sensor-based interaction (SI)* represents interactions of implicit nature [20] based on sensor devices. An example is "proximity interaction", where the simulation triggers events when a sensor detects the presence of a user.

3.6   Context-Awareness

Context-awareness (CA) refers to acquiring and using context information in simulation activities. The simulation is able to sense context information through several means, such as: (1) The physical place where the game happens may host physical objects that are equipped with sensors (e.g. smart objects in [9]). These devices may be connected to other similar objects and to game servers; (2) The player carries or wears devices that sense context from the environment and/or from the player; and (3) The game queries remote information about the player based on the player identity (e.g. social network profiles).

In this regard, *Dynamic Content Generation (DCG)* refers to creating game content dynamically through context. The simulation also may use context to adapt rules, change simulation behaviour, and virtual world content (*Gameplay adaptability – GpA*).

3.7   Resilience

Resilience (Res) refers to how a game is able to cope with technology uncertainties (i.e. in sensors and networking) to prevent them from breaking immersion and the simulation experience. These uncertainties stem from inherent technology component limitations such as accuracy, precision, response time, and dependability. For example, in PV the tracking problem is a key issue as: (1) sensor technologies ignore physical world boundaries; (2) sensor technologies may not be able to track objects moving above a certain speed threshold. We identify three important aspects for resilience: *Uncertainty handling policy (UHP)*, *Game activity pacing (GAP)*, and *Mixed-reality consistency (MRC)*.

Uncertainty handling policy (UHP) refers to specific strategies a simulation may use to handle uncertainties. Valente et al. [9] discussed five general strategies to approach these issues (e.g. hide, remove, manage, reveal, exploit). *Game activity pacing (GAP)* refers to how the pacing of activities might interfere with the operations of specific technologies (e.g. sensors), and vice-versa, and what to do about this issue.

Mixed-reality consistency (MRC) refers to how a game keeps the physical and virtual worlds superimposed and synchronized (in real-time) without negative side-effects that a player might perceive. For example, a key element in the PV pipeline is tracking of physical objects and physical elements (e.g. architecture). PV may use different approaches, such as sensors or computer vision. A PV simulation can process tracking through the mobile user equipment (e.g. "inside processing" in portable HMDs, cameras, and computers) or through a dedicated infrastructure (e.g. "outside processing" using cameras fixed in the physical infra-structure and dedicated computers).

4 Case Study

This section describes briefly how the aspects that Sect. 3 describes apply to a proof-of-concept PV demo that we developed in previous works [4] (as a "live-action virtual reality game"). In this game demo the player carries a smart object that simulates a gun. The player wanders around a small room freely, shooting virtual aliens that try to invade the environment. The physical room is equipped with several infrared markers that are used in the mapping (*Virtual world generation*) and tracking processes (*Mixed-reality consistency*). The tracking hardware consists of a portable computer and an Oculus Rift device equipped with two regular cameras (one for each eye), which have been modified to capture infrared light only.

Virtuality. Considering *Virtual world generation (VWG)*, the application requires a pre-processing step to build the virtual world. In this process, a user (non-player) walks in the physical environment wearing the tracking hardware to scan all infrared markers fixed on the room walls. The system uses this information to create the first version of the 3D world. Later, a designer tweaks this 3D model manually. Considering *Virtual content presentation (VCP)*, the demo provides information through the HMD and headphones. During our preliminary tests, one player (out of twelve) experienced adverse effects such as headaches and disorientation.

Sociality. Considering *Social presence*, in the current version there is only one active avatar (the player character) in the game stage, which means that *Social presence* does not apply. Regarding *Ethical concerns*, we plan to create an evaluation plan to assess how these experiences might affect players when we test this application with a broader audience.

Spatiality. Considering *Mobility*, the current version takes place in a 5 m × 5 m room. The demo does not use redirected walking techniques to simulate a larger environment.

Communicability. Considering *Connectivity*, in the current version the simulation does not use networking as the mobile player equipment is self-contained (i.e. performs all processing). However, we are experimenting with environment devices and smart objects spread in the room that communicate with the player equipment using radio frequency modules and Wi-Fi. Considering *Game stage communication*, it does not apply to the current version.

Interaction. The demo uses tangible interaction – the player manipulates a smart object as a gun.

Resilience. As a proof-of-concept, the demo does not implement *Uncertainty handling policy*. However, we are working on "manage" strategies [9] as "fallback options" for networking operation: the player equipment communicates with smart objects through RF modules (the fastest option), if this option does not work adequately then the game tries Wi-Fi; if this also fails then the game tries Bluetooth. Considering *Game activity pacing*, the speed that the player moves the gun object has not affected how the game operated. However, we are still experiencing issues if the player equipment loses sight of the infrared markers. Considering *Mixed-reality consistency*, tracking errors accumulate as the player moves in the environment as the system uses relative position of some markers in the tracking process. To solve this issue, the environment contains special markers that contain absolute physical position, which the tracking system uses to correct tracking information.

Context-Awareness. *Dynamic content generation* does not apply to the demo. Considering *Gameplay adaptability*, the current version does not use it. However, we are experimenting with temperature sensors to change virtual world colours according to physical temperature (Fig. 4). In Fig. 4, the laptop displays what the player sees through the HMD. To the left of the player's hand, there is an environment device (a heater) that becomes a fireplace in the virtual world. In this example the player equipment contains a temperature sensor. The demo senses the current temperature and modifies the fireplace animation according to this information: if the temperature is higher, then the virtual fireplace gets bigger.

Fig. 4. A player in the test room with a heater on the ground and her correspondent HMD view

5   Conclusions

In this paper we started to conceptualize a new paradigm that has emerged recently through the new trend of affordable HMD devices coming to the market, as well as the availability of fast wireless networking, wearable technology, and context-aware devices. In previous works [3], we started exploring this new entertainment paradigm as "live-action virtual reality games". However, instead of providing formal definitions about this kind of application, in this paper we set out to identify an initial set of characteristics (i.e. quality requirements) that may contribute to implement this new paradigm. We believe that this approach may lead to more practical results (e.g. helping designing and developing these applications) instead of trying to formulate abstract definitions – this is an approach that echoes other works about fuzzy definitions in game research such as "pervasiveness" [21].

The initial set of aspects that we presented is not a complete set, but it is a starting point to foster discussion and further research agendas. Also, these aspects do not exist in isolation as several of them have interdependences and specific game features may require several aspects. For example, in a work in progress we are experimenting with ultrasonic sensors to detect player presence, so as to open a door in a game activity and play a sound in a loudspeaker. This is a simple example of *Game stage communication* that requires *Context-awareness* and *Interaction* (e.g. proximity interaction).

Future works include elaborating questions to assess the characteristics, refining this initial set, discovering interdependences, discovering more characteristics, developing applications based on this material, analysing other applications that share similar concerns, and feed all this material back again in this research process.

Acknowledgments. The authors thank CAPES, FINEP, CNPq, FAPERJ, and NVIDIA for the financial support to this paper.

References

1. The VOID: The vision of infinite dimensions. https://thevoid.com/
2. Artanim: Real Virtuality. http://artaniminteractive.com/real-virtuality/
3. Valente, L., Clua, E., Ribeiro Silva, A., Feijó, B.: Live-action virtual reality games. Departamento de Informática. PUC-Rio, Rio de Janeiro (2015)
4. Silva, A.R., Clua, E., Valente, L., Feijó, B.: An indoor navigation system for live-action virtual reality games. In: Proceedings of SBGames 2015, pp. 84–93. SBC, Teresina (2015)
5. Milgram, P., Colquhoun Jr., H.: A taxonomy of real and virtual world display integration. In: Ohta, Y., Tamura, H. (eds.) Mixed Reality, pp. 1–26. Springer, Berlin (1999)
6. Walther, B.K.: Notes on the methodology of pervasive gaming. In: Kishino, F., Kitamura, Y., Kato, H., Nagata, N. (eds.) ICEC 2005. LNCS, vol. 3711, pp. 488–495. Springer, Heidelberg (2005)
7. Guo, B., Zhang, D., Imai, M.: Toward a cooperative programming framework for context-aware applications. Pers. Ubiquit. Comput. **15**, 221–233 (2010)
8. Nevelsteen, K.J.L.: A Survey of Characteristic Engine Features for Technology-Sustained Pervasive Games. Springer International Publishing, Cham (2015)

9. Valente, L., Feijó, B., do Prado Leite, J.C.S.: Mapping quality requirements for pervasive mobile games. Requirements Eng. 1–29 (2015)
10. Steinicke, F., Ropinski, T., Bruder, G., Hinrichs, K.: The holodeck construction manual. In: ACM SIGGRAPH 2008 Posters, pp. 97:1–97:3. ACM, New York (2008)
11. Bruder, G., Steinicke, F., Valkov, D., Hinrichs, K.: Augmented virtual studio for architectural exploration. In: Proceedings of Virtual Reality International Conference (VRIC 2010), pp. 43–50. Citeseer, Laval (2010)
12. Paul, P., Fleig, O., Jannin, P.: Augmented virtuality based on stereoscopic reconstruction in multimodal image-guided neurosurgery: methods and performance evaluation. IEEE Trans. Med. Imaging **24**, 1500–1511 (2005)
13. Kim, S., Lee, Y., Woo, W.: How to realize ubiquitous VR?. In: Pervasive: TSI Workshop, pp. 493–504 (2006)
14. Dey, A.K.: Understanding and using context. Pers. Ubiquit. Comput. **5**, 4–7 (2001)
15. Sanchez-Vives, M.V., Slater, M.: From presence to consciousness through virtual reality. Nat. Rev. Neurosci. **6**, 332–339 (2005)
16. Wolbert, M., Ali, A.E., Nack, F.: CountMeIn: evaluating social presence in a collaborative pervasive mobile game using NFC and touchscreen interaction. In: Proceedings of the 11th Conference on Advances in Computer Entertainment Technology, pp. 5:1–5:10. ACM, New York (2014)
17. Madary, M., Metzinger, T.K.: Real virtuality: a code of ethical conduct. recommendations for good scientific practice and the consumers of VR-technology. Front. Robot. AI. 3 (2016)
18. Steinicke, F., Bruder, G., Jerald, J., Frenz, H., Lappe, M.: Estimation of detection thresholds for redirected walking techniques. IEEE Trans. Vis. Comput. Graph. **16**, 17–27 (2010)
19. Ishii, H., Ullmer, B.: Tangible bits: towards seamless interfaces between people, bits and atoms. In: Proceedings of the SIGCHI conference on Human factors in computing systems, pp. 234–241 (1997)
20. Rogers, Y., Muller, H.: A framework for designing sensor-based interactions to promote exploration and reflection in play. Int. J. Hum Comput Stud. **64**, 1–14 (2006)
21. Nieuwdorp, E.: The pervasive discourse: an analysis. Comput. Entertain. **5**, 13 (2007)

Short Papers

Metry Mouse Missions: An Interactive, Geometric Obstacle Course of Daredevil Proportions

Günter Wallner[1]([✉]), Lauri Galbreath[2], and Simone Kriglstein[3]

[1] University of Applied Arts Vienna, Vienna, Austria
guenter.wallner@uni-ak.ac.at
[2] New York University, New York City, USA
lauri.galbreath@nyu.edu
[3] Vienna University of Technology, Vienna, Austria
simone.kriglstein@tuwien.ac.at

Abstract. Educational games have started to establish themselves as a fruitful complement to traditional teaching methods since they can enhance motivation and actively engage learners with the subject matter. While educational games targeted toward single players still prevail, recent years have also witnessed a growing interest to incorporate collaborative elements into educational games to take advantage of the positive effects associated with collaborative learning.

In this paper we introduce *Metry Mouse Missions*, an educational game which fosters collaborative problem-solving and engages young people, aged 8–11 years old, in the construction of complex geometric models through the interactive adventures of a daredevil mouse. A central aim of *Metry Mouse Missions* is to provide an inviting interface that supports exploration and intellectual curiosity about geometric constructions.

Keywords: Game-based learning · Collaborative learning · Geometry

1 Introduction

While educational games have established themselves as a promising complement to traditional education methods there still exists only a limited number of educational games to date which include a collaborative dimension (cf. [10]). While empirical studies have shown that collaborative learning can be a very effective form of learning (see, e.g., [4]), designing collaborative educational games is not a straightforward endeavor as it has been shown that the effectiveness of collaborative learning depends upon a variety of factors (cf. [1]) such as group composition and the quality of the interactions between the collaborators.

In this paper we describe *Metry Mouse Missions*, an educational game currently in development and intended to convey geometric concepts to young people aged 8 to 11 years. The goal of the game is to successfully maneuver a stunt

G. Wallner et al. (Eds.): ICEC 2016, LNCS 9926, pp. 201–204, 2016.
DOI: 10.1007/978-3-319-46100-7_17

mouse across obstacle courses composed of varied terrain, fire, and piranhas. For that purpose, players must unlock shapes and construct *obstacle tacklers* by correctly answering geometry-related questions about each desired game component. *Metry Mouse Missions* encourages students to work in pairs and promotes sustained collaborative problem solving. Friendly competition is encouraged.

2 Related Work

Given the vast amount of literature on game-based learning and collaborative learning environments a comprehensive review of related work is beyond the scope of this paper. We will thus limit our discussion to a few educational games concerned with teaching concepts of geometry. Examples in this area include the work of Ketamo [2] who described an adaptive geometry game for handheld devices. Sedig [8], in turn, introduced a game-based learning environment called *Super Tangrams* which helps children to understand transformation geometry, a topic which has also been addressed by *DOGeometry* [9]. Also worth mentioning is the work of Kiili and Ketamo [3] who developed a game where children learn by teaching an octopus about geometrical shapes. The latter also has a collaborative element which gives players the possibility to have their octopus compete against those trained by other players. However, each player has to train the octopus individually while in *Metry Mouse Missions* players have to work together to master an obstacle course.

3 Theoretical Framework

Metry Mouse Missions is developed with an eye towards inclusivity and constructivist learning principles. Central to a constructivist learning environment is that learners are able to choose and develop their own learning goals, and that the environment can be adapted to the uses learners put to it. The role of declarative knowledge, like facts and figures, and other forms of cognitive content, are used to help *construct* new worlds that reflect diverse perspectives; they are not the end in themselves, as an instructionist learning environment would have it.

Particularly useful in conceptualizing the *flow* of cognition in this learning game is Perkins' [7] conception of the *access characteristics* of knowledge, which looks at four categories of relevant knowledge (viz., knowledge, representation, retrieval, construction). Users must learn to utilize the tools of the system through physical and mental means, and construct something completely unique within it. Immediate feedback, active questioning, and interactivity increase mindfulness and intrinsic motivation [5]. Generative processing is facilitated in the game through multimedia, personalization, guided activity, feedback, and reflection [6]. The intention is to create an interactive environment that helps users develop more complicated schemata around geometry. Rewards (e.g., animations of the mouse running the obstacle course, cool things to make, racing other users) are designed into the system to keep users motivated and excited to see what comes next.

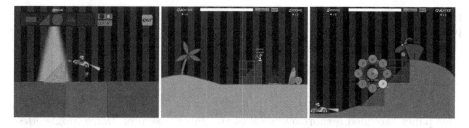

Fig. 1. Left: A tackler has been placed in front of the water hole to allow *Metry Mouse* to safely jump over it (single-player mode). Middle: The tackler for this fire obstacle is currently build by the other player and is therefore locked (two-player mode). Right: A player attempts to solve a question regarding the number of sides of the shape. The circle in the middle displays the amount of time left (two-player mode).

4 Game Design

The game consists of a collaborative two-player mode and a single player mode which is meant as a tutorial and preparation for the two-player mode. In both modes the player is challenged through a number of racetrack obstacle courses in need of various user-built contraptions (e.g., ramps, bridges) to help a stunt-mouse overcome obstacles like holes, fire-pits, water holes, or hills (see Fig. 1). These contraptions have to be built in an editor – called the *Obstacle Tackler* – by arranging basic geometric shapes – that is squares, right-sided triangles, and quadrants – in a proper way. Once the obstacle tacklers are successfully built the users may personalize their contraptions by spray painting with patterns and various color combinations. However, to place the tackler on the race track the player must unlock it first, by answering three questions about the geometric relationships involved in the construction (e.g., determining the area and circumference of a shape; recognizing the number of right angles in a shape, etc.). Each level in the game requires new tacklers to be built in order for *Metry Mouse* to successfully complete the race and reach the cheese located at the end of the race track.

In the single-player mode the user is aided in this process by a book, which collects all the built tacklers and gives information about the geometric relationships and equations. The two-player mode is different to the single-player mode in the sense that it limits the time available to build tacklers and answer questions. This has been done to ensure a fluent game experience for both players. Secondly, to provide incentive for both players to actively take part in the game, players can collect stars for building tacklers (the faster a tackler is built the more stars it is worth) and answering questions. In the latter case, a correct answer is worth a certain amount of stars, depending on the difficulty of the question. A wrong answer will reduce the amount by one and the players can try again, until all stars are used up in which case the level has been lost. Stars also influence the current status of the player, reaching from *Boss Clown* to *Dare Devil*. Beside the number of stars, the game keeps track of various statistics for each player (e.g., number of tacklers built, number of correct answers given, mostly played level) which can be viewed before challenging another player. Figure 1 shows screenshots of the game from the single-player and the two-player mode.

5 Conclusion

This paper provided a short overview of the game design of *Metry Mouse Missions* and the theoretical foundations on which its design is based. Future work will need to determine the effectiveness of the game in reaching the learning objectives by conducting user studies with young learners.

References

1. Dillenbourg, P.: Over-scripting CSCL: the risks of blending collaborative learning with instructional design. Three worlds of CSCL. Can we support CSCL?, pp. 61–91 (2002)
2. Ketamo, H.: An adaptive geometry game for handheld devices. Educ. Technol. Soc. **6**(1), 83–95 (2003)
3. Kiili, K., Ketamo, H.: Exploring the learning mechanism in educational games. J. Comput. Inf. Technol. **15**(4), 319–324 (2007)
4. Kyndt, E., Raes, E., Lismont, B., Timmers, F., Cascallar, E., Dochy, F.: A meta-analysis of the effects of face-to-face cooperative learning. Do recent studies falsify or verify earlier findings? Educ. Res. Rev. **10**, 133–149 (2013)
5. Malone, T.W., Lepper, M.R.: Making learning fun: a taxonomy of intrinsic motivations for learning. Aptitude Learn. Instr. **3**(1987), 223–253 (1987)
6. Moreno, R., Mayer, R.E.: Techniques that increase generative processing in multimedia learning: open questions for cognitive load research. In: Plass, J.L., Moreno, R., Brünken, R. (eds.) Cognitive Load Theory, pp. 153–177. Cambridge University Press, New York (2010)
7. Perkins, D.N.: Person-plus: a distributed view of thinking and learning. Distributed Cognitions: Psychological and Educational Considerations, pp. 88–110 (1993)
8. Sedig, K.: From play to thoughtful learning: a design strategy to engage children with mathematical representations. J. Comput. Math. Sci. Teach. **27**(1), 65–101 (2008)
9. Wallner, G., Kriglstein, S.: Design and evaluation of the educational game DOGeometry: a case study. In: Proceedings of the 8th International Conference on Advances in Computer Entertainment Technology, ACE 2011, pp. 14:1–14:8. ACM (2011)
10. Wendel, V., Gutjahr, M., Göbel, S., Steinmetz, R.: Designing collaborative multiplayer serious games. Educ. Inf. Technol. **18**(2), 287–308 (2013)

Little Fitness Dragon: A Gamified Activity Tracker

Isabelle Kniestedt$^{(\boxtimes)}$ and Marcello A. Gómez Maureira

University of Malta, Msida MSD 2080, Malta
ikniestedt@gmail.com, ma.gomezmaureira@gmail.com
http://www.um.edu.mt/

Abstract. We propose the design of an activity game and virtual pet for smart-watches that combines casual game design principles, lessons from fitness trackers, and location-based features. Players take care of a newly hatched dragon that grows and changes depending on their activities, reflecting their general fitness in a playful and encouraging manner. Where most virtual companions are aimed at children, we designed this game with young adults in mind. An early PC prototype was tested by ten members of this target group to gauge interest and inform design iterations. The general design of the game and the virtual dragon were mentioned as strong points, while the emulation on the PC was considered not intuitive. Upcoming prototypes will be tested on smart-watches, with the ultimate goal of exploring the impact of connecting a virtual pet to the physical location of a player on engagement and activity levels.

Keywords: Applied gaming · Games for wearables · Activity tracking · Virtual pet

1 Introduction

In recent years wearable fitness trackers and smart-watches have become more widely used and increasingly sophisticated. No longer are users limited to simple step counters; with devices like the Pebble and Apple Watch we now see smart-phone functionality integrated with fashionable technology that fits unobtrusively on our wrists.

Our goal is to explore the novel interaction possibilities that smart-watches provide and how they may be used to improve people's lives. In that light we have begun development on *Little Fitness Dragon*, and activity game for mobile phones and smart-watches. By building on existing research and incorporating lessons from the casual game industry, we aim to develop an engaging wellness tracker that encourages its players to be active on a regular basis by combining a virtual pet with location-based game mechanics. The novelty of this game lies in grounding a virtual character in a player's physical surroundings, as well as utilizing modern wearables which so far remain underused, both for gaming purposes and in research relating to activity trackers.

© IFIP International Federation for Information Processing 2016
Published by Springer International Publishing AG 2016. All Rights Reserved
G. Wallner et al. (Eds.): ICEC 2016, LNCS 9926, pp. 205–210, 2016.
DOI: 10.1007/978-3-319-46100-7_18

This paper describes the preliminary design and conception of a PC prototype for the game. The prototype was tested with a small selection of participants, some of whom had game design experience. This was done purposefully to better inform the design of the game before moving forward with its development. We conclude this paper with our plans for future work and follow-up studies.

2   Related Work

Over the last decade researchers have studied both the successes and the limitations of wearable fitness devices. One documented project is *Fish'n'Steps* [7], which used a wearable pedometer and linked a user's daily step count to the growth and happiness of a virtual fish. The digital fish tank was displayed in a common area of the test participants' office space, and users were required to check in on a daily basis to log their activity. Out of 19 participants, several increased their daily step count over the testing period of six weeks. Another relevant example is UbiFit [3]. It aimed to encourage users to monitor their own activity and to implement varied activities into their lives on a daily basis. It did this through a glanceable display background on the user's mobile phone showing a garden, which would change depending on the level of activity and the variety of activities the user participated in that week. Users of the glanceable display were able to maintain their activity levels over a period of several months (which included holiday weeks), while that of test participants not using the display dropped significantly. While these projects showed positive results, commercial activity trackers often end up being abandoned by their users. Barriers to continued use are that the devices do not record all physical activity, are inaccurate, do not provide a social functionality, or that the devices themselves are ugly or impractical [5].

The *Tamagotchi* showed many years ago that users can grow attached to a digital creature or pet. Research has begun to explore this further, for instance with testing the use of virtual pets to influence changes in behavior. A study with 39 adolescents determined that those with a virtual pet providing positive and negative feedback on their breakfast habits were twice as likely to eat breakfast than those in the control group [1]. With the continued development of mobile devices, location-based games and apps have also become more common. *Gaea* [2] uses mobile phones and a public display in a location-based multiplayer mobile game that encourages the public to recycle. Another interesting case of using location-based game features for encouraging behavior can be seen in the overnight commercial success of *Pokemon Go*, which has players walking long distances in their quest to 'catch them all' [8].

3   The Design

Little Fitness Dragon (LFD) is a game for both smartphones and smart-watches. While it works as a self-standing application on mobile phones, it can use more accurate sensors when used in combination with a smart-watch (i.e. the heart

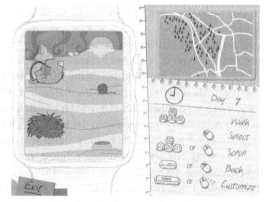

(a) Photograph of mock-up implementation.   (b) Screenshot of the prototype application.

Fig. 1. Target platform mock-up (left) and prototype screenshot (right)

rate monitor and step counter). It makes use of the GPS sensor in the mobile device to create a casual gaming experience that combines aspects of virtual pets, location based gaming, and activity tracking.

Its goal is to stimulate regular activity and it is aimed at young adults with a sedentary lifestyle who wish to increase their daily activity level. While much of the existing research, especially that related to virtual pets to stimulate lifestyle changes [1,6], has been focused on children, we argue that the use of virtual characters and 'cute' graphics can be just as effective in adults, as is illustrated by the wide appeal and success of casual games like *Peggle* and *Farmville*.

In LFD, players are tasked with taking care of a newborn dragon, which is always visible when the game is open (see Fig. 1a). The fully animated dragon keeps track of a player's activity (e.g. calories burned and step count), and will grow and change depending on the player's activity level. A player who moves the minimum recommended daily amount will have a calmer, more relaxed dragon, while a player who exercises a lot will have a more energetic dragon. A similar approach was used in Fish'n'Steps and showed that users were pleased to see their progress reflected in the growth of their virtual fish. The study discovered that negative feedback for underperformance could lead to feelings of guilt and reluctance to return to the application. By having the dragon's behavior change with the user's activity level we provide an abstract way for users to reflect on their performance without negative connotations. The dragon will always be excited to see its owner and encourage them to engage, lowering the barrier to return to the game when it has not been used in a while.

During walks the player may come across 'resource locations', where he or she can find ingredients to use in the game. These locations are generated by the game, following certain constraints (e.g. keeping a minimum distance between locations). They can vary in type (and therefore resources that may be found there), and are discovered by coming in close physical proximity of their GPS coordinates. One aspect of the game is a compass screen on which players can see both visited and unvisited resource locations in their surroundings. Whenever the player comes across a resource location, they will be prompted by their dragon for an interaction or mini-game. Mini-games are optional and not necessary to complete for those who simply wish to collect the resource. For these players they will have a simple interaction with the dragon, after which it will return to them with a resource its managed to hunt, depleting the location for that day. Locations can be revisited on a daily basis to collect more resources and enable players to replay the corresponding mini-game.

Resources can be used to cook and craft items for the dragon, e.g. toys and different nests. Each dragon has different preferences for food and items. Additionally, feeding the dragon different types of food allows players to gradually change its appearance, e.g. color, scales, horns, wings. The default view of the game shows the dragon's den, where the player can feed their dragon and place toys and other items for it to play with. Tapping the dragon shows a zoomed in view of what it is currently doing, e.g. eating, sleeping, or playing, as well as the progress towards the daily activity goals. Here the player can also interact with their dragon to which it will respond with different animations.

By developing for current day smart-watches we can overcome some of the barriers encountered in previous studies [5], such as inaccurate tracking or the need for additional tracking devices. Furthermore, the availability of a high-resolution display allows us to provide players with appealing graphics and positive reinforcement. During the development of this project we follow theory-based design principles for apps that track daily activity levels [4], for instance by making use of 'abstract' and 'reflective' data in showing the player's performance through changes in the dragon rather than numbers and statistics. We expect that basing the design of LFD on these principles will make it an encouraging activity companion, while the addition of location-based play creates a real-world connection to an otherwise virtual creature.

4   Player Experience

To test the viability of the design we created an initial prototype for PC systems using *GameMaker Studio* (see Fig. 1b). While this prototype could not be used to test the effectiveness of the game as an activity tracker (as it lacks the mobility necessary to collect meaningful data on the subject), we consider this as the first step in the development process. With this basic prototype we created a functional discussion point with other designers and were able to gauge initial user response to the game concept.

Care was taken to simulate the controls and mechanics of the intended design as intuitively as possible in a PC application, while giving a clear idea of the intended game play and aesthetics. A tutorial explained the game, while daily exercise was emulated by adding an avatar on a map screen that was controlled with the keyboard. A total of ten people played the game with ages ranging between 21 and 32, all with relatively high gaming literacy or a background in game development. Feedback was collected in open discussions with the testers, first allowing them to freely voice their initial impressions of the game and then asking more specific follow-up questions. With two of the testers, both working in game development, a more in-depth interview took place to ask about suggestions for the next stage of development.

All ten testers responded positively to the prototype, with the only negative comments referring to the PC controls not being intuitive. The combination of activity tracking with casual game play was mentioned as an interesting idea that testers could see themselves using in their lives. Testers specifically enjoyed the style and quality of the aesthetics, as well as the design of the dragon. Several concerns also came to light during the discussions. The user interface, in the prototype presented in 800 by 600 pixels resolution on a computer display, showed to potentially become too cluttered on a smaller display, especially that of a smartwatch. It also became clear that the initial plan of using resources for both cooking and crafting, and the large amount of available resources planned resulted in an overly complicated system. The compass also needed to be redesigned, as players were observed to not understand the representation of themselves and the resource locations.

It is possible that the high levels of gaming literacy of our participants influenced the receptiveness to the proposed game concept. This was a conscious decision, however, as at this stage it was deemed important to discuss potential issues in the game's design. We argue that game literate participants are better equipped to provide in-depth comments. They furthermore tend to be more critical, as they tend to spend a lot of time interacting with games and technology. Overall, we feel the prototype served its function as a discussion point for desired features and showed a positive interest in further development of the game.

5   Future Work

The next step is the creation of a second prototype for the target platform that has the basic functionality needed to test the game as an activity tracking tool. Based on the comments received during the initial test we will be making several changes to the design as well. One such change is that while we at first intended the game to be completely self-standing on smart-watches, it has become clear that the extra screen space offered by mobile phones will be needed to include all the features we envision. Core features will work independently from the phone on the smart-watch side, while some non-essential features will be available on the phone side and data is synced between the two. Additionally we will be streamlining the design of the resources and crafting mechanics, and focus on increasing interaction with and feedback from the dragon. We will also implement a reward mechanic that can take stationary activities (e.g. gym activities) into consideration for users who do not have a watch with a heart rate monitor.

The main limitation of the prototype is that it could not be used to test the validity of the design as a wearable activity tracker. We argue, however, that there is merit in testing games and applications before considering them for further study. Although we could not yet test the validity of the game as an activity tracker, we were able to gauge the interest in the design from our target audience. More importantly, it allowed us to identify issues and make design changes that would have been more costly at a later stage of the projects, or could have hampered our research further down the line. We argue that the use of early prototypes like these can improve the quality of both future research and the applications produced for it.

Our next study will focus on testing the efficacy of this second prototype. We will continue to involve users over the course of the development, although as we move forward we will also be including those less used to playing games. Later on we also see potential of using the game to explore the potential impact of connecting the physical environment to the virtual domain in regards to player engagement and activity levels, specifically compared to virtual companions that do not react to the player's physical environment.

References

1. Byrne, S., Gay, G., Pollack, J., Gonzales, A., Retelny, D., Lee, T., Wansink, B.: Caring for mobile phone-based virtual pets can influence youth eating behaviors. J. Child. Media **6**(1), 83–99 (2012)
2. Centieiro, P., Romão, T., Dias, A.E.: A location-based multiplayer mobile game to encourage pro-environmental behaviours. In: Proceedings of the 8th International Conference on Advances in Computer Entertainment Technology, p. 31. ACM (2011)
3. Consolvo, S., Klasnja, P., McDonald, D.W., Avrahami, D., Froehlich, J., LeGrand, L., Libby, R., Mosher, K., Landay, J.A.: Flowers or a robot army? encouraging awareness & activity with personal, mobile displays. In: Proceedings of the 10th International Conference on Ubiquitous Computing, pp. 54–63. ACM (2008)
4. Consolvo, S., McDonald, D.W., Landay, J.A.: Theory-driven design strategies for technologies that support behavior change in everyday life. In: Proceedings of the SIGCHI Conference on Human Factors in Computing Systems, pp. 405–414. ACM (2009)
5. Harrison, D., Marshall, P., Bianchi-Berthouze, N., Bird, J.: Activity tracking: barriers, workarounds and customisation. In: Proceedings of the 2015 ACM International Joint Conference on Pervasive and Ubiquitous Computing, pp. 617–621. ACM (2015)
6. Hswen, Y., Murti, V., Vormawor, A.A., Bhattacharjee, R., Naslund, J.A.: Virtual avatars, gaming, and social media: designing a mobile health app to help children choose healthier food options. J. Mob. Technol. Med. **2**(2), 8 (2013)
7. Lin, J.J., Mamykina, L., Lindtner, S., Delajoux, G., Strub, H.B.: Fish'n'Steps: encouraging physical activity with an interactive computer game. In: Dourish, P., Friday, A. (eds.) UbiComp 2006. LNCS, vol. 4206, pp. 261–278. Springer, Heidelberg (2006)
8. Novak, M.: Sore legs become pandemic as Pokemon Go players accidentally get exercise. http://gizmodo.com/sore-legs-become-pandemic-as-pokemon-go-players-acciden-1783402931. Accessed 20 July 2016

Promoting Stretching Activity with Smartwatch - A Pilot Study

SinJae Lee[1,2], SangBin Kim[2], and JungHyun Han[2(✉)]

[1] Samsung Electronics Co. Ltd., Suwon, Korea
[2] Korea University, Seoul, Korea
jhan@korea.ac.kr

Abstract. It has been claimed that wearable devices are useful for healthcare applications by providing functionalities such as idle alerts, pedometer, heart-rate measurement, and calorie calculation. However, these functionalities have the limitations of providing only passive assistance. In order to prompt users to do physical activities, we developed a prototype application for active assistance, which works on smartwatch devices. It guides users to stretch their arms periodically during their daily lives. For effective guidance, we integrated motion recognition and gamification elements. We performed a user study to confirm the usefulness of our approach.

Keywords: Smartwatch · Physical activity · Stretching · Motion recognition · Hidden Markov Model · Gamification

1 Introduction

In recent years, the field of wearable technology has grown rapidly especially for wrist-worn devices such as smartbands and smartwatches. Since the devices are integrated with not only high-performance CPU and GPU but also accurate micro-electromechanical system (MEMS) sensors, it is possible to implement various services on user's wrist, which include idle alerts, pedometers, exercise recording/management, and calorie monitoring, claiming to assist in healthcare.

The medical community has reported that sedentary work over many hours can be very harmful to health [1,6]. It is generally recommended that workers do not remain in the same posture for long periods at the workplace [2,7], and the public have thus taken an interest in wearable devices that can help in this context. Such devices often adopt an idle alert function to tell users to move or change their posture. However, we believe it is difficult for these functionalities to effectively encourage physical activities. We call them *passive assistance*. In this paper, we propose an *active assistance* functionality that can effectively prompt the users physical activities.

Promoting physical activities has mainly been studied from the perspective of games [3,5,8]. However, game activities have their own limitation that people

© IFIP International Federation for Information Processing 2016
Published by Springer International Publishing AG 2016. All Rights Reserved
G. Wallner et al. (Eds.): ICEC 2016, LNCS 9926, pp. 211–216, 2016.
DOI: 10.1007/978-3-319-46100-7_19

are made to get fully devoted to them in a certain place and for a certain period of time. Our approach presented in this paper aims at promoting physical activities using wearable devices in daily environments.

We have developed a prototype application based on smartwatches. It prompts physical activity by informing the users that it is time to stretch, guiding and evaluating their motion, and providing feedbacks. Additionally, gamification elements are added to further motivate the users' activities. Our approach is the first study to prompt physical activity and evaluate it using a wearable standalone device.

2   Active-Assistance Operations

The objective of our work is to investigate whether it is possible to effectively prompt physical activities by promoting arm stretching with the assistance of a wrist-worn smartwatch (Fig. 1-(a)).

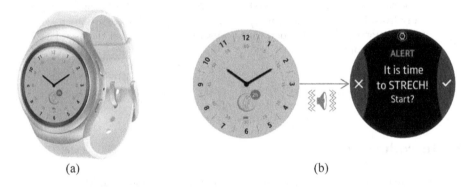

(a)   (b)

Fig. 1. A smartwatch and its interface. (a) Smartwatch. (b) The watchface mode reminds the user of stretch.

In the smartwatch, the watchface mode provides *reminder* when the user has not stretched for a certain period of time. See Fig. 1-(b). In this study, the watchface mode is set to provide reminders between 10 am and 6 pm, when the user is assumed to be working at his or her chair. The stretching reminder is set off one hour after the last stretching time. The user can perform arm stretching according to the application's direction or turn down the reminder message. The reminder time is then updated to one hour later.

Figure 2 shows the arm-stretching flow guided by the application. If the user accepts the reminder message, stretching guide is provided, as illustrated in Fig. 2-(a). The first layer of the guide provides character images together with simple text whereas detailed text is given in the second layer that can be accessed by scrolling. The way to stretch is explained with spreading/shrinking wave animation of circles, as shown in Fig. 2-(b) and -(d). At the peak state of

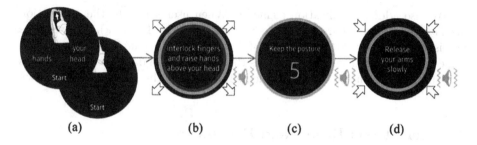

Fig. 2. User interface for arm-stretching flow.

stretching, the user is supposed to retain the stretched posture for five seconds. Figure 2-(c) shows the five-second countdown animation. Haptic feedback is provided at the start and end times so that the user does not need to take a look at the display during stretching.

3   Evaluation and Feedback

The user's stretching motion can be represented by sequential time series data. We used a Hidden Markov Model (HMM) algorithm [4], which processes sequential data in real time on embedded systems. We acquired the accelerometer data at 100 Hz and used a Kalman filter to compensate for the noise in the raw sensory data. The observation vector, containing acceleration and some processed data, was evaluated in real time during the stretching action. When the users action was done, we compared the probability given by the motion recognition algorithm with the proper threshold to determine whether the user succeeded or failed. For this purpose, we need off-line pre-training stage and per-person training stage. Ten volunteers were involved in the pre-training stage. Each volunteer provided ten motions for the vertical stretch. We assume that the arm movement is symmetric and can safely rely on the data from a single sensor on one wrist.

Fig. 3. Gamification elements. (a) For the success case, the progress bar is displayed at the boundary area. (b) The fail case. (c) Daily goal achievement.

We also added gamification elements. When user succeeds, the application displays the progress bar for the pre-set daily goal. See Fig. 3-(a). The progress bar is increased by 20 % per successful stretching motion. When the goal is achieved, the application congratulates the completion of daily goal and displays a virtual reward. In the current implementation, it is the gold medal, as shown in Fig. 3-(c).

4   User Study: Result and Discussion

We conducted an experiment to assess our approach of providing stretch reminders, guiding the motion, and evaluating the user's motion. The smartwatch used in the experiment is Samsung Gear S2[1] with Tizen OS (wearable profile version 2.3.1). The prototype application is implemented in C++ for the native environment[2]. Before and after the experiment, participants were asked to fill in questionnaires. We informed the participants that the acquired data would only be used for the present study.

4.1   Procedure

We recruited 17 participants (15 males and 2 females) aged 23 through 41 (with M 29.875 and SD 4.177). They included graduate students, engineers, and office workers. The participants were paid $10 for their involvement. Nine out of them had experiences in healthcare services based on mobile or wearable devices.

We first conducted an initial survey before the experiment. Then, after being instructed in the usage of the application, the participants performed a training for stretching activity in order to enhance the motion recognition rate. The experiment lasted three days, during which the participants wore the device and continued their normal daily activities. The application recorded the log data during the experiment, e.g., how many times stretching was done, whether the user failed or succeeded, etc. After the experiment, we extracted the log data from the device and asked the participants to fill in the final questionnaire.

4.2   Questionnaire and Result

The initial questionnaire asked participants how much time they typically spend doing sedentary work and how frequently they do stretching per day. The participants do approximately 8.5 hours of sedentary work and stretch on average 1.84 times per day.

We analyzed the recorded log data. For three days of experiment, the participants received on average 7.147 reminder messages per day, of which 64 % were accepted. On average, they attempted 18.201 stretches per day. In the three-day experiment, the goal (at least five intermittent stretching motions) was achieved for two days on average. See *Data analysis* part of Table 1.

---

[1] http://www.samsung.com/global/galaxy/gear-s2/.

[2] https://developer.tizen.org/development/api-tutorials/native-application.

The result of the final questionnaire is shown in *Questionnaire analysis* part of Table 1: (1) The "effectiveness of stretching" is meant to measure the personal perception on how much the muscles seem to be relaxed as a result of stretching; (2) With respect to the "effect of gamification," the participants were asked how much they were motivated by the reward, i.e., gold medal for achieving daily goal; (3) The final question asked the participants whether, if given a chance, they intend to use same application in the future.

Table 1. Results of the experiment. The values of the *Questionnaire analysis* show 5-point Likert-scale from 1 (low) to 5 (high)

Data analysis	M	SD
Number of reminders per day	7.147	2.398
Number of stretches per day	18.201	7.968
Number of daily goal achievement	2.000	1.110
Questionnaire analysis	M	SD
Effectiveness of stretching	4.000	0.791
Effect of gamification	3.059	0.899
Intention to reuse	4.471	0.514

4.3 Discussion

In general, we received positive responses from the participants. According to the results, the participants performed stretches as much as 18 times per day. Recall that, in the initial survey, they answered that they stretched on average 1.84 times over 8 hours. They also appraised highly the effectiveness of the stretch-promoting system and most of them wished to use this kind of application again.

The gamification element was expected to motivate the user to perform stretching more actively, but the score on "effect of gamification" (M 3.059 and SD 0.899) does not lead to the conclusion. It can be analyzed from two perspectives. First of all, adding gamification elements might not be effective for prompting physical activities, as claimed by [9]. Secondly, the reward in the current prototype system, the gold medal, is too simple to be assessed. When the prototype application is extended into a pervasive game, a more elaborate rewarding system could be added and evaluated more formally.

5 Conclusion

We have presented an attractive approach to encourage user's physical activity by using smartwatch-based prototype application. During the experiment, participants wore a smartwatch which reminds stretching time periodically.

The experimental results show that participants were made to conduct more stretching activity and provided positive feedback for our approach although the static time-based reminder might be able to annoy them when they do not want to stretch.

We concluded that it is possible to encourage user's physical activity with an active assistance manner for people wearing smart wearable devices. We are currently extending the system and also designing more elaborate experiments.

Acknowledgement. This work was supported by Institute for Information & Communications Technology Promotion (IITP) grant funded by the Korea government (MSIP) (No. R0115-15-1011) and the National Research Foundation of Korea (NRF) grant funded by the Korea government (MSIP) (No. NRF-2016R1A2B3014319).

References

1. AOA: Standing Up for Your Health. http://www.osteopathic.org/osteopathic-health/about-your-health/health-conditions-library/general-health/Pages/sedentary-lifestyle.aspx
2. COMCARE: Sedentary Work (2016). https://www.comcare.gov.au/preventing/hazards/physical_hazards/sedentary_work
3. Consolvo, S., Klasnja, P., McDonald, D.W., Landay, J.A.: Goal-setting considerations for persuasive technologies that encourage physical activity. In: Proceedings of the 4th International Conference on Persuasive Technology, p. 8. ACM (2009)
4. Françoise, J., Schnell, N., Bevilacqua, F.: A multimodal probabilistic model for gesture-based control of sound synthesis. In: Proceedings of the 21st ACM International Conference on Multimedia, pp. 705–708. ACM (2013)
5. Marshall, S.J., Norman, G.: Using wireless technology to promote exercise and fitness. Lecture Notes on Wireless Healthcare Research, p. 77
6. Owen, N., Healy, G.N., Matthews, C.E., Dunstan, D.W.: Too much sitting: the population-health science of sedentary behavior. Exerc. Sport Sci. Rev. **38**(3), 105 (2010)
7. Pronk, N.P.: Reducing occupational sitting time and improving worker health: the take-a-stand project, 2011. Preventing Chronic Dis. **9**, E154 (2012)
8. Tabak, M., Dekker-van Weering, M., van Dijk, H., Vollenbroek-Hutten, M.: Promoting daily physical activity by means of mobile gaming: a review of the state of the art. Games Health J. **4**(6), 460–469 (2015)
9. Zuckerman, O., Gal-Oz, A.: Deconstructing gamification: evaluating the effectiveness of continuous measurement, virtual rewards, and social comparison for promoting physical activity. Pers. Ubiquit. Comput. **18**(7), 1705–1719 (2014)

Evaluation and Redesign of a Curriculum Framework for Education About Game Accessibility

Thomas Westin[1(✉)] and Jerome Dupire[2]

[1] Department of Computer and Systems Science, Stockholm University, Kista, Sweden
thomasw@dsv.su.se
[2] CNAM/CEDRIC, 292, rue St Martin, 75003 Paris, France
dupire@cnam.fr

Abstract. Game Accessibility (GA) has been brought to the front of the video game landscape thanks to a recent but major change in the US law called the Communications and Video Accessibility Act; GA is now a legal obligation for game developers in the US. However, there is a gap between legislation and practice of GA. This study is based upon a previous tentative curriculum framework (TCF) for GA. The questions are: What are the opinions among educators and game developers regarding the TCF? How could the TCF be redesigned? To answer the questions, the TCF was surveyed with practitioners and researchers in the GA community. This paper presents an evaluation and redesign of the TCF, divided into different categories, depending on the students' profiles, scopes and skills. Furthermore, how the curriculum content can be created and shared is also discussed, as well as future work.

Keywords: Game Accessibility · Game education · Curriculum Framework

1 Introduction

Game accessibility (GA) has been researched since the dawn of the computer and video game industry and there is a significant amount of publications, see e.g. [1, 2]. However, only a limited number of titles from the mainstream game industry offer even basic accessibility features. In the USA, the Communications and Video Accessibility Act (CVAA) [3] is about to change this situation: game consoles and distribution platforms now have to be accessible and, from January 2017, game software also has to be accessible. As USA is one of the largest markets for games in the world, the CVAA have already had international impact; two of the major game consoles were patched with accessibility features for the first time in 2015.

However, if these legal provisions are genuine progress and recognition, there is still a gap between the aims and the means. Indeed, game accessibility is still not an identified part of the video game curriculum around the world and students are often not aware of game accessibility at all. This study is a follow-up on a tentative curriculum framework (TCF) [4], defined as a "modular structure that support creating and sharing educational resources, as well as teaching and learning about game

© IFIP International Federation for Information Processing 2016
Published by Springer International Publishing AG 2016. All Rights Reserved
G. Wallner et al. (Eds.): ICEC 2016, LNCS 9926, pp. 217–222, 2016.
DOI: 10.1007/978-3-319-46100-7_20

accessibility" [4]. In the framework learning outcomes were related to three outcome requirement levels: (1) Introduced (I) outcomes are not examined, i.e. the outcome does not have to be part of an assignment but could be included in some lecture or reading material; (2) Transitional (T) outcomes may be examined, optional by the course designer, where the student may have to show that s/he has acquired knowledge, skills and/or attitudes; and (3) Emphasized (E) outcomes have to be examined, required to pass the course; the examination is focused on the complex integration of knowledge, skills and attitudes regarding the learning outcome. The requirement levels were adapted from [5]. As the TCF was an interpretation of results in the first study, the research questions in this follow-up study are: What are the opinions among educators and game developers regarding the TCF? How could the TCF be redesigned?

2   Method

An online survey based on the tentative curriculum framework [4] was sent for evaluation to (1) twenty-three persons who answered the survey in the first study [4] and agreed to participate in this follow-up study; (2) fifteen participants at the IGDA Game Accessibility SIG Roundtable at Game Developers Conference 2016; and (3) two others who had actively asked to be included. In total, the survey in this paper was sent to forty people, of which one e-mail address bounced, and sixteen persons responded within two weeks' time. The survey[1] was mainly composed of closed questions to minimize time required to fill it in. People were asked to say if they agreed, disagreed or did not know, about each learning outcome and the relation to requirement levels (I, T, E) in the curriculum framework. The questions were repeated for each category (designer basic, engineer basic, and advanced levels). Open questions allowed them to share any comment about their choices for each category, as well as a final generic question about the study. In contrast to the first study, this follow-up study required each respondent to fill in their name and e-mail, in case we needed some further clarification of their answers. This may have affected the number of responses.

3   Results and Analysis

First, some interesting suggestions appeared in the open text fields, such as inviting impaired people during a course in order to see and understand what their real situation is regarding video games and/or the environment. Another respondent reflected upon the implications of doing this in practice *"because of logistical complexity"*. Still, a suggestion could be to try and perform some participatory design at least once during a curriculum.

---

[1] https://goo.gl/r514LU.

3.1   Basic Level for Designers

Most respondents (13 of 16) considered history important for designers. All (16 of 16) agreed that introduction of scope of issues, a transitional outcome of know-how of solutions, and emphasis on basic concepts and needs of disabled was adequate. Interestingly, one respondent disagreed to put emphasis on design methods for designers, while the others (15/16) agreed. Only 6/16 agreed that introduction of funding was important and 11/16 agreed that legislation was important. Almost all (15/16) agreed that experience of disability was important.

The quantitative data were confirmed by quotes from the open questions. For instance, scope of the issues but also experience of disabilities were clearly supported: *"The key at a basic level is to emphasize the issue, to make it personal"*. Also, the disagreement but also uncertainty (don't know) regarding funding was clearly expressed: *"To be aware of the cost of providing accessibility is more relevant in my opinion"*. Furthermore, regarding legislation and funding: *"Areas around legalisation & funding are very country dependent. Games are multi-national. The issues are multi-national."*. Funding was included in the survey due to the commercial nature of computer games, and legislation was motivated by international impact of the CVAA. Another reply reflects on the process of learning from basic to advanced levels: *"Awareness of legislation and funding are important, but seem like they might work better as material that is covered toward the end of the curriculum"*. Finally, a comment regarding history of game accessibility: *"History is important, but maybe provided anecdotally throughout. Perhaps it could be emphasized alongside legislation and funding"*. A suggestion may be to merge these learning outcomes with related topics.

3.2   Basic Level for Engineers

Two learning outcomes were agreed by the same number of respondents as for designers: issues (16/16) and funding (6/16). Six learning outcomes had similar numbers of agreements as for designers: legislation (12/15), experience (14/16), know-how (15/16), basic concepts (14/16), needs (13/16), and design methods (13/16). Interestingly, more respondents agreed that history was important for designers (13/16) than for engineers (9/16). This may be better understood based on this comment: *"Proper execution of the design is important, so knowing what the issues are and also the proper solutions seem to be the most important."*. One respondent suggested that if engineers know the issues and follow the design by designers who are aware of e.g. history, it may be enough. However, this may also be viewed as too focused on utility alone.

3.3   Advanced Level for Designers and Engineers

The advanced level contains two less learning outcomes than the basic level; the items basic concepts and needs of disabled are supposed to be part of the basic level courses and thus, do not appear here. Most of the respondents agreed about the relevance of all seven learning outcomes. However, one respondent said: *"Legalisation & Funding is a non-issue for design & engineer"*. Still, while legislation is only formally relevant in countries with legislation for game accessibility, funding is needed for all professional game developers. Furthermore, for smaller, independent developer teams, there may not be a specific in-house person to manage legislative issues, which may make this relevant for both engineers and designers at the advanced level. It would be interesting to discuss these particular learning outcomes more with professionals in the game industry.

4 Discussion

The framework builds upon eight components in the UNESCO toolkit of curriculum design [6]. The framework focuses on three of these as explained in [4], represented by Sects. 4.1–4.3 below.

4.1 Broad Learning Objectives and Outcomes

The main goal of the framework is to raise awareness about game accessibility among both professional and aspiring game developers. Based on the UNESCO toolkit [6] overall objectives and outcomes are knowledge, understanding, skills, values and attitudes. These are represented by the names of learning outcomes in Table 1, either directly (e.g. 'know the scope', 'understand basic concepts') or indirectly (e.g. 'know-how', 'able to apply', which implies skills). To change values and attitudes may require longer time and should thus be an integral part of all learning outcomes. Still, to gain experience of disabilities through various forms of simulations and participatory design may have a more direct relationship to changing values and attitudes.

Table 1. Redesigned curriculum framework. Modifications marked in *italic text*.

Learning outcomes – in arbitrary order	Basic level – for designers	Basic level – for engineers	Advanced level – for all
1. Understand basic concepts	E	E	$(E)^a$
2. *Know the needs of disabled*[b]	E	E	$(E)^a$
3. Able to apply design methods	E	T	$(E)^c$
4. *Know the scope of issues*[d]	I	I	E
5. Experience of disabilities	I	I	T
6. Know-how of solutions	T	E	$(E)^c$

[a]Include only in advanced level if there is no prerequisite basic level course
[b]May also include game accessibility history and legislation where applicable
[c]Include only if it has not been emphasized at the basic level
[d]May also include awareness of funding and economic issues for both developers and gamers

4.2 Structure of the Curriculum Content, Learning Areas and Subjects

According to UNESCO [6] the framework should describe the structure of content, as well as the subject or learning areas. A brief description of each learning area, presented as outcomes in Table 1 is: (1) Basic concepts are e.g. disability, accessibility and universal design; (2) Needs of disabled are grounded in research involving people with disabilities; (3) Design methods describe how games can be made more accessible; (4) The scope describe the relevance of issues; (5) Experience of disabilities aims to change values and attitudes by gaining empathy through e.g. simulating disabilities; (6) Know-how of solutions is how to practically implement game accessibility. Given the varied opinions about history, funding and legislation, those are now integrated as optional parts of needs and scopes outcomes (Table 1). One option is to cover these subjects as side literature or further readings, another is to have them part of the curriculum with examination, based upon the goals of a specific course. If there is no basic level course, then concepts and needs should also be included in the advanced level, which is why E is marked with a parenthesis: (E).

For instance, a game designer who wants to learn the basics and validate the competence must only learn basic concepts, needs of disabled and be able to apply design methods. An engineer can do the same but switch design methods with know-how of solutions. The advanced level is the most flexible. Any advanced student, who has passed a basic level course, can ignore the basic concepts and needs of disabled. Furthermore, an advanced game designer who has taken the basic level course must only learn the scope of issues and know-how of solutions. An advanced engineer who has taken the basic level course needs learn the scope of issues, but also design methods. This enables an advanced level student to fill the gap between basic level designers and engineers as they have insights into both design methods and implementation of designs (or solutions).

It is important that the framework is modular, to be flexible and applicable for both students and autodidacts working in the game industry. The redesigned framework (Table 1) does not say in which order the various learning outcomes should be addressed at each level. It does have a progression from basic to advanced levels regarding the three outcome requirement levels (introduced, transitional, and emphasized). However, the learner could take an advanced level course without having to take the basic level course, although the course will then naturally be harder and take longer time. Furthermore, to learn the basics, the introductory and transitional level outcome requirements could also be ignored, as those are not (required to be) examined.

4.3 Standards of Resources Required for Implementation

As the curriculum framework aims to provide a structure for sharing and creating Open Educational Resources (OERs), there must be proper acknowledgement and use of the content. Furthermore, all the content must be easy to find based upon user profile, e.g. designers / engineers / advanced, teacher / student qualifications etc. The resources have also to be accessible according to W3C presentation [7] and web content [8] accessibility guidelines. The community of educators must agree upon which standards to use and to what extent, in collaboration with disabled. All formats of OERs must be editable and have support for accessibility, as far as possible. To implement the framework a number of Open Educational Resources (OERs) have to be developed by the community of educators in games. An important part is to map out the types of resources which look to be the more suitable and/or usable, regarding the different learning outcomes. Matching between each learning outcome and the most relevant or usable types of resources is also necessary.

5   Conclusions and Future Work

Based upon the opinions of respondents, we have confirmed the design of the tentative curriculum framework presented in [4] with some modifications (Table 1). To put the redesigned framework into practice, various existing and future resources can be mapped to learning outcomes, as discussed in Sect. 4.3. Future work is to investigate what formats and licenses to use for OERs that can be accepted by all educators, be most useful for game developers and students, and be as accessible as possible. We will build different use cases in an online deposit and design the corresponding interfaces and architecture, before evaluating their usability and efficiency. This needs to be done in collaboration with both game industry, academia and disability organizations.

References

1. Yuan, B., Folmer, E., Harris, F.: Game accessibility: a survey. Univ. Access Inf. Soc. **10**, 81–100 (2011)
2. Westin, T., Bierre, K., Gramenos, D., Hinn, M.: Advances in game accessibility from 2005 to 2010. In: Stephanidis, C. (ed.) Universal Access in HCI, Part II, HCII 2011. LNCS, vol. 6766, pp. 400–409. Springer, Heidelberg (2011)
3. FCC: FCC extends ACS waiver for video game software (n.d.,). https://www.fcc.gov/document/fcc-extends-acs-waiver-video-game-software. Accessed 04 Jan 2016
4. Westin, T., Dupire, J.: Design of a curriculum framework for raising awareness of game accessibility. In: Miesenberger, K., Bühler, C., Penaz, P. (eds.) ICCHP 2016. LNCS, vol. 9758, pp. 501–508. Springer, Heidelberg (2016). doi:10.1007/978-3-319-41264-1_68
5. Maki, P.L.: Assessing For Learning: Buidling A Sustainable Commitment Across The Institution, 2nd edn. Stylus Publishing, Sterling (2010)
6. UNESCO: Curriculum Design. Activity 1: The structure of a curriculum framework (n.d.,). http://www.ibe.unesco.org/fileadmin/user_upload/COPs/Pages_documents/Resource_Packs/TTCD/sitemap/Module_3/Module_3_1_concept.html. Accessed 10 Jan 2016
7. W3C: W3C Presentation guidelines (n.d.,). http://www.w3.org/WAI/training/accessible. Accessed 02 Sep 2015
8. W3C: Web Content Accessibility Guidelines (WCAG) Overview (n.d.,). https://www.w3.org/WAI/intro/wcag. Accessed 04 May 2016

Mindtraining: Playful Interaction Techniques for People with Dementia

Elisabeth Hackner and Michael Lankes$^{(\boxtimes)}$

Department of Digital Media, University of Applied Sciences Upper Austria,
Softwarepark 11, 4232 Hagenberg, Austria
elisabeth.hackner@students.fh-hagenberg.at, michael.lankes@fh-hagenberg.at

Abstract. The paper presents the preliminary studies regarding applicable interaction techniques in the field of tablet games for dementia. Serious games in the dementia context are a well-researched topic. However, there is very little knowledge about performing gestures and interactions on tablet computers by users suffering from dementia. Since they already encounter many restrictions, a touch interface might be another obstacle. Tablet games often require a different kind of interaction, such as single tap, swipe, or drag and drop. We developed the Android application *Mindtraining* for dementia patients, which integrates multiple interaction techniques. The purpose of the tablet game is to facilitate an intuitive and efficient usage of gestures for people with early- and middle-stage dementia aged over 65 years. In our study we will investigate how people with dementia perform different gestures and how much help they need each time they use the application.

Keywords: Serious games · Dementia · Alzheimer's disease · Tablet interaction · Cognitive impairment · Tablet activation

1 Introduction

The number of people with dementia, especially Alzheimer's disease (AD), is increasing and no cure has yet been found [6]. In addition to medicine-based therapies, also non-medicine-based therapies exist to slow down the progress of the disease. Current studies present a meaningful integration of tablet computers, such as iPads, into the therapy context with the aim of benefiting cognitive abilities or acting as trigger for the patient [2,8]. Particularly mobile games show great potential to stimulate dementia patients [1,4]. An advantage of mobile technology is that the hardware is affordable and easy to handle as no external input control (such as a mouse or a keyboard) is needed. Studies often choose children games and educational games for evaluation in the dementia context [1,2]. Although these types of games seem to be easy to use, they still often require too complex interactions or result in a cognitive overload for people with dementia. A major problem is that most technologies are not designed for people with cognitive disabilities and therefore making operating the device very hard to use.

G. Wallner et al. (Eds.): ICEC 2016, LNCS 9926, pp. 223–228, 2016.
DOI: 10.1007/978-3-319-46100-7_21

Many dementia patients, especially people over an age of 65 years, also suffer from visual and/or hearing impairment due to their advanced age. However, mobile applications integrate assistive technologies very infrequently. These applications need to fulfill special requirements to ease the usage for people who are cognitively impaired. Basically, designing for dementia patients means moving back in time and thinking of events that happened in the past of one individual and the respective generation [1]. Metaphors, which are frequently used in mobile applications, have to tie in with the level of knowledge, the experiences and the cultural background of earlier years. Required gestures for touch displays have to be simple or alternatively be explained in a tutorial-like style. As dementia patients tend to have almost no short-term memory, they might need a tutorial with every time they use the application.

In this paper, we present preliminary findings of interaction techniques in the tablet game *Mindtraining* in terms of ease of use and how good dementia patients are able to remember different kinds of gestures. The application serves as an interactive playful photo album, which shows various content on each page and integrates multiple different gestures, such as tap, drag and drop, and swipe. As there seems to be an absence of best-practice approaches for interaction techniques on tablet devices we focus on a mixture of gestures in our application. Intuitive interaction techniques could support a more independent usage of applications on tablets. Caretakers would benefit from this, as they cannot afford the time to provide technical support and training for every single patient. Already a small amount of additional workload for nurses can be an obstacle for using a beneficial serious game in a nursing home.

2 Related Work

A dementia disease can affect multiple cognitive abilities, such as memory, attention, language, reasoning, judgment, reading, and writing [9]. Recent research shows that video games with cognitive content have the potential of delaying the cognitive decline [1]. But only a few games were created for the target group dementia patients in mind, addressing their specific health restrictions.

In a research project, a mobile app was developed that offered personalized music based on the patient's life, with a special focus on usability [7]. Music and photos also played an important role in a pilot study, where tablets were used in dementia therapy for over three months [1]. In this study, they proposed listening and singing to music or watching photos (animals, patients themselves, family, children, babies, etc.) and videos as initiating and ending practice in therapy. This inspires communication and affects the patient's mood in a positive way. In the same study they mentioned that the caretaker had to give continuous positive feedback, especially at the end of the tablet therapy to motivate and encourage the patient. Games, which integrate continuous positive feedback and encouragement, would relieve the caretaker [1].

Software, especially games, for dementia is a well researched area and there are many recommendations available for developing dementia games [5,8]. However, there seems to be a lack of guidelines for interaction techniques - especially regarding touch interfaces. Senior people might not have any prior knowledge of operating touch devices. Hence, performing different gestures in an application might be already too complex for people with dementia. The developed prototypes in past research projects integrate different interaction techniques, either input with mouse and keyboard, WiiMote controller, touch or ecological gestures. In conclusion, all researchers of the prototypes tried to find a simple and natural way to interact with the respective system to reduce the cognitive overload for people with dementia. Either touch interaction or ecological gestures seemed to be the most successful interaction paradigms. These do not require any external controller, such as a mouse or keyboard. In a study with mobile games and elderly people, the participants reported that it is much easier to touch the objects on the screen than using a mouse [10]. Learning how to interact with a software system is a complex task, in particular for users, who never used computer systems before. Yet, studies have shown that elderly people with dementia are willing to learn new technologies [3,11]. In another study with dementia patients, half of the participants had never used a mobile device before. However, all of them indicated that they would like to see more technology and believed they could benefit from it [4]. Moreover tablets cover many positive features like high-quality responsiveness multi-touch screen, mobility, accessibility and ease of aquition [8].

3   Game Prototype Mindtraining

Based on related work, we established the requirements for *Mindtraining* and extended the application with different interaction techniques. The requirements include: (1) providing visual and auditory help; (2) matching the mental model with the conceptional model; (3) giving motivational messages and positive feedback when achieving a goal or making a mistake; (4) providing short and simple messages; and (5) counteracting the declining cognitive abilities of the persona [1,3,5]. *Mindtraining* is an interactive photo album with a playful integration of cognitive games. A photo album is an item, which is also known from the earlier years of nowadays dementia patients, hence it should present a good mental model for the players. Visual aids, especially photos, can stimulate the memories and are therefore a proofed concept in dementia therapy [1]. Playing the game requires different gestures and interaction techniques. In the album you have to swipe through the pages, tap on photos to see them in full screen and use tap for turning on and off a music radio. The radio plays songs of the earlier years of the patients and should serve as alternate stimulation of the user. Also a cognitive game with completing of sayings is implemented on multiple pages with two different scenarios: (1) tapping on the right answer, (2) dragging the right answer to a target location. Wordplays, including sayings, are widely used in mind training therapies for dementia patients to exercise their mind.

The system is complemented with a logging module which tracks the interaction of the user and logs the data in JSON format to files on the device. The module logs single tap, double tap, long press, swipe from left to right and vice versa, swipe from top to bottom and vice versa and dragging interactions of drag-gable elements. The logging is applied to the following view types of Android: `TextView`, `Image`, `Button`, `ImageView` and `ImageButton`.

Our objective is to investigate how people with dementia cope with different gestures in a mobile playful application. On the one hand it is interesting how good people can remember gestures and how intuitive they are. On the other hand we want to find out if one of the gestures might be easier to perform than another one and give recommendations of applying gestures in a mobile application.

4   Preliminary Study

The application was tested by eight participants, see Fig. 1 (age: 56–90, gender: 3 male, 5 female). Three of the participants have early-stage dementia, one has middle-stage dementia, the others don't have dementia. The results of these tests were used to optimize the application and eradicate remaining usability problems of *Mindtraining*. The device used is a 10.1" sized ASUS MeMO Pad 10 Android tablet. A protection case covers the back of the device, which firstly gives additional grip and secondly provides a stable base to position it on a table in the right angle.

Fig. 1. Typical setting of the field tests: Subject playing the game, a carer sitting next to her and supporting her when questions arise and the observer in the background, taking notes.

In total, four main iterations, each included planning, implementing, testing and evaluation, took place. Besides adapting sizes for fonts and graphics, two important issues were optimized during these iterations. At first people were instructed which gestures had to be performed, such as tapping on a photo or swiping for flipping a page. When it came to dementia patients, switching between the different gestures caused problems. As they had learned that swiping from right to left resulted in the intended outcome, they also tried swiping on photos and buttons. To solve the cognitive overload of switching between different gestures, simple animations for tapping and swiping were implemented at the desired positions to provide a visual instruction how to perform the gesture on the element. This optimization showed that dementia patients needed fewer instructions from the caretaker on how to interact with the different elements.

The second main usability problem, which had been observed, is that a single tap is often difficult to perform by elderly people including dementia patients. The main issues are sideslipping of the finger and the duration of the tap. Also the user sometimes touches the screen with the fingernails, which has no effect on a capacitive display. With Android's standard functionality of clickable elements the action is only executed when performing a single tap on the element. To solve this issue we extended Android's standard functionality for clickable elements in a way that these elements also react to gestures, such as swipe, double tap and long press. The logging module tracks, which gesture has been performed on an element. This will allow an analysis of the usage of gestures afterwards. Due to the single tap problem, the scenario with dragging the right answer to a target location in the sayings game, could be performed much faster and more fluently than single tapping on the right answer.

As next step, a field test with three participants with early-stage dementia with 75–90 years in age, will be conducted to observe the interactions. The test will take place in a small day-care facility where dementia patients get cared for three times a week. To examine which gestures on a tablet device are best suited for this target group, we integrated an automatic logging module in the final prototype. The logging module tracks how a user interacts with visible elements on the screen. Additional to the logging module, an observation protocol will serve as a documentation of qualitative data during the field test.

5   Conclusion and Future Work

In this paper we presented the purpose of serious games in the dementia context and introduced *Mindtraining*, an Android application that facilitates an intuitive usage of gestures. Software design guidelines for people with dementia are a common topic in research, but there seems to be a lack of recommendations when it comes to touch devices and their interaction techniques. In our application we are tracking and observing the user's interaction with the tablet to find out which gestures can be performed better than others. The next step will be conducting a field test with dementia patients and analysing the used interactions in the application *Mindtraining*.

References

1. Aktivierung von Menschen mit Demenz im Pflegeheim. ZQP-Studie (2014)
2. McCallum, S., Boletsis, C.: A taxonomy of serious games for dementia. In: Schouten, B., Fedtke, S., Bekker, T., Schijven, M., Gekker, A. (eds.) Games for Health, pp. 219–232. Springer Fachmedien, Wiesbaden (2013)
3. Lim, F.S., Wallace, T., Luszcz, M.A., Reynolds, K.J.: Usability of tablet computers by people with early-stage dementia. Gerontology **59**, 174–182 (2013)
4. Kong, A.P.-H.: Conducting cognitive exercises for early dementia with the use of apps on iPads. Commun. Disord. Q. **36**(2), 102–106 (2015)
5. Bouchard, B., Imbeault, F., Bouzouane, A., Menelas, B.-A.J.: Developing serious games specifically adapted to people suffering from Alzheimer. In: Ma, M., Oliveira, M.F., Hauge, J.B., Duin, H., Thoben, K.-D. (eds.) SGDA 2012. LNCS, vol. 7528, pp. 243–254. Springer, Heidelberg (2012)
6. Alzheimer's Disease International: global knowledge, dementia statistics. http://www.alz.co.uk/research/statistics
7. Nezerwa, M., Wright, R., Howansky, S., Terranova, J., Carlsson, X., Robb, J., Coppola, J.F.: Alive inside: developing mobile apps for the cognitively impaired. In: IEEE Long Island Systems, Applications and Technology Conference (LISAT), pp. 1–5. IEEE (2014)
8. Tomé, R.M., Pereira, J.M., Oliveira, M.: Using serious games for cognitive disabilities. In: Ma, M., Oliveira, M.F., Baalsrud Hauge, J. (eds.) SGDA 2014. LNCS, vol. 8778, pp. 34–47. Springer, Heidelberg (2014)
9. Gogia, P., Rastogi, N.: Clinical Alzheimer Rehabilitation. Springer Publishing Company, New York (2008)
10. Cota, T.T., Ishitani, L., Vieira Jr., N.: Mobile game design for the elderly: a study with focus on the motivation to play. Comput. Hum. Behav. **51**, 96–105 (2015)
11. Lauriks, S., Reinersmann, A., Van der Roest, H.G., Meiland, F.J.M., Davies, R.J., Moelaert, F., Mulvenna, M.D., Nugent, C.D., Dres, R.M.: Review of ICT-based services for identified unmet needs in people with dementia. Ageing Res. Rev. **6**(3), 223–246 (2007)

User Interface Prototyping for Handheld Mobile Augmented Reality Applications

Antonia Kampa[✉], Kathrin Stöbener[✉], and Ulrike Spierling[✉]

Faculty of Design, Computer Science, Media, Hochschule RheinMain,
University of Applied Sciences, 65195 Wiesbaden, Germany
{antonia.kampa,kathrin.stoebener,ulrike.spierling}@hs-rm.de

Abstract. We introduce MockAR, a prototyping application for designing user interfaces for mobile handheld Augmented Reality, to be used by non-programming media designers. It has been successfully employed in the project SPIRIT, which develops location-based AR storytelling for outdoor historical sites, including complex interaction and navigation features based on mobile phone sensors and markerless image recognition.

Keywords: Augmented reality · User interface design · Prototyping

1 Introduction: AR User Interface Design Prototyping Tool

Interaction with Augmented Reality (AR) and the need for appropriate user interfaces have been topics of research for several decades [4, 6, 8] . However, available design frameworks mainly target expert developers and -users such as programmers. There are no standard or commonplace user interaction metaphors, as it has widely been a niche topic. For a long time, AR has also been associated with special devices such as head-mounted displays and extra hardware for tracking or tangible interfaces [6]. Only recently, new kinds of mobile apps for off-the-shelf phones and tablets become widespread. They include AR in form of a visual overlay of digital information on real objects or landmarks on a camera image. For entertainment and education purposes, such AR applications are to be conceived in a consumer market. This development produces an increasing need for non-programmers, such as media designers, to tackle AR elements as new media to be included in the conception and design of communication with their target groups. Like in other areas of media conception, interface design and graphics, designers need easy to use prototyping tools.

In the research project SPIRIT, a location-based mobile AR application has been developed that includes AR video overlay on specific spots of a cultural heritage site. Visitors shall experience entertaining on-the-spot storytelling, together with scavenger-hunt-like spatial interactions and information seeking, based on mobile device sensors. Storytellers and UI designers have been involved in the design of UI features integrated with the interactive story's concept. Figure 1 shows an early functional prototype, that had to be redesigned for more user guidance. This interdisciplinary development

G. Wallner et al. (Eds.): ICEC 2016, LNCS 9926, pp. 229–234, 2016.
DOI: 10.1007/978-3-319-46100-7_22

afforded several stages of prototyping before the system's full implementation [1]. Easy prototyping of location-based AR experiences requires tools that go beyond existing approaches. As a side result in the SPIRIT research project, we developed the AR UI prototyping tool MockAR for the project's non-programming designers. It supports the widely known principle of 'wire framing', used to draft and test so-called click dummies in early development stages [9]. MockAR plays back image sequences that can be experienced based on a wide range of user interactions using handheld devices' sensors.

Fig. 1. Early functional prototype of the SPIRIT application

2   SPIRIT: Outdoor Cultural Heritage AR Video Entertainment

The SPIRIT AR application delivers location-based stories, targeted at outdoor and indoor cultural heritage education on site. The goal is to achieve a feeling of 'presence' on the spot supported by interaction with the application, so that visitors can engage with their historical surroundings. The AR overlay consists of pre-produced video snippets [10] representing 'spirits of the past' at the location of their former living (compare Fig. 1). Technically, the developed AR system relies on GPS and image recognition to trigger content, using no dedicated markers, but reference images found in the physical environment. This technological vision of a natural seamless interaction is at the same time a challenge for designing the right affordances for users, as there are no technically given 'calls to action' for finding the right spots. While there are no standards, UI designers need to be included in the design process, to come up with innovative ideas. Therefore, an interdisciplinary user interaction design process is needed.

2.1   Augmented Reality User Interaction in SPIRIT

While several common AR interaction styles are not necessary, such as manipulating 3D objects, there are other challenges for users to be addressed in a user interface, like orientation in the environment and interacting with spirit videos.

In the SPIRIT scenario, the main AR user interaction consists of pointing the camera towards interesting surroundings, anticipating that (markerless) image recognition leads to a trigger for content. Users need to steady their mobile device until the recognition algorithm has successfully captured 'reality', which can then be overlaid with information, videos or other media assets. In practice, a user searches the whole area for suitable visual backdrops that could serve as image triggers, with the help of a UI that supports the right anticipation. On success, ghost-like characters as semi-transparent video deliver story content in form of dialogues, while users keep the camera focus on the triggered backdrop also accessing limited dialogue functions. In summary and besides this basic interaction loop, user actions include:

- walking between specific outdoor locations relevant for the told story,
- searching visual backdrops as image triggers (finding interesting story locations),
- tapping on buttons in a conventional GUI-like interface,
- tilting the mobile device up and down, changing between augmented story and a general GUI.

Further, we develop and evaluate novel input styles using different sensors, such as turning around like in a panoramic image, turning at specific angles up to 360°, or pitching and shaking the mobile device. We also test setting a timer for automatic displays without a trigger image, for example as several step-by-step hints and instructions, helping the user to find the right locations and backdrops.

2.2 User Interface Design Prototyping Versus User Interface Development

For the above-mentioned interactions, the mobile application needs to be equipped with various UI elements offering meta-information and hints for the user. As there is not a straight-forward standard solution, several optional creative design ideas are developed. In a cycle of design and formative evaluation, these alternatives need to be tested long before final implementation. In traditional interactive media (such as for desktop, web and touch applications using point-and-click or tap interaction), so-called wireframes are created with basic tools [9] as simple as for example MS-PowerPoint. The result can be experienced clicking linearly through ideal progressions of use, mostly at the desktop. This approach has been used at first, however it is limited for experiencing location-based AR issues. These include the difference between lighting and readability conditions indoors vs. outdoors (see Fig. 2), the handling of the device including holding its weight and reach space for touch interaction, as well as issues concerning the specificity of the outdoor location, far away from office space. To fill this gap, we developed MockAR, an application to be used for low-fidelity prototyping of UI design alternatives.

Fig. 2. Mockup UI evaluation indoors (left) and outdoors (right).

3   User Interface Wire Framing for AR Technology

An increasing number of wireframing tools for non-programmers exist, suggesting that creative design and programming tasks are distributed to different persons in a team [3, 5, 7]. However, these lack the possibility to test the above-mentioned issues of mobile AR, while dedicated AR tools are programming libraries [8, 11]. The WozARd [1] prototyping tool for non-programmers provides AR, however, it is limited by its Wizard of Oz concept relying on a supervisor. In short, we did not find suitable tools enabling non-programmers to quickly test and evaluate AR user interaction ideas, which motivated the development of MockAR.

3.1   MockAR Details

MockAR engages non-programmers in the UI design process of AR interactions, making this task accessible to a wider group of creators used to wireframing. MockAR emulates AR effects by displaying a linear order of semi-transparent images in front of camera-captured video. It makes full use of available sensors of mobile devices as input options to advance the image sequence. The image succession is determined by alphabetical order of image file names (0–9, A–Z). Transition between two images is set by an inter-action keyword (e.g. *shake, pitch, turnL, turnR, tap)* contained in the last six letters of the file name. In SPIRIT, we used MockAR with interactions like tapping on screen (default), shaking, pitching by 90°, turning the device left and right (Fig. 3), and setting a timer. A *six digit number* sets timed image transitions in milliseconds. Technical skills needed for using MockAR are image editing, changing filenames, saving files on an Android device and installing and starting the Android app on a mobile device. Therefore we assume MockAR is easy to use for non-programming user interaction designers.

Fig. 3. Example user interactions from left to right: tap, shake, pitch, turn left & turn right

Utilizing devices' sensor data, we use basic Android Software Development Kit [2] functions to access device coordinates, such as of the accelerometer for detecting movements in landscape mode, as well as the camera2 package for capturing video used as AR background overlaid by a FrameLayout displaying transparent PNG images. Images are kept in a specific folder on the device's SD-card. After reading file names and finding interaction keywords, a listener on specified device sensors or the timer in milliseconds is set. Figure 3 shows user interactions, and Fig. 4 user interaction keywords in the last six characters of the image file name. MockAR displays the transparent PNG image files from left to right.

001_entrance_log
o_001500.png

002_welcome_tap
.png

003_look_right_in
_front_of_you_pit
ch.png

004_look_over_to
_your_right_turnR
.png

005_mix_it_well_s
hake.png

006_look_over_to
_your_left_turnL.
png

Fig. 4. Image file names with specifying user interaction keywords

3.2 Proof of Concept

Figure 5 shows an example of how MockAR has been successfully used to evaluate creative ideas. Designers came up with the idea to conceive the app generally as metaphorical 'magic equipment', asking a user to apply 'energy' in order to visualize a spirit. The question then was how 'applying energy' can be performed. One idea was to let the user shake the tablet (Fig. 5, upper row from left to right). Alternative ideas included using two thumbs to swipe at the same time, or, just standing still and waiting while pointing at a backdrop (Fig. 5, lower row from left to right).

Fig. 5. Two alternative actions to evoke the visualisation of spirits, tested with MockAR

A non-programming media artist quickly built the alternatives by creating illustrations and including the according keywords for interaction into the filenames of an ordered image sequence. In fact, this way we found that shaking the device in this situation has been experienced as unnatural and difficult by test users. With the help of MockAR, such ideas could be tested and filtered in an early phase of development, when implementation of the more complex interactions was yet to be done. Also other quick prototyping of UI element positions and the sequencing and duration of video snippets saved time in the collaboration with the programmers.

MockAR was also tested in a student project involving four non-programmers in AR application design. Due to the simplified approach, they were able to build alternative design interactions within 20 min each. After building a series of designs, MockARs users requested further functionalities regarding non-linear playback and gesture input, which will be set on the development agenda.

4   Conclusion

MockAR has been developed as a side endeavor that became necessary within the project SPIRIT, while designing for a complex and novel user interaction in location-based AR with handheld devices. As recently, this area of development appears to prosper as a new field for media designers, easy-to-use prototyping tools for non-programmers are needed. MockAR established an iterative and interdisciplinary design and communication process within the project, which proved to be more difficult when designers had to wait for implementation by the AR developers.

Acknowledgements. This work has been funded (in part) by the Federal Ministry of Education and Research (BMBF) in Germany (03FH035PA3). We thank all project members for their support.

References

1. Alce, G.: Prototyping methods for augmented reality interaction. ACM Siggraph Comput. Graph. **39**(1), 17–22 (2015)
2. Android SDK, sensors overview in android software development (2016). http://developer.android.com/guide/topics/sensors/sensors_overview.html
3. Aurasma development kit (2016). https://www.aurasma.com/
4. Bai, Z., Blackwell, A.F.: Analytic review of usability evaluation in ISMAR. Interact. Comput. **24**(6), 450–460 (2012)
5. Balsamiq. Rapid, effective and fun wire framing software. Balsamiq (2016). https://balsamiq.com/
6. Billinghurst, M., Grasset, R., Looser, J.: Designing augmented reality interfaces. In: ACM SIGGRAPH Computer Graphics - Learning through computer-generated visualization. vol. 39, no. 1, February (2005)
7. Layar, augmented reality, interactive print (2016). https://www.layar.com/
8. MacIntyre, B., et al.: DART: a toolkit for rapid design exploration of augmented reality experiences. In: Proceedings of the 17th annual ACM Symposium on User Interface Software and Technology. ACM (2004)
9. Snyder, C.: Paper Prototyping: The Fast and Easy Way to Design and Refine User Interfaces. Morgan Kaufmann Publishers, Boston (2003)
10. Spierling, U., Kampa, A.: Structuring location-aware interactive narratives for mobile augmented reality. In: Mitchell, A., Fernández-Vara, C., Thue, D. (eds.) ICIDS 2014. LNCS, vol. 8832, pp. 196–203. Springer, Heidelberg (2014)
11. VUFORIA SDK. Vuforia play mode for unity (2016). https://developer.vuforia.com/library/articles/Training/Vuforia-Play-Mode-for-Unity

Designing Shared Virtual Reality Gaming Experiences in Local Multi-platform Games

Stefan Liszio$^{(\boxtimes)}$ and Maic Masuch$^{(\boxtimes)}$

Entertainment Computing Group, University of Duisburg-Essen, Duisburg, Germany
{stefan.liszio,maic.masuch}@uni-due.de

Abstract. Designing multiplayer virtual reality games is a challenging task since immersion is easily destroyed by real world influences. However, providing fun and social virtual reality experiences is inevitable for establishing virtual reality gaming as a convincing new medium. We propose a design approach to integrate social interactions into the game design while retaining immersion, and present design methods to implement this approach. Furthermore, we describe the game design of a collaborative local multi-player/platform virtual reality game to demonstrate the application and effectiveness of our methods.

Keywords: Virtual Reality gaming · Multiplayer · Immersion · Presence · Game design · Player experience · Social interaction

1 Make or Break: Social Interaction vs. Immersion

Virtual Reality (VR) games are able to create unique realistic experiences in fictional worlds to an extent that is out of reach for traditional gaming systems. One of the main contributing factors for a compelling virtual reality gaming experience (VRGX) is the system's ability to shift the user's perceptive and cognitive attention from the real to the virtual world to elicit *sensory* [14] and *cognitive* [13] immersion. Hence, any action or event happening in the real world might destroy this illusion. This holds for any interaction with other social entities, which make the real world become salient again. This is why VR is often perceived as being a solitary technology, which isolates a single individual in an artificial environment [4]. On the other hand, social interactions while gaming are considered a key factor for joyful gaming experiences [8]. Some authors are of the opinion that there is a contradiction between social interactions and cognitive immersion [15]. In contrast, Cairns et al. [2] state that without social interaction some games would not be fun at all. According to the authors, only

S. Liszio, M. Masuch—We wish to thank K. Alt, N. Bloch, F. Born, J. Feuerbach, T. Günter, H. Häuser, F. Münch, A. Schröder, P. Sykownik, and especially E. Meinike for their participation and commitment in the development of *Lunar Escape*.

G. Wallner et al. (Eds.): ICEC 2016, LNCS 9926, pp. 235–240, 2016.
DOI: 10.1007/978-3-319-46100-7_23

such interactions which do not happen within the game's context are a potentially disruptive influence on cognitive immersion. This argument is supported by a study on the disruptive factors on presence (i.e. feeling of actually being in the virtual world [7]) by Slater and Steed [14]. One of the most reported reasons for breaks in presence was the hearing of background noises such as people talking. Then again some participants mentioned the wish to share their experience as a cause for the perceived break in presence. In line with these findings, it was found that players experience higher levels of cognitive immersion when playing with others [2]. To solve this issue, the other players must become part of the game in a such way, that any interaction becomes an action intrinsic to the gameplay. We assume that cognitive immersion in digital games can be preserved and become a shared experience, if all interactions between players are expressed through game mechanics. Taking this as a design paradigm, we are able to design multiplayer VR games, which provide a rich social VRGX to all players without cutting down immersion.

2 Expanding the Game Space

Following the design paradigm set up in this paper, social interaction has to be integrated as a core mechanic of the game, meaning that it is essential for the game design to work. If game related social interaction takes place beyond the virtual game world, as this is the case in local multiplayer games, it is necessary to push the game's boundaries [6,11] beyond the mere virtual game world. We call this approach the *expansion of the game space* . The systematic expansion of the game space is comparable to the basic idea of pervasive gaming and mixed reality gaming. These genres expand the *magic circle of play*, either socially, spatially or temporally [10] to combine natural world interactions with digital game elements [3]. Including player interactions in the physical world as a game mechanic makes the game happen in both worlds: the virtual and the real world. Hence, the game space is stretched out to allow all players to enter the game world, whether they access it using a head-mounted display (HMD) or any other gaming device. Applying this idea to VR gaming implicates that not only what happens in VR is part of the game, but also all related actions and events happening outside. It is possible that multiple players become part of the game and share the same gaming experience facilitated by the cognitive immersion stimulated by the game [2]. A shared cognitive immersion is the foundation of live action role-playing games or even traditional pen and paper role-playing games. The latter game genre demonstrates that sensory immersion is not crucial, although it can facilitate and enrich the experience (e.g. costumes, props). With regard to (partly) digital games, alternate reality games show that it is possible to create engaging games, which emerge to the physical world, blurring the line between reality and fiction. Popular examples are the location-based mobile games *Ingress*, and the recently in 2016 released *Pokémon GO* developed by Niantic Inc. The success of these games proves that highly immersive experiences depend more on factors like storytelling, and social interaction than on the technological characteristics of the medium itself.

2.1   Design Methods

The following methods and techniques help designers of VR games to implement our approach of the expansion of the game space.

Unification. Unification is a game design technique where in a first step a fitting and homogeneous theme for a game is identified [12]. In the second step, every detail of the game is designed along this theme. Thus, all elements of a game from interface to visuals and music must reinforce the game's theme. If possible, even the surrounding real world environment should be arranged and shaped accordingly. For VR games this is a promising approach since today's VR systems do not exhibit a level of sensory immersion high enough to make the necessary hardware components completely "invisible" to the user (i.e. "illusion of non-mediation" [9]). If the designer manages to find an explanation for these deficiencies which fits the game's theme and story, they may even facilitate the theme. Thus, instead of trying to make the player believe there is no VR system, explain its existence with the game's theme. It is then possible to strengthen cognitive immersion and to compensate lacks in sensory immersion.

Storytelling. Good storytelling establishes an emotional bonding with the virtual world and its inhabitants and involves the player in the unfolding story [6]. Storytelling evokes cognitive immersion on the player, because it gives meaning to the actions and events happening in the virtual world. For VR games, storytelling is important, because the main characteristic of VR games over traditional games is that the player can find herself literally in the middle of the story. Furthermore, it has been shown, that the ideas and emotions transported by the story are equally important for the experience of presence like the VR system's technical qualities [1]. Storytelling stimulates the human imagination while the individual properties of the transporting medium become subordinated. Because VR entertainment is a quite unexplored new medium yet, designers have to learn how to craft intriguing stories tailored for VR. Storytelling supports the unification of the game's theme by involving the player mentally and emotionally.

Stimulated Communication. Verbal communication is a common form of social interaction found in many games. Provoking game-related chat while the game is actually running can reciprocally amplify unification. Thus, the storytelling should provide a common vocabulary to the players. Then again, if all player communication is consistent with the theme, this supports the occurrence of a unified or homogeneous gaming experience. A recent example for a local multiplayer (VR) game, which stimulates verbal communication between the players is the award-winning *Keep Talking and Nobody Explodes* developed and published by Steel Crate Games in 2015. The VR player has to defuse a bomb with the instructions given by a second player, who is outside the VR and cannot see the bomb. Real-world communication is the main mechanic in this game, therefore it is impossible to leave it out without breaking the game.

Player Roles and Mutual Dependencies. Assigning identifiable roles to certain players allows the game designer to equip each individual player with special abilities, tasks and objectives, information about the current game state, and views on the virtual game world. This is a prerequisite to establish mutual dependencies between all players. Depending on the structure of interaction between the players and the game system [6] this asymmetric distribution of abilities and information can force players either to collaborate or to compete. The result are complex and dynamic game-related interactions, which make the shared gaming experience unique. Giving players the opportunity to choose roles that fit their individual play styles enhances the gaming experience and strengthens the player's involvement.

Combination of Multiple Platforms. Using diverse game controllers and displays can support the game's theme and establishing player roles. Further, to date it is unlikely to find more than one HMD per household. Hence, game concepts which consider one player wearing a HMD and others participating in the game with alternative hardware are preferable. This technological setup can be used to implement the aforementioned design elements *mutual dependencies* and *player roles*. However, complexity and implementation efforts might increase. The advantage of private input and output devices lies in the possibility to provide each player with individual abilities, views on the game world, or an asymmetric information distribution [5].

3   Social VR Game Case Study: Lunar Escape

As a case study, we designed the collocated multiplatform VR game *Lunar Escape*, using the design methods presented before. In this collaborative game, one player wears an *Oculus Rift DK2*, while two others play on tablet PCs. Verbal communication between all players is essential to achieve the goal. The players have to find all parts of their broken space ship on a foreign planet to fix it.

3.1   Player Roles and Game Mechanics

Lunar Escape is playable with three active players. Each player has to choose a distinct role, which is associated with unique abilities, tasks, and perspectives on the game world, as well as a certain input and output device.

Mech-Operator. The Mech is a robot remotely controlled by the VR player by using a *Razer Hydra* motion and orientation detection game controller. This special controller was integrated to provide a natural and intuitive VR interface and to support the game's futuristic theme. Any movement of the player's arms is mapped to the arms of the Mech (Fig. 1). The Mech is armed with shields and different weapons to defend against enemies. It can carry things and use a tool to repair the shipwreck. The Mech-Operator is not able to change weapons or tools

Fig. 1. *(A)* View of the Mech-Operator with tools for carrying things selected. *(B)* The Copilot interacts with a GUI on a tablet PC to gain energy from minerals. *(C)* The scout views the drone he's steering and has to collect the green minerals.

on her own. Therefore, she has to communicate with the Copilot. Additionally, shields, walking, and firing needs energy, which has to be produced and managed by the Copilot. The Mech-Operator's main objective is to find and collect all the wreckage to repair the space ship. The player has no other information about the game state (i.e. energy status, navigational information).

Copilot. The Copilot manages the internal systems of the Mech using a tablet PC. He is not able to interact with the virtual world directly. However, the Copilot has the most information about the current game state, such as energy and ammunition level, available Scout drones, as well as a minimap of the virtual world, which is updated with new information gathered by the Scout. The player has to provide necessary information to her teammates by direct communication. A major task of the Copilot is to select the weapons or tools as called by the Mech-Operator. Further, the Copilot has to gain energy from minerals for the Mech to walk and shoot, or for repairs. To do this, she has to repeat increasingly difficult visual patterns displayed on the tablet PC in time (Fig. 1).

Scout. The Scout steers an unmanned reconnaissance drone to discover the planet. The player uses a tablet PC as input and output device and has an isometric view on the drone and the world below (Fig. 1). The drone is controlled by tilting the tablet, e.g. by tilting the tablet PC forward, the drone moves in the same direction. The player can use a grappler to collect minerals from the ground. In addition, the Scout can launch fireworks to distract enemies from itself or the Mech. Further, the Scout has to explore and discover the planet in search of the lost wreckage and enemy hordes. As soon as the Scout spotted a part of the ship, the position is shown on the Copilot's minimap.

4   Conclusion

With the design of the social multi-platform VR game *Lunar Escape*, we have proven our design approach to include social interaction in the real and the virtual world as an intrinsic game design feature. Playtest sessions were characterized by vivid game-related communication and deeply focused, engaged play. We assume that the players experienced high levels of immersion and social presence and an overall positive shared VRGX. Encouraged by these results, we believe that the expansion of the game space allows designers to create compelling VR games that are social, immersive, and fun.

References

1. Baños, R.M., Botella, C., Alcañiz, M., Liaño, V., Guerrero, B., Rey, B.: Immersion and emotion: their impact on the sense of presence. Cyberpsychol. Behav. Impact Internet, Multimedia Virtual Reality Behav. Soc. **7**(6), 734–741 (2004)
2. Cairns, P., Cox, A.L., Day, M., Martin, H., Perryman, T.: Who but not where: the effect of social play on immersion in digital games. Int. J. Hum. Comput. Stud. **71**(11), 1069–1077 (2013)
3. Cheok, A.D., Yang, X., Ying, Z.Z., Billinghurst, M., Kato, H.: Touch-space: mixed reality game space based on ubiquitous, tangible, and social computing. Pers. Ubiquit. Comput. **6**(5), 430–442 (2002)
4. Crecente, B.: Nintendo's Fils-Aime: Current state of VR isn't fun (2015). http://www.polygon.com/2015/6/18/8803127/nintendos-fils-aime-current-state-of-vr-isnt-fun. Accessed 19 May 2016
5. Emmerich, K., Liszio, S., Masuch, M.: Defining second screen gaming: exploration of new design patterns. In: Chisik, Y., Geiger, C., Hasegawa, S. (eds.) Proceedings of the 11th Conference on Advances in Computer Entertainment Technology, pp. 1–8. ICPS, ACM, New York, NY, USA (2014)
6. Fullerton, T.: Game Design Workshop: A Playcentric Approach to Creating Innovative Games, 2nd edn. Elsevier, Amsterdam (2008)
7. Heeter, C.: Being there: the subjective experience of presence. Presence: Teleoperators Virtual Environ. **1**(2), 262–271 (1992)
8. Lazzaro, N.: Why we play: affect and the fun of games: designing emotions for games, entertainment interfaces, and interactive products. In: Sears, A., Jacko, J.A. (eds.) The Human Computer Interaction Handbook, pp. 155–176. Erlbaum, New York (2008)
9. Lombard, M., Jones, M.T.: Defining presence. In: Lombard, M., Biocca, F., Freeman, J., IJsselsteijn, W.A., Schaevitz, R.J. (eds.) Immersed in Media, pp. 13–34. Springer International Publishing, Cham (2015)
10. Montola, M.: Exploring the edge of the magic circle: defining pervasive games. In: Alexanderson, D. (ed.) Proceedings of the 6th Annual Digital Arts and Culture Conference (2005)
11. Salen, K., Zimmerman, E.: Rules of Play: Game Design Fundamentals. MIT Press, Cambridge (2004)
12. Schell, J.: The Art of Game Design: A Book of Lenses. Elsevier, Amsterdam (2008)
13. Sherman, W.R., Craig, A.B.: Understanding Virtual Reality: Interface, Application and Design. Computer Graphics and Geometric Modeling. Morgan Kaufmann, San Francisco (2003)
14. Slater, M., Steed, A.: A virtual presence counter. Presence: Teleoperators Virtual Environ. **9**(5), 413–434 (2000)
15. Sweetser, P., Wyeth, P.: Gameflow: a model for evaluating player enjoyment in games. Comput. Entertainment **3**(3), 3 (2005)

Identifying Onboarding Heuristics for Free-to-Play Mobile Games: A Mixed Methods Approach

Line E. Thomsen[1], Falko Weigert Petersen[1(✉)], Anders Drachen[1], and Pejman Mirza-Babaei[2]

[1] Department of Communication, Aalborg University, Copenhagen, Denmark
Line.e.thomsen@outlook.dk, Falko@Weigert.dk, Drachen@hum.aau.dk
[2] Faculty of Business and Information Technology, University of Ontario Institute of Technology, Oshawa, Canada
Pejman.Mirza-Babaei@uoit.ca

Abstract. The onboarding phase of Free-to-Play mobile games, covering the first few minutes of play, typically sees a substantial retention rate amongst players. It is therefore crucial to the success of these games that the onboarding phase promotes engagement to the widest degree possible. In this paper a set of heuristics for the design of onboarding phases in mobile games is presented. The heuristics are identified by a lab-based mixed-methods experiment, utilizing lightweight psycho-physiological measures together with self-reported player responses, across three titles that cross the genres of puzzle games, base builders and arcade games, and utilize different onboarding phase design approaches. Results showcase how heuristics can be used to design engaging onboarding phases in mobile games.

Keywords: Mobile games · Flow · Psycho-physiological measures · User experience · Heuristics · Onboarding phase · Free to play · Game user research

1 Introduction

The Free-to-Play (F2P) business model has become increasingly popular when it comes to mobile games, and currently dominates the market. However, thousands of F2P mobile games exist, suffering from discoverability issues, and are characterized by imbalances in player retention [1]. Appsee [2] noted that the retention rate of mobile games is relatively low and only 28.60 % of players return to the game after one day [2]. The reasons for the typical low retention rates varies, but one of the four most common reasons is a poorly designed onboarding experiences [2]. The onboarding phase is thus an important element for capturing and retaining new players but to the best knowledge of the authors, no heuristics have yet been developed for purpose of designing the onboarding phase. This paper will therefore focus on developing onboarding heuristics for mobile games in order to provide the industry with a set of guidelines worth considering when designing a mobile game. The exact duration of the onboarding phase of a F2P mobile game varies across titles, but in collaboration with the developers at King

© IFIP International Federation for Information Processing 2016
Published by Springer International Publishing AG 2016. All Rights Reserved
G. Wallner et al. (Eds.): ICEC 2016, LNCS 9926, pp. 241–246, 2016.
DOI: 10.1007/978-3-319-46100-7_24

and Norsfell, seven minutes were established as a generic timeframe among the evaluated games. Broadly speaking, the onboarding phase lasts from the first time a player starts the game until the basic mechanics have been utilized.

The presented heuristics were formed based on an experimental study that evaluated three mobile titles: Candy Crush Jelly Saga (King 2016), WinterForts and Pogo Chick (Norsfell 2016). Two lightweight psycho-physiological measures, GSR and PPG were combined with abbreviated versions of the Flow State Scale (FSS) [3], using this as a proxy measure of engagement, as well as post-session walkthroughs and user-generated engagement graphs. These data were combined to develop an understanding of the features of the three games which influence flow and user experience, and jointly permitted the definition of heuristics that focus on fostering engagement of players during the onboarding phase. Because this is a short paper, the focus is on the study's results rather than the utilized method.

(1) *Candy Crush Jelly Saga* is a puzzle game where the objective is to match three or more pieces of candy in a row, in order to spread jelly and hereby win the levels. (2) *WinterForts* a base builder game where the game objective is to build, maintain, construct alliances and attack enemies. (3) *Pogo Chick* is an arcade-style game where the player controls a chick on a pogo stick through a track of obstacles. The onboarding phases of the three titles are highly diverse as they use three onboarding styles.

Through the study of related work, the focus was on research concerning heuristics in games, psycho-physiological methods in Games User Research (GUR) and the use of Flow theory in game evaluation. **Heuristics in games:** Within the context of digital games, multiple sets of heuristics have been developed and related studies suggest that heuristics are excellent at identifying playability issues in prototypes [4]. However, during a comparison of two set of playability heuristics, Korhonen et al. [4] found that the amount of heuristics should not be too vast as redundancy then might occur and that they should be presented similarly to Nielsen's usability heuristics [4]. **Psycho-physiological measures in games:** The domain of psycho-physiological research has been described as being concerned with trying to decipher mental processes, by measuring the body's signals and thereby finding links between them [5]. Emotions are a core element in experience and using psycho-physiological measures to recognizing a user's emotional state, is utilized across fields that share related psycho-physiological states, e.g. arousal [5]. While a full breakdown of all relevant related work on psycho-physiological measures in GUR is out of scope here, a mention is made of work that utilizes the same measures in surrounding fields. In a similar study, using a Cinema setup, [6] used ECG and GSR to measure implicit psychological constructs and found physiological observations are better suited for observation of e.g. archetypes, than introspective reports. PPG is like ECG a measure that equally can be used to calculate an HRV score, which is a widely used scale to measure arousal. However, determining whether a psycho-physiological response is related to an event or non-specific can be a challenge due to the many-to-one relationship [7]. **Flow:** Flow theory was developed by Csikszentmihalyi [8]. The focus of the work, is the relationship between intrinsically motivated behavior and the associated satisfaction from performing actions in their own right, as compared to the accomplishing of a goal. According to Csikszentmihalyi the concepts of Flow consist of nine dimensions [8]. These nine dimensions are adopted in the FSS, originally developed for measuring Flow in sports

[3], but adopted for use in digital games by Kivikangas and further validated by Nacke et al. [9]. The FSS measures the nine dimensions of Flow, via 36 questions. Related surveys developed specifically for games, are targeting the user experience more broadly than Flow but still includes elements of the nine dimensions. The *Game Experience Questionnaire* [10] and *The Game Engagement Questionnaire* [9] are psychometric instruments for game user experience assessment. However, the FSS is the only frequently used questionnaire utilized for the evaluation of Flow experience [9]. A short versions of the *Game Experience Questionnaire*, termed the *Post-Game Experience Questionnaire* (PGQ) [10], covers the user experience dimensions of Positive and Negative effect, Tiredness and the feeling of Returning from a Journey. The PGQ was adopted here as a proxy measure of the user experience.

2 Method and Data Analysis

In brief, the participants played the onboarding phase of three different mobile games, which possess different onboarding styles. The participants played the onboarding phase of each game, without prior experience with the games. GSR and HRV data was collected during the play session, while questionnaires, interviews and engagement graphs data was collected post play. Psycho-physiological measurements measures were used as one interest was in knowing if these could be used to evaluate engagement and experience of mobile games. The experimental setup was based on a within-subject design where each participant was exposed to three different onboarding phases.

The participants included 21 females (75 %) and 7 males (25 %). The age of the participants ranged from 20–37 years (mean = 25.25; SD = 3.63). Demographic data was collected as well as information on prior game experiences.

Skin conduction levels were measured using a Bitalino GSR sensor. Interbeat interval was recorded by a Merlin-digital Heart Rate Monitor. An IPad mini 3 was used for the test sessions. Before each play session a three-minute baseline was recorded, where after the participants played the onboarding phase of one game. The post-play sessions consisted of multiple steps: (a) drawing first Engagement Graph; (b) FSS questionnaire; (c) stimulated recall; (d) drawing second Engagement Graph; (e) PGQ questionnaire. This approach was followed for each onboarding phase condition.

Data analysis consisted of multiple steps: (a) post-session processing of the psycho-physiological data; (b) evaluation of the FSS and PGQ surveys; (c) explorative content coding of the post-session interviews; (d) evaluation and comparison of the engagement graphs with GSR and HRV composite graphs; (e) comparative and correlational analysis across the qualitative and quantitative measures. The GSR data was first visually inspected for logging gabs, where after the data was normalized using an algorithm that was used in similar analysis by Mirza-Babaei et al. [10]:

$$GSR_{Normalized} = \frac{\left(GSR_{(t)} - GSR_{Min}\right)}{\left(GSR_{Max} - GSR_{Min}\right)} \tag{1}$$

GSRMin and GSRMax refers to the minimum and maximum GSR value in a certain time frame and *GSRt* is the GSR data point in the middle of the time frame [10]. The GSR and HRV data was divided into smaller time windows that were based on the game design. Based on these time frames, graphs were created to visualize the normalized GSR and HRV scores. The GSR and HRV graphs were compared to the engagement graphs, created by the game designers and participants (Fig. 1).

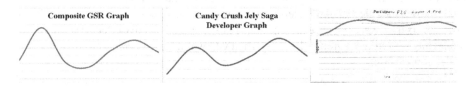

Fig. 1. Example of the three different graph types, Composite GSR (Left), Developer Engagement Graph (Middle), Player drawn Engagement Graph (Right).

In order to check the reliability of the PGQ and FSS, Cronbach's alpha was calculated. For the FSS the average score was .64 (SD = .42) while the PGQ had an average score of .71 (SD = .13). In order to investigate which of the three games induced the highest Flow score, the average score across all Flow dimensions was calculated. A comparison of overall Flow and PGQ scores is displayed in Table 1.

Table 1. Average FSS score for the three tested games and the PGQ dimension positive and negative game experience

Game	Average flow scores	PGQ positive dimension	PGQ negative dimension
Candy Crush Jelly Saga	3.84 (SD = 1.03)	2.27 (SD = 1.19)	1.52 (SD = .94)
WinterForts	3.11 (SD = 1.26)	1.74 (SD = .95)	2.04 (SD = 1.40)
Pogo Chick	3.04 (SD = 1.30)	2.08 (SD = 1.40)	1.83 (SD = .99)

The video recordings were meaning condensed and then coded by the means of an open coding. The engagement graphs were further analyzed by comparing them to the statements given during the interviews. The sentiments describing the participant's experience of the onboarding phase and thus the graphs, were used to analyze which game element created an enjoyable onboarding phase. Based on the analyzed data several onboarding heuristics were identified.

3   Identifying Onboarding Heuristics

The following top level categories were identified through the open coding: (1) Game context, (2) Music, (3) Learnability, (4) Rewards System (5) Relatedness (6) Mastering Controls (7) Game Objective and (8) Progress Overview. The categories 1, 2 and 3 seemed to be related to the device being mobile and the context thus ever-changing. The players were e.g. conscious of not disturbing their surrounding while playing and also needed games that can be played despite of interruptions caused by their surroundings. 4,5 and 8 are related to the games providing valuable and meaningful feedback for the players in order for the players to be able to relate to a game they never played before. Lastly, 6 and 7 are related to the game mechanics, where the controls need to be manageable and the games objective needs to be clear to the player. Additionally, several of the categories identified (4, 6, 7 and 8) in the open coding showed a shared relationship with the nine dimensions of Flow and a selective coding was therefore performed to investigate if more categories would uncover. The selective coding uncovered the supplementary categories Immersion and Autonomy. The categories 6, 7 and 8, initially found during the open coding, were refined and renamed: Skill Level, Clear goal and Clear feedback and Progression.

The heuristics identified in the empirical data will know be presented. The description of each heuristic follows the style of Nielsen's [4]. The heuristics are: **Clear goal**: Players should have a clear understanding of the games goal; this can be established in the beginning or during gameplay. **Autonomy:** Players should feel in control when playing. Missing autonomy can cause a negative game experience. **Skill Level:** The game should match a player's skill, without being too hard or easy. **Relatedness:** Players need to feel an association with the game. The player thus needs to feel that e.g. the theme, visual design and genre of the game is relatable. **Clear feedback and progression:** Players should receive information about how well they are during and when succeeding in a goal. **Game context:** The game needs to allow varying contexts and for disturbances without the players making irreversible mistakes that permanently ruins the player's game experience. **Learnability:** Players should be able to learn core game mechanics quickly during the onboarding phase, to ensure that they know how to play the game. **Music:** Music in the game can help support the game genre and environment but usages of sound depends on the surrounding context, as the players can be cautious about causing disturbance. **Rewards system:** Rewards needs to have value and purpose for the player. Through the onboarding phase the player needs to learn the reward system and find the rewards desirable to obtain when playing. **Immersion:** Immersion can be the outcome of a well-designed onboarding phase.

4   Discussion and Future Work

The goals of this study was to identify which elements that create an enjoyable onboarding phase, and based on this identify heuristics. Furthermore, lightweight psycho-physiological measures were utilized to investigate if it was possible to utilize the techniques in a mobile game setting. It was concluded that these measures of arousal appear to correlate with the self-reported data and that the high-frequency measures can be used to obtain insights into the specific causes of arousal. This result parallels previous work in other types of games [5, 9]. During the evaluation of the three games, the most common problem identified was a lack of autonomy. When players were forced to perform certain actions, the participants expressed a negative game experience. Furthermore, some of the identified heuristics are share with related literature (e.g. Clear Goal and Autonomy) on playability heuristics [4], which indicates that the heuristics, presented here, might be more generic across games and platform. Even though several sets of heuristics have been developed, none of them are focusing on the onboarding phase of mobile games. The heuristics thus contributes with knowledge within a relatively undiscovered research area. As the presented heuristics still are at an early stage, future work will focus on testing and evaluating them in order to create more refined and effective heuristics, which enables the development of better onboarding phase and increases player retention rate. Additionally, this study indicated that lightweight psycho-physiological and self-reported data can support each other in the evaluation of the onboarding phase of mobiles games, as they can pinpoint even small game events that causes high or low arousal, which will be elaborated further in the future. In conclusion, the three tested games had very different onboarding phases, which helped identifying the elements that created a more or less enjoyable experience for the players. This formed the basis for identifying the 10 onboarding design heuristics. However, future research has to be conducted to refined and evaluate the heuristics further.

References

1. Hadiji, F., Sifa, S., Drachen, A., Thurau, C.: Predicting player churn in the wild. In: Proceedings of the IEEE Computational Intelligence in Games, pp. 1–8 (2014)
2. Appsee Insights. http://blog.appsee.com/blog/2015/10/13/gaming-app-user-retention-only-22-return-after-one-month/
3. Jackson, S.A., Marsh, H.W.: Development and validation of a scale of measure optimal experience: the flow state scale. J. Sport Exerc. Psychol. **18**, 17–35 (1996)
4. Korhonen, H., Paavilainen, J., Saarenpää, H. Expert review method in game evaluations: comparison of two playability heuristic sets. In: Proceedings of the 13th International MindTrek Conference, pp. 74–81 (2009)
5. Ivonin, L., Chang, H.M., Díaz M., Català, A., Chen, W., Rauterberg, M.: Traces of unconscious mental processes in introspective reports and physiological responses. PLOS ONE **10**(4), e0124519 (2015). (pp. 1–3)
6. Csikszentmihalyi, M.: Beyond Boredom and Anxiety. Jossey-Bass, San Francisco (1975)
7. Nacke, L., Lindley, C.A.: Flow and immersion in first-person shooters: measuring the player's gameplay experience. In: Proceedings of the 2008 Conference on Future Play: Research, Play, Share, pp. 81–88. ACM, Toronto (2008)
8. Isselsteijn, W., de Kort, Y., Poels, K., Jurgelionis, A., Bellotti, J.: Characterizing and measuring user experiences. In: Proceedings of ACE Conference 2007, The International Conference on Advances in Computer Entertainment, vol. 3, issue no: 8, pp. 33–39. ACM, Toronto (2007)
9. Brockmeyer, J.H., Fox, C.M., Curtiss, K.A., McBroom, E., Burkhart, K.M., Pidruzny, J.N.: The development of the Game Engagement Questionnaire. J. Exp. Soc. Psychol. **45**, 624–635. (2009). Oxford University Press, Oxford
10. Mirza-Babaei, P., Wallner, G., McAllister, G., Nacke, L.E.: Unified visualization of quantitative and qualitative playtesting data. In: CHI 2014 Extended Abstracts on Human Factors in Computing Systems, pp. 1363–1368. ACM, New York (2014)

A Revisit of the Measurements on Engagement in Videogames: A New Scale Development

Amir Zaib Abbasi[1(✉)], Ding Hooi Ting[1], and Helmut Hlavacs[2]

[1] Department of Management and Humanities,
Universiti Teknologi PETRONAS, Tronoh, Malaysia
amir_zaib_abbasi@yahoo.co.uk
[2] Research Group Entertainment Computing,
University of Vienna, Vienna, Austria

Abstract. This research article attempts to conceptualize and operationalize the concept of engagement in videogame-play as consumer videogame engagement that comprises both psychological and behavioral dimensions. Accordingly, this study has developed a scale for measuring consumer videogame engagement through following the steps of scale development. Next, the study has collected data on two samples. Besides, this study has applied SPSS 22.0 version and SEM-PLS approach to analyze the data on two samples and to validate the construct of consumer videogame engagement. Based on the study results, an instrument has proven to be a valid source for measuring engagement in videogames as well as a reflective-formative and multi-dimensional construct. This study contributes to the videogame literature as it considers consumer videogame engagement as a multi-dimensional construct comprising on cognitive, affective and behavioral engagement. It further validates the scale of consumer videogame engagement as reflective-formative model among videogame players.

Keywords: Engagement · Videogame engagement · Consumer videogame engagement · Cognitive engagement · Affective engagement · Behavioral engagement · Reflective-formative model · Scale development process

1 Introduction

Literature indicates that several studies have put their efforts to develop an instrument to measure engagement in videogame playing. Among all the studies, a study by [1], was the first research who developed an instrument to measure the subjective experience of videogame-play based on these dimensions *"gameflow, cognitive-absorption and presence"* and named it as game-experience questionnaire or GEQ. Another subsequent study done by [2] who developed a scale named as game engagement questionnaire or GEQ with combination of four constructs *"flow, presence, absorption and immersion"* to measure player's engagement in videogame. Again, this study has also used almost similar dimensions as it was used in the following study [1]. In similar vein, a recent study [3] has reviewed the model of game engagement construct given by [2]. In this study, the author has discussed that three of the dimensions of game

© IFIP International Federation for Information Processing 2016
Published by Springer International Publishing AG 2016. All Rights Reserved
G. Wallner et al. (Eds.): ICEC 2016, LNCS 9926, pp. 247–252, 2016.
DOI: 10.1007/978-3-319-46100-7_25

engagement questionnaire such as *"flow, immersion and presence"* [2] are interrelated to the subjective experience of videogame-play but absorption is similar to flow construct so, it is better not to consider in the measurement of game-engagement questionnaire. According to [3], a new revised construct of game-engagement comprises the following dimensions *"flow, presence, involvement and immersion"* that can be applied to examine the subjective experience of videogame play.

Doing a critical review of prior researches that have developed and used engagement scale in their studies. The current study has concluded with the following limitations; first, this study finds that mostly studies have only considered psychological constructs (*flow, presence and absorption*) and have ignored the importance of using behavioral dimensions to examine the subjective experience of videogame play as well as measure the player' engagement in video games [1–3]. Secondly, these studies have not properly conceptualized and operationalized the term engagement and immersion in their studies.

Moreover, several studies have stated that engagement in videogame, is a multi-dimensional construct [4, 5]. Among these studies, only a study by [4] who really captured the meaning of engagement on a multi-dimensional level. But, the problem with the following study [4] is, authors have misspecified the construct of game immersion as reflective-reflective construct (*A reflective measurement model is; when items share a common theme, items are exchangeable and deleting or adding an item does not change the conceptual meaning of the construct* [6]) on first and second order construct. Rather, the construct of game immersion seems to be as reflective-formative construct that means reflective on first order and formative on second order construct (*A formative measurement is; when items do not require to have a shared common theme, items are not replaceable and deleting and adding an item can change the conceptual meaning of the construct* [6]). The decision behind calling a game immersion construct as reflective-formative was drawn on basis of reviewing the following study [6] that has discussed the important decision rules for specifying the construct as reflective or formative.

Therefore, the current study considers the limitations of past studies and takes an initiative to first conceptualize and operationalize the term engagement in videogames as *"consumer video-game engagement"* and develops a new scale with combination of psychological as well as behavioral dimensions in order to measure engagement in videogame-playing in more advanced level. Moreover, this study aims to validate a newly developed construct among the videogame consumers. The present study is first in videogame literature which considers both psychological and behavioral dimensions for measuring consumer video-game engagement. Secondly, this study considers the importance of both reflective and formative constructs in explaining and measuring the construct of consumer videogame engagement on higher order construct. Thirdly, this study applies the concept of marketing and consumer research, especially the definition of consumer engagement and its related dimensions (cognitive, affective and behavioral) that have been discussed in the following studies [7, 8] in order to conceptualize and operationalize the construct of consumer videogame engagement.

2   Conceptualization of Consumer Videogame Engagement

This study follows the definition of engagement given by [7, 8] as *"Engagement is a multidimensional construct which is subject to a context-specific expression of relevant cognitive, emotional, and behavioral dimensions"*. The author of the study [8], has further added that engagement is a process which reveals as a result of two-way communications between the engagement-subject (consumer/customer) and a particular engagement-object such as a product, service or a brand, which leads to generate consumer engagement states *(cognitive, affective and behavioral)*. On the basis of above stated definition, this study conceptualizes consumer videogame engagement as *"A psychological state that triggers due to two-way interactions between the consumer and videogame product, which generates different level of consumer engagement states (cognitive, affective and behavioral)"*.

3   Scale Development and the Validation of Consumer Videogame Engagement

This study adopts the scale development procedure given by [9, 10]. This study first compiles the measurement scales as already reported in the literature which is specifically relevant to the following dimensions: conscious-attention, absorption (cognitive engagement), dedication, enthusiasm (affective engagement), social interaction and interaction (behavioral engagement). The items on the following dimensions such as conscious attention, six items (Items 1 to 6) from [11], item7 from [12] and item8 from [13] are adapted in this study. Absorption scale adapted from [14]. Whereas, dedication items as item1 from [15] and item2 to item7 from [16] and the items of enthusiasm are adapted from the study of [11]. However, social connection scale is adapted as item1 to item4 from [11] and remaining items 5,6 and 7 from [17]. Finally, interaction scale is adapted from [14]. Overall, the study has generated 39 items, which were further evaluated for the content validity by 4 PhD students and two experts to assess the content of consumer videogame engagement. Based on their comments, this study has revised certain items.

For first-time data collection, 200 questionnaires were distributed among university teenage students who play videogames aged 16-19, out of which 160 questionnaires were returned with a response rate of 80 %. Out of 160 questionnaires, 134 valid cases were left after treating the missing values and biased responses. The data were further analyzed for exploratory factor analysis (EFA) as well as for internal consistency and the results are shown in the Table 1. After finding the satisfactory results, this study continued to second-time data collection, 350 questionnaires were distributed and collected 290 responses with response rate of 83 %. After treating missing values and biased responses, we were left with 265 valid cases that were used for further analysis.

SEM-PLS *(Structural equation modeling-partial least squares)* was employed to validate the construct of consumer videogame engagement because, it has both reflective and formative constructs [18]. For reflective construct, this study involves the estimation of internal consistency, convergent validity and discriminant validity.

Table 1. Shows results of both first and second time data collection

Construct	Items	Study one: N=134		Study two (N=265): Convergent Validity			
		EFA Loadings	C.Alpha	CFA Loadings	C.Alpha	CR	AVE
Absorption	When I am playing this video-game, I forget everything else around me.	0.82	0.83	0.73	0.84	0.89	0.61
	Time flies when I am playing this video-game.	0.63		0.73			
	When I am playing this video-game, I get carried away.	0.93		0.83			
	It is difficult to detach myself from playing this video-game.	0.82		Deleted			
	When I am playing this video-game, I feel immersed.	0.48		0.80			
	I feel happy, when I am playing this video-game intensely.	Deleted		0.81			
Conscious Attention	I like to know more about this video-game.	0.87	0.89	Deleted			
	I like to learn more about this video-game.	0.92		0.82	0.88	0.92	0.74
	I notice information related to this video-game.	0.83		0.85			
	I pay a lot of attention to anything about this video-game.	0.74		0.88			
	I keep up with things related to this video-game.	0.65		0.88			
Dedication	This video-game inspires me.	0.71	0.84	0.84	0.86	0.91	0.71
	I am enthusiastic about playing this video-game.	0.85		0.85			
	I am proud of playing this video-game.	0.65		0.84			
	I find this video-game full of meaning and purpose.	0.84		0.84			
	I am excited when playing this video-game.	0.82		0.82			
Enthusiasm	I spend a lot of my discretionary time playing this video-game.	0.8	0.85	0.75	0.86	0.90	0.65
	I am heavily into playing this video-game.	0.91		0.85			
	I am passionate about playing this video-game.	0.67		0.84			
	I enjoy spending time playing this video-game.	0.52		0.81			
	I try to fit playing this video-game into my schedule.	0.85		0.77			
Interaction	In general, I like to get involved in the discussions about this video-game playing.	0.75	0.88	0.83	0.88	0.91	0.68
	I am someone who enjoys playing this video-game with others like-minded video-game players.	0.73		0.81			
	I am someone who likes actively participating in the discussions about this video-game playing.	0.95		0.87			
	In general, I thoroughly enjoy exchanging ideas on this video-game with other video-game players.	0.84		0.82			
	I often participate in activities relating to this video-game.	0.77		0.79			
Social Connection	I love playing this video-game with my friends.	0.91	0.86	0.89	0.83	0.90	0.75
	I enjoy playing this video-game more when I am with others.	0.91		0.85			
	Playing this video-game is more fun when other people around me play it too.	0.88		0.86			
	I receive social fulfillment from playing this video-game.	0.59		Deleted			

Whereas, the evaluation of a formative construct follows different guidelines like testing of multicollinearity, indicator weights, and redundancy analysis.

Initially, a reflective measurement model was assessed for its convergent validity and achieved confirmatory factor loadings (CFA) greater than 0.70, composite reliability ranged from 0.89 to 0.92, while AVE were in between 0.61 to 0.75. All criteria of convergent validity were met. Discriminant validity was evaluated through newly introduced method called Heterotrait-Monotrait ratio (HTMT) of correlations [19] and found that all values have passed the critical value of HTMT .85 as in Table 2.

Table 2. Discriminant validity (HTMT Ratio)

	Absorp	ConsAtten	Dedicate	Enthusi	Interact	SocialConn
Absorp						
ConsAtten	0.683					
Dedicate	0.656	0.836				
Enthusi	0.806	0.73	0.697			
Interact	0.582	0.618	0.654	0.661		
SocialConn	0.414	0.576	0.46	0.561	0.621	

This study has assessed the three criteria for the evaluation of formative measurement model as suggested by [20]. The first criteria is to assess the convergent validity also termed as redundancy analysis. The results indicate that the path coefficient between consumer video-game engagement and global measure is 0.826, which is higher than the threshold value of 0.80 as recommended by [20] and thus, depicting that the formative constructs have achieved the convergent validity. Second, the study has checked the collinearity issues and found that there is no multicollinearity issue because, all values shown in the Table 3, are below the threshold value of 5 as suggested by [20]. Third, this study has assessed the significance of indicator weights as shown in the Table 3 and found that formative constructs are highly significant at 0.00 level.

Table 3. Evaluation of formative constructs

Construct Scale	Measurement model	Items	Weights	Full Collinearity (VIFs)	T - Values	P-Values
Cognitive Engagement	Formative	Absorption	0.40	3.1	3.16	0.00
		ConsAtten	0.71		6.91	0.00
Affective Engagement	Formative	Dedication	0.50	3.3	4.90	0.00
		Enthusiasm	0.62		6.12	0.00
Behavioral Engagement	Formative	Interaction	0.78	1.7	10.15	0.00
		Social connection	0.34		3.51	0.00

4 Conclusion

This study first conceptualized operationalized the construct of consumer videogame engagement then developed a scale for measuring consumer video-game engagement. The scale was first validated through EFA and reliability test. Second, the data were recollected on more respondents for measuring CFA and reflective measurement model on first order. All results met the criteria for the assessment of reflective measurement model then second order were created on a formative level. Formative measurement model was assessed on basis of three criteria given by [20] and results met the criteria for the evaluation of a formative model.

References

1. Jennett, C., et al.: Measuring and defining the experience of immersion in games. Int. J. Hum Comput Stud. **66**(9), 641–661 (2008)
2. Brockmyer, J.H., et al.: The development of the Game Engagement Questionnaire: a measure of engagement in video game-playing. J. Exp. Soc. Psychol. **45**(4), 624–634 (2009)
3. Procci, K.C.: The Subjective Gameplay Experience: An Examination of the Revised Game Engagement Model (Ph.D. Diss). University of Central Florida Orlando, Florida (2015)

4. Cheng, M.T., She, H.C., Annetta, L.A.: Game immersion experience: its hierarchical structure and impact on game-based science learning. J. Comput. Assist. Learn. **31**(3), 232–253 (2015)
5. Silpasuwanchai, C., et al.: Developing a comprehensive engagement framework of gamification for reflective learning. In: Proceedings of the 2016 ACM Conference on Designing Interactive Systems, pp. 459–472 (2016)
6. Jarvis, C.B., MacKenzie, S.B., Podsakoff, P.M.: A critical review of construct indicators and measurement model misspecification in marketing and consumer research. J. Consum. Res. **30**(2), 199–218 (2003)
7. Brodie, R.J., et al.: Customer engagement: conceptual domain, fundamental propositions, and implications for research. J. Serv. Res. **14**(3), 252–271 (2011)
8. Hollebeek, L.D.: Demystifying customer brand engagement: exploring the loyalty nexus. J. Mark. Manage. **27**(7–8), 785–807 (2011)
9. Churchill Jr, G.A., A paradigm for developing better measures of marketing constructs. J. Market. Res. **16** 64–73 (1979)
10. Tsaur, S.-H., Yen, C.-H., Yan, Y.-T.: Destination brand identity: scale development and validation. Asia Pacific J. Tourism Res. **21** 1–14 (2016)
11. Vivek, S.D., et al.: A generalized multidimensional scale for measuring customer engagement. J. Market. Theory Pract. **22**(4), 401–420 (2014)
12. Qin, H., Patrick Rau, P.-L., Salvendy, G.: Measuring player immersion in the computer game narrative. Intl. J. Hum. Comput. Interact. **25**(2), 107–133 (2009)
13. Wiebe, E.N., et al.: Measuring engagement in video game-based environments: investigation of the user engagement scale. Comput. Hum. Behav. **32**, 123–132 (2014)
14. So, K.K.F., King, C., Sparks, B.: Customer engagement with tourism brands scale development and validation. J. Hosp. Tourism Res. **38**(3), 304–329 (2014)
15. Schaufeli, W.B., et al.: The measurement of engagement and burnout: A two sample confirmatory factor analytic approach. J. Happiness Stud. **3**(1), 71–92 (2002)
16. Cheung, C.M., et al.: Promoting sales of online games through customer engagement. Electron. Commer. Res. Appl. **14**(4), 241–250 (2015)
17. Kemp, E.: Engaging consumers in esthetic offerings: conceptualizing and developing a measure for arts engagement. Intl. J. Nonprofit Voluntary Sector Market. **20**(2), 137–148 (2015)
18. Hair, J.F., Ringle, C.M., Sarstedt, M.: PLS-SEM: Indeed a silver bullet. J. Market. Theory Pract. **19**(2), 139–152 (2011)
19. Henseler, J., Ringle, C.M., Sarstedt, M.: A new criterion for assessing discriminant validity in variance-based structural equation modeling. J. Acad. Mark. Sci. **43**(1), 115–135 (2015)
20. Hair Jr., J.F., et al.: A primer on partial least squares structural equation modeling (PLS-SEM). Sage Publications (2013)

Geometric Representations for Subjective Time in Digital Narratives

Nikitas M. Sgouros[⊠]

Department of Digital Systems, University of Piraeus, 185 32 Piraeus, Greece
sgouros@unipi.gr

Abstract. Subjective time refers to our living experience of time. We develop subjective timescapes i.e., spatial representations for time as experienced by story characters. Each such timescape describes how a character perceives and shapes story time. We show how these spatial constructions are compatible with relevant psychological and phenomenological studies on subjective time. Timescapes allow us to model characters as operating from particular temporal perspectives mediated by memory and anticipation at various points in a story and to provide geometric mappings of these concepts. We apply these ideas in a visualization environment for digital narrative plot structures.

Keywords: Time · Narrative · Visualization · Experiential aspects

1 Introduction

Most of the current research and applications of time focus on representing and managing "clock" time, i.e. fixed periodic structures such as the 24-h standard or the calendar system. However, there is another equally important notion of time, that we call "subjective" time, and describes our awareness of precedence or succession, duration, simultaneity and tempo of events, the feeling of presence, and the establishment of temporal perspectives on events and behaviour. In contrast to its clock counterpart, subjective time is qualitative in nature [1], different for each individual and with no rigid linear structure. Subjective time exerts considerable influence on motivation, planning and execution of purposeful activity [4]. We describe the construction of subjective timescapes, i.e., spatial representations for the experience of time in story characters. We develop geometric perspectives for representing the flow of time, temporal dilation and segmentation in episodes. We provide geometric mappings that make these phenomena examinable and allow the creation of alternative character-centric micro-narratives describing how characters experience time. Current narrative systems focus on supporting inferential aspects of stories by reasoning about plans and actions from character goals using variants of plan-based AI methods [3]. They seek to formalize the notion of clock time and to provide means for reasoning about the temporal aspects of knowledge. Time in their stories is something external and

© IFIP International Federation for Information Processing 2016
Published by Springer International Publishing AG 2016. All Rights Reserved
G. Wallner et al. (Eds.): ICEC 2016, LNCS 9926, pp. 253–259, 2016.
DOI: 10.1007/978-3-319-46100-7_26

disassociated from what is happening in the story. In contrast to these systems our approach seeks to represent how story events interact with the experience of time in characters.

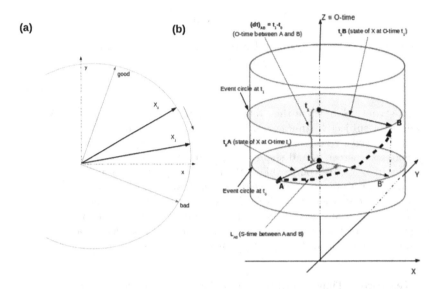

Fig. 1. (a) Atemporal representation for the state of character X on the unit circle (b) C-time interval $(dt)_{AB}$ and S-time segment AB for X corresponding to events at C-times t_0 and t_1. X's state follows the helical trajectory of the S-time curve from A to B by simultaneously rotating with an angle ϕ and translating by $(dt)_{AB}$ on the z-axis. (Color figure online)

2   Character State and Subjective Time

A narrative can be analysed as a sequence of events describing the goals and actions of a set of characters and the complications arising from them. Given such a goal-oriented structure we represent character state in terms of his current disposition towards various goals, i.e. his perception of how near or far he currently is towards their adoption and/or attainment and of how interrelated these goals are. We model character state as a unit vector in a 2-D real vector space lying on an horizontal unit circle centered on the character (see Fig. 1(a)). Thus, character state and goals are mapped to particular directions of motion in space. This configuration reflects the character's perception of goal-driven behavior as motion in a particular direction. Pairs of goals that are opposite to each other and, therefore, pose a dilemma for a story character, are mapped to orthogonal vectors in this space and define a basis for this vector space. The configuration of such a basis encodes the semantic opposition of its goals as a left-right antithesis that reflects a common story metaphor of a dilemma as a forking path of two orthogonal directions forward. As an example, Fig. 1(a) depicts the state and goals for a character X. X is confronted with two possible and contrasting goals (becoming either good or bad). We represent such a moral viewpoint with a basis M consisting of two orthogonal unit vectors (vectors are written in bold) **good** and **bad** denoted in red in Fig. 1(a). A state X_0 of X is a vector which can be described in terms of M as a linear combination of the vectors **good** and **bad**. Such a combination indicates that X has two potential goals of being either "good" or "bad" while also describing his current disposition towards them. By disposition we refer to the distance of his current state from either of the goal vectors in M, which reflects how close he is towards adopting or achieving that particular goal. This distance is captured by the dot product between his current state vector and the particular goal vector. X can change his disposition towards his goals. Such change is represented as a rotation of his state vector. Rotation can be instantaneous, as in the case of character decisions, or gradual, as a result of action execution. For example, by reneging on a promise X can change his state from X_0 to X_1, thus rotating his state vector closer to the **bad** goal (see Fig. 1(a)) and increasing his disposition of achieving this goal. We model the perception of state change from the perspective of the character involved as being proportional to the angle of rotation between his initial and resulting state.

We develop two main structures for representing subjective time. The first one, which we call clock time (**C-time**), refers to the temporal placing of events by an external observer using a clock. We represent the C-time for such an event as a point on the z-axis of a 3-D coordinate system (see Fig. 1(b)). We use C-time to signify that an outside uninvolved observer experiences E as preceding all events with higher z-coordinates and succeeding all events with lower ones. Also important is the difference between the C-times of successive events as this indicates the amount of time such an observer perceives as having expired between two successive events in relation to the time intervals between the other pairs of successive events in the sequence. Consequently, C-time exhibits the linearity of clock time. The second structure of time, which we call subjective time (**S-time**), is different for each character involved in the event sequence and corresponds to his perception of the temporal features (placing, duration, simultaneity) between successive events at each point in the sequence. More specifically, we represent each event by the effects it has on the states of the characters. Therefore, each event is a slice of C-time represented as a unit circle (such as the one in Fig. 1(a)) centered on the C-time axis and vertical to it. Each such circle contains the character states that result from the event actualization. The representations of all events are stacked on a cylinder of unit radius and height h, where h is equal to the difference between the C-times of the last and the first event in the story. We model the trajectory of S-time for character X by the sequence of the geodesics (shortest paths) on the surface of this cylinder formed by connecting the endpoints of successive state vectors of X. The duration of the S-time for X between any two successive events E1 and E2 is equal to the length of the geodesic connecting the endpoints of his state vector at events E1 and E2. Let A and B be the endpoints of the state vector for X at successive

C-times t_0 and t_1, respectively, where $t_1 > t_0$ (see Fig. 1(b)). The length L_{AB} of the geodesic between A and B represents the duration of the S-time interval separating successive events at clock times t_0 and t_1 according to X. In order to compute L_{AB} let us assume that B at t_1 results by an event that forces X's state at t_0 to transform to the one at t_1 following a helical trajectory with a rotation angle of ϕ radians ($0 \leq \phi < 2\pi$) around the z-axis and a simultaneous translation of $(dt)_{AB}$ units on the z-axis where $(dt)_{AB} = t_1\text{-}t_0$ is the C-time interval between A and B. If we then flatten our event cylinder to a square we compute L_{AB} as: $L_{AB} = \sqrt{(dt)_{AB}^2 + \phi^2}$. According to this relation S-time maintains the phenomenology of the flow of time in which events seem to constantly approach an agent from the future, are actualized in the present and recede to the past because S-time duration between two events is proportional to the duration of the C-time $(dt)_{AB}$ separating them. Furthermore, S-time duration between successive events for X is proportional to the rotation angle ϕ separating X's state vectors in these events. Because we model X's perceived amount of state change among these events as being proportional to this angle ϕ, the duration of the S-time between them is also proportional to the change in X's state. Consequently, between two pairs of successive events separated with equal C-time intervals, X will perceive the pair in which his state rotates more as lasting longer than the other one. This allows us to embed in a character an experience of duration compatible with the one posited by the contextual change model in the psychology of time in which estimates of duration of an event in which a person does not need to estimate its duration is proportional to the number of changes observed during an interval [5]. We are not interested in the absolute value of S-time, only in the qualitative relations (comparisons and proportionality) between various S-times. Our ability to generate and process temporal experiences presupposes our ability to apprehend event sequences as episodes (i.e. coherent event sequences that are extended in time). We adopt the phenomenological notion of temporality in which coherency refers to the meaning established by the character for the events in question [2]. We use the notion of distance between the state of a character X and a goal in his goal space, as captured by the dot product between these two vectors, to establish our notion of temporal coherency. In particular, during each event X experiences his state as staying invariant, moving closer or away from a goal **G**. We capture this experience by comparing the value of the dot product between **G** and the agent state vector at the current C-time point t_i with its corresponding value at the previous C-time point t_{i-1} in the event sequence. If the value at t_i is greater-than, less-than or equal to the previous one at t_{i-1} then the agent experiences his state to converge, diverge or stay invariant, respectively, with respect to **G**. A sequence of events in which the agent experiences his state to only converge, diverge or remain stable with respect to a goal forms an episode.

3   An Example

Our story example involves three characters; Joe, Bob and Ann. This story plot has been automatically produced by QuNE, a narrative generation system based

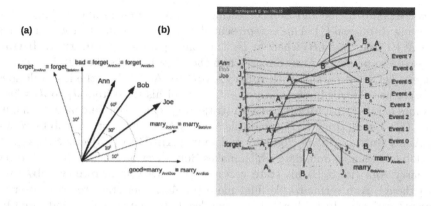

Fig. 2. (a) Initial configuration for the example love story ("≡" denotes coincident vectors) (b) Subjective timescapes for the characters in the example love story.

on spatial representations of purpose and quantum theory [6]. The goal structure (see Fig. 2(a)) motivating their behaviour consists of five bases. The first one is Morality (which is common to all three characters with two vectors **good** and **bad**). We also use two bases describing what it means for Ann to try to marry or to forget any of the other characters (bases AnnJoe with **marryAnnJoe** and **forgetAnnJoe** and AnnBob with **marryAnnBob** and **forgetAnnBob** for Joe and Bob respectively), and two bases describing such an involvement for Joe (bases JoeAnn with **marryJoeAnn** and **forgetJoeAnn**) and for Bob (basis BobAnn with **marryBobAnn** and **forgetBobAnn**). The orientation of these bases indicate that for both Joe and Bob trying to marry Ann is regarded as primarily 'good' while forgetting her as primarily 'bad'. Ann has a positive view for marriage since for her trying to marry either Joe or Bob is definitely 'good' and forgetting either of them is definitely 'bad'. Initially both Joe and Bob are more prone to decide to try marrying Ann. Ann seems more likely not to try marrying either one of them. There are four possible story developments: Date, Serenade, Duel and Marriage. Date involves Ann and one of the other guys causing each one of the state vectors involved to rotate by a random angle (dating is unpredictable). Serenade results in increasing the probability for Ann to decide and marry her serenader. Duel implicates two guys resulting in the winner trying to marry Ann and in the loser deciding to forget her. Finally, Marriage occurs when both characters decide to do so. Figure 2(b) depicts the S-time structure of this story based on the configuration of Fig. 2(a) that is reproduced as the Event 0 (E0) circle in Fig. 2(b). Figure 2(b) depicts the trajectory of Ann's state by the sequence A_0A_8, the one for Bob with the sequence B_0B_9 and the one for Joe as J_0J_8. Most of these pairs of successive points (e.g. A_4A_5) are connected with line segments whose length indicates the duration of the S-time interval between successive events for the character involved. The ones not connected (e.g. B_1, B_2) describe instantaneous character decisions and therefore lie on the same event circle. Figure 2(b) assumes equal C-time intervals between the story events.

E1 corresponds to Joe and Bob contesting for Ann. Bob wins and decides to try marrying Ann (goal G). This is represented as the instantaneous rotation of his state at E1 from B_1 to B_2 where at B_2 it becomes parallel with **marryBobAnn**. Bob seeks to persuade Ann to marry him therefore he seeks through his actions to make her state parallel with **marryAnnBob**. At E1 Joe (the loser) decides to forget her. This is indicated by the rotation of his state from J_1 to J_2 which becomes parallel with **forgetJoeAnn** (trajectory $J_2 J_8$). Bob serenades Ann four times (E2-5, trajectory $B_2 B_6$) and this arouses Ann's interest for Bob by rotating Ann's state gradually closer to goal **marryAnnBob** (trajectory $A_1 A_5$). In E6 Bob and Ann go on a date which makes Bob waver on whether he should try to marry Ann (in $B_6 B_7$ his state vector rotates away from **marryBobAnn**), even though Ann seems to like him more (in $A_5 A_6$ her state rotates closer to **marryAnnBob**). In E7 both characters decide to marry. This is indicated by the rotation of Bob's state from B_8 to B_9 becoming parallel to **marryBobAnn** and Ann's from A_7 to A_8 becoming parallel to **marryAnnBob**. Each character experiences a different micro-narrative stemming from his partitioning of time into episodes during the event sequence. In particular, at the end of the story Joe divides his experience into two episodes. The first one consists of the sequence $J_0 J_1$ and the second one of $J_2 J_8$. This is the case because between J_1 and J_2 Joe reaches the goal of forgetting Ann. Ann partitions her experience in three episodes. The first one consists of the sequence $A_0 A_6$, the second one of $A_6 A_7$, and the third one of point A_8. This is the case because in A_6 Ann's state changes from converging towards **marryAnnBob** to becoming invariant with respect to it, while in A_8 Ann decides to marry Bob. Analogously, Bob partitions his experience in five episodes, $B_0 B_1$, $B_2 B_6$, $B_6 B_7$, $B_7 B_8$ and B_9. Other micro-narratives also emerge. For example, during E1-7 Joe perceives Ann's state to rotate away from his and vice versa signifying a growing rift between the two, while on the other hand the states of Bob and Ann move close to one another signifying a gradual rapprochement. In general, subjective duration for Ann and Bob is greater than Bob, since the length for $J_0 J_8$ is less than either $A_0 A_8$ or $B_0 B_9$ indicating greater effort for Ann and Bob than Joe.

Acknowledgments. Presentation of this paper was partially supported by the University of Piraeus Research Center.

References

1. Wittmann, M.: Felt Time: The Psychology of How We Perceive Time. MIT Press, Cambridge (2015)
2. Husserl, E.: Phenomenology of Internal Time Consciousness. Indiana University Press, Indiana (1964)
3. Young, R., et al.: Plans and planning in narrative generation: a review of plan-based approaches to the generation of story, discourse and interactivity in narratives. Sprache und Datenverarbeitung **37**(2) (2013)
4. Baron, S., Miller, K.: Our concept of time. In: Mölder, B., Arstila, V., et al. (eds.) Philosophy and Psychology of Time. Studies in Brain & Mind, vol. 9. Springer, New York (2016)

5. Zakay, D.: Relative and absolute duration judgments under prospective and retrospective paradigms. Percept. Psychophysics **54**(5), 656–664 (1993)
6. Sgouros, N.M.: Psychagogy and quantum theory as conceptualizations for serious entertainment and its narrative. Entertainment Comput. **15** (2016). Elsevier

Productive Gaming

Ulrich Brandstätter$^{(\boxtimes)}$ and Christa Sommerer

Interface Culture, University of Art and Design Linz, Linz, Austria
{Ulrich.Brandstaetter,Christa.Sommerer}@ufg.at

Abstract. Video games can be appropriated for productive purposes. Commercial games and game engines are often used for video productions, and game development companies provide development kits and modding environments to gaming communities and independent developers. With gamification, game principles are deployed in non-game contexts for benefits beyond pure entertainment. Most approaches are more focused on using games and their design elements rather than the process of playing. We propose a video game category wherein productivity is achieved by playing video games, and present a forthcoming productive game as an example.

Keywords: Serious games · Media production · Video games · Play

1 Introduction

We propose a new video game category for video games that yield productive results by being played: *productive gaming* transforms playing activities into creative processes, facilitating creations with validity beyond game virtualities. In the language of McLuhan and Nevitt, who conceived the concept for electronic technology in 1972, we allow gamers to become *Prosumers* [1], i.e., consumers turned into producers.

The proposed video game category increases the value propositions[1] of video games. Implicitly, *"all games express and embody human values"* [3]. However, with the exception of serious games [4], the explicit gain of playing video games beyond pure recreation is disputable: as Malaby points out, play dissociates from everyday life by being consequence free and pleasurable and, especially, dissociates from work by staying within a *magic circle* [5]. Caillois divides play and productivity, and implies that game play must not become productive or be conducted in pursuit of profit, otherwise it becomes corrupted [6]. Consequently, the conjunction of play and productivity makes the introduction of specific framework conditions necessary. These are described as a set of attributes that apply to video games that enable productive gaming. However, we refrain from giving

---

[1] *"[...] a game's value proposition is in how it might make its player think and feel and fun is the ultimate emotional state that they expect to experience as a consequence of playing."* [2].

© IFIP International Federation for Information Processing 2016
Published by Springer International Publishing AG 2016. All Rights Reserved
G. Wallner et al. (Eds.): ICEC 2016, LNCS 9926, pp. 260–265, 2016.
DOI: 10.1007/978-3-319-46100-7_27

an ultimate definition to describe productive gaming. The reasoning behind this approach is given by Wittgenstein, who argues that *"elements of games, such as play, rules, and competition, all fail to adequately define what games are"* [7], and by Sutton-Smith, who considers the description and definition of play and games in non-paradoxical terms almost impracticable [8].

Games facilitating productive gaming are serious games with additional characteristics:

- productivity is a subject matter of the game, not to be enforced as game goals, but enabled as goals of the meta game.
- Consistently, productivity is not reflected in victory conditions, creational objectives are set and determined before or during play sessions by the players themselves, who retain unrestrained artistic freedom.
- Creation processes are aligned towards (and do not break) the game flow.
- Gameplay results are perceivable without the game and, ideally, even without knowledge of the game.

These nominal characteristics describe a non-exclusive video game category with emphasis on the game-play. Consistently, productive gaming requires games that provide mechanisms to start and realize creative processes, but also constructive-minded players.

In this paper, we describe related work with a concise disambiguation in Sect. 2. In Sect. 3, we provide a more detailed introduction to productive gaming. We then present Forever loops (Sect. 4), an ongoing project that facilitates productive gaming for the creation of audio-visual compositions. In Sect. 5, we discuss our findings and conclusions and present suggestions for future work.

2 Related Work

We differentiate from similar concepts using the previously introduced productive gaming characteristics. A related concept can be found in the industrial use of construction games, e.g. the utilization of *Lego* [9] for architectural prototypes, or using *Minecraft* [10] (in creative mode) as a 3D modeling environment. In both cases, productivity is a subject matter. The main distinction originates from the objectives. The industrial use of construction games typically involves predefined ambitions given by constituents, whereas in productive gaming the players themselves determine creational objectives before or during play. Another approach can be found in human-based computation games, or games with a purpose, where *"people playing computer games could, without consciously doing so, simultaneously solve large-scale problems"* [11]. Here, human game interaction is used to acquire labeling data for specific meta game goals, such as the analysis of gene sequences in *Play to Cure: Genes in Space* [12]. By being played, results with validity beyond the game virtuality are achieved. However, the creational goals usually are fixed by the developers and cannot be influenced by the players. A different, yet very popular concept is the utilization of game engines and modifications for media productions, e.g. *Machinima* communities using suitable computer games for video productions. Here, results typically are perceivable without the game and yield audio-visual makings. Nevertheless, productivity is achieved by using games rather than playing games. Finally, we dissociate productive gaming from gamification (i.e., the use of game design elements in non-game contexts [13]) because the latter usually aims at goal-oriented play: *"Finally, academic as well as industry critiques of gamified applications have repeatedly emphasized that these focus almost exclusively on design elements for rule-bound, goal-oriented play (i.e., ludus), with little space for open, exploratory, free-form play (i.e., paidia)"* [14].

3 Productive Gaming

A game example facilitating productive gaming can be found in *Sim Tunes* [15]. It resembles a drawing game in which players populate a canvas with up to four virtual bugs of different color. These AI-controlled bugs traverse the displayed virtual space and trigger music playback. Specific pixel colors represent different musical notes that are played by the instrument according to what is assigned to the bug. In terms of our proposed characteristics, Sim Tunes does not employ victory conditions, i.e., players set their own objectives and produce audio-visual creations by playing the game.

In general, productive gaming is closer to free form (*paidia*) than to more structured (*ludus*) playing and takes advantage of the games also being simulations: *"[...] Espen Aarseth has argued that [...] simulation is what drives most" serious games" [...]. In simulations, and I quote, "knowledge and experience is created by the player's actions and strategies". Aarseth calls for recognition of simulation as "a major new hermeneutic discourse mode, coinciding with the rise of computer technology, and with roots in games and playing."* [16]

The proximity to simulations makes a clear distinction from productivity software necessary. Barr describes the main differences as follows: *"First, the motivations for playing video games differ from productivity application use. Specifically, players play games for their own sake, while they generally use productivity applications to achieve some other task. Second, video game interfaces are not neutral, presenting carefully designed narratives and complex graphics to the player. Third, video games frequently dictate goals to players, while productivity applications generally facilitate user goals. Finally, video game designs purposefully involve conflict and constraints on the player, while productivity applications are designed to minimize them."* [17] Juul and Norton consider game obstacles and challenges as the distinguishing features of games as opposed to usability for productivity software [18]. For our purposes, the capability of seducing users into a lusory attitude [19] is the distinctive feature, i.e., play requires a proper mindset and engagement, which is established upon and complements game rules [20]. Concerning both the level of engagement and the level of game structure, productive gaming involves substantial oscillation effects on the paidia-ludus continuum [21] and play structure flexibility. During play sessions, users experiment and play with the simulations without pre-defined goals, and then apply their discoveries and new techniques to their performances.

In this context, the notion of serious storytelling must be contemplated, as well as its relation between serious games and productive games. Serious story-telling refers to *"storytelling outside the entertainment context, where the narra-tion as artefact is impressive in quality and relates to a matter of importance and seriousness."* [22] A narrative, i.e. the *"[...] chain of events related by cause and effect occurring in time and space and involving some agency"* [23], is important for both serious storytelling and productive gaming. Serious storytelling con-stitutes a broader concept with several application scenarios, including serious games, but also eLearning, qualitative journalism, virtual training environments, or forensics. Productive gaming on the other hand builds upon serious games and at the same time concerns only a subset.

4   Forever Loops

Forever loops by Marlene and Ulrich Brandstätter is a productive gaming project that produces audio-visual compositions. The underlying simulation involves an interface that primarily comprises graphical gears, as shown in Fig. 1.

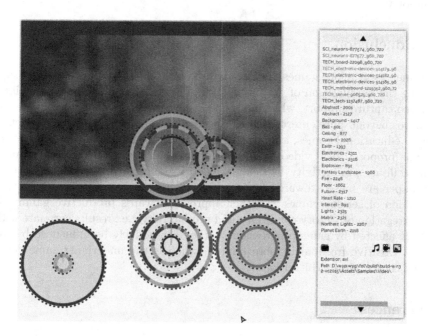

Fig. 1. Forever loops screen-shot. A gear train comprising multiple interconnected gears is playfully arranged and programmed by a user. The canvas in the upper left corner gives a visual representation of the audio-visual composition. The window to the right is required for media selection.

Relevant mechanisms are based on real-world gears and their machinery, which is well known and understood by most people. Users begin with a fundamental understanding of the system mechanics, which quickly evolves into impressive skills regarding (musical) composition and performance. Concerning productivity, the virtual gears can be interfaced with audio-visual material, including sounds, images, and videos. Playback of the media goes hand in hand with playfully arranging gears and gear trains with their respective programming.

Game play results include musical compositions, video remixes, slide shows, VJ acts, and even performances. In contrast to other productivity games, including the aforementioned Sim Tunes, players can import and are encouraged to use personal media material. On top of this, satisfactory results can be exported as a video file at user request, which can than be viewed without the game and even without knowledge of the game.

Users are encouraged to experiment with the underlying physics of the gear simulation, and to use their findings to produce new compositions at their own pace. A central aspect of our approach is the rejection of the notions of winning or losing. From a design perspective, it is common for video games to blur the borders between interface and game play [18]. Here the gear wheels and their mechanics become the central interface, and are tightly interwoven with the game-play.

5   Conclusion

To some extent, video games are already used for productive purposes, e.g., supporting the modification of existing games, asset export and import capability, or video capture support, which are popular game features that facilitate usage scenarios beyond pure entertainment. Specific video game genres, such as active games, educational games, and art games, attempt to offer additional benefits.

The proposed new video game category specifically describes video games that facilitate productivity by being played. Productive games as described in this paper are biased towards free-form play and can be considered as a specialization of serious games. Another approach towards productive gaming is the segregation of victory conditions and productivity, i.e., results correlate with and are affected by game progression, as they can actively be influenced by the player. Creative freedom is more limited, whereas the underlying game genre can be chosen more arbitrarily.

References

All links were last followed on July 17, 2016.

1. McLuhan, M., Nevitt, B.: Take Today: The Executive As Dropout. Harcourt, Brace, Jovanovich, Incorporated (1972). ISBN: 9780151878307
2. Ermi, L., Mäyrä, F.: Fundamental components of the gameplay experience: analysing immersion. In: DIGRA (2005)
3. Flanagan, M., Niessenbaum, H.: Values at Play in Digital Games. The MIT Press, Cambridge (2014)

4. Laamarti, F., Eid, M., El Saddik, A.: An overview of serious games. Int. J. Comput. Games Technol. **2014**, 11:11–11:11 (2014). Article ID 11 http://dl.acm.org/citation.cfm?id=2728206
5. Malaby, T.M.: Beyond play: a new approach to games. Games Cult. **2**, 95–113 (2007)
6. Caillois, R., Barash, M.: Man, Play, and Games. University of Illinois Press, Urbana (1961). ISBN: 9780252070334
7. Wittgenstein, L.: Philosophical Investigations. Blackwell Publishers, Oxford (1953)
8. Walther, B.K.: Playing and gaming reflections and classifications. Int. J. Comput. Game Res. **3** (2003)
9. Christiansen, O.K., TheLegoGroup: Lego (1949)
10. Persson, M., Mojang, Bergensten, J., Zetterstrand, K., Toivonen, M., Rosenfeld, D.: Minecraft (2009). https://minecraft.net/
11. von Ahn, L.: Games with a purpose. Computer **39**(6), 92–94 (2006). doi:10.1109/MC.2006.196, ISSN: 0018-9162
12. CancerResearchUK. Play to cure: genes in space (2014)
13. Deterding, S., Khaled, R., Nacke, L., Dixon, D.: Gamification: toward a definition. In: CHI Gamification Workshop Proceedings, Vancouver, BC, Canada (2011)
14. Deterding, S., Dixon, D., Khaled, R., Nacke, L.: From game design elements to gamefulness: Defining "gamification". In: Proceedings of the 15th International Academic MindTrek Conference: Envisioning Future Media Environments, MindTrek 2011, pp. 9–15. ACM, New York (2011b). ISBN: 978-1-4503-0816-8
15. Iwai, T., Mace, H., Itoh, B., Delvi, U., Martin, J., Maxis: Simtunes (1996)
16. Rockwell, G.M., Kee, K.: The leisure of serious games: a dialogue. Game Studies: Int. J. Comput. Game Res. **11** (2011). http://www.bibsonomy.org/bibtex/27f014bc2f7ef4b5ff248a10e523823af/dblp
17. Barr, P.: Video game values play as human-computer interaction. Ph.D. thesis, Victoria University of Wellington (2007)
18. Juul, J., Norton, M.: Easy to use, incredibly difficult: on the mythical border between interface and gameplay. In: Proceedings of the 4th International Conference on Foundations of Digital Games, FDG 2009, pp. 107–112. ACM, New York (2009). ISBN: 978-1-60558-437-9
19. Sommerer, C., Brandstätter, U., Mignonneau, L.: Aesthetics of interactive art: Art-game interfaces. In: Handbook of Digital Games and Entertainment Technologies (2015)
20. Salen, K., Zimmerman, E.: Rules of Play: Game Design Fundamentals. MIT Press, Cambridge (2004). ISBN: 9780262240451
21. Jensen, G.H.: Making sense of play in video games: ludus, paidia, and possibility spaces. Eludamos. J. Comput. Game Cult. **7**, 69–80 (2013)
22. Suhonen, J., Lugmayr, A., Sutinen, E.: Serious storytelling - serious digital story telling. In: Proceedings of the 7th International Workshop on Semantic Ambient Media Experiences (SAME 2014), Ambient Media Usability, Interaction, and Smart Media Technologies (2014)
23. Wilkens, T., Hughes, A., Wildemuth, B.M., Marchionini, G.: The role of narrative in understanding digital video: an exploratory analysis. Proc. Am. Soc. Inf. Sci. Technol. **40**(1), 323–329 (2003). doi:10.1002/meet.1450400140, ISSN: 1550–8390

Solving the Sophistication-Population Paradox of Game Refinement Theory

Shuo Xiong[1]([⊠]), Parth Pankaj Tiwary[2], and Hiroyuki Iida[1]([⊠])

[1] Japan Advanced Institute of Science and Technology, Nomi, Japan
{xiongshuo,iida}@jaist.ac.jp
[2] Shri Mata Vaishno Devi University, Katra, India
parthpankajtiwary@gmail.com

Abstract. A mathematical model of game refinement was proposed based on uncertainty of game outcome. This model has been shown to be useful in measuring the entertainment element in the domains such as boardgames and sport games. However, game refinement theory has not been able to explain the correlation between the popularity of a game and the game refinement value. This paper introduces another aspect in the study of game entertainment, the concept of "attractiveness" to reasonably explain the sophistication-population paradox of game refinement theory.

Keywords: Game refinement theory · Physical model in game · Attractiveness of board like games

1 Introduction

The dynamics of decision options in the decision space has been investigated and we observed that this dynamics was a key factor in gauging game entertainment. Then Iida et al. [1] proposed the measure of the refinement in games. The outcome of interesting games is always uncertain until the very end of the game. Thus, the variation in available options stays nearly constant throughout the game. In contrast to this, one player quickly dominates over the other in uninteresting games. Here options are likely to be diminishing quickly from the decision space. Therefore, the refined games are more likely to be seesaw games. We then recall the principle of seesaw games [3].

Based on the principle of seesaw games, Iida et al. [4] proposed a logistic model of game uncertainty. From the players' viewpoint, the information on the game result is an increasing function of time (the number of moves) t. We further define the information on the game result as the amount of solved uncertainty $x(t)$. Game information progress presents how certain is the result of the game in a certain time or steps. Let B and D be the average branching factor and the average number of the depth of game, respectively. If one knows the game information progress, for example after the game, the game progress $x(t)$ will be

© IFIP International Federation for Information Processing 2016
Published by Springer International Publishing AG 2016. All Rights Reserved
G. Wallner et al. (Eds.): ICEC 2016, LNCS 9926, pp. 266–271, 2016.
DOI: 10.1007/978-3-319-46100-7_28

given as a linear function of time t with $0 \leq t \leq B$ and $0 \leq x(t) \leq B$, as shown in Eq. (1).

$$x(t) = \frac{B}{D} t \qquad (1)$$

However, the game information progress given by Eq. (1) is usually unknown during the in-game period. Hence, the game information progress is reasonably assumed to be exponential. This is because the game outcome is uncertain until the very end of game in many games. Hence, a realistic model of game information progress is given by Eq. (2).

$$x(t) = B(\frac{t}{D})^n \qquad (2)$$

Here n stands for a constant parameter which is given based on the perspective of an observer in the game considered. Then acceleration of game information progress is obtained by deriving Eq. (2) twice. Solving it at $t = T$, the equation becomes:

$$x''(T) = \frac{Bn(n-1)}{D^n} t^{n-2} = \frac{B}{D^2} n(n-1).$$

It is assumed in the current model that the game information progress in any type of games is happening in our minds. We do not know yet about the physics in our minds, but it is likely and we propose that the acceleration of information progress is related to the force in mind. Hence, it is reasonable to expect that the larger the value $\frac{B}{D^2}$ is, the more the game becomes exciting due to the uncertainty of game outcome. Thus, we use its root square, $\frac{\sqrt{B}}{D}$, as a game refinement measure for the game considered [4]. We show, in Table 1, a comparison of game refinement measures for traditional board games [4].

Table 1. Measures of game refinement for traditional board games

	B	D	$\frac{\sqrt{B}}{D}$
Chess	35	80	0.074
Go	250	208	0.076
Shogi	80	115	0.078

2   Attractiveness in Board Like Games

One of the limitations of the game refinement value is that it fails in explaining the disparity in the population of fans and players of some of the games with equal or higher game refinement value. For example, GO has a higher game refinement value than soccer, but soccer still attracts a far greater population of fans and players than GO. We define this limitation of game refinement theory as the **sophistication-population** paradox that we will address in the course of this paper. Therefore, this section draws upon the limits of game refinement theory and then proposes a notion of attractiveness in game playing. A mathematical model of attractiveness for board like games is proposed.

Game refinement theory has expressed the relationship between uncertainty of outcome and game progress, a game outcome can be considered based on two factors: skill and chance. In the balanced game, the game outcome is decided by players' skill and chance which incorporates some stochastic events, events which cannot be controlled or predicted. For chess, in the ideal situation, the top player or AI can always select the best moves at any time in the game, and all of players choices or branching factor are decided by players consideration, while we calculate game refinement value by the formula $R = \frac{\sqrt{B}}{D}$.

Similar to the branching factor, we introduce a new concept known as "attractiveness branching factor". If there is an element in the game which can neither be controlled or predicted by audience as well as the players, we refer to that element as the element of attractiveness. Generally, there are three situations which will develop the game uncertainty.

3   Physical Model of Attractiveness in Board Like Games

We take in consideration the human thinking process in the traditional board games, intelligent players would follow such a process as shown in Fig. 1. For example in chess, the average branching factor (say B) is about 35 [6], but out of these choices, many moves are not reasonable to Play. After filtering out some of the existing options based on players' skill, we will be left with a smaller set of plausible moves which we define as "b". Generally, a player is not always aware of the best choice available in b where $b \geq 2$, so he takes a chance, which as a result introduces a chance element in the game. By plausible consideration of available moves depending on the skill of the player and taking some chance, a player decides his final move [2,7].

Fig. 1. A model of thinking process in traditional board games

Almost all traditional board games fall in the category of strategic games, and a pre-dominant way of approaching or playing these games is using the concept of **Convergence**. It is a very integral aspect of human thinking process, everyday humans are faced with situations where they have a lot of possible options which can be pursued, but somehow these options are narrowed down to a smaller set based on the existing laws and morality because not all options are plausible.

Board games are the same, in order to win the game players need thought to filter their strategy, this thought process is a typical convergence process [7]. Therefore we refer to the thought process as the resistance force in game process and we redefine the formula for force as follows [5].

$$\mathbf{F - f = ma} \tag{3}$$

In Eq. (3), $F = m \times R^2$, $a = r_0^2 = (\frac{1}{D})^2$. Consider chance element and skill element, while $B = b$ in Fig. 1, we have $a_b = r^2 = (\frac{b}{D})^2$. By substituting all the values in Eq. (3), separately for skill and chance we obtain the set of Eq. (4).

$$\begin{cases} f_s = F_s - m \times r^2 = m \times R^2 - m \times r^2 \\ f_c = F_c - m \times r_0^2 = m \times r^2 - m \times r_0^2 \end{cases} \tag{4}$$

Therefore, the total resistance force will be the sum of equations in Eq. (4), which is described as $f = F - m \times a = f_c + f_s$.

By the theorem of impulse, we have the following formula.

$$J = \int_{t1}^{t2} f dt = f \Delta t = mv$$

For game refinement theory we have $v = \frac{f \Delta t}{m}$, while the F is replaced by F_s (the force by skill) and F_c (the force by chance), the formula will be changed as follows.

$$f \Delta t = (f_s + f_c) \Delta t = mv$$

In anytime for one deterministic game, "mass" will not be changed, therefore in any time duration Δt, we have

$$v = \frac{(f_s + f_c) \Delta t}{m} = \frac{f_s \Delta t}{m} + \frac{f_c \Delta t}{m} = v_s + v_c$$

Then according to Fig. 2, for the v_c part, the "attractiveness theory" will be obtained. In game refinement theory, the v is $\frac{B}{D}$; while v replaced by $v_c + v_s$, the refinement theory will be $\frac{B}{D} = \frac{B_c + B_s}{D} = \frac{B_c}{D} + \frac{B_s}{D}$. B_c means the branching factor which was controlled by chance element in game and B_s means the branching factor which was controlled by player's skill. Then we call the B_c as a new parameter character $B' + 1$, which changes the "branching factor" into "the branching factor which players cannot control or predict", "1" means the final determined movement. Then we can apply the likeness game refinement theory as shown in Eq. (5). In Eq. (5), B' means "attractive branching factor", D means "Depth" of game.

$$A = \frac{\sqrt{B'}}{D} = \frac{\sqrt{B_c - 1}}{D} = \frac{\sqrt{b - 1}}{D} \tag{5}$$

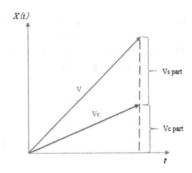

Fig. 2. The speed of attractiveness

4   Application of Attractiveness Theory

We consider three situations: the traditional board games; the games in which information cannot be observed in-game time (non-stochastic incomplete information game); the games in which only stochastic events occur (stochastic complete information game), then we choose Shogi (Japanese Chess) and StarCraft II HOS version as the benchmark for our mathematical model.

From the master's point of view, there are only a few plausible candidates to play at each position in chess [7]. In this study we assume that it may be equal to $\log_3 B$ in the sophisticated boardgames such Shogi and Go. Using this assumption we have the following conclusion. In Shogi the game attractiveness value equals to $A = \frac{\sqrt{B_c - 1}}{D} = \frac{\sqrt{4-1}}{115} = 0.015$, whereas the game refinement value is 0.078.

The attractiveness scaling factor of any game is given by Eq. (6).

$$P_{asf} = \frac{Game\ attractiveness\ value}{Game\ refinement\ value} \tag{6}$$

So, the attractiveness scaling factor of Shogi is 19.3 %. Similarly, we can calculate the attractiveness value for StarCraft II HOS version as shown in Table 2 [8]. The higher the attractiveness value of the game, the larger the population of fans and players the game will attract.

Table 2. The three properties of different game

Game	R value	A value	P_{asf}
Shogi	0.078	0.015	19.3 %
StarCtaft II	0.0695	0.0266–0.0423	38.27 %–60.86 %

5   Conclusion

In this paper, according to the Newton's classical mechanics we have found the meaning of Mass and Force in games. Then based on the theorem of impulse, we educed the property, concept and value of "attractiveness" to explain the sophistication-population paradox put forth by the game refinement value. We introduced the concept of "attractiveness scaling factor", which can be used to show whether a game is compatible for a novice or a weaker player or not. Higher the attractiveness scaling factor more chance a weaker player will have of winning the game. The lower attractiveness factor means the game will shift towards a more skill based game outcome and hence there will be less chance for novice or weaker player to win the game. Usually a high attractiveness scaling factor of a game will attract more fans and players population. This as a result explains as to why Shogi and Go even after having a really high game refinement value and sophistication still attract a much smaller fans and player population when compared to the more popular games of similar game refinement value such as soccer.

Acknowledgments. This work is funded by a grant from the Japan Society for the Promotion of Science (JSPS), in the framework of the Grant-in-Aid for Challenging Exploratory Research (grant number 26540189) and Grant-in-Aid for JSPS Fellow.

References

1. Iida, H., Takeshita, N., Yoshimura, J.: A metric for entertainment ofboardgames: Its implication for evolution of chess variants. Entertainment Computing Technologies and Applications, pp. 65–72 (2003)
2. Allis, V.L., van den Herik, H.J., Herschberg, I.S.: Which Games Will Survive? In: Levy, D.N.L., Beal, D.F. (eds.) Heuristic Programming in Artificial Intel Ligence 2: The Second Computer Olympiad, pp. 232–243. Ellis Horwood Ltd., Chichester (1991)
3. Cincotti, A., Iida, H., Yoshimura, J.: Refinement and complexity in the evolution of chess. In: Proceedings of the 10th International Conference on Computer Science and Informatics, pp. 650–654 (2007)
4. Iida, H., Takahara, K., Nagashima, J., Kajihara, Y., Hashimoto, T.: An application of game-refinement theory to mah jong. In: Rauterberg, M. (ed.) ICEC 2004. LNCS, vol. 3166, pp. 333–338. Springer, Heidelberg (2004)
5. Tait, P.G.: Newton's Laws of Motion. A. & C, Black (1899)
6. Matsubara, H., Iida, H., Grimbergen, R.: Chess, Shogi, Go, natural developments in game research. ICCA J. **19**(2), 103–112 (1996)
7. de Groot, A.D.: (1965). Thought and Choice in Chess, later published from Amsterdam Academic Archive (2008)
8. Xiong, S., Iida, H.: Attractiveness of real time strategy games. In: ICSAI 2014, pp. 264–269. IEEE (2014)

Cultural Visualisation of a Cultural Photographic Collection in 3D Environments – Development of 'PAV 3D' (Photographic Archive Visualisation)

Artur Lugmayr[✉], Adam Greenfeld, Andrew Woods, and Pauline Joseph

Curtin University, Perth, Australia
{artur.lugmayr, adam.greenfeld, andrew.woods,
pauline.joseph}@curtin.edu.au,
http://www.curtin.edu.au/vismedia

Abstract. This demonstration illustrates the possibilities of new 3D technologies in conveying large scale historical photographic databases in interactive 3D virtual environments. We illustrate the visualization of the State Library of Western Australia (SLWA)'s photographic collection containing over 1 million photographs dating back to the 1850s utilizing Curtin's Hub for Immersive Visualization and eResearch (HIVE). Our application was intended to explore the possibilities in visualizing cultural data sets on the HIVE's Cylinder, a 3 m high, eight-meter diameter, and 180° cylindrical projection surface. Our demonstration illustrated the potentials of virtual environments in creating interactive information designs for photographic imagery, which can be explored according location, time-period, creator, and subject.

Keywords: Cultural visualization · Computer graphics · Virtual environments · Oculus rift · 3D · Cultural collections · Photographic archives

1 Introduction

The aim of the project was the development of a prototype to serendipitously navigate and visualize the image archives that is the photographic collection of the State Library of Western Australia (SLWA). The intended audience for the discovery and engagement with this collection are the general public users of the SLWA. With these aims, the objective was the creation of a proof of concept prototype to:

(1) explore the capabilities and suitability of Curtin University's Hub for Immersive Visualisation and eResearch (HIVE) [1];
(2) create a prototype that extends existing similar undertakings based in 2D towards large screen 3D displays;
(3) the exploration of Virtual Reality (VR), in particular large immersive 3D displays as a tool for visualizing large-scale image databases; and

© IFIP International Federation for Information Processing 2016
Published by Springer International Publishing AG 2016. All Rights Reserved
G. Wallner et al. (Eds.): ICEC 2016, LNCS 9926, pp. 272–277, 2016.
DOI: 10.1007/978-3-319-46100-7_29

(4) the creation of an appealing and easy to use prototype to illustrate information design aspects for representing large scale image databases in 3D.

The main components of the system architecture (as illustrated in Fig. 6) consist of the large scale photographic archive collection of the SLWA. The archive contains over one million photographs going back almost a century and each photograph holds a little piece of Western Australia's historical memories covering events, places, buildings, lifestyles, people and families to list a few. The PAV-3D project attempted to create a prototype that illustrates the capabilities of presenting images and associated metadata in a virtual environment, instead of creating a simple web-interface prototype for presenting the archive content (The flowchart is presented in Fig. 1).

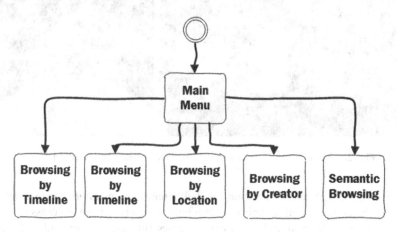

Fig. 1. Flowchart of the prototype software

2 Related Works

The demand for accessing digital photographic collections housed by cultural institutions and utilizing it in digital humanities and visualization projects is increasing. With this application, we explore the possibilities of immersive environments in digital humanities [2, 3], or [4]. For example, DX Labs in cooperation with the State Library of New South Wales (SLNSW) [5] created the Loom digital interface, which is "a multi layered visualization experiment" that enables news ways of exploring the digitized images of the SLNSW [5]. The Loom online interface offers users different viewing experiences to explore photographic collections in chronologic order based on time, location and topics in a 2D web-space. 3D representations have been considered in form of a projection of Sydney, utilizing location based information of photographic materials. Of the 14,664 digitized images in the SLNSW's collection, 3,287 images are accessible via LOOM, of which 1,396 have been tagged [5].

3   Implementation of 3 Scenarios

The Curtin HIVE was used to develop the virtual reality environment [1]. Our target display was the Cylinder, which is a projection surface stretching 3 m high, and 8 m in diameter. The Cylinder is back-projected, and immerses the user within a 180° cylindrical projection surface. By using 3D glasses, the user is fully immersed into the 3D environment, which is projected onto the display surface (see Fig. 2).

Fig. 2. Curtin's Hub for Immersive Visualisation and eResearch (HIVE)

Figures 2, 3, 4, 5 and 7 illustrate the 3 different demonstrators for the variables location, subject, and timeline. This project involved expertise from the cross discipline areas of data visualization and information studies (library, records and archives) at Curtin. Visitors to libraries and archival intuitions are increasingly expecting a virtual experience when interrogating search interfaces in these institutions to explore their vast information collections. There is an expectation to interact with the search catalogues to serendipitously discover items of interest that fulfils the users' everyday life information needs. These user expectations align closely with information seeking experiences increasingly provided by museums for its visitors.

Fig. 3. Scenario 1 – browsing by timeline

Fig. 4. Scenario 2 – browsing by subject

Fig. 5. Scenario 3 – browsing by location.

There are requirements for interacting with the search catalogue using as many human senses as possible: eyes, hands, nose, mouth, ears. Sensory engagement with the collection using mediums of vision and touch are paramount in most cases. Such user experience expectations require future graduates in library and archives professions to be aware and equipped with skill sets in the visual media and data visualization disciplines. Hence, this project offered an opportunity to explore what these skill sets are and to learn from the expertise of the discipline of visual media. Further, to investigate if there are opportunities for offering information studies graduates with elective study pathways in visual media.

4   Discussion and Conclusions

It's evident, that through the emergence of today's digital photographic equipment, and the multi-faceted possibilities to share visual data that currently more visual content is available than ever before [6]. We focused on an advanced information design to develop a visualization prototype of the State Library of Western Australia (SLWA)'s over 1 million photographs, dating back to the 1850s, and holding a little piece of Western Australia's history covering events, locations, buildings, persons, and families. The basic architecture of the implementation is illustrated in Fig. 6.

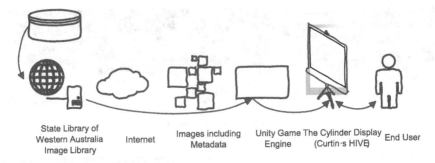

State Library of
Western Australia   Internet   Images including   Unity Game The Cylinder Display End User
Image Library   Metadata   Engine   (Curtin·s HIVE)

Fig. 6. Architectural overview of PAV-3D

From the information design perspective, the image archive could be browsed in 5 modalities: timeline, location, keywords, creator, and semantic browsing. The last modality is currently still in implementation stage, and will not be available for the demonstration. As core platform for the implementation of the prototype, we have been utilizing Unity. Our prototype was based on the metadata available through the library API's. For the scope of the prototype, we simplified the basic metadata to allow an easier implementation of the software. Example metadata is illustrated in Table 1.

Table 1. Example metadata for a library database entry.

Filename	Description	Location			Date	
slwa_b38000000_22	312750PD: House, 240 Newcastle Street, North-bridge,	- 31.945338 -	115.859459	19840500	0/5/1984	May '84

Fig. 7. PAV-3D browsing by images from one creator.

References

1. C. HIVE. http://humanities.curtin.edu.au/research/centres/hive/
2. Lugmayr, A., Teras, M.: Immersive interactive technologies in digital humanities: a review and basic concepts. In: Proceedings of the 3rd International Workshop on Immersive Media Experiences, pp. 31–36 (2015). http://doi.acm.org.dbgw.lis.curtin.edu.au/10.1145/2814347.2814354
3. Lugmayr, A., Bender, S.: Free UX testing tool: the LudoVico UX machine for physiological sensor data recording, analysis, and visualization for user experience design experiments. In: Proceedings of the SEACHI 2016 on Smart Cities for Better Living with HCI and UX, pp. 36–41 (2016). http://doi.acm.org/10.1145/2898365.2899801
4. Lugmayr, A., Stockleben, B., Scheib, C., Mailaparampil, M., Mesia, N., Ranta, H.: A comprehensive survey on Big Data research and it's implications - what is really 'new' in Big Data? It's cognitive Big Data. In: Proceedings of the 20th Pacific-Asian Conference on Information Systems (PACIS 2016) (2016). http://www.pacis2016.org/abstract/Index
5. S.L. of New South Wales, LOOM. http://dxlab.sl.nsw.gov.au/loom
6. Schmidt, E.: Every 2 Days We Create As Much Information As We Did Up To 2003 (2010). http://techcrunch.com/2010/08/04/schmidt-data/

Posters

Enrichment of Story Reading
with Digital Media

Pedro Ribeiro[1]([⊠]), Ido Iurgel[1], Wolfgang Müller[2],
and Christian Ressel[1]

[1] Rhine-Waal University of Applied Sciences, Friedrich-Heinrich-Allee 25,
47475 Kamp-Lintfort, Germany
{pr,ii,cr}@hsrw.eu
[2] University of Education Weingarten, Leibnizstr. 3,
88250 Weingarten, Germany
mueller@md-phw.de

Abstract. Reading is no more limited to the physicality of the book whether it is screen or paper. Digital media's potentialities represent an opportunity to leverage a novel reading-experience. We envision that a more joyful and immersive reading-experience can be promoted by interacting with the reading space. Reading can be enriched by controlling digital media infrastructures that contextually react to the reading performance and the narrative. In this paper, we present a prototype and a key scenario, which demonstrate that digital enrichment promises new ways of experiencing a story. Furthermore, we explore the features which characterize this concept and we envision its potential roles.

Keywords: Reading · Stories · E-books · Augmented reading · Digital media

1 Introduction

Reading is a vital skill to function in today's society. But why do we read? What are the reasons? In a research, Clark and Rumbold [5] explain the link between reading enjoyment and reading motivation and stated that readers who are intrinsically motivated are more likely to benefit from enjoyment and achieve a deep learning.

Nowadays, we witness to a shift in the way we read and in the materiality of the book brought about by digital technology. E-books are a digital replication of a paper book that in some cases is augmented with functionalities such as dictionary or games. Typically, these augmentations happen in the same medium where the text is. But how can we foster enjoyment and meet the reader's motivations better without compromising the reading performance? In this paper, we describe a concept that aims to allow the interaction with the reading space just by reading. In this space, digital media infrastructures react to the reading performance and the narrative, promoting enjoyment and immersion.

A significant number of studies have investigated how to digitally augment the book. The MagicBook project [4] explored the potential of augmented reality to enrich the reading-experience. Since then, several academic and commercial books employed augmented reality. Recently, researchers developed the SequenceBook [10], an interactive book with blank pages that serves as medium for a dynamic projection. Another

G. Wallner et al. (Eds.): ICEC 2016, LNCS 9926, pp. 281–285, 2016.
DOI: 10.1007/978-3-319-46100-7_30

interesting concept explored the experience of a textbook with a fold-out screen-margin extension [6, 7]. The margin space allows complementary content.

A small number of studies have been done in the area of automated environments that reacts to the reading activity. Back et al. (1999) presented The SIT book [2], a prototype, able to use the reader hands' speed as control parameter for a narrative soundscape. Later in 2005, Bahna and Jacob presented a system [3] in which extra information is peripherally conveyed through a video projection. In 2013, Alam et al. proposed the augmentation of an e-book reading-experience by controlling haptic and audio-visual interfaces existing in a living room [1]. Finally, Schafer et al. developed a system that uses a multimedia room to transform an interactive read-aloud experience, providing feedback that supports children's enjoyment and meaning-making [8].

2 Prototype

Story reading enrichment (SRE) means to synchronize the reading with one or more digital media experiences. A SRE system must allow (1) the definition of how digital media infrastructures will respond to the reading performance and narrative; (2) the control and perception of a SRE. In order to explore the SRE, we developed a prototype composed by a Tablet and a Smart bulb. The Tablet displays the story, identify the reading position and control the bulb. In order to obtain, the reading position, the system employs speech recognition. Then, depending on the specification of how the light must behave, in a specific reading position, the Tablet controls light's properties.

3 Scenario

Emma uses a Tablet to read "The Hobbit" [9] to her son Matt. Matt can see on his Tablet a map of "Middle-earth". He easily realizes where they stopped and by touching the spot, the text appears on both Tablets. The room turns dark, and a cavern soundscape can be heard. When Emma mentions a character, she also associates it to a light (by pointing the lamp). The Light reflects the character's emotions. While reading, the riddles' "battle", the lights of Bilbo and Gollum start to oscillate between white (fear), yellow (joy) and red (angry). At the same time, a melody intensifies the drama. Later, Matt uses the map to jump to a beloved section, where dwarves sing in choir. Matt can then see a lyric and starts to read it. Matt follows a word highlighting feature, which provides the correct pace. When Matt starts to read, a melody starts playing. The longer Matt respects the pace, the more instruments and voices densify the music. By reading correctly he unlocks different music channels, coming from different positions. This game progressively immerses him in a joyful environment.

4 Story Reading Enrichment: Features

Based on the scenario, we identified the four main features of a SRE:

Required attention: Reading is a high attentional activity, demanding constant foreground visual attention. The SRE must be able to display information both to the *peripheral attention* and to the *foreground attention.* Peripheral interaction aims to subtly augment the reality with the narrative's context, e.g. white light to reflect the fear felt by Bilbo. On the other hand, the interaction can obviously encompass a more concrete stimulation e.g. an image of a frightened Bilbo, providing an interactive context that supports the storytelling or meaning-making.

Virtuality: The SRE is characterized by its virtuality and can vary in a continuum that ranges between (a) *real environment* (b) *virtual environment*, wherein the inter-medium is characterized by a *mixed reality experience.*

Locus of agency: A SRE can be *proactive* and/or *reactive.* In the simplest usage, a SRE shall be *proactive,* because whenever the reader is focused on reading, an implicit enrichment must happen e.g. melody intensifying the drama. On the other hand, enrichment can be reactive when a reader explicitly requires enrichment e.g. storyteller that uses SRE to complement his performance - make a gestures to set all lights off.

Interactivity: SREs can be controlled and perceived by readers through a multi-modal interaction. Regarding the control of a SRE, the reading position and performance can be detected through different input modalities (touch, speech recognition, eye gaze direction, gesture recognition or even emotion recognition). The perception of a SRE can be promoted by different modalities such as visual, auditory, haptic, etc.

5 Story Reading Enrichment: Roles

Based on the SRE's features, we envision roles with a focus on multiple aspects of the intrinsic motivation [5] such as curiosity, involvement or social interaction.

Meaning-making: What if the reader does not know a specific object or idea? In order to foster the *curiosity* and to avoid losing *involvement*, the SRE can function as a facilitator of meaning-making e.g. when several characters are introduced in a short amount of text, reader may benefit from additional digital media. This kind of SRE can be explicitly initiated by the reader or implicitly through concentration sensing.

Intensification/clarification: Another way to promote *involvement,* is by intensifying the reading. A scene can be intensified through music targeting an emotional state or a fictional genre. The SRE can also serve as a clarification to interpret text. A good example is, when a figure of speech like irony or metaphor is used.

Support: In another perspective the SRE can support the reading performance. This functionality is characterized by a playful manner of using a SRE, targeted to extend the reader's expressivity e.g. a storyteller controlling the SRE through gestures or speech. This supportive role shall promote social activities such as storytelling.

Training: The SRE as a playable environment can be used in a gamified experience e.g. rewarding by mastering reading and interpretation skills. Another example is to encourage a focused reading, by providing a SRE based on neurofeedback technic.

Topography: The SRE can also be used to simplify the text navigation. We believe that, if the reader can use a simple metaphor to map and mark the written content, we can promote a feeling of being in control of the reading. An example is the creation of a virtual map where the reading-experiences or digital marginalia are mapped.

Inspiration: The SRE can also spark the imagination. When an author deliberately describes a scene, in an ambiguous way, he is challenging reader's imagination. SRE can have the mission of supporting the imagination challenge. For example, by allowing readers to decide in which kind of virtual environment they want to read (forest, city, etc.) or by synchronizing the SRE with the narrative and reading performance.

Cumulative reading: The SRE must be able to learn from each reading session and enhance the reader's capacity to recall/relate thoughts and emotions from previous readings and adapt SRE's behaviours based on reader's preferences.

6 Conclusion

In this paper, we explore a concept that employs digital media infrastructures, that react to the reading performance and the narrative, promoting a more joyful and immersive reading-experience. Based on the user experience envisioned through a key scenario, we analyse the principal features of a SRE and discuss how SRE can assume a variety of roles, promoting experiences that aim to match readers' intrinsic motivations. This paper highlights the potential and open questions of this concept. It also serves as a conceptual framework for developing SREs. Further work will involve building a functional SRE system that allows the proof-of-concepts development. Furthermore, evaluations will be performed to understand how to effectively enrich the story reading and to identify story genres' constraints and side effects.

References

1. Alam, K.M., Rahman, A.S.M.M., Saddik, A.E.: Mobile haptic e-book system to support 3D immersive reading in ubiquitous environments. ACM Trans. Multimedia Comput. Commun. Appl. **9**, 1–20 (2013). ACM, New York
2. Back, M., Gold, R., Kirsch, D.: The SIT book: audio as affective imagery for interactive storybooks. In: CHI 1999 Extended Abstracts on Human Factors in Computing Systems, pp. 202–203. ACM, New York (1999)
3. Bahna, E., Jacob, R.J.K.: Augmented reading: presenting additional information without penalty. In: CHI 2005 Extended Abstracts on Human Factors in Computing Systems, pp. 1909–1912. ACM, New York (2005)
4. Billinghurst, M., Kato, H., Poupyrev, I.: The MagicBook: a transitional AR interface. Comput. Graph. **25**, 745–753 (2001). Elsevier
5. Clark, C., Rumbold, K.: Reading for pleasure: a research overview. ERIC (2006)
6. Figueiredo, A.C., Pinto, A.L., Zagalo, N., Branco, P.: Bridging book: a not-so-electronic children's picturebook. In: Proceedings of the 12th International Conference on Interaction Design and Children, pp. 569–572. ACM, New York (2013)
7. MFA Thesis: Marginalia. http://www.chrisrbecker.com/marginalia
8. Schafer, G., Green, K., Walker, I., Fullerton, S.K., Lewis, E.: An interactive, cyber-physical read-aloud environment. In: Proceedings of the 2014 Conference on Designing Interactive Systems, pp. 865–874. ACM, New York (2014)

9. Tolkien, J.R.R.: The Hobbit. HarperCollins, London (1996)
10. Yamada, H.: SequenceBook: interactive paper book capable of changing the storylines by shuffling pages. In: CHI 2010 Extended Abstracts on Human Factors in Computing Systems, pp. 4375–4380. ACM, New York (2010)

Vancouver Maneuver: Designing a Cooperative Augmented Reality Board Game

Alexander Golombek, Michael Lankes$^{(\boxtimes)}$, and Jürgen Hagler

Department of Digital Media, University of Applied Sciences Upper Austria,
Softwarepark 11, 4232 Hagenberg, Austria
S1410628004@students.fh-hagenberg.at,
{michael.lankes,juergen.hagler}@fh-hagenberg.at

Abstract. In this paper we present *Vancouver Maneuver*, a game for mobile devices using Augmented Reality software to create a cooperative board game experience. Utilizing principles from both digital and analogue board game design, a hybrid game design approach is proposed in order to identify applicable mechanics. By doing so we combine the physical and social aspects of co-located tabletop gaming with the computing power and aesthetics of digital games.

Keywords: Augmented Reality · Board games · Co-located play

1 Introduction

With recent developments in the field of smartphones or tablets, the market for mobile computer games is still growing. Technological improvements, both regarding computing power and the handling of advanced 3D graphics, make it possible for game developers to create games with demanding hardware specifications in mind. Current generations of mobile devices even allow Augmented Reality (AR) applications to be available for a majority of smartphone users.

According to Zagal et al. [1] all games have their roots in the physical world, whether it is sports on wide fields or strategical board games with game pieces. While digital games tend to be more solitary and are experienced individually, traditional games are often played with others. When looking at digital games, the majority of games are played on desktop computers or game consoles, and are either singleplayer games or multiplayer online games where players interact on a mediated basis. One reason for this can be seen in the nature of how computers are typically used—one user at a time and physically separated from other players. Handheld everyday devices like smartphones, on the other hand, break up these restrictions. AR can combine co-located, collaborative gaming, like it is associated with board games, with the processing power and the possibilities of real-time visual feedback known from digital games. The idea is to take the basic concept of a board game and use the device to source out tasks like checking rules, calculating scores and resources or apply chance based numbers.

© IFIP International Federation for Information Processing 2016
Published by Springer International Publishing AG 2016. All Rights Reserved
G. Wallner et al. (Eds.): ICEC 2016, LNCS 9926, pp. 286–289, 2016.
DOI: 10.1007/978-3-319-46100-7_31

Apart from utilizing well established mechanics from digital games, new concepts and ideas can be introduced, since the combination of analogue and digital games is more as the sum of its parts.

2 Related Work

For mobile AR settings there are several interaction studies like gesture tracking or works related to traditional image and marker tracking (e.g. Peitz et al. [2]) or the recognition of finger movement via camera [3]. With all these new concepts being available, it is the main challenge for game designers to work with the technology and develop applicable games that use them extensively. There also have been studies regarding actual game piece tracking in order to maintain a certain physicality [4]. A new medium will always take some time to explore its full potential, and work like *Art of Defense* by Duy-Nguyen et al. [5] demonstrates how the use of tangible objects is a step in the right direction. As the team explicates in their paper about the game, tangible elements are a vital part in AR games in order to interact with the merged environments of reality and the virtual world. *The Sphero* [6] is an AR installation that focuses on the physical environment around players and thus increases immersion and enjoyability. However, until now, apart from the technological advancements in the mobile AR game domain, little is known about the design approaches and procedures.

3 Our Game Design Approach: Vancouver Maneuver

Designing an AR board game contains practices from both design fields, since developers create games with the physical and social dimension of board games in mind, while simultaneously having the tools and experience of digital game development at their disposal. As a starting point for our game design approach we picked one specific form of game: the cooperative puzzle. While competitive games also have a strong social component they often tend to cause tactical avoidance of conversation and self-restraint. Since it is a common approach for board games we began with an analogue paper prototype which then got transferred into a digital one. Based on these findings we created our game prototype of *Vancouver Maneuver (VM)*. Each player controls a burglar via his/her mobile device, working together to get a key and open a safe. Obstacles include security cameras, laser sensors and locked doors. By rotating rooms players solve different puzzles with increasing difficulty (see Fig. 1).

When thinking about board games and its differences in comparison to digital games, there are three interdependent factors to account for regarding game design: the general setting of players, the physicality of game pieces and the social interaction [7]. Regarding the first factor the obvious design choice for *VM* was to position the two player opposite to one another to establish differing vantage points onto the game board in order to encourage social interaction. For example one player has vision over a certain area of the game world and has to describe it to his teammate. Apart from the physical vantage point AR can

Fig. 1. The board as seen through a mobile device (left) and the screen view (right).

achieve this through different renderings on the respective players device. There are parts of the game world which are only visible to one player, regardless of his position, but rather linked to his avatar. This also helps to engage the players in real-world movement, an aspect that other AR games like *BloxAR* [8] also valued highly.

The second big aspect of board games is the physicality of game pieces and their interaction. In *VM* this factor is covered by separate board tiles for each rotatable room (see Fig. 2). One thing to take account is the mobile device itself. Players tend to look through their virtual camera very often, so a secondary interaction with the other hand is not easy to manage – especially for new players. While interaction with real world objects is mandatory, it is still more reliable to fall back on well-known interaction methods players know from traditional video games. For example, an earlier prototype had single markers on the board to be pushed around like conventional pegs. While this added an additional layer of physical interaction, the flow of the game was much better when players controlled their avatar with pointing the cursor to the desired field on the grid.

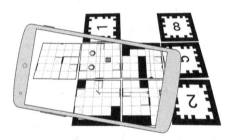

Fig. 2. Diagram of different image trackers representing rooms.

The third and most important part is the social interaction between players. For *VM*, cooperation is inherent regarding basic gameplay, since players get confronted with the same problems at the same time. Examples are the previously mentioned vantage points that require describing elements to a teammate or demanding switch puzzles. Moreover you have individual tasks to perform with your avatar while coordinating those with your teammate. The main challenge for collaborative play forms the solving of puzzles by observation and discussion. It aims at a certain level of difficulty that is sufficient enough to force players to share information and argue over the best line of action [1].

4   Conclusion and Future Work

Mobile gaming is more prominent than ever, and with the current and future technology in smartphones there is a lot of potential regarding AR. While technical improvements are important, it is equally vital to catch up with the design side of this new medium. We have discussed that a hybrid approach between analogue board games and digital games opens up a research field on its own, since it is more than just a simple combination of two game types. *VM* addresses this issue and first play tests show that the approach is very promising. However, it is only the first step toward gathering knowledge regarding the creation and design of AR board games. The next steps will therefore be a refinement of the game design based on thorough formalized and controlled play testing. To take into account all social experiences and receptions of the game, we plan to set up different game sessions with both dedicated desktop and mobile AR versions of the game in order to compare traditional video gaming to the AR board game. Overall this work provides an illustration of our design experience and hopefully will serve as inspiration for other games of similar type to be developed.

References

1. Zagal, J.P., Rick, J., Hsi, I.: Collaborative games: lessons learned from board games. Simul. Gaming **37**, 1 (2006)
2. Peitz, J., Björk, S., Jäppinen, A.: Wizard's apprentice gameplay-oriented design of a computer-augmented board game. In: Proceedings of the 2006 ACM SIGCHI International Conference on Advances in Computer Entertainment Technology (2006)
3. Hürst, W., Vriens, K.: Mobile augmented reality interaction via finger tracking in a board game setting. Workshop Paper (2013)
4. Molla, E., Lepetit, V.: Augmented reality for board games. In: 9th IEEE International Symposium on Mixed and Augmented Reality (ISMAR) (2010)
5. Nguyen, D., Raveendran, K., Xu, Y., Spreen, K., MacIntyre, B.: Art of defense: a collaborative handheld augmented reality board game. In: Proceedings of the 2009 ACM SIGGRAPH Symposium on Video Games (2009)
6. Jones, B., Dillman, K., Manesh, S.A., Sharlin, E., Tang, A.: Designing an immersive and entertaining pervasive gameplay experience with spheros as game and interface elements. In: Proceedings of the First ACM SIGCHI Annual Symposium on Computer-Human Interaction in Play, CHI PLAY 2014 (2014)
7. Andersen, T.L., Kristensen, S., Nielsen, B.W., Grønbæk, K.: Designing an augmented reality board game with children: the battleboard 3D experience. In: Proceedings of the 2004 Conference on Interaction Design and Children (2004)
8. Bakker, N.C., da Camara, J., van Elsas, H.L.J., Spek, G., van Baar, I.J., Kybartas, B., Bidarra, R.: BloxAR: augment your social life! In: Proceedings of the First ACM SIGCHI Annual Symposium on Computer-Human Interaction in Play, CHI PLAY 2014 (2014)

Author Index

Printed in the United States
By Bookmasters